D1087603

POLITICAL THOUGHT IN
MEDIEVAL ISLAM

POLITICAL THOUGHT IN MEDIEVAL ISLAM

AN INTRODUCTORY OUTLINE

BY

ERWIN I. J. ROSENTHAL

CAMBRIDGE
AT THE UNIVERSITY PRESS
1968

PUBLISHED BY
THE SYNDICS OF THE CAMBRIDGE UNIVERSITY PRESS

Bentley House, 200 Euston Road, London, N.W.1
American Branch: 32 East 57th Street, New York, N.Y. 10022

© CAMBRIDGE UNIVERSITY PRESS 1958

Standard Book Number: 521 06131 8

First edition	1958
Reprinted	1962
Reprinted with corrections	1968

320.95
R815

First printed in Great Britain at the University Press, Cambridge
Reprinted in Great Britain by John Dickens & Co. Ltd., Northampton

To
MY WIFE

CONTENTS

AUTHOR'S NOTE

THIS book was substantially completed at the beginning of 1955, and any literature on the subject published after this date could not be considered.

I should like to record my grateful appreciation to the Syndics of the Cambridge University Press, for help in revising the typescript and also to the Staff of the Press, who have so expertly piloted the book through all its stages.

My special thanks go out to a learned friend who wishes to remain unnamed, for compiling the index.

NOTE ON THE SECOND IMPRESSION

In reprinting the opportunity has been taken to correct misprints and errors and to rephrase a few sentences.

NOTE ON THE THIRD IMPRESSION

This reissue has made possible the inclusion of references to relevant literature (confined to new critical editions and/or translations of texts) which has appeared since the book was first published. For reasons of economy the notes remain after the text, yet they form an essential part of the book and the reader is asked to pay them due attention.

NEW YORK — E. I. J. R.
November 1967

ABBREVIATIONS

ACR Erwin I. J. Rosenthal, *Averroes' Commentary on Plato's "Republic"* (Cambridge University Press, corrected reprint, 1966).

AH Anno Hijrae.

AIJT E.I.J.R., "Avicenna's Influence on Jewish Thought" in *Avicenna: Scientist & Philosopher*, ed. G. M. Wickens (London, 1952).

BSOAS *Bulletin, School of Oriental and African Studies*, London.

C.E. Common Era.

EI *Encyclopaedia of Islam.*

GAL C. Brockelmann, *Geschichte der arabischen Literatur* (Leiden, 1943–9), 2 vols., and Supplementary vols. I, II, III (Leiden, 1937–42).

KAF E.I.J.R., 'Ibn Jaldūn's Attitude to the Falāsifa' in *Al-Andalus*, XX, 1, 1955.

KGS E.I.J.R., *Ibn Khaldûn's Gedanken über den Staat* (München und Berlin, 1932).

M E.I.J.R., "Maimonides' Conception of State and Society" in *Moses Maimonides*, ed. I. Epstein (London, 1935).

MGWJ *Monatsschrift für Geschichte und Wissenschaft des Judentums.*

MSOS *Mitteilungen des Seminars für Orientalische Sprachen der Universität Berlin.*

NE Aristotle, *Nicomachean Ethics.*

PF E.I.J.R., "The Place of Politics in the Philosophy of Al-Fārābī" in *Islamic Culture*, XXIX, 3, 1955.

PG E.I.J.R., "Politische Gedanken bei Ibn Bāǧǧa" in *MGWJ*, 1937, 3.

PIB E.I.J.R., "The Place of Politics in the Philosophy of Ibn Bājja" in *Islamic Culture*, XXV, 1, 1951.

PIR E.I.J.R., "The Place of Politics in the Philosophy of Ibn Rushd" in *BSOAS*, XV, 2, 1953.

RSO *Rivista degli Studi Orientali.*

SAIPT E.I.J.R., "Some Aspects of Islamic Political Thought" in *Islamic Culture*, XXII, 1, 1948.

ZDMG *Zeitschrift der deutschen Morgenländischen Gesellschaft.*

INTRODUCTION

ISLAM is the youngest of the great world religions. Although Arabia is its cradle and its inspiration, it owes in its theology a good deal to Judaism and Christianity, and its way of life centred in and regulated by an all-embracing law has many features in common with the Jewish way of life. Muḥammad, its founder-prophet, grew to maturity in daily contact with Jews and Christians.

Yet, although Jewish and Christian elements can be found in Muḥammad's teaching and in Muslim ritual and law, Islam is not simply the sum total of foreign elements. For Muḥammad brought his own personality to bear upon what he saw and heard and argued about. In their transformation these foreign elements blended with Arabian features into something peculiarly its own, another child of the desert, of the Semitic genius for religion.

From its beginnings in the Arabian desert, Islam looked out on the world that surrounded the Arabs. Religious zeal increased the power of its arms and brought it victory over many lands and nations of different cultures and civilizations, of different faiths and customs. It has always been willing to accept ideas and institutions from those it vanquished. But in acceptance it has adapted and transformed its inheritance. Not always able to work the various strands into a harmonious whole, Islam has never yet lost its identity, even if instead of fusion and synthesis there resulted only fruitful and peaceful co-existence. This holds good for every manifestation of Muslim life and thought. The hard core of Muḥammad's teaching and its interpretation gave Islam that coherence and stability which enabled it to control its receptiveness, and to draw into its Arabian foundation, elements from highly developed nations and systems which enriched and ennobled it. In Arabia in the first place, Judaism and Christianity had to be faced in matters of doctrine and ritual; Zoroastrianism offered the next challenge in Iran, as did Sassanian ideas and practice of government; Byzantium supplied more than administrators. Indian and especially Persian literature, Persian historiography, Greek and Hellenistic philosophy, Jewish and Roman law, Greek medicine and natural sciences, not to mention Indian and Byzantine art and architecture, all have a share in the complex fabric of Islamic civilization. It is not the least important and attractive feature of the Muslim genius that it was able to accommodate all these strangers and make them feel at home. It made no great demands on converts: "There is no God but Allah and Muḥammad is his prophet" were the magic words that opened the gates of the spacious house of Islam to the *ahl al-kitāb*, those who possessed a book, that is, a revelation. Refusal to accept Islam was not punished by death in their case; they were granted protection against payment of poll-tax, which helped to fill the coffers of the Muslim treasury. With the others it was conversion or the sword. The Oneness and Unity of God and Muḥammad as his prophet had to be acknowledged, a reasonable enough price to pay for a share in the privileges of the Muslim community, especially in the time of its empire-building, with the promise of rich booty and high office.

Mutual adaptation proceeded apace, naturally not without opposition. The astonishing result, Islamic culture and civilization, justified Arab open-mindedness, generosity, desert hospitality carried into urban life, and intellectual curiosity of beduins who were attracted by the refinement and glitter of Iran and Byzantium. The title of a remarkable book by A. Mez, *The Renaissance of Islam*, reflects the rich flowering of the spirit at the height of the Abbasid caliphate in Baghdad.

Islam is a religious way of life which contains diverse elements all bound together in a certain unity of outlook by the common belief in God and his prophet who had received a revelation—the final revelation—in the form of the Qur'ān, "the precious Book". The exemplary life of the prophet, his Sunna, and Hadith, a body of authentic traditions going back to Muḥammad, and his work for the Muslim "Community of the Faithful", were combined with the Qur'ān, and all three served as sources of the *Sharī'a*, the prophetically revealed law of Islam. This law bound and united all Muslims, were they Arabs, Persians or Turks, and others who had embraced Islam either by force or of their own free will. This *Sharī'a* is the rock of Islam, or to be more precise, of Sunnī or orthodox Islam, to the exclusion of the *Shī'a*, which owes allegiance to 'Alī and not to the orthodox caliphs. It comprises many sects differentiated by their recognition of different descendants of 'Alī as their imams, and by different doctrines.

Political thought in medieval Islam, the subject of this book, offers a classic example of the power of Islam to develop a system and a theory of its own and to relate to them systems, theories and ideas which are brought to Muslims from without. Political thought at first centres round the caliphate and is, in fact, a theory of the caliphate, its origin and purpose. Naturally this theory of the *Khilāfa*, developed by the jurists, is also our starting point; we take our bearings from it, just as the Muslims did, and in relation to it we describe and evaluate theories of Muslim writers on history and government. The art of government, as distinct from its theory, does not concern us directly, but only in so far as the writers of the so-called "Mirrors for Princes" offer advice to rulers on the basis of a political theory.

The inclusion of Ibn Khaldūn, the only political thinker in the strict sense of the term in Islam, requires no justification. In the first place, he bases his theory on observation of past and present Muslim states; in the second place, or rather on a par with the first reason, he is convinced of the superiority of the *Khilāfa*, based on the *Sharī'a*, over the power state, which he analyses and defines. That his investigation has led him to develop general principles of government going beyond the confines of Islam only adds to the importance of his theories, and brings into clearer relief their Islamic background.

The "Mirrors" illustrate the adaptability of Islam in the direction of Iran and of a typically Persian literary *genre*; but the *Falāsifa*, that is, the Muslim religious philosophers, are in a very special way the best qualified exponents of an attempted synthesis between two cultures and ways of life. The relatively large space allotted to a discussion of their views is justified for several reasons. First, their political philosophy represents the encounter of the political philosophy of Plato and Aristotle with the theory of the *Khilāfa* on home ground, that is, on the sure foundation and against the rock-like background of the *Sharī'a*, which is equally binding for all Muslims. Next, their political philosophy is, like that of their Greek masters, an integral part of their general philosophy, but is at the same time largely conditioned by their recognition of the authority of the *Sharī'a*. Further, and as a result, they make a determined attempt at a real synthesis between Platonic and Islamic concepts on the basis of the common ground of the central position of law in the state, and despite the existence of fundamental differences. They make this attempt as philosophers and as students of Aristotle's theoretical and Plato's practical philosophy rather than as theologians or jurists. There are differences among them, and variations will be noted in the reception of Plato's political philosophy by various thinkers, ranging from mere illustration in Avempace to almost complete synthesis in Averroes, who is at the same time perhaps the most thorough and convinced Muslim of them all. Lastly, they are considered as *Muslim* philosophers, which means that their metaphysical standpoint is not one of complete independence, but is conditioned by the *Sharī'a* of Islam. This results in a limitation in the character, quality and range of their speculation imposed by the overriding authority of the *Sharī'a*. If inconsistencies are viewed with the eyes of Muslims, it will be found that they are more apparent than real.

Consequently, my starting point in the treatment of the political philosophy of Al-Fārābī, Avicenna and Averroes, excepting Avempace, is Islam, not Aristotle, because I am convinced that they were Muslim philosophers first and followers of their masters Plato and Aristotle second. Two sovereign worlds of the spirit meet in their minds and they try to harmonize revelation, in the form of prophetic law, with reason, in the form of the *Nomos* of the Greek city-state. If priorities must be established, supremacy belongs to the revealed law of Islam. In this sense only have the *Falāsifa* a place in a study which deals with political thought in medieval Islam. What is more, from the point of view of political theory their importance cannot be exaggerated, although they have had no influence on the course of events in the Islamic state at all, so far as our present knowledge allows us to judge. Their impact on the political thought of later jurists is, however, not negligible. But we do not measure ideas and their value by the impact they have made on the general run of humanity alone. It is in this field of political thought that the challenge of sovereign reason in the shape of philosophy has been met most vigorously and successfully by the *Falāsifa*. They were more than theologians and jurists; and they were also more than independently speculating philosophers in the wake of Plato, Aristotle and their Hellenistic commentators and continuators. Their independence as philosophers may, however, be questioned in the field of metaphysics.

I have had to restrict my range of inquiry to representative exponents of *Sunnī* Islam as far as constitutional law is concerned. Shīʿī doctrine is mixed with a number of extra-Islamic ideas and notions and is too complicated to be treated in this first conspectus of political thought in Islam without further research on the lines of R. Strothmann's work.

In explanation of the sub-title of the book I would say that at the present stage of our knowledge of the relevant texts a more ambitious undertaking is out of the question. Many of these texts are not available in critical editions; and even where we have them they have not yet been sufficiently studied under the aspect of politics. With the *Falāsifa* there are additional difficulties to be met. The correct and definitive evaluation of their work requires a varied expert knowledge such as hardly any student of Islamic thought possesses. One has to be Arabist, classicist, historian of ancient and medieval philosophy and expert in Islamic and general medieval history to grasp fully the antecedents of Islamic philosophy and the combinations of ideas stemming from Greek and Hellenistic philosophy.

A precise knowledge of the many elements, some of them from Iran and even from India, which have gone into Hellenistic philosophy and theosophy, is especially important. For they have a large share in the mystical branch of Islamic philosophy which in its theory of knowledge is relevant to the theory of prophecy as evolved by Al-Fārābī and developed by Avicenna, and to the latter's own theory of knowledge. Political philosophy is only a branch of general philosophy; its greater importance is due to the religio-political, unitary character of Islam.

For all these reasons, the interpretation of the political theories of the Muslim religious philosophers, offered under the general heading of "The Platonic Legacy", is provisional. But I hope by isolating, as far as this is possible, the political ideas properly so called, to give the reader an introduction to the more detailed study and appreciation of the subject in Islam. For this reason I have included a discussion of the theory of the caliphate (as evolved by some of the principal jurists), of government, and of the power-state. It would be pleasing to an orderly mind, especially one attuned to the concept of evolution, if it were possible to show that there is a steady evolution from the theological-juristic by way of the political-historical to the scientific-realistic approach to politics in Islam. But this cannot be established without clear documentary evidence which I have not so far discovered. Students of, and experts in *Fiqh*, among the writers on politics other than the jurists, are naturally aware of the existence of the acknowledged interpretation of constitutional law, the more so since they as Muslims are themselves guided in their thinking and investigations into politics by the *Sharī'a*. Ibn Khaldūn was certainly familiar with the theory of the *Khilāfa* no less than with some writings of the *Falāsifa*. This holds good at least for Avicenna, it applies much less, if at all, to the political treatises of Al-Fārābī, and certainly does not extend to Averroes' commentaries on the *Republic* and the *Nicomachean Ethics*.

The *Falāsifa*, with the exception of Avempace, are strongly under the influence of the *Sharī'a*, but also under that of Plato and Aristotle. That their thought is considered against the background and under the aspect of the Platonic legacy seems justified in view of the nature of their writings on politics, which are all based on Plato's *Republic* and *Laws*. This is not to deny or minimize the importance of Aristotle's *Nicomachean Ethics*, which is so evident in the case of Al-Fārābī and Averroes. But, apart from serving as the theoretical basis for their reception and adaptation of Platonic ideas, this work as a part of Aristotle's whole philosophy is used mainly as a corrective of Plato's views, as expressed in the *Republic*. It is no exaggeration to speak of a renaissance of Plato's political philosophy in Islam. The danger of isolating political from general philosophy is, I trust, much reduced by a treatment such as I have adopted.

Moreover, by confining myself to an investigation into the documentary evidence for Platonic ideas and arguments in the political writings of the principal *Falāsifa*, I hope to show the impact which Plato's political philosophy made on Islam. It has been accepted in some of its fundamental features without some of its basic assumptions. For example, the existence of slavery and Plato's neglect of the third class of citizens of his *Republic*, a point noted with disapproval by Averroes, found as little favour with the *Falāsifa* as Plato's idea of the community of women. The *Falāsifa* were equally conscious of the gulf between their superior intellectual powers and the inability of the masses to rise beyond persuasion and imagination, to the exclusion of real intellectual understanding. But as Muslims the *Falāsifa* accepted the masses as their equals in faith, albeit a naïve, unquestioning, even an unintelligent faith, and they shared with them, as far as we know, the observances of Muslim ritual. Nor did they deny them a share in the happiness and bliss promised to all Muslims in return for obedience to the will of God, as laid down in the teachings and regulations of the divinely revealed law. But Plato's political philosophy helped them all to see the political character and significance of their own law more clearly.

It has often been stressed that Islam is like a vast mansion containing many rooms, not all of which are interconnected. There is good reason to assume that Muslim theology and law developed long after Muḥammad, and that his immediate successors, the first four caliphs, were idealized by later generations of Muslim theologians, jurists and historians. This applies particularly to the *Sunnī* theory of the *Khilāfa*, and it is well known what a gulf separates this ideal theory from political reality. But it should be emphasized that this book is concerned with political theory only, which was worked out at a time when the actual caliphate little resembled the ideal picture drawn by writers on constitutional law. But it is precisely this picture of the *Khilāfa*, as demanded by the (ideal) *Sharī'a*, which is the centre of gravity and the point of reference for all Muslim writers who are concerned with political theory. Unless this is realized neither the religious philosophers of Islam, the *Falāsifa*, nor Ibn Khaldūn can be properly understood.

Since a large part of this book is devoted to an exposition of the political thought of the *Falāsifa* and of Ibn Khaldūn the results of historical and literary criticism cannot enter our discussion, the more so since they in no way affect the attitude of these authors; not only the ideal, but also the authoritative character of the *Sharī'a* as the ideal constitution of the ideal state is an axiom with them no less than with the jurists. We must realize that no matter what modern research has established with regard to the origin and development of Muslim law and its threefold foundation in Qur'an, Sunna and Hadith, it is, in a Muslim's consciousness, divine law, perfect and binding on all members of the Muslim community. Otherwise we cannot hope to understand what was in the minds of the Muslim writers whose political thought we consider. Our interpretation must take full account of their basic attitude.

A final observation concerns the character of Islam in relation to politics as understood by Western students. Unless we grasp this character we cannot appreciate the significance of the caliphate as it is presented in the theory of the *Khilāfa*, which serves as introduction and background to this book.

Islam knows no distinction between a spiritual and a temporal realm, between religious and secular activities. Both realms form a unity under the all-embracing authority of the *Sharī'a*. L. Massignon's definition of Islam as "une théocratie laïque égalitaire" correctly expresses this idea of Allah's sovereign law revealed through his messenger, the prophet Muḥammad, to mankind. Spiritual and temporal are the two complementary sides of the religious law. The caliph or *imām* is as vicegerent of the prophet the defender of the faith, charged with the implementation of the law by safeguarding the welfare of the believers in this world and, by enforcing obedience to it, ensuring their salvation in the world to come. All believers, caliph as well as labourer, are equal before the law of God. Muslims owe obedience to the caliph only inasmuch as he is instrumental in applying this law. At least in theory, the power of the caliph is conditional upon his faithful discharge of his duty: to guard the law and enforce its application in the life of the Community of the Faithful founded by Muḥammad. The Prophet is credited with the Hadith: *dīn wadawla* (or *dīn wamulk* or *dīn wasulṭān*), "religion and ('secular') power are twins". This means that *dīn wadawla* are the two sides of the *Sharī'a*. Usually the complement of *dīn* is *dunya* (this world); *dīn* means religion, not church, and is not contrasted with *dunya* which it comprises. The opposite of *dunya* is *ākhira*, the world to come. Both are contained in the *dīn*. It is unfortunate that we must use Western terms to translate the Arabic ones, for in so doing we distort their original meaning and give them a Christian connotation. A Muslim's life—ideally at least—is ruled in its entirety by the *Sharī'a*, which lays down precise rules and regulations governing his relations with God as well as with his fellow-Muslims and non-Muslims. We are used to term the former 'religious' and the latter 'secular'. But where a religious law is all-comprehensive, this distinction falls to the ground. Politics is part of religion, so to speak; in other words, politics, *siyāsa*, or *siyāsat al-dunya*, is the scene of religion as life on this earth as long as the law of the state is the *Sharī'a*. This state is the *Khilāfa* or *Imāma*, and if we must operate with our Western terms, it may be defined as a spiritual and temporal unity. Hence where the phrase "religious and political" is used in this book, this special unity should be taken as implied.

In further justification of the introductory and provisional nature of this study I would point to the paucity of existing literature on the theology, law and philosophy of Islam in so far as it affects the subject under review.

A. von Kremer's *Geschichte der herrschenden Ideen des Islam* (1868) and *Culturgeschichte des Orients* (1875), an excellent pioneering effort at a time when many important and essential Arabic texts were unknown or not available in critical editions, have held the field for many years. Advance has been slow and followed the emergence of textual, historical and literary criticism. Many a distinguished scholar preferred the self-sacrificing task of providing the student of Islam with reliable critical editions of the vast source material dispersed over the libraries of three continents, to an exposition of the various aspects of Islamic culture. The more texts are made available and evaluated the greater becomes our insight into the origin and development of Islam. We need think only of the epoch-making researches of Wellhausen, Winckler, Goldziher, Noeldeke, V. V. Bartold and C. H. Becker to realize the complex fabric of Islamic civilization. In our context, Goldziher's critical understanding of the development of Muslim theology and law has led later scholars in the field to the important recognition of the predominantly theoretical character of the *Sharī'a* as the ideal norm of the *Umma* (Muslim nation). J. Schacht has developed Goldziher's ideas in his important book, *The Origins of Muhammadan Jurisprudence*, and A. Guillaume's *The Traditions of Islam* is indispensable for the correct understanding of the Hadith (tradition). When we add Sir T. W. Arnold's *The Caliphate*, which is based, as he says himself, on Goldziher's and Becker's researches, we have reliable means at our disposal to study the caliphate in its constitutional aspects. We are further helped in this task by D. Santillana's *Istituzioni*, Sir Hamilton Gibb's study of Al-Māwardī, M. Henri Laoust's monograph on and translation of Ibn Taymīya, E. Tyan's *Le Caliphat* and Louis Gardet's important *La cité musulmane*, which appeared after I had already drafted the whole book and, in particular, completed the chapter on the caliphate. (See my review of *La cité musulmane: vie sociale et politique* in *The*

Islamic Quarterly, II, 3, 1955) and many important studies by other scholars like Louis Massignon, R. A. Nicholson, H. Corbin and A. J. Arberry.

To turn to the *Falāsifa*, it will be remembered that their political thought has attracted the attention of scholars only for the last two decades. The absence of critical editions of some of their writings is acutely felt. Fr. Dieterici edited in 1895 Al-Fārābī's *Ideal State* from the then known manuscripts in London and Oxford, and although we know from M. Steinschneider's invaluable monograph *Alfarabi*, published in 1869, how important this Muslim philosopher is for the history of philosophy in Islam and for the history of the reception of Platonic and Aristotelian ideas by the *Falāsifa*, the description and evaluation of Al-Fārābī's political philosophy has only begun with L. Strauss's *Philosophie und Gesetz* and my *Maimonides' Conception of State and Society*, both published in 1935. Reference to preliminary studies is made in the appropriate sections in this book. Important contributions by the greatly missed Paul Kraus, by Fr. Rosenthal, R. Walzer and S. Pines touch upon the subject of this book, and a relevant study by S. Pines (*Nature et Société: problèmes de philosophie politique des Arabes*) will be published soon. A critical edition of Al-Fārābī's *Compendium Legum Platonis* by F. Gabrieli has recently added an important text for study (*Plato Arabus III* of the *Corpus Platonicum Medii Aevi*, ed. R. Klibansky, Warburg Institute, London, 1952). We owe to Asín Palacios editions of Ibn Bājja's treatises which allow us, within the limits of their intelligibility, to assess their significance for political philosophy in Islam. The position is better in the case of Ibn Rushd thanks to Mueller, Gauthier, Bouyges, S. van den Bergh, G. F. Hourani and others.

My edition of the Hebrew version of Ibn Rushd's commentary on Plato's *Republic* has now appeared. This text is the basis for the subsequent chapter on Ibn Rushd.

Lastly, my *Ibn Khaldūns Gedanken über den Staat* (1932) forms the basis of the chapter "The Theory of the Power-State", supplemented by a fresh study of the *Muqaddima*, a critical edition of which, based on Quatremère's, is being prepared by Prof. Ṭanjī. A reliable text is not only essential for a correct understanding of Ibn Khaldūn's thought, but also for the evaluation of his influence on modernist thinkers like 'Ālī 'Abdu-l-Rāziq and Rashīd Riḍā. An important English translation by Prof. Fr. Rosenthal has now appeared.

PART ONE

CONSTITUTIONAL LAW AND MUSLIM HISTORY

CHAPTER I

THE QUEST FOR HAPPINESS

I. THE MEDIEVAL ATTITUDE

POLITICS, Plato's royal art, is defined by Aristotle in his *Nicomachean Ethics* as "the most authoritative of the sciences" and its object as the supreme good which man desires for its own sake.[1] This good is equated with happiness as the result of action, and though men differ in their desires and their objects, such as pleasure, honour or the life of contemplation, according to their lights, they all seek the highest good in their quest for happiness. Ordinary men seek pleasure or honour for their own sakes, but also for the sake of happiness. This view of Aristotle's became the common property of the Middle Ages. Yet the philosopher aims at practical or moral and theoretical or intellectual perfection. That perfection is happiness *par excellence*.

Medieval thinkers, Muslim, Jewish and Christian alike, conceived of this happiness in relation to God, and for them its consummation consisted in the love of God. They were, with few exceptions, concerned not so much with the individual and his perfection but rather with the group, the religious society in the state governed by divine law. They agree with Aristotle that "the good of the state is manifestly a greater and more perfect good".[2] But by giving the highest good a religious content by relating it to the God of revelation in the form of law, they transformed the merely metaphysical concept of their teacher into a religious value. Thomas Aquinas formulated it thus: "The ultimate end of everything is its completion....Man's last end, therefore, does not consist in the total and collective good of the universe, but in God." And "the love of God is the end of all human activity and desire".[3]

The Muslim philosophers with whom alone we are concerned in this book all concentrate their attention upon "the attainment of happiness", a phrase which is actually the title of one of Alfārābī's political treatises to be discussed later.[4] *Sa'āda* is, unlike the Greek εὐδαιμονία of which it is a translation, the Islamic form of happiness, and Miskawaih (d. 1030) in his book *Tahdhīb al-akhlāq* defines the happiness of the philosopher as practical and theoretical perfection in one. Both are interdependent. The latter is attained through knowledge of "existing things", the former through ethical perfection—to which his book is devoted. Political government is necessary to achieve practical perfection. Moral education should lead us to obedience to God as our final welfare.[5] Fakhr al-Dīn al-Rāzī (d. 1209) is of the opinion that only prophetic revealed law enables man to live in society. Without political-social organization man cannot reach his destiny. Maimonides among the Jews likewise assigns to intellectual perfection the highest stage, necessarily preceded by ethical perfection. Only their combination can lead to the love of God by imitating his ways. Happiness is the result of action directed towards God.[6]

Thomas Aquinas, Maimonides and Averroes are agreed that the knowledge of God is the fulfilment of rational man's quest for happiness. Happiness, the highest good of the religious society and of its individual members, is the central problem of political thought in medieval Judaism, Christianity and Islam. It is the task of the state to guarantee not only life and property through justice and equity but also the happiness of its citizens. In Islam the ruler combines political with spiritual authority; in Christianity the functions are divided between the emperor and the pope; in Judaism authority rests with the rabbis until the Messianic kingdom is established. But in all three religions the divine law rules supreme, at least in theory, and is never lost sight of as the ideal. This happiness, though derived from Greek political philosophy, was given a fuller and deeper meaning by extending it to the whole of society though confining its highest degree, its most perfect form, to the intellectual *élite*, the religious philosophers.

Huizinga rightly says of Dante, the most profound Christian political thinker of the Middle Ages, that "the imperative demand of universal human culture as the principle of the community remains one of the most significant sayings of Dante's incomparable genius".[7] In defining "civilization" Huizinga says that it emphasizes that man is a citizen and a member of a community bound and protected by law. In support of his definition he quotes Dante as saying that "the fundamental basis of imperial majesty, i.e. world monarchy, therefore truly rests upon the necessity of human civilization which is ordered and directed towards one end: the happy life".[8] Ibn Khaldūn defines civilization in strikingly similar terms, as we shall see later in the chapter devoted to his theory. This happy life is, according to Dante,[9] the "good life" in that providence has set man a twofold aim: earthly happiness and the bliss of life eternal, which is the joy of contemplating God.[10] Earthly happiness is attained, with the help of philosophy, in the realization of the moral and intellectual virtues. But only if we are guided by the divine light, and if we practise the cardinal virtues of faith, love and hope, can we reach the heavenly paradise, the life of eternal bliss. These virtues are beyond the reach of human reason; Dante finds them taught in the Christian scriptures and formulated in Christian theology. Judaism teaches love of God, love of neighbour and Messianic hope and redemption.

Despite all doctrinal differences and distinctions caused by different political systems and a different historical situation there is agreement in the Middle Ages on the end of man as a rational, religious creature within the religious society and state. This agreement consists chiefly in the common concept of God as the God of revelation, the personal Creator-God who rules the universe and man in it, who demands of man faith and obedience to his will expressed in a law which is designed to guarantee man's well-being in this world and his happiness in the world to come. The law is revealed to a prophet and mediated by him to the people conceived of as "a kingdom of priests, a holy nation" by Jews, as the "church of Jesus Christ" by Christians, and as the "community of the faithful" by Muslims. This law alone guarantees the twofold happiness of which Dante speaks no less than do Maimonides, Averroes, Ibn Khaldūn or the Muslim jurists and theologians. It is binding on the few elect philosophers and the masses alike, and its truth is assured by its divine character.

2. LAW, DIVINE AND HUMAN

The central problem of medieval religious philosophy is that of faith and reason, or better, revelation and reason. According to Aristotle's formulation, which goes back to Plato, man is a *zoon politikon*, a political being; hence this problem assumed the concrete form of the distinction between divinely revealed law and human, man-made law. As such it engaged the minds of the speculative religious thinkers of medieval Judaism, Christianity and Islam. But they were not the first to encounter it, for the challenge to revelation and its truth had already been met by Jewish-Hellenistic philosophy in the first century of the common era. Although it is very difficult to trace any direct influence of Philo of Alexandria on medieval thought, it is possible that some of his ideas were transmitted to the Middle Ages through Stoic and Syrian-Christian philosophers. Be that as it may, the fact remains that Philo was compelled to vindicate the superiority of revelation over the philosophy of Plato by postulating the supremacy of God's wisdom over man's reason. The *Torah* (Law) of Moses, revealed by God to the prophet, is superior to the law which Plato's philosopher-kings lay down with the help of their human reason.[11] A religious element, it is true, is not absent in Plato,[12] who likens the political activity of the philosopher to a "ministering to the gods". But Plato's god is not the personal God of revelation, of righteousness and justice, of love and mercy, the creator of heaven and earth and of man in his image, in whom Jews, Christians and Muslims believed.

St Augustine encountered the same challenge in the *Enneads* of Plotinus, whose concept of emanation is probably responsible for the Muslim philosophers' theory of prophecy, which will engage our attention later on; for Al-Fārābī seems to have taken an adaptation of *Enneads* IV–VI to be Aristotle's *Theology*.[13] In Islam the problem of revelation and reason presents itself chiefly as the contrast between the divine and human law. It is therefore necessary to state the problem briefly here and to give its detailed presentation later. Etienne Gilson[14] speaks of

> two distinct orders of assent: religious faith and rational knowledge. I know by reason that something is true because I *see* that it is true: but I believe that something is true because *God has said it*. In those two cases the cause of my assent is specifically different, consequently science and faith should be held as two specifically different kinds of assent....If they are two distinct species of knowledge, we should never ask one of them to fulfil what is the proper function of the other.... According to its very definition, faith implies assent of the intellect to that which the intellect does not see to be true....Consequently, an act of faith cannot be caused by rational evidence, but entails an intervention of the Will.

Whilst the distinction between will and intellect is valid and whilst faith is an act of will, I believe it is true to say, in the light of the contrast established by Jewish and Muslim medieval thinkers between divine law and human law, that for them (*a*) the act of faith comes first and assent second—though assent is no less necessary for man as a rational being—and (*b*) since faith is faith in a God who reveals his will through prophetic law, it implies acceptance of the revealed word of God as a law which tells us not only what we shall do but also what we shall believe. It commands us to know and to love God as much as is in our power. Once we are as believers *under* the law we cannot forgo a rational inquiry into its teachings. But since our rational faculty is limited, and ultimate authority and sovereignty belong to God and not to our reason, there are revealed truths which, as Gilson expresses it, we *believe* because God has spoken them. In other words, there are not only beliefs and convictions but also commandments which are inaccessible to demonstrative argument. The word of God is a command and must be obeyed.

If we are to understand the medieval mind correctly, and in particular the impact on it of Greek-Hellenistic philosophy, we must be aware that the emphasis of medieval thinkers is placed on the comprehensive character of divinely revealed law in relation not only to happiness, but to a twofold happiness, as stated earlier: the happiness of the body belonging to this world, and the happiness of the soul belonging essentially to the next world, though it has taken temporary abode in the body here. The difference between divine and human law goes back ultimately to a different concept of God. As Gilson put it succinctly:[15] "At the summit of the Aristotelian universe is not an Idea but a self-subsisting and eternal Act of thinking. Let us call it Thought: a divine self-thinking Thought." On the other hand, according to him, "A Christian's philosophical first principle had to be one with his religious first principle, and since the name of his God was 'I am' [i.e. the God of the Hebrew Bible] any Christian philosopher had to posit 'I am' as his first principle and supreme cause of all things, even his philosophy."[16]

This means that revelation conditions philosophical speculation, prescribes its scope and content, and imposes certain limits on its subject-matter. Gilson speaks of Christian philosophy as having arisen "at the juncture of Greek philosophy and of the Jewish Christian religious revelation, Greek philosophy providing the technique for a rational explanation of the world, and the Jewish-Christian revelation providing religious beliefs of incalculable philosophical import".[17] When Gilson says of Augustine that his problem was "to express the God of Christianity in terms borrowed from the philosophy of Plotinus",[18] he expresses an idea which applies to all religious thinkers, Jews, Christians and Muslims alike, who have had to meet the challenge of Greek-Hellenistic philosophy.

As a general principle, this means that in assessing the character and meaning of medieval philosophy we have to remember that its representatives clothed indigenous beliefs and convictions in the language of Greek-Hellenistic philosophy. In doing so they modified, adapted and transformed the meaning of that terminology. God as the "first cause" or the "prime mover" is at the same time the "I am", the God of justice, righteousness, love and mercy, the personal God of revelation. The problem is naturally not confined to any particular period in history but presents itself again and again, particularly when a new philosophical movement takes shape. The religious mind reacts to its challenge in much the same way, by taking its stand on the personal God of revelation, as we can see from Pascal's answer to Descartes: "The God of Christians is not a God who is simply the author of mathematical truths, or of the order of the elements; that is the view of heathens and Epicureans...; but the God of Abraham, the God of Isaac, the God of Jacob, the God of Christians, is a God of love and of comfort, a God who fills the soul and heart of those whom he possesses."[19]

But to revert once more to the Middle Ages, Gilson's view may again be adduced that St Thomas Aquinas (like Averroes), grants that revelation is true, but does not take it for granted. "No man would ever admit that God has spoken, unless he had solid proofs of the fact....If truly God has spoken, his revelation must needs be true, and it is necessary for us to believe it. For this is the proper aim and scope of revelation to provide all men, philosophers or not, with such knowledge of God, of man and of his destiny, as is required for their eternal salvation."[20]

It follows that for medieval man revelation and reason are not mutually exclusive, but pursue one and the same aim, man's happiness, though by different paths. The religious philosophers insisted on the superiority of revelation as containing absolute truth, for although reason arrives at the same truth (since truth is one and indivisible) it does so only after a long search. Yet human reason is inferior to divine wisdom, and thus man needs God's guidance, especially in matters beyond his reason and made known to him only by prophetically revealed law. But philosophy is the best means for explaining by demonstrative argument what it is within man's rational faculty to grasp. The disciples of Plato and Aristotle who had studied Plato's *Republic* and *Laws* and Aristotle's *Nicomachean Ethics* were convinced that only the prophetic lawgiver was qualified to promulgate, on the basis of truth revealed, a law that would lead man to perfection and happiness here and in the hereafter. The Greek *Nomos* was the product of human reason and fell short of this divine purpose.

In Judaism, thinkers before Maimonides distinguished in the *Torah* of Moses between precepts of reason and precepts of revelation. Through experience human reason would eventually have arrived at certain precepts since society cannot exist without the prohibition of murder, theft and adultery. These laws are common to all nations and usually (though not in Judaism) thought of as falling within natural law. Laws of revelation stem from God's mercy and goodness. Man cannot understand their reasons but must obey them because they are commanded by God for man's good. Maimonides rejects this division and replaces it by a division into ceremonial precepts not accessible to human reason, and judicial precepts within reach of human understanding; unlike Thomas Aquinas, he includes moral precepts among the latter.

The division of precepts into kinds, whatever they are called, is important for the distinction between divine and human law. Maimonides stresses—as his Muslim teachers, Al-Fārābī and Avicenna, and his contemporary Averroes, had done—the necessity of law for human existence in a state, and in this sense he is a disciple of Plato and Aristotle, who helped him to realize more fully and to stress the political character of the divine law. He assigns to the law of human origin the aim "only to ensure the good order of the state and of its affairs and to remove from it injustice and strife...to arrange well relations between men...and to obtain for them what they conceive to be happiness...". By contrast a law is divine "all of whose directions have regard for the welfare of physical [material] concerns...as well as for the establishment of ⟨right⟩ convictions; which, in the first place, provide sound opinions about God and the angels..., and is intent on making man wise, understanding, alert and observant, so that he gains true knowledge of reality".[21] He speaks of the double purpose of the law: "the welfare of the soul and the welfare of the body". This is guaranteed only by "the true law, which...is the sole and unique one, namely, the law of Moses: it brings us the twofold perfection".[22] Or, "The Torah has given us the most important of the true ideas by which we reach ultimate perfection, and called upon us to believe in them in general, viz. in the existence of God, his unity, knowledge, power, free will and eternity; which we can only understand after a careful study of other ideas. There are still other notions, belief in which is necessary for the best order of the state."[23] Ultimate human perfection—that of the soul—is possible only in the ideal state, which is governed by prophetic law, which Maimonides contrasts with "the laws of political governments, like the laws of the Greeks which are made by political leaders and not by prophets".[24]

The perfection of the soul, intellectual perfection, is not attainable by philosophy alone, for it depends on right beliefs and convictions taught only in God's law as revealed through prophecy. The masses must be satisfied with these sublime notions in the form of parables, but the metaphysician must penetrate to the inner, hidden meaning which he explains with the help of demonstrative argument. Philo of Alexandria had already spoken of philosophy as "the bondwoman of wisdom", that is, of scripture. The figurative interpretation of scripture might sometimes do violence to the plain meaning of the text so as to harmonize the Bible, or the Qur'ān, with Aristotle, but their divine origin and obligatory character were accepted by all Jews and Muslims, heretics notwithstanding. The divinely revealed prophetic law was the ideal constitution of the ideal state; only this law could guarantee the highest good of all believers, be they philosophers or ordinary citizens of the Jewish community or of the Islamic state. It is with the Islamic state that this book is concerned.

CHAPTER II

THE CALIPHATE: THEORY AND FUNCTION

> "THE science of law is the knowledge of the rights and duties whereby man is enabled to observe right conduct in this life, and to prepare himself for the world to come." Ḥanafī definition of *Fiqh*.

BEFORE Muḥammad preached Islam—submission to the will of Allah[1]—the Arabs were organized in tribes, which were divided into clans or families. The desert with its oases does not permit a social and political organization larger than the family, the clan or at most the tribe. To achieve a larger and higher unity, a force is needed which is capable of binding together men of differing customs and traditions. The message of the prophet, gathered in the Qur'ān, provided this cohesion and, with the more material inducements of booty and landed property as the result of the holy war (*jihād*) on behalf of Allah, succeeded in winning the allegiance to Islam of independent, proud, born warriors. Muḥammad's success was such that under his successors the community of believers was extended far beyond the Arabian peninsula and finally consolidated in the vast Islamic empire in Asia, Africa, Spain and Sicily.

How was it that the message claimed by the messenger of Allah to be God's final revelation to mankind proved acceptable not only to pagans, but also to Christians, Jews and Zoroastrians—all three possessors of a book of revelation, *ahl al-kitāb*—and to Buddhists? How could Islamic civilization bind together so many divergent ethnic groups, some of which were so superior in their way of life to their conquerors? To suggest that the spread of Islam by conquest was part of the general movement of migration of peoples only partly accounts for this astounding historical phenomenon, as does the prevailing political situation. The more important factor is the religious law of Islam, for which a divine origin was claimed and which was designed to cover all manifestations of human life. Its sources, apart from the Qur'ān, are the Sunna, which is the record of the Prophet's life in thought and action, and Hadith, authentic tradition. The *'ulamā*, the spiritual leaders of the *umma* or *jamā'a*, the Muslim community, evolved the *Sharī'a*, the way leading to Allah, out of these three sources, by interpretation with the help of *qiyās*, analogy. Only in this way could the universal validity and application of the divinely revealed law in ever-changing circumstances be secured and preserved. These interpretations were collected and codified in the *Fiqh*-books of four schools, recognized as orthodox and named after their founders Ḥanafī, Mālikī, Shāfi'ī and Ḥanbalī. From these *Fiqh*-books can be learnt the constitutional law of Islam, as well as from special treatises emanating from the four schools and devoted to the theory and practice of the *khilāfa*, the caliphate.[2]

But before the brief outline given below of the political teaching contained in the *Sharī'a* two observations essential for its understanding must be made. One concerns the *Sharī'a* itself and the other the Western student of it. Islamic law underwent a long development from the days of Muḥammad and his companions until its codification by the four schools in the eighth and ninth centuries of the common era. Just as the Sunna arose out of the Qur'ān, so the Hadith represents the authoritative interpretation of the Sunna. Many a tradition owes its existence to the need of finding "scriptural" authority and warrant for a situation, a decision or an institution in political reality. For the *Sharī'a* was the ultimate norm and the only common standard to be applied to a life lived under widely different circumstances. It was the task of the Muslim jurists to integrate the political, social and economic life of their age into the religious law of Islam. They had not only to watch over the unimpaired authority of the *Sharī'a*, they had also to bring constitutional theory into line with political reality. This meant in practice that they had to achieve a reconciliation between the caliph as the highest authority in theory, and the sultan or emir as the actual wielder of power, by accommodating both under the Islamic law, which insisted on the unity of power spiritual and temporal. It was this compromise that saved and preserved the caliphate as an institution and, what is more, as a universal idea after the extinction of the Abbasid caliphate in 1258.

Muslim law does not differentiate between authority and power. The *Sharī'a* knows of only one supreme authority, that of the *imām*. He, in turn, can delegate all or part of his authority to his appointed ministers, governors and generals. Even those who "appointed" themselves sought *ex post facto* investiture in exchange for their recognition of the caliph's authority.

This leads us to the second point. In spite of an apparent similarity between some of the functions of caliph and of pope, the basis and nature of the Islamic and Christian states are fundamentally divergent. Both states, it is true, claim world-wide authority and power under God. Both are guided and determined by a central religious idea, which is represented by rulers whose functions, rights and duties at a first glance strike the historical observer as similar, if not identical. But the analogy of certain functions of caliph and pope, of priest and *imām*, of king and emir must not blind us to the fundamental difference between the corresponding offices and their holders in Islam and Christendom. In reality, the theoretical justification and practical application of the offices of the vicar of Christ and the vicegerent of the Prophet Muḥammad are based on different spiritual and theological premisses and different historical-political conditions. There are no two swords, a spiritual and a temporal, in Islam. Consequently there is no separation between state and church. In theory at least the offices of caliph and emir are united in one and the same person. In practice, the caliph often delegates his temporal authority to an emir, who exercises effective power but recognizes the spiritual authority of the caliph. This may be nothing more than a legal fiction; but it alone guaranteed the unity of Islam under the overall authority of the *Sharī'a*. This is not to deny that there were struggles for power in Islam, especially between weak caliphs and strong emirs backed by their military strength as generals, who usurped political power. But there was never a struggle, like that between pope and emperor in the Christian West, arising from different theories and their interpretation. There is no rival claim between the divine law of the church and the law of the state because Islam knows only one law, the divinely revealed *Sharī'a*, which holds sway over political life no less than over social, economic and cultural life. Life is one and indivisible; religion pervades and determines all its aspects. The whole of life is ordered by the religious, all-embracing divine law. The authority and validity of this law were never questioned by any effective Muslim ruler, no matter what his own practice was. He could not abrogate the religious law, though he might at times set it aside. The unchallenged exercise of political power could not clear him from offences against the *Sharī'a*, though the caliph would not dare to challenge him for want of effective power.

How the Muslim jurists dealt with this important problem in an age of weak central authority in a far-flung empire we shall see in the course of our discussion of the theory of the *khilāfa*.

An independent political philosophy is not to be expected. The existence of the state as the political organization of the *umma* or *jamā'a*, the Muslim community, is taken for granted. The jurists do not ask whether and why there must be a state; they are only concerned with the application of the *Sharī'a* to the body politic. Life has to be regulated in such a way that Muslims can prepare themselves for the world to come in willing submission to the will of Allah as laid down in the *Sharī'a*. The state presided over by the caliph as "Commander of the Faithful" is to guarantee the maintenance of pure Islam in conformity with its law, to protect the faithful and defend them against heretics and unbelievers. The world is divided into *dār al-Islam*, the territory over which Islamic rule extends, and *dār al-ḥarb*, the remaining lands to be won over to Islam, if need be by war after peaceful conversion has failed. *Jihād*, the "holy war" to spread the true faith in Allah over the whole earth and thus reduce and finally eliminate the *dār al-ḥarb*, is one of the basic duties for every Muslim. *Jihād* is to be waged against infidels and heretics.

Prayer, fasting, the giving of alms, poll-tax of the protected non-Muslims like Jews, Christians and Zoroastrians, are thus as much the concern of the Muslim state as the administration of justice, of finance and military organization. They all combine to make up the life of the members of the *umma*, bound to Allah. It is the task of the *khilāfa* to preserve the *umma* intact, free from disunity, strife and heresy. The caliphate has thus clearly defined duties as an institution in law, classified and codified in *Fiqh*. The *umma* is a living reality created by the prophet who, transcending family, clan and tribe, invited all Arabia to form the "Community of Muslims" (*Ummat al-Islam*). The brotherhoods inaugurated by him (*mu'ākhāt*) were associations of like-minded "believers" (*mu'minīn*) which he valued more highly than mere blood-brotherhood.[3] The concept of the *umma* has remained the one unifying factor amidst the diversity of the peoples of the Islamic empire. We must, therefore, never lose sight of the significant fact that this *umma* originated in the small band of the first followers of Muḥammad, the nucleus of that Medina for which he drew up what is called the "Statute of Medina".[4] The term *umma* denotes originally a religious community, not necessarily of Muslims, since it is applied to the Jews of Medina who are an *umma* in themselves, and in the "Statute" form together with the *mu'minīn*, the believers (in Allah),[5] the *ummat al-Islam* "apart from the men (*min dūna-l-nās*)", that is, all mankind outside the community of Muḥammad in Medina. "Community" is here used by Muḥammad in a religious, social and political sense, granting certain privileges to and imposing certain duties on all its members, Muslims, Jews and pagans. Among the privileges we find mutual protection (*dhimma*), and among the duties common war against a common enemy (*jihād*).

In a very real sense, the constitution of Muḥammad in Medina is the model for the constitution of the Islamic empire, since it already contains two important elements, *jihād* and *dhimma*, though both concepts have undergone transformation and expansion. *Jihād* came to comprise all non-Muslims with the exception of the *ahl-al-kitāb* who were protected, *dhimmīs*. Originally *jihād* was confined to a declared enemy, and *dhimma*, in the combination *dhimmat-Allah* meant mutual protection of all members of the *umma* of Medina. The core of this *umma* was, of course, formed by the "believers". As Wellhausen puts it: "faith is the link, the faithful are the standard-bearers of unity"[6] and "political unity aimed at becoming a unity of faith".[7] That means that Muḥammad's original mission as a purely religious call inevitably attained its consummation in a political organization, which naturally tended to consolidate itself by excluding all non-Muslims. Hence Muḥammad's war against the Jews who refused to give up their faith, the free practice of which was originally guaranteed them, and the reduction of the status of Jews, Christians and Zoroastrians to that of *dhimmīs*, of protected, second-class citizens of the Islamic state. At that stage they were no longer entitled or obliged to take part in *jihād* and share in its spoils. Their contribution to the treasury of the *ummat al-Islam* of Medina as equals was by payment of a poll-tax (*jizya*), demanded of inferior citizens by law. This change expresses perhaps most strikingly the unity of the political and the religious as the characteristic and peculiar feature of Islam and of the Islamic state, symbolized in the institution of the caliphate as the essence as well as the outward form of the *umma*. The office is more important than its holder, therefore the institution survived the extinction of the Abbasid caliphate. But since it is described in concrete terms of the functions of its representative we turn now to their definition and exposition.

The caliph is the defender of the faith, the dispenser of justice, the leader in prayer and in war, all in one. He is bound by the *Sharī'a* to the loyal, effective discharge of these duties, either in person or by delegating his authority to his appointed officials, chief among them the vizier and the *qāḍī* or judge, or more often to the sultan or emir who has usurped effective power by force. Everything connected with these offices of state is a part of constitutional law and is treated in the *Fiqh*-books under *khilāfa*.

The caliphate as an institution is based upon the Qur'ān: *Sūra* II, 28 attests to its divine origin and *Sūra* XXXVIII, 25 stresses the caliph's duty to act as a judge in these words: "Oh David! verily, we have established thee a vicegerent (*khalīfa*) in the earth, judge thou truthfully between men...." The nature of the caliph is clearly defined here: he is the vicegerent of Muḥammad the messenger of Allah; thus he commands spiritual authority and is at the same time temporal ruler and judge like David. Obedience to Muḥammad and those in authority is derived from *Sūra* IV, 62. In theory Islam is an absolute theocracy; in fact it is an absolute monarchy limited only by the caliph's dependence on the decisions of the *'ulamā*, from the time of Mu'āwiya onwards. According to Muslim tradition only the first four successors of Muḥammad were caliphs in the strict sense; with Mu'āwiya, *mulk* (absolute monarchy) arose. Yet some of the Abbasid caliphs came up to the standard required of the *imām* as "Commander of the Faithful", and although the distinction between *imāma* and *mulk* is of great importance for political theory and practice alike, we must not forget that the real meaning of the *khilāfa* is God-centred rule in conformity with the *Sharī'a*.

The interpretation of the *Sharī'a* undertaken by Sunnī jurists of the four recognized schools is, however, a compromise between the ideal norm and political reality. Its aim was clearly twofold: to vindicate and uphold the divine purpose of the Muslim state and to give support to the Abbasid caliphs in their struggle against both Sunnī and sectarian (*Shī'ī* in the first place) challenges to and encroachments on their authority.[8] A theory of government was evolved under pressure of rival claims to power. The treatises of the Abbasid period must thus be read in the light of this constitutional struggle; they reflect the existing political situation in the Islamic empire notwithstanding their theoretical superstructure in defence of the valid teaching of Qur'ān, Sunna and Hadith. This is true of the Ḥanafī Abū Yūsuf Ya'qūb's (731–98) introduction to his *Kitāb al-kharāj* which he wrote at the behest of the caliph Hārūn al-Rashīd, and also of two later authors contemporary with each other: the Shāfi'īs Al-Māwardī (991–1031) and Abū Manṣūr 'Abd al-Qāhir b. Ṭāhir al-Baghdādī (d. 1037); also of their fellow-Shāfi'īs Al-Ghazālī (d. 1111) and Badr al-Dīn Ibn Jamā'a (1241–1333); and of the Ḥanbalī Ibn Taymīya (d. 1328). The ideal Muslim state as *imāma* was as strongly upheld by the only Muslim thinker who developed an independent political theory, Ibn Khaldūn (1332–1406), when he contrasted it with the *mulk* as a man-made, exclusively this-worldly, temporal state. Leaning on his predecessors, he nevertheless formulated the difference in origin, development and purpose of the respective states within a philosophy of history built around the power-state and power-politics. He did this in a manner both concise and—as far as the power-state is concerned—novel, reaching beyond his own age and Muslim civilization. He approached past and contemporary history as an empiricist and was interested in the law governing history and politics, unlike the Muslim jurists, especially Al-Māwardī, on whose exposition of the *khilāfa* he drew extensively.

I. AL-MĀWARDĪ

We begin with Al-Māwardī's *Ordinances of Government* (*al-aḥkām al-sulṭānīya*)[9] which were written, as Professor Sir Hamilton Gibb has shown,[10] in an attempt to assert the authority of the Abbasid caliphs against the Buwaihid emirs who were in effective control of their state. The moment was auspicious in that Sultan Maḥmūd of Ghazna, though in unchallenged power over Persia, raised the prestige of the caliph in Baghdad by professing his loyalty to the house of Abbas. Al-Māwardī's treatise was intended as the theoretical basis for the delimitation of the spheres of authority between the caliph, in charge of religious affairs, and the emir, in effective control of civil administration on the basis of a negotiated agreement.

We might well ask: if effective power was so firmly in the hands of the Buwaihid emirs, why should they have agreed to recognize the supreme spiritual and temporal authority of the Abbasid caliph, to mention his name in the Friday prayer and to make a treaty with him? The answer makes plain the specific character of the Islamic state as a religious-political unity under the authority of Muslim law which bound rulers and ruled alike. If the rulers wanted to stay in power unchallenged and unhindered they dared not ignore the fundamental principle that the authority conferred by the *ijmāʿ* (*consensus*) of the *umma* or *jamāʿa*, the Muslim community, upon the lawful caliph was the only authority in law to which a Muslim would and could submit. To be clothed with the mantle of legality was worth a contract confirming their *delegated* authority and freeing them from the stigma of rebellion or usurpation. Only in this way could the unity of the community of the faithful under their commander be preserved. The task of the Sunnī jurists was thus not to formulate and interpret the doctrine of the *khilāfa*, but to harmonize an existing historical-political situation with the *Sharīʿa* by interpreting Qur'ān, Sunna and Hadith in the light of political reality in order to preserve the unity of the Muslim community. Hence the detailed exposition of the conditions required of the caliph, of his functions and those of the officers under his authority, both spiritual and temporal (or rather, religious and civil).[11]

Al-Māwardī insists on the necessity of the imamate and, by way of preamble, states with the authority of the Qur'ān: "the imamate is established to replace prophecy in the defence of the faith and the administration of the world."[12] *Ijmāʿ* is required to make the contract binding between the *umma* which confers the imamate and the *imām* who administers it. Next, he asks whether the imamate is demanded by reason or by the *Sharʿ* and declares for the latter. His justification is derived from the Qur'ān (IV, 62) and is directed against the Muʿtazilites—the first Muslims to establish a speculative theology, or rather an anti-Aristotelian religious philosophy—and against the *falāsifa* or philosophers influenced by Plato, Aristotle and their Neoplatonic successors and commentators.

In almost the same terms as are used later by the *falāsifa* and Ibn Khaldūn, he draws a distinction between government based on reason and the higher form of government based on revealed law. The first merely guards against mutual injustice, strife, discord and anarchy, while the second provides for the positive enforcement of law and justice in mutual confidence and friendship. Most important of all, the divinely revealed law enables the governor to administer religious affairs and prepare man for the hereafter.[13] The imamate is established by a contract between two parties: the *imām* and the *jamā'a*. To be able to rule efficiently and to defend the faith the *imām* must satisfy seven conditions, and the first of these is *'adāla*, justice, since his primary function is the administration of justice, according to the verse in the Qur'ān quoted above. Next, he must possess *'ilm*, knowledge of tradition, enabling him to make independent decisions and pass judgement on points of law (*ijtihād*).[14] In practice, this was the task of the *mujtahids*, the professional jurists, and their successors, the *muqallids*; these latter relied in their decisions entirely upon their predecessors instead of going back to the sources of law. The caliph must be physically and mentally fit to discharge his duties as ruler, and he must possess courage and determination to protect the territory of Islam and wage holy war (*jihād*) against its enemies and against the infidels. He must also be a descendant of the Quraish.

Ibn Khaldūn, who elaborates generally on these seven conditions,[15] goes into great detail on this question of descent. He traces its origin to the *anṣār*, the companions of the prophet, who is credited with the *hadith*: "The imamate belongs to the Quraish." He cites in support the *Ṣaḥīḥ* of Al-Bukhārī, one of the authentic collections of traditions, and discusses at great length the importance of belonging to a strong group animated by *'Aṣabīya*, the corporate sense common to a family, clan or tribe which gives the group staying power and the drive born of a common outlook. The coherence of a group is impaired by the weakening of this force, to the point where common action finally becomes impossible. Ibn Khaldūn believed this to be an inevitable process like all other natural forces.

That some jurists denied the necessity of descent from the Quraish was proof for him of the decline and disappearance of the '*Aṣabīya* among the Quraish, rendering them incapable of rule over their tribe, the Muḍar, and through it over the community of the faithful.[16]

Al-Māwardī, like Al-Baghdādī, insists on the election of the caliph by qualified electors.[17] This is directed against the *Shī'a* which practised the method of designation. It ignores Umayyad and Abbasid practice as well. The elector must possess '*adāla* and be conversant with the conditions laid down as necessary for the caliph. Both qualifications were often absent, and after a ruling of Al-Ash'arī Sunnī jurists had to be satisfied when at least one qualified elector[18] had made the election. Even the nomination of a successor by the ruling *imām*, for example of a son—not necessarily the firstborn—by his father, had to be condoned. The jurists were simply guided by historical precedent. They were engaged in a rationalization of the actual historical situation, and relied on the authority of the historians of the caliphate, like Ibn Sa'd, Ibn Hishām, Ibn al-Athīr, Ṭabarī and others.

We must not expect from these writers the historical sense or the power to criticize their sources which we demand today. We must accept their habit of interpreting events of the past in the light of their contemporary experience, and of basing their accounts partly on spurious traditions (hadiths) and apocryphal stories. But even though tendentiousness sometimes triumphs over authenticity, and pious legend often replaces reality, we do learn how they pictured to themselves and for their readers and hearers the life, manners and actions of Muḥammad and his companions, and of the Umayyad and Abbasid caliphs, especially if we take into account the poets as well. It stands to reason that their biographies and histories contain material which would not pass muster when examined by modern textual, literary and historical criticism. But this did not deter the writers on constitutional theory and practice from basing their theories on the history of the caliphate so presented. They sought and found justification for the course of that history in Sunna and Hadith, authentic and imaginary. What appears to us as pious fraud, as born of political expediency, as condoning aggression and brute force must be set against the overriding principle ruling the guardians and interpreters of Muslim law: to preserve the unity of the Muslim community under the authority of the *khalīfa* whose religious aura increased in proportion to the decrease of his effective power and authority.[19]

They were after all not political philosophers, and politics as a discipline did not interest them. They were exponents of one of the four recognized schools of law, and politics found a place in the *Fiqh*-books mainly because of its combined religious and legal aspects, embodied in constitutional law, and because the caliphate, as the frame within which the life of the *umma* was lived, was the successor of Muḥammad's religious-social-political community of the faithful. Muslim constitutional law is the result of the confrontation of the *Shar'*—the ideal, divinely revealed law—with the historical and political reality of the Islamic empire, which was made up of pre-Islamic Arabian, Byzantine, Persian and Roman elements.

Faced with the need to justify two forms of caliphal succession, by election or by designation, jurists had to lean on the historians, who were no more expert in constitutional theory than they themselves were skilled in historical criticism. These historians were not guided by an authoritative political theory based on the *Sharī'a* when they were writing their chronicles and histories. And notwithstanding exceptions like Ibn al-Ṭiqṭaqa or Ibn Khaldūn we must not overlook their partisanship, so evident in the idealization of the four "right-guided" first caliphs, or in their open or ill-concealed hostility to the Umayyads.

The principle of the election of a caliph is thus based on the historians' description of the choice of Abū Bakr by five companions of Muḥammad and of the choice of Uthmān after 'Omar had laid a charge on six, including Uthmān himself, to elect one among their number as his successor. This choice had to be confirmed by the people. In technical terms, this means that election takes place by *bay'a*, investiture with the electors' oath of loyalty, to be followed by *bay'a* in public, expressing the *ijmā'* of the community.[20]

If a choice had to be made between two candidates the electors were guided by the circumstances of the time. Political unrest or external danger tipped the scales in favour of courage and determination. Otherwise a learned candidate was preferred, who was better able to guard the community against heresy and error, the foremost duty of the caliph as the defender of the faith.[21]

The duties of the commander of the faithful naturally derive from the conditions he must fulfil, which will therefore be discussed in detail presently. Once elected and invested the caliph binds himself to the *jamāʿa* by a contract (*ʿahd*) guaranteeing loyal fulfilment of his duties and receiving in exchange a binding promise of obedience. The contract can be concluded only after the investiture (*bayʿa*) by the *ahl al-ḥall wa-l-ʿaqd* "the people (with power) to bind and to loosen". He cannot be replaced even by a man more worthy than himself, unless he forfeits the imamate by loss of freedom. This can come about in either of two ways: he may be made prisoner and thus unable to exercise his functions, or the seizure of effective power by an emir may place him under restraint. In the latter case the *preferable* candidate must appear on the scene after the investiture (*bayʿa*) and the conclusion of the contract (*ʿahd*) between *imām* and *jamāʿa* have taken place. It is not impossible that behind the terms *preferred* (*mafḍūl*) and *preferable* (*afḍal*) there is concealed the struggle between a lawful *imām* and a pretender who contests the caliphal dignity. This pretender may already be an emir or sultan. If it were to come to an open struggle and the pretender were to win, the lawful caliph would either be made prisoner or placed under restraint, and he would consequently forfeit his dignity. In such a contingency the usurper must be recognized. Here theory is made to suit an existing political emergency which can only be terminated by legalizing usurpation.[22]

Hence the importance of the right choice of those to whom he delegates some of his functions. The Buwaihid emirs illustrate this vividly by their "loyalty", which was embodied in the agreement which they concluded with the Abbasids. It is this precedent which guided Al-Māwardī and Al-Baghdādī in their exposition of constitutional law and their concentration on the respective administrative functions of caliph and emir.[23] But while they were at one in demanding the institution of the caliphate and in insisting on the election of the caliph, they differed in their attitude to the existence of two *imāms* at the same time. Al-Māwardī, in opposition to Al-Ashʿarī, forbids it, recognizing only the Abbasid caliph in Baghdad to the exclusion of the Umayyads in Spain and the Fatimids in Egypt. Al-Baghdādī, though not approving, nevertheless permits it on condition that they are far apart from each other,[24] thus simply recognizing an established fact. Such an attitude shows to what extent jurists allowed themselves to be influenced by political reality and to what extreme lengths they were prepared to go in jeopardizing the theoretical ideal. Moreover, the Qur'ān enjoins obedience to "those who exercise authority" (IV, 62). This is adduced irrespective of the clearly intended meaning of authority as *lawful* authority.

We have noted that there are differences of opinion as to how the office of caliph or *imām* is obtained. Apart from election, a caliph can be chosen and invested as the result of his designation by the reigning caliph. This is expressed by the term *'ahd*, and the designated successor is styled *walī-l-'ahd*, "heir-presumptive".[25]

This type of succession is again justified by historical precedent, but this time without scriptural warrant. Al-Māwardī adduces two examples from the early period of Islam: Abū Bakr's designation of 'Omar, accepted by the Muslim *jamā'a*, and Uthmān's succession to 'Omar. The second example is strange, since 'Omar's appointment of six companions (the *ahl al-shūra*) who were to consult with each other to choose one of their number as his successor is usually claimed to constitute an election, not a designation. These two acts serve Al-Māwardī as precedents to legalize the hereditary transfer of the dignity of *imām* within the Abbasid dynasty, whose interests he promoted. The precedents are valid because they were set by the first two of the four *khulafā rāshidūn* ("right-guided" caliphs), who are universally acclaimed as shining examples of the ideal Muslim ruler. The Umayyads were "kings", founders and promoters of *mulk*, political authority built on power. The jurists are at pains, as Al-Māwardī clearly shows, to qualify their recognition of designated succession by stipulating that the reigning *imām* should choose the best fitted and qualified person as his successor. According to the majority of jurists,[26] this successor is the legitimate *imām* even without the formal consent of the electors prescribed by the *Shar'*, provided always that his investiture is followed by the conclusion of the contract (*'ahd*). He may or may not be a son or relative of the reigning caliph. This is in agreement with pre-Islamic tribal practice among the Arabs. But the history of both the Umayyad and Abbasid dynasties shows that sons—not necessarily the firstborn since there is no right of primogeniture in Islam—or kinsmen were invested with the imamate.

Al-Māwardī discusses frankly and fairly the different opinions of the jurists on whether or not the caliph is entitled to designate one of his sons or relations as his successor and whether he acts legally in doing so. This difference of opinion reflects different attitudes to the institution of the caliphate and to its nature. Those who recognize the absolute authority of the caliph as head of the Muslim nation naturally concede him the right, in his capacity as ruler, to appoint a successor. Those who do not recognize his authority as absolute justify their opposition by declaring that family considerations must not weigh with the caliph, who is bound by law to choose one who fulfils the conditions laid down for the holder of the office of *imām*. He is clearly under the law and his authority subordinate to that of the law. In theory they are certainly right. Others concede the reigning caliph the right to designate his father, but not his son. All other relations are accounted as non-kinsmen for this purpose.

The safeguards which Al-Māwardī stipulates, such as the consent of the person designated as successor, and his compliance with the required qualifications for the office of *imām*, are purely theoretical and merely serve further to clothe hereditary succession with the mantle of legality.[27]

The principle of election is explicitly affirmed in the case of a caliph who chooses two heirs without assigning priority to one of them. After his death the electors must exercise their prerogative and choose one of them; as historical precedent 'Omar's charge to the companions to elect a successor is again quoted. We see from this example that 'Omar's action can be used for both types, election and designation, although in the latter case the choice between more than one candidate is left undecided. It seems that Al-Māwardī favoured election proper.

The electors can act only after the caliph's death. During his lifetime his authorization is required unless he is no longer in effective control. In this case a situation has arisen which is equivalent to his death.[28]

A further important element is now introduced into the theory of the *khilāfa*: it is the public welfare (*maṣāliḥ 'āmma*). It determines the order of priority when making provision for three successive heirs presumptive. The authority for such a threefold designation is, naturally, again a historical precedent. This time

Muḥammad's successive designation of generals in the field is the source, and what he decrees for the emirate—the *Amīr* is originally and primarily a military leader—is transferred to the imamate. Here we must remember that the title *Amīr al-mu'minīn* given to the caliph denotes his function as leader in the *jihād*, the holy war. As we have seen, this is one of his principal qualifications. Significantly, Al-Māwardī claims that this practice, well established under the two dynasties, was recognized as valid by the *'ulamā* of the time. Hārūn al-Rashīd is said to have consulted the most excellent *'ulamā* of his time before he designated three of his sons as his possible successors. This step was taken in case premature death or disqualifying incapacity removed the caliph-designate before the death of the reigning caliph, who wanted to make sure of dynastic succession by designating more than one person in a certain order of priority.[29] The example of Hārūn al-Rashīd shows the practice which has become established: consultation with the *'ulamā* so as to be in conformity with the *Shar'*, a formal act of designation in their presence followed by the *bay'a* of the *'ulamā* as the *ahl al-ḥall wa-l-'aqd*. *Bay'a* signified the recognition of the caliph-designate and the promise of loyal obedience to him.[30]

Al-Māwardī's claim that such an act of designation is in the public interest simply superimposes on the caliph's regard for dynastic power and influence the general welfare of the *umma*.

Of equal interest and importance is the general contention that once the caliph has died and one of his heirs-presumptive has succeeded him, the new caliph is free to appoint his own successors by designation. He is not bound by the designation of his predecessor since he is now the only supreme authority and is entitled to exercise the caliph's prerogative and powers.[31]

Al-Māwardī shows that he could appreciate the force of political necessity and dynastic considerations when, for example, he defends Al-Manṣūr's efforts to persuade 'Īsa b. Mūsa voluntarily to renounce his designation as second in succession by the preceding caliph As-Saffāḥ, in favour of Al-Mahdī, Al-Manṣūr's own choice. Yet he quietly re-enters the realm of ideal theory in assigning ten principal duties of public concern to the caliph.

The first is to guard the faith based on its established principles and on the consensus (*ijmā'*) of the first Muslims (*salaf al-umma*). As mentioned before, this condition presupposes the quality of *'ilm* to be understood as expert knowledge of the tenets and traditions of Islam, and the ability to expound and defend them against heretics. That this duty heads the list is indicative of the emphasis the Abbasids laid on the spiritual side of their office.

Next, he must execute and preserve justice, in conformity with his own *'adāla*, that is to say, he should have a good character, and be just, honourable and right-minded.

Defence of the territory of Islam, protection of life and limb, and guarantee of the livelihood of the Muslims comes third, reflecting the qualification of *kifāya*, or the satisfaction of all the requirements of the material side of his office.

Fourthly, he is obliged to see that punishment for offences is meted out in accordance with the prohibitions of Allah, and that the rights of his subjects are upheld.

From the realm of justice we move to that of military action, the garrisoning of frontiers and especially the waging of *jihād* against those who have been invited to accept Islam but have refused, until they have either been converted or have accepted the status of protected non-Muslim *ahl al-kitāb* (Jews, Christians and Zoroastrians) as *Dhimmīs*. From here we proceed to the religious obligations of *fay'*, the just distribution of booty from the *jihād*, and of *ṣadaqāt*, the giving of alms, charity.

This is followed by the responsibility for sound financial administration and for the judicious selection of competent, loyal officials. This duty is no doubt implied in his *kifāya*.

Lastly, the caliph is enjoined to extend his personal supervision to public affairs and to apply himself to the government (*siyāsa*) of the nation (*umma*, the Muslim community), and to the defence of religion (*milla*). In support Al-Māwardī cites Qur'ān, XXXVIII, 25: David, as the *khalīfa* on earth, has to decide justly between men and must not follow his passions, for they deflect him from the path of God.[32]

It is evident that these ten duties are all religious, being directly related to God and likened to a walking in "the path of Allah". Although they are divided into religious duties in the narrow sense, and judicial, administrative, financial and military duties, they are all complementary and all derived from the divine institution of the office of *khalīfa* or *imām*. They show quite clearly the unity of religion and politics, of the spiritual and temporal, or religious and secular aspects of a life centred in and leading to God. The theory of the caliphate is clearly modelled upon the primitive *ummat al-Islam* of Muḥammad in Medina. Historians and writers of "Mirrors for Princes" stress the divine origin of the caliphal office,[33] and in the later Abbasid period the designation *khalīfat Allah* for the caliph has gained wide currency, in marked distinction from the insistence of earlier periods that the caliph was only the *khalīfa* of the Prophet (as was suggested in the saying attributed to Abū Bakr in which he refused to be called the vicegerent of Allah).

Finally, Al-Māwardī reviews the conditions for the effective maintenance of the office of *imām* and discusses what constitutes a valid ground for its forfeiture. This is physical or mental unfitness, and here he takes the opportunity to stress once more that the caliph must be able to interpret the faith correctly and that he must have freedom of movement and be unencumbered by restraint or violence. There can be little doubt that the contemporary situation is largely responsible for this detailed and precise exposition.

Reverting to the problem of the accession to power, we note in conclusion that it is unanimously held that the office-holder possesses authority only if he is confirmed in office by the *ijmā'* of the community. The community acts under divine guidance and its agreed choice and recognition are therefore infallible. Muḥammad is credited with the saying: "My community will never agree upon an error." On this all schools are agreed, and parallels between Shāfi'ī and Ḥanbalī expositions of constitutional law are numerous, as can be seen from the treatise of Ibn Abī Ya'la b. al-Farrā (990–1065), which bears the same title as Al-Māwardī's.

The two hundred years which separate the death of Ibn Abī Ya'la b. al-Farrā and the birth of another Ḥanbalī jurist of far more colourful personality, Ibn Taymīya, brought important political and spiritual developments which naturally made their mark on the minds and expositions of writers on Muslim constitutional law. Two Shāfi'īs are of paramount importance and deserve special attention, Al-Ghazālī and Ibn Jamā'a.

2. AL-GHAZĀLĪ

The gulf that separates the classical theory of the *khilāfa* based on the ideal *Shar'* from the political reality of the Abbasid caliphate dominated by the Seljuq sultanate is manifested perhaps most strikingly in the utterances on the *imāma* of the celebrated Shāfi'ī theologian, religious philosopher and mystic Abū Ḥāmid al-Ghazālī.[34] More than any other jurist mentioned in this survey, his utterances must be understood against the background of contemporary political and religious controversies and struggles. His personality and his quick reaction to spiritual trends and political movements and situations have left their unmistakable mark on every word he wrote. Ibn Rushd (Averroes) opposed him, and his verdict that Al-Ghazālī was all things to all men is certainly coloured by polemics.[35] Besides, consistency must not be expected when inconsistency passed unnoticed in the mind and conscience of medieval thinkers, least of all in Islam, which managed to accommodate within itself many contradictory systems of thought. Al-Ghazālī is not alone in changing his mind or his allegiance to ideas and to those who hold them. His friends of yesterday became his opponents more than once, perhaps with rather too great ease. But there can be little doubt that he was sincere in his search for God and wholehearted in his allegiance so long as it lasted. In examining his utterances on politics this means that we must take into consideration the time and circumstances no less than the purpose he had in mind when making them. Then, we are not surprised to find, in his *K. al-iqtiṣād fī-l-'itiqād*, an exposition of the nature and purpose of the *imāma* as orthodox and classical as that of Al-Māwardī; yet his *K. al-mustazhirī* is generously tempered with political realism and preparedness to make concessions to expediency. Later, in his *Iḥyā al-'ulūm*, he bows to the actual power of the Seljuq sultanate in his attempt to preserve the institution of the caliphate as the symbol of the unity of the Muslim community.

In the *K. al-iqtiṣād fī-l-'itiqād* he speaks as a jurist, and there is significance in his initial claim at the beginning of the third chapter "On the *imāma*" that its investigation was a matter for jurisprudence, not for practical affairs (*muhimmāt*) nor for metaphysics (*ma'qūlāt*). He thus denies the philosophers the right to examine the *imāma* in the light of Greek political philosophy, no doubt having Ibn Sīnā in mind. He makes this clear by stating that "it is not required by reason, but by the (divine) law (*Shar*ʿ)",[36] just as Al-Māwardī had.[37] It is a view which agrees with his assertion in the introduction to Part II (Metaphysics) of his *Maqāṣid al-falāsifa*, that politics as the first of the three practical sciences aims at "man's welfare in this world and bliss in the next, attainable only if government is rooted in the legal and completed by the political sciences (*ʿulūm sharʿīya, ʿulūm siyāsīya*)".[38]

That he wanted to remove the problem of the *imāma* from the realm of practical politics is understandable when we remember that the purpose of the *K. al-mustazhirī* is to establish the legitimacy of the Abbasid caliph Al-Mustazhir against the opposition of the *Bāṭinīya* sect who recognized his Fatimid rival.[39] Since effective power was exercised by the Seljuq sultan, Al-Ghazālī had to base his claim for the Abbasid caliph's legitimacy on *Fiqh*.

For this reason, the necessity of the *imāma* and the qualifications and duties of the *imām* or caliph are justified in almost identical terms in both treatises, though Al-Ghazālī is less exacting in his demands on the caliph in the *K. al-mustazhirī*. The *imāma* is necessary because it is of advantage and keeps away damage in the world;[40] it is an indispensable institution of Muslim life demanded by the *ijmā*ʿ of the community, after the death of Muḥammad, when the maintenance of the religious and political order made the immediate investiture of the *imām* imperative.[41] But the *ijmā*ʿ of the *umma* is not sufficient, for "the good order[42] of religion" is obtained only "by an *imām* who is obeyed". In fact, "the good order of religion is possible only through the good order of the world", which, in turn, is dependent on an "*imām* who is obeyed". The word *imām* is replaced by *sulṭān*, a few lines farther down. That he means by *sulṭān* "authority, power", and not "the man in power, the ruler", is clear from the Hadith he quotes in his support: "Religion and ⟨temporal⟩ power are twins"[43] and the continuation: "therefore it is said that *dīn* is the foundation and *sulṭān* is the guardian."[44] This is orthodox doctrine, maintaining the religious-political unity of Islam. Yet the stress on power is significant even though it is only a means to an end, this end being the good order of religion with ultimate happiness (*saʿāda ākhira* or *s. quṣwā*[45]) as final goal, "and this is undoubtedly the aim of the prophets".[46]

Having demonstrated the necessity of the imamate, Al-Ghazālī proceeds to enumerate the virtues by which the *imām* must be distinguished in order to lead those entrusted to his care to the goal which the *Sharī'a* has set for man. Although we meet with the qualifications stipulated by Al-Māwardī, they are partly modified to meet the general political situation and the particular case of Al-Mustazhir.

Ability to wage *jihād* is conditioned by the possession of prowess and courage (*najda wa-shajā'a*). It has always been considered one of the foremost duties of the caliph. But Al-Ghazālī, faced with a young caliph and a powerful Seljuq master, explains away its absence in Al-Mustazhir by pointing to the *shawka*, the force and power of the Seljuqs which guarantees the *najda* required of the caliph. He wants to think of them not as independent rulers but as the loyal servants of the caliph.

In the same way he disposes of the awkward condition of *kifāya*, the competent discharge of the duties of government and administration. The requirements of the law are fulfilled as long as the caliph is supported by experts and a conscientious vizier.

He treats *'ilm* in the same way. Al-Ghazālī finds an ingenious and spirited defence for the caliph who lacks the power of *ijtihād*, the prime constituent element of *'ilm* which, he avers, does not mean theological authority. There was no command of the lawgiver to this effect, nor is this quality required in the public interest (*maṣlaḥa*). In matters of effective power the caliph leans on the strongest, the Seljuqs; in matters of statecraft on the wisdom of his vizier. Why should he then not rely on the expert *'ulamā* of his time in matters of *'ilm*? Hence the advice to the caliph to consult his *'ulamā* and act upon it, being so to speak a *muqallid* who relies on the authority of others better qualified.[47]

Al-Ghazālī would rather have *taqlīd* (reliance on (previous) authority) than have the state upset and disturbed by the deposition of a caliph who is incapable of *ijtihād* and the appointment of a candidate who would fulfil this requirement. Such a lenient interpretation of the *Sharī'a* could hardly be justified as contributing to the "good order of religion" which he so often stresses, and *dīn* looks more like a stepbrother than a twin of *sulṭān* or *mulk*.

To compensate for this lax application of the *Shar'* Al-Ghazālī introduces *wara'*: fear of God, a pious way of life, and the refraining from dubious practices as the fourth moral quality required of the *imām*. Whereas the three others are of public concern and of importance both for religion and government, piety is an entirely personal matter.[48] That Al-Ghazālī should stress it is not only a sign of his own piety, but also a reflection of the state of affairs at the time when the caliph ruled only by delegated authority, but was useful as an example of personal religion.

The caliph is enjoined to delegate authority to one possessed of *shawka*, who in return swears him allegiance. Al-Ghazālī has the Seljuqs in mind. The fiction is maintained, however, that ultimate responsibility rests with the caliph, who is entitled to the homage and obedience of the great men of the realm and of "those with power to bind and to loosen". It is he, not his delegate, the wielder of effective power, who restrains men from bloodshed and ensures their welfare in this world and in the future life (*ma'āsh wa-ma'ād*). He must consult the *'ulamā* and act on their advice.[49] Al-Ghazālī never tires of pointing this out.

That he should impress upon Al-Mustazhir his obligation to study the law (*Shar'*) assiduously, because he can count on the obedience of his subjects only if he lives and governs in accordance with the regulations of the *Sharī'a*, is what one would expect a Muslim spiritual leader to recommend to his sovereign. Such advice is a usual ingredient of "Mirrors for Princes" and ethical treatises. Both genres have been cultivated in abundance by Muslim men of letters. Al-Ghazālī is no exception. That the *imāma* based on justice (*'adāla*) is the highest form of *'ibāda*, of service of God, follows from what he has said about *dīn wa-dunya*. Knowledge and application of the *Sharī'a* are the caliph's sure guides in his august office. Knowledge (*ma'rifa*) and service of God (*'ibāda*) guarantee the good order of religion (*niẓām al-dīn*).[50]

The caliph is confined to "religious" duties in the strict sense of the word. He is enjoined to concentrate on the study of the law (*Sharī'a*) and to practise the religious virtues of piety, humility, charity and compassion as the *khalīfat Allah*. For this reason, Al-Ghazālī concentrates in the third part of his chapter "On the *imāma*" in the *K. al-iqtiṣād* on an exposition of the *'aqīda*, faith and religious conviction, of the *ahl al-sunna*, the orthodox Muslims, concerning the *ṣaḥāba*, the companions of Muḥammad, and the *Khulafā rāshidūn*. In the *K. al-mustazhirī* the caliph is asked, in a manner reminiscent of the "Mirrors for Princes", to heed the advice to rulers of earlier religious teachers, and to be guided by the wise sayings of just *imāms* of the past.

But Al-Ghazālī goes a long way further. With great courage (or is it cynicism?) he introduces a new way of designating a new caliph by recognizing in law an existing practice, the designation by the sultan who is in effective power and is the actual ruler.[51] With complete frankness, he draws the logical conclusion from the existence of a weak, powerless caliph and a strong sultan in effective control of government and administration. It is clear from a remark at the end of the second of the three parts into which he divides his discourse on the *imāma* in the *K. al-mustazhirī* that he was fully aware of the complete absence of the conditions necessary for a fully functioning caliph and that the *imāma* in his day was really a sham. This is acknowledged in his *Iḥyā*, when he says that the Abbasid caliph is the lawful occupant of the office of *imām* by contract and as such bears the responsibility which goes with it. But the function of government is carried out by sultans who owe him allegiance. Government is in the hands of those who are backed by military force. The caliph is, in his definition, he to whom the wielder of force gives his allegiance. As long as the authority of the caliph is thus recognized, government is lawful. The alternative, if such a government built on brute military force were declared illegal, would be chaos and lawlessness. Public welfare and its institutions like the judiciary, finance (with responsibility for collection of the taxes imposed by the *Sharī'a*) and police would be utterly disregarded. There can be no question even of deposing a tyrannous sultan. For it would be extremely difficult to unseat him while he has the army behind him; disorder and confusion would be the only result. Order and the welfare of the state must be safeguarded. Al-Ghazālī simply repeats here what he had already said of the inadvisability of deposing a caliph lacking the qualification of *ijtihād*, transferring it to the sultan who must consequently be left in authority and rendered obedience. Al-Ghazālī does not actually quote Qur'ān IV, 62 in support of his contention, but contents himself with applying early Hadiths, claiming obedience to the caliph, to the temporal rulers who have usurped power and are in effective control of the government. His definition of the sultan is equally revealing. The sultan is the man in control of affairs who owns allegiance to the *imām* and grants him his prerogatives, that is, he mentions the caliph's name in the address (*khuṭba*) during the public Friday prayer and mints coins bearing the name of the reigning caliph (*sikka*). His orders and judgements are valid wherever he holds sway.[52]

3. IBN JAMĀʿA

Another Shāfiʿī, Badr al-Dīn Ibn Jamāʿa (1241–1333)[53] takes and further develops, in his treatise devoted to constitutional theory and administrative law,[54] the views previously expressed by Al-Ghazālī. It is based on Qur'ān, Sunna, the examples (*āthār*) of the companions of the Prophet, and the utterances (*aqwāl*) of the *ʿulamā* of the lands (of Islam). Of its seventeen chapters the first five concern us in particular; they deal with the necessity of the *imāma*, the conditions and duties of the *imām*, and the regulations governing his office[55] and those of his principal ministers. It is here that a further source for his exposition is discernible, his personal experience as *qāḍī*, coupled with a clear insight into the mechanism of the political life of his time.

He justifies the necessity of the *imāma* with verses from the Qur'ān, couching their interpretation in religious and ethical terms. The treatise begins with XXXVIII, 25, followed by XXII, 42, and the comment that God lends his support to those kings who fulfil four conditions: prayer, almsgiving, commanding what is pleasing to God and forbidding what is displeasing to him.

The duties of the *imām* are summarized as "the defence of the *dīn* (religion), the warding off of offenders, granting compensation to those wronged [...], and establishing right. For herein consists the welfare of the lands, the security of the subjects, and the stemming of the tide of corruption ⟨and decay⟩. The affairs of mankind are in good order only if a sultan devotes himself to their administration (*siyāsa*) and to their protection exclusively."[56]

Ibn Jamāʿa then adds to the argument from necessity a religious one: the institution of the *imāma* is also an act of God's grace. The high quality of the ruler, styled "the shadow of God on earth", reflects on the ruled. A just ruler guarantees just subjects.[57] More important than these pious platitudes or, more positively, than this ideal picture of the caliph, is his view, expressed in the name of some sages (*ḥukamā*), that forty years of tyranny from the sultan are better than the abandonment of his subjects for one hour. This establishes the principle of acquiescence in bad rule which we have already met with in Al-Ghazālī's *Iḥyā*.[58] Authority is preferable to anarchy. The old-established principle that the caliph can be deposed if he acts contrary to the *Sharī'a*, or that if he issues regulations contrary to it he must be disobeyed, has been quietly abandoned in favour of obedience to any lawfully constituted authority. It is for this reason that all jurists, no matter how far they were prepared to compromise with the source of effective power, insisted on the investiture of the *imām* and on his supreme authority in theory. They accepted as lawful first partial and, later, complete delegation of the functions of government, even to a usurper—as long as he swore allegiance to the caliph.

Ibn Jamā'a, writing a treatise on constitutional law, naturally mentions election as one method of installing a caliph. But following Al-Ghazālī he declares force to be a lawful second method. Like Al-Ghazālī he stipulates ten qualifications in the candidate for the *imāma* compared with Al-Mawārdī's seven. The three additional qualifications are that the candidate must be a male, a Muslim and free.

He departs from Al-Māwardī and other earlier jurists in two important points. He includes designation of a successor by the reigning *imām* in the method of election. By subdividing the first method into election and designation, he arrives at three methods like Al-Ghazālī; but his third method goes beyond that of his predecessor since he terms it forceful seizure, which is naturally not the same as Al-Ghazālī's designation of a caliph by the sultan who wields effective power. Ibn Jamā'a obviously has in mind a powerful military leader usurping the supreme authority by appointing himself to the office of *imām*.

In addition to recognizing usurpation *de jure* he dispenses with the conclusion of a contract between *imām* and *jamā'a*, the Muslim community. This is his second point of departure. The election is valid and lawful if followed by the investiture, *bay'a*; it need not be confirmed and sealed by the *'aqd* (contract). *Bay'a* thus implies the obedience of the whole community and not only of the *ahl al-ḥall wa-l-ʿaqd*, provided he is the only *imām* at the time.[59] He concedes that disobedience towards Allah on the part of the *imām* absolves the community from obeying him. Wherein such disobedience consists he does not make explicit. But he asserts that obedience to authority (*amr*) is a religious duty since it is commanded in the Qur'ān (IV, 62). He declares this verse to mean that God coupled the duty of obedience to those who are in command (or authority) with that to him and to his Prophet-messenger. Hence it is an absolute duty. Therefore, obedience to the caliph is identical with obedience to God, and the *bayʿa* rendered to the caliph actually equals *bayʿa* to God.

The third method, *bayʿa* through force, is effected by the "coercion of the wielder of force" (*qahru-ṣāḥibi-l-shawka*), either if there is an *imām* whom he has overpowered or if there is no *imām* in office at the time. Self-investiture by armed force is lawful, and obedience is due to such a ruler "so that the unity of the Muslims is assured and that they speak with one voice".[60]

Purely political considerations alone would not have induced Ibn Jamāʿa to condone and recognize as lawful the imamate of usurpation by military force. His chief concern was undoubtedly to preserve the unity of the Muslim community and Islam as the unifying bond.[61] But it must be admitted that he compromised to an astonishing degree with political realities and stretched his concept of legality very nearly to breaking-point. For he actually ruled that if one usurper is challenged and vanquished by another, the first is deposed and the second becomes *imām* in his place, "for the sake of the welfare of the Muslims and of their unity". Legalized expediency is still expediency, and the flouting of the *Sharīʿa* remains unmitigated, no matter how punctiliously formalities are observed, for very little, if any, meaning can attach to a *bayʿa* in such circumstances.

By letting the "king-maker" make himself "king", Ibn Jamāʿa has thus come to the end of the road on which Al-Ghazālī had already far advanced. He did so quite unashamedly and openly without trying to accommodate the ideal theory to political reality. A further concession to political practice can be seen in the legalizing of a general delegacy of authority "as is the custom of kings and sultans in our time". This means that such a *khalīfa* of the *imām* has authority, delegated authority, to appoint judges and governors (or prefects) and to be himself in charge of the army and the treasury, in peace and in war against enemies and heretics. Apart from Quraishite descent he must possess the same qualifications as the *imām* in whose place he rules, no doubt a purely theoretical demand in the interests of the supreme authority of the *Sharī'a*. We must see in this an attempt to make the usurpation of power appear legal by associating it with the vizierate of delegation or the general emirate.[62]

The wheel has come full circle, and the caliph has become in law what he has been for a long time in fact, a mere figurehead. According to the *Sharī'a*, not only judges but all government functionaries derive their authority direct from the caliph; otherwise their acts and actions are null and void. That Ibn Jamā'a legalized a delegation of all caliphal prerogatives and duties to the wielder of effective power shows, to my mind, concern, at least in theory, for the rule of law, the divinely revealed *Shar'*. Dispensing with the condition of Quraishite descent may be intended to help preserve the Abbasids in at least formal possession of the caliphal dignity, provided the usurper was satisfied with exercising full authority as the Abbasid caliph's vicegerent. It would then be another instance of regard for the *Sharī'a*. Delegation of authority can certainly be accommodated within the law more rightfully and easily than *de jure* recognition of usurpation of the highest authority by force of arms. This, however, Ibn Jamā'a has also conceded.

Closer attention to the problems connected with such a general delegacy of authority shows Ibn Jamā'a's deep concern for Islam and its *Shar'*. The caliph (*khalīfa*) *must* entrust the king (*malik*) with the administration of the territory which he has subdued by force of arms, and call for obedience to this ruler in order to avoid opposition, disunity and a split in the nation (*umma*). "The delegation of power becomes thereby sound, effective, lawful government." If the usurper lacks the necessary qualifications, the caliph is permitted to proclaim his investiture, but he must designate a representative or vicegerent capable of "conducting the affairs of state in the interests of religious and worldly welfare".[63] There is, in principle, no difference between a territory far away from the central government and the entire realm of Islam, as the reference to precedents established by the Prophet shows.

Ibn Jamā'a's stark political realism is tempered with the theologian's and the jurist's concern for the mutual duties between sultan/caliph and community. They number ten on either side and are derived from Qur'ān and Hadith.

His definition of those who exercise authority is cautious: "they are the *imām* and his representatives according to the majority. But it is also said that they are the *'ulamā*."[63]

Describing the *imām's* representatives, Ibn Jamā'a begins, like Al-Māwardī, with the vizier, and justifies the institution of the vizierate by the inability of the *imām* or sultan to attend to all matters of religion (*milla*) and of the welfare of the nation (*umma*) which are entrusted to him. The sovereign, therefore, needs the help of a *wazīr* who shares with him the supervision of all affairs of state (*naẓar*), and the administration (*tadbīr*, government).[64] The vizier is responsible for the just and efficient administration of justice and finance under the sovereign, who can depose him. Like Al-Māwardī, Ibn Jamā'a distinguishes between a vizierate of delegation (*tafwīḍ*) and of execution (of the orders of the caliph/sultan, *tanfīdh*). The former implies independent conduct of all affairs of state; such a vizier-in-charge is practically independent, exercising full power and authority, guided by his own *ra'y* and *ijtihād*, that is, independent opinion, judgement and decision, as long as he keeps the sovereign fully informed of his actions. Hence, he must possess the same qualifications as the caliph himself, except descent from the Quraish. The caliph has the right and the duty to examine carefully, in the light of his *ra'y* and *ijtihād*, the vizier's actions and then to confirm what he approves and to revoke what he disapproves.[65] This is the meaning of sovereignty; ultimate responsibility rests with the caliph even if he delegates full powers to his vizier.

The vizier of the second kind is merely executing the sovereign's orders, without any independence or power to change anything his master has decided and commanded.[66]

Ibn Jamā'a also follows the same orthodox doctrine in respect of the institution of the emirate, although he departs in important details from Al-Māwardī, with whom he agrees in distinguishing between a general and a particular emirate. The former is "a *khilāfa* whose holder is placed in command by the *amīr al-mu'minīn*". He derives this from the precedent of 'Omar.[67] The first of the three kinds of "particular emirate" is "the general supervision (*naẓar*) of the affairs of a country..., these are the kings and sultans according to what is done (*'urf*) at the present time".[68] The term *'urf* must be read in conjunction with the continuation "and they have been previously mentioned and described". It will then be clear that "kings and sultans" are fulfilling the functions of the vizierate of delegation which is recognized in the *Sharī'a*, although they have actually conquered the territories over which they rule by force of arms,[69] and their usurpation has been legalized by the *imām*'s formal delegation of authority. Ibn Jamā'a's argument thus falls in the category of *ḥiyal* or legal devices. For he terms contemporary practice *'urf*, and identifies it with the general emirate which he apparently equates with this vizierate. The only, but vital, difference between the vizier or emir and "the kings and sultans" is that the caliph of the former retains his independent and full ultimate authority, whereas that of the latter is a mere figurehead. Ibn Jamā'a clearly realizes this by not demanding of the caliph, who invests the usurper with delegated authority, any examination of the latter's actions by means of his own *ra'y* and *ijtihād*, with resultant approval or disapproval.

The second kind of "particular emirate" consists in the supervision of the army or of the finances of a particular territory or of the police. The third kind is restricted to the command of part of the army, as was the custom in Egypt, Syria and the other Muslim lands in Ibn Jamā'a's own time. It is represented by those invested with a military fief for purposes of *jihād*. All three kinds go back to the practice of the Prophet.[70] Precedent is used here to justify not only the *Sharī'a*, but also contemporary practice, which is in this way legalized.

That his own sympathies and his own interest were with the *'ulamā* becomes abundantly clear from the fifth chapter "On the preservation of the rules of the *Sharī'a*". It begins with the fundamental statement that "the most powerful means to preserve empires is the *Sharī'a*: it is the documentary proof (*ḥujja*) which the Prophet-messenger brought and established ⟨as law⟩, and which he commanded to be obeyed and preserved. It is the most direct way to God, for it is built on revelation (*waḥy*) and divine communication (*tanzīl*). All good results from obeying it and all evil from disregarding it."[71] He asserts that "the Prophet has established defenders who keep alight its flame, the kings and emirs, and supports the learned *imāms*[72] who guard its word of command".[73] After defining their character and function he assigns them the duties of *qāḍī* (judge), *mufti* (in charge of legal decisions, *fatwā*), police (*wilāyatu-l-ḥisba*), supervision of pious bequests (*awqāf*) and of the welfare of orphans and other helpless people. The first two offices require knowledge of *Fiqh*, its *uṣūl* (roots, principles) and *furū'* (branches, derivations), but it is also lawful for the *imām* to charge other persons with the three last named. They are listed in order of importance, first place going to the judges, who must combine probity with intelligence, suitability and health. The duties of the police indicate the religious and political nature of Islam and the Muslim state; they are threefold and comprise the supervision of the strictly religious duties, such as ritual purity, prayer, etc., as well as public morals; of measures and weights in accordance with the usage of the country, of trade and commerce, goods and prices; and lastly of matters "which are common to the law of God and of his servants" concerning slaves and *Dhimmīs*, for example.[74]

All this, and his exposition of financial and military administration, including the rules of warfare and the employment of ruses, is again good classical doctrine and need not concern us in detail. But in conclusion we have to consider once more the ideal duties of the *imām* as demanded by the ideal *Shar'*.

It is noteworthy that Ibn Jamā'a stresses the religious and legal side of the *imām's* office and duties. He insists on the recognition of his exalted rank and demands reverence and respect for him, no doubt as a counter to the caliph's loss of effective political power. The overruling consideration is the welfare of the Muslim nation and the good order of religion.[75] Of the ten duties of the *imām* towards his subjects special mention must be made of his responsibility for the preservation of religion as expressed in its principles and articles of faith. He must guard Islam against heresy and defend it against attack, in close co-operation with the *'ulamā*. He must observe the ritual of Islam and see that prayer, fast and pilgrimage are generally performed. He must concern himself with the religious law (*shar'*) and its application and administration by expert, trustworthy and loyal *'ulamā*. At least once a year he must engage in holy war (*jihād*). He must apply the law impartially to all Muslims, high and low, rich and poor. Almsgiving and its fair distribution in accordance with the conditions laid down in the *Sharīʿa* is his duty. All his duties culminate in his rule of justice.[76]

This is good orthodox doctrine, as we know it from Al-Māwardī. But it is difficult to see how the caliph can fulfil his duties, unless the fiction is insisted upon that ultimately he alone is responsible for the government even if he has delegated all his functions to a *malik* who in turn, by delegated authority, appoints judges and the other officials and functionaries.

In praise of justice Ibn Jamāʿa quotes extensively from philosophy (or wisdom, *ḥikma*) and Hadith in the style of the "Mirrors for Princes"; for example, "the justice of the king is the life of the subjects and the spirit of the realm...",[77] or "the welfare of the subjects and the culture of the countries are grounded in justice".

That he mentions Chosroes and other "infidel" kings is evidence of the influence of these "Mirrors", which we shall discuss later. He sums up by stating: "they who did not believe in reward and punishment knew that on justice depended the wellbeing of their kingdom, the preservation of their dynasty and the culture of their territory."[78]

From all this he draws the interesting conclusion that the laws of the prophets and the views of the philosophers agree that "justice is the cause of the increase of blessings and of the growth of prosperity, but that injustice and tyranny are the reason for the destruction of empires".[79]

He is again on classical ground when he stresses the equality of the *imām* with all other Muslims in rights and duties. The sultan is obliged to place himself in the same position before God as are his subjects and representatives before him. He must obtain the good advice of the *ʿulamā* for his legal enactments.[80] In this vein he deals with the institution of vizier and other offices of state, as previously described, following Al-Māwardī on the whole.[81] It can only have one meaning: to secure the preservation of Islam and its law in spite of the many compromising concessions to the political exigencies of the times. Or it may be that, in setting out the principles and practice of constitutional law, Ibn Jamāʿa, while taking into account the adverse position of the caliphate in his own day, wanted to provide a basis for the time when the caliph would once more be master in his own house and state and would be able to rule in accordance with the regulations of the *Sharīʿa*, explained to him by the *'ulamā*. How else are we to understand his panegyric on the *Sharī'a* quoted above?[82]

Yet, it can hardly be denied that the cleavage between the demands of the *Sharī'a* and political reality was both complete and irremediable in his day, and any attempt, no matter how ingenious, at an accommodation which would be both intellectually honest and politically effective, was bound to fail; that is, if we judge the attempt by our modern standards of intellectual and moral integrity and consistency, and disregard human nature and the conditions prevailing in Ibn Jamā'a's time. Even so, Ibn Jamā'a overstressed the legality of usurpation, and his implied identification of the delegation of authority between vizier, emir and the ruler (*sulṭān* or *malik*), whose seizure of power the caliph legalized, is equivocal and rather dubious compared with Al-Māwardī. The same possibly applies also to the titles by which he designates the *imām*, despite his definition of *sulṭān*.[83]

4. IBN TAYMĪYA: THE RULE OF THE DIVINE LAW

In clinging fast to the ideal *Shar'* all the jurists and theologians discussed so far had to fall back on compromise. The deeper the cleavage between the demand of this ideal law and the political reality, the more extensive and dangerous this compromise became. The jurists' principal concern was with authority and power which were, from the point of view of the *Sharī'a*, in the wrong hands. In their recognition of an existing state of affairs they were driven to drop more and more of the conditions stipulated for the caliph and of the regulations concerning his installation, not to mention his deposition.

But although they bowed all too deeply to expediency and brute force they strove successfully to preserve the unity of the Muslim community (defections of sectarians and heretics notwithstanding) and the framework of the ideal Muslim polity. In a very deep sense this fiction was more real than the transitory political structure of the Abbasid empire.

If Ibn Jamā'a felt the need to condone and legalize usurpation of the supreme executive authority of the *Sharī'a*, he hoped to accommodate the military power of the sultan under the law and thereby vindicate its authority. His contemporary Ibn Taymīya tried to escape from the vicious circle in which Ibn Jamāʿa and his predecessors were caught, by concentrating on the *Sharīʿa* and its application to the life of the community with the religious fervour and reforming zeal characteristic of Ḥanbalism at that time.[84] In attitude, approach and treatment he stands in marked contrast to the other jurists. The title of his treatise must be understood as his programme: *Siyāsa sharʿīya*, administration according to and by means of the *Sharīʿa*; it implies that he is concerned in the first place with the rule of the divinely revealed law. The *Sharīʿa* is the supreme authority, the exclusive and complete guide of the *umma* of Islam, of the *ahl al-sunna wa-l-jamāʿa*.[85] While acknowledging the necessity of "political" authority he recognizes the *de facto* power of the ruler of the day and the necessity of obedience to authority in the interests of the *Sharīʿa* and for the benefit of the community. He ignores the problem of the *khilāfa* altogether, denies its necessity (though for other reasons than the Khārijites) and is very critical of its theoretical foundation. He does not insist on the ideal qualifications of the *imām*, in fact he never discusses them. He dispenses with the election and even the designation of the caliph: God designates the sovereign through the infallible voice of the community, the *ijmāʿ*. It is clear from this attitude that the centre of gravity has shifted from the *khilāfa* and the *khalīfa* to the community, whose life must be regulated by the divine law. At the same time he pleads for close co-operation between the *imām*—the necessary authority—and the community. He accepts the state as it is and is entirely interested in just government on that basis, whether the *imām* is legal or illegal as far as his assumption of power and authority is concerned, in fact even if he enjoys neither and is a mere figurehead. Hence Ibn Taymīya stresses insistently the religious duties of all Muslims, rulers and subjects alike. This is tinged with a certain political realism, since he is concerned with the maintenance and good order of the political framework so that all Muslims may attain the bliss of the world to come. It is the governor's duty to improve the material and spiritual conditions of the people in preparation for the future life.

In his concern for the reform of individual and communal life he became a forceful advocate of a reform of the administration in the spirit of the ideal *Sharīʿa*. This brought him continually into conflict with the authorities and frequently into prison and eventually to his death. As a Ḥanbalī theologian and jurist he was opposed to everything which could not be traced to or substantiated by the Sunna, and he fought consistently against *bid'a*, innovation. He combined this rigid attitude to a pure Islam with an open mind towards Greek-Hellenistic political thought, like Naṣīr al-Dīn Ṭūsī.[86] Both are indebted to Al-Fārābī in the first place.

Ibn Taymīya begins his exposition of the principles and practice of government based on the *Sharī'a* with a theological premiss; he stresses the absolute unity of God (*tawḥīd*) in a chapter significantly entitled *siyāsa ilāhīya wa-ināba nabawīya*, "divine government and prophetic vicegerency", underlining the theocratic character of Islam. Like all writers on constitutional law he invokes Qur'ān IV, 61 f. with its command to obey God, his Prophet, and those who exercise authority. But obedience is dependent on justice, and if those in authority (he does not ask how they got there) act as they ought not to act, one must still obey those orders which are in agreement with the commandments of God.[87] Those in authority are the civil, military, fiscal and religious functionaries, who are all "the representatives of God to his creatures" under the political and religious unity of Islam.[88] "On justice rests the preservation of both worlds; this world and the hereafter do not prosper without it."[89] Therefore "God sent prophets and books so that men should administer justice (*qisṭ*) with regard for the rights of God and his creatures."[90] In another place he formulates the need for justice thus: "to judge according to justice, to render dues to those who have a claim on them, constitute the essential principles of just government (*siyāsa 'ādila*) and the very purpose of public office."[91]

The religious character of government is stressed in a series of statements which, though dealing with one or the other aspect of religion and politics, all converge on their inter-connection. "To govern the affairs of men is one of the most important requirements of religion, nay, without it religion cannot endure. . . . Only through association (*ijtimā'*) can the sons of Adam enjoy well-being, for they have need of one another. . . . A ruler (*ra's*) is indispensable for their social life. The duty of commanding the good and forbidding the evil cannot be completely discharged without power and authority. The same applies to all religious duties (holy war, pilgrimage, prayer, fast, almsgiving), to helping those who are wronged, and to meting out punishment in accordance with the legal penalties. . . ."[92] "The purpose of public office is to further the religion and the worldly affairs of man (*iṣlāḥ . . . dīnahu wa-dunyahu*) . . . when the pastor exerts himself in proportion to his ability to further both, he is one of the most excellent fighters on the path of God."[93]

"The exercise of authority is a religious function and a good work which brings near to God, and drawing near to God means obeying God and his Prophet."[94] This is and remains the primary duty of every Muslim, and it is with Muslims and their duties that the state is concerned which Ibn Taymīya wants to see administered in accordance with the *Sharī'a*. Hence his preoccupation with the more strictly religious duties of prayer and holy war in particular, suitably supported by Hadiths;[95] and his conviction that the welfare of a country depends on obedience to God and his Prophet, on condition that there is a properly constituted authority which "commands the good and forbids the evil" and is capable of enforcing the prescriptions of the former and the penalties for disobeying the latter.[96]

Authority is the complement of a hierarchy which is demanded by reason no less than by revelation. The *Sharī'a* entrusts power (*sulṭān*) and wealth (*māl*) with the service of God, and this ensures the good order of religion and of the world. "Religion without *sulṭān*, *jihād* and *māl* is as bad as *sulṭān*, *māl* and *ḥarb* without *dīn*."[97]

This being so, it is very important to choose the right people for office. Ability and loyalty are the two outstanding qualities demanded of men in public office. But Ibn Taymīya is realist enough to suggest that ability to fill an office—courage and bravery in a war-leader, judgement and power of enforcement in a judge—is more important than piety and loyalty if nobody can be found who combines all requirements. In support he appeals to the Sunna: Muḥammad was always guided in the choice of a leader by the welfare of the *umma* as the overriding consideration, even if his subordinates were to surpass him in knowledge and faith. If no one person is available who possesses in himself all the qualities needed for an office one has to appoint as many as together are endowed with them. This idea is strongly reminiscent of Al-Fārābī[98] and goes back ultimately to Plato, as does the idea of men forming an association to help each other to satisfy their needs.

The religious fervour and reforming zeal characteristic of this theologian and jurist found wide scope in every sphere of religious, social and political life. But although he absolved Muslims from obeying orders contrary to the commandments of God he did not advocate open rebellion, as is clear from his fear of anarchy.[99] Instead, he appealed to those in authority to observe the virtues of sincerity, of fear of and trust in God, of charity and patience, and to be well disposed towards their subjects.[100] This would enable them to practise the foremost political virtue, justice, and thus to keep free from corruption and to control their greed.[101]

We remember that justice is the principal "political" virtue in Plato and Aristotle as well. This justice, embodied in the law of the state, provides the common ground between Greek and Muslim political philosophy, as we shall see later on.[102] The integrity of the officials is essential for the preservation of public order and morale, and since the governor of the Muslim state is obliged to "command the good and forbid the evil" the political organization of the Muslim community is superior to that of any other state.[103] Justice has its origin and justification in the command of God.

The head of the state and his subordinate officials should always be guided by the demands of Qur'ān and Sunna. But if the governor, for any reason, does not know what their teaching is or how to apply it to a particular problem, he must ask the advice of the *'ulamā*, skilled in the *Sharī'a* and its interpretation, for "the Prophet says: Religion is good counsel".[104] If faced with a problem for which no revelation was received, the ruler should follow the advice of him who tells him what Qur'ān, Sunna or *ijmā'* of the Muslims demand. He must follow no one else even if he were the mightiest in religion and worldly affairs. In case of disagreement among the Muslims, he must ascertain the opinion of all and then follow that which is nearest to the teaching of Qur'ān and Sunna.[105]

This counsel of perfection coming from a Ḥanbalī jurist is, however, balanced by a realist's knowledge of human nature. Just as those in authority can fulfil the demands of their office only so far as is in their power, so God has imposed on man only what he can do.[106]

It is clear from Ibn Taymīya's advice to rulers that he did not consider the quality of *ijtihād* essential in the *imām*, but was prepared to let him practise *taqlīd*, as did Al-Ghazālī.[107]

It cannot be ruled out that, in common with the jurists whom we have already considered, Ibn Taymīya was interested in strengthening the influence and power of the *'ulamā*. He says not only that the two classes in authority are the emirs and the *'ulamā*,[108] but maintains also that the "doctors of the law" became the heirs and guardians of the Prophet's legacy after the Golden Age of Islam under the four "right-guided" first caliphs.[109] No doubt he would have liked them to be the effective leaders of the *umma*, whose life ought to be ruled by the *Sharī'a*. If they were to exercise authority, they would certainly be in a position to carry out those reforms in public and private life which Ibn Taymīya advocated and considered necessary in the interests of a pure Islam and of the good order and welfare of those who practised it. Hence his plea for justice in legislation affecting family and economic life, his condemnation of prostitution and of wine-drinking, and his efforts to stop them. The "doctors of the law" as guardians and interpreters of the *Sharī'a*, and given authority to administer it, particularly in the office of judge, are undoubtedly the natural representatives of administration and legislature in the Muslim state, the government of which is termed *siyāsa shar'īya*. Ibn Taymīya may have intended, by casting the *'ulamā* for this role, to link a reformed *umma* to the Golden Age of Islam under the four first caliphs who followed directly after the Prophet himself.[110] He allows for human limitations, both in the extent of obedience to divine command and in the discharge of authority in accordance with that command. This speaks for his common sense and political realism and also explains his definition of one of the three groups into which he divides men. He calls it *umma wasaṭ*, "the nation of the middle road" or, perhaps rather, "the just, equitable nation" "who care for the material and spiritual affairs of the community and for the maintenance of religion". Such a people alone enables a *siyāsa dīnīya*, religious government, to function.[111] *Wasaṭ* may well represent Aristotle's *mesotes*, the mean between two extremes, and it may point to Al-Fārābī, an affinity with whose political philosophy M. Laoust has rightly detected in Ibn Taymīya.

But it must not be overlooked that despite possible points of contact between the political philosophies of the two men there is also, and this is more important, a fundamental difference. Ibn Taymīya, the theologian, is certainly at variance with Al-Fārābī, the philosopher, as far as the latter's identification of the Platonic philosopher-king with the Islamic prophetic lawgiver is concerned. Since this forms the centre-piece of Al-Fārābī's doctrine, a brief discussion of this point is necessary, in anticipation of a full exposition in chapter VI.

Al-Fārābī sees in prophecy a natural, psychological phenomenon: perfect imagination combined with perfect rational perception in one person. The Muslim concept of prophecy is at most implied in this equation of prophet and lawgiver in the person of Muḥammad. It is not easy to harmonize this theory with the concept of prophecy as we meet it in the Qur'ān, except by allegorical interpretation. According to *Sūra* LVII, 25 ff., God sent his prophets to the Hebrews, Christians and Arabs with a revelation in the form of a Book (*kitāb*). This book—the Torah of Moses, the Gospel of Jesus and the Qur'ān of Muḥammad—is the hall-mark and proof of prophecy. Muḥammad "the seal of the prophets" says of God (v. 25): "and we sent down to you ⟨the community of the faithful⟩ the Book ⟨the Qur'ān⟩ and the balance ⟨of justice⟩ so that men might take care of justice." This passage, together with the saying, "the two pillars of religion are the Book and the Sword", define the nature of Islam and of Muḥammad's prophecy. Ibn Taymīya and Al-Fārābī no doubt agree as to the essence and effect of Muḥammad's prophecy, but Ibn Taymīya differs from Al-Fārābī in his idea and definition of prophecy. Muḥammad, the messenger of Allah, is clothed with divine authority to govern the Muslim community as spiritual and temporal ruler according to the law which was revealed to him and which he promulgated as the constitution and law of the *ummat al-Islam*. Together with all the other prophets he stands under the direct orders of God. This not only distinguishes him from the philosopher who can by his own efforts reach the stage of prophecy, provided his imagination and his intellect are of the highest perfection, but it also enables him to make his law serve the material and spiritual needs of his community. Fulfilment of the law leads them to God through a life of justice in this world; it secures them the future life and thus the attainment of the highest good. For Ibn Taymīya, the Prophet of Islam is the supreme spiritual guide (*murshid*); in direct communion with God he is a creative, independent legislator (*mujtahid*) who clothes his decisions with divine authority and infallible validity. He is the ideal ruler of the ideal community.

The parallel with Plato's ideal state as described in the *Republic* and the *Laws* is apparent, and it is for this reason that Platonic political ideas, to some extent modified by Aristotle's *Nicomachean Ethics*, gained entry into Muslim political thought. But this must not blind us to the fundamental differences which are naturally more in evidence in Ibn Taymīya than in Al-Fārābī and in Ibn Rushd (though to a lesser degree).

Thus it is conceivable that Ibn Taymīya's two classes in authority, the *'ulamā* and the emirs, at least partly correspond to Plato's philosopher-kings and guardians.[112] Other parallels, mentioned earlier, may be recalled: the necessity of association and of authority, or Ibn Taymīya's idea of hierarchy among men and Aristotle's ruler-ruled or master-servant relationship. But it would be wrong to speak here of Greek influence in the sense of a transformation and change of Islamic notions or even of a blending of Islamic with Greek-Hellenistic thought such as undoubtedly occurred with the *Falāsifa*.[113] I am more inclined to see in it an analogy, a mode of expression adopted by the jurists in an attempt to counter the philosophers and their challenge. The possibility, however, cannot be excluded that the political thought of the *Falāsifa*, which owes so much to Plato and Aristotle, sharpened the eyes of the jurists writing on constitutional problems and led them to appreciate the theoretical basis underlying the struggle for power in their day. Since most of them were actively engaged in the administration, contact with Greek political thinking may have helped them to realize more clearly the "political" significance and indeed relevance of the *Sharī'a*, for the vindication and ultimate authority of which they strove as officials, teachers and authors.

What stands out in Ibn Taymīya's approach and treatment is his emphasis on the ideal Muslim community under the ideal prophet/lawgiver/ruler; his appeal to Qur'ān and Sunna and not to historical precedent; his insistence on the realization of the *Sharī'a* through the *umma wasaṭ* who co-operate with those in authority by obedience to lawful command and by example in piety; and finally—underlying them all—the central place he assigns to the *Sharīʿa*. The *khilāfa* or *imāma* as the battleground between *imām* and emir or sultan is outside his concern. Authority interests him only in so far as it is indispensable for the good order and welfare of the *umma* in this world, and for the fulfilment of the basic Islamic duties in order to ensure the good working of the political and religious unity of Islam, *ṣalāḥ al-dunya wa-l-dīn* (welfare of the world and of religion).

This, then, is in outline the principal content of the theories of some leading theologians and jurists in the Muslim state based on the divinely revealed law.

The essence of the *Sharīʿa*-state may be summed up in the classic formulation of Ibn Khaldūn, in anticipation of the full treatment of his political theory in chapter IV: "...if, however, the laws ⟨of the state⟩ were laid down by God through a ⟨divinely commanded⟩ lawgiver, it is a religious administration (*siyāsa dīnīya*) useful in this world and in the hereafter. This means that this world alone is not man's aim, for it is altogether useless and vain, seeing that its end is death and destruction.... Therefore man's aim is religion which leads him to happiness in the hereafter as the way to 'God who owns everything in heaven and on earth' (*Sūra* XLIII, 53)... the lawgiver knows best what is of advantage to the people in matters of the hereafter which are hidden from them... the intention of the lawgiver is the welfare of man in the hereafter, and it is necessary, in accordance with the religious laws (*sharāʾiʿ*), to bind the people to the ordinances of the *Sharīʿa* in the affairs of their life in this world and in the hereafter. This authority is in the hands of the *ahl al-sharīʿa*, namely the prophets, and those who stand in their place in this matter, namely the caliphs.... The *khilāfa* is in essence the vicegerency of the lawgiver (*ṣāḥib al-sharʿ*) in order to defend the faith (*dīn*) and to govern the world (*dunya*) with its help."[114]

Ibn Khaldūn reproduces the classical theory of the jurists, seeing in the caliphate the frame within which the *Sharīʿa* determines the life of the Muslim community and ensures the Muslim's happiness in the world to come. A glance at the date of the first exposition of the theory of the *imāma*, Al-Māwardī's *Al-Aḥkām al-sulṭānīya*, is revealing; it helps us to realize the close connection between political theory and practice. For Al-Māwardī died almost a century after the institution of the *Imārat al-umarā* (chief emirate) had assumed the character of what is later known as the sultanate, at the end of the caliphate of Rāḍi.[115]

In 940 began the decline of the Abbasid caliphate and the struggle between the caliph and the sultan (or emir) for effective exercise of authority and power. Hence the preoccupation of the jurists with the *imāma*, its origin, scope, and responsibilities, and with problems of election, designation and investiture, conditioned by the struggle between the *imām* and the effective ruler. They had to keep faith with the ideal *umma* headed by an *imām* with sole supreme authority, and to preserve the inheritance of Muḥammad and his *ummat al-Islam*. How they discharged their responsibility we have seen in our general survey.

Only Ibn Taymīya ignored the political struggle and tried, by his concentration on the *Sharī'a*-government for the *umma*, to create the conditions necessary for the reconstitution of a Muslim community guided by the Sunna of the Prophet. By his attempt at reform and a re-statement of the essential Muslim virtues and duties, he pointed beyond the existence of the already more than shadowy caliphate to a new relationship, a new bond between the *umma* and its *Sharī'a*. The vitality and, indeed, the survival of Islam depend on a Muslim community closely knit together by a law that works. But since his reforms tended to lead back to a golden but primitive past through his narrow interpretation of what constitutes Sunna and what *bid'a* (innovation), his plea for a *siyāsa shar'īya* went unheeded, and his appeal to the *umma wasaṭ* met with little or no response. The legacy of Byzantium and Iran had transformed the original *umma* into a highly sensitive and differentiated society, living in the midst of a developed civilization that could no longer be reduced to the level of a primitive community living the life of simple, sincere piety and devotion. Yet Ibn Taymīya's idea of the *umma* living by the *Sharī'a* is sound, and alone promises stability and permanence amidst the transitoriness of the political organization in the form of a caliphate, which instead of being a unitary centralized "City of God on earth" suffers from the dualism of a weak caliph dominated by a strong sultan. If the *Sharī'a* is to be the authoritative law of the land, only a real community can overcome the rift created by the division of power and authority, spiritual and temporal, which runs counter to the very basis of Islam as a religious and political unity.

Wahhābism, the movement which was built on Ibn Taymīya's theology and organized itself in the kingdom of Sa'ūdī Arabia, could succeed in the primitive, simple conditions it found there, but it is no solution in conditions such as modern civilization has created.

But since his *Siyāsa shar'īya* does not depend on the *imāma*, it is possible that a modern reinterpretation of the *Sharī'a* would succeed in making it the instrument which would guide the *umma* in the way Ibn Taymīya intended, but which he missed by his backward gaze.

CHAPTER III

GOVERNMENT

I. THE VIEWS OF A UTILITARIAN MORALIST

Siyāsa, government, is determined by the *Sharī'a* and, according to the Muslim jurists, falls to the caliph or *imām*. But whilst the Islamic, that is the religious and political, character of the state is assumed as a matter of course by all Muslim writers, jurists, historians, philosophers and moralists, the meaning and content of *siyāsa* undergo significant changes in the course of Islamic history and under the impact of the decreasing coherence of the Abbasid caliphate. The *imāma*, though presupposed, gives way to the *mulk*, literally "kingdom", in the thought and reflections of writers on morals and politics. They are interested in the actual state and principally in its effective ruler. (*Siyāsa* as *siyāsa madanīya*, politics, as seen by the Muslim philosophers influenced by Plato and Aristotle, will occupy us later in this book.)

This can easily be seen in the *Al-Fakhrī* of Muḥammad b. 'Alī b. Ṭabāṭaba known as Ibn Al-Ṭiqṭaqa.[1] The book was written in 1302 for, and named after, the ruler of Mosul "who governs the people and directs the affairs". Its main part is a straightforward history, from the first four caliphs to the last of the Abbasid caliphs. It is of little originality, but, through its practical purpose as a guide for his prince, of some importance. Its utilitarian tendency is reinforced by an introduction dealing generally with "royal politics". Although he writes as a staunch adherent of 'Alī, his Shī'ī bias rarely gets the better of his balanced judgement. This may be due to his primary interest in the personalities and events he describes, judged by the standard of political success or failure. In his portrayal of caliphs and viziers and in his account of their rule he relies mainly on anecdotes and poems. While we cannot expect accurate historical reporting or disinterested factual evaluation, he affords us, by his vivid, colourful and entertaining style and diction, a lively impression of how the rulers and their viziers struck the contemporary story-tellers and poets. In this way, a clear picture emerges of what constitutes the *malik mu'aẓẓam*, the eminent king, or *malik fāḍil*, the excellent king. That he calls his momentary patron, the "king" of Mosul, by the former term goes without saying, but, apart from obvious flattery, this designation comprises all the good qualities which Ibn al-Ṭiqṭaqa demands of the good and successful ruler. His Shī'ism does not influence the character of his general remarks, which alone concern us in this context. It may, however, partly account for the disregard he shows for the theory of the *khilāfa* and of the *salṭana*. In his introduction he does not hesitate to emphasize his conviction that this history of the dynasties is useful for rulers and their chief ministers; for this reason he has covered in one treatise the history not only of the "great" dynasties of the Umayyads and Abbasids, but also that of the Buwaihids, Seljuqs and Fatimids under the Abbasids. The usefulness consists in his description of "the qualities ⟨of kings⟩ and of the foundations of government and the tools of authority". The author gives advice as a moralist on the qualities required in a ruler, his conduct, his relations with his subjects and their duties towards him.[2] In brief, he treats of "the principles of government and rules of conduct from which we derive advantage in events and affairs, in the government of the subjects, in the protection of the state (*mulk*, kingdom) and in the improvement of morals and behaviour".[3] This part of the book is a kind of "Mirror for princes and magistrates" such as the Persians wrote in pre-Islamic times with consummate literary skill, to be imitated under Islam, as we shall see later in this chapter. Islamic historiography as a whole is strongly influenced by that of Persia, which is characterized by its moralizing, edifying and entertaining tendencies.

Although the *khilāfa* remains the ideal state for Ibn al-Ṭiqṭaqa, he is chiefly concerned with the *mulk*, such as that over which his patron holds sway. He is not interested in the origin, character and purpose of the state, nor can we expect a systematic treatment of the topics of practical politics. But his general observations and remarks in this part of the book, and also between anecdotes and in verses here and there in its main part, betray a certain political realism, a realistic attitude which takes for granted the Islamic background of the absolute monarchy under consideration. His judgement is guided by moral principles, and a high moral standard of conduct is demanded of rulers and subjects alike. To make better men of his subjects is one of the foremost tasks of the ruler, together with dispensing justice. For morality is not merely man's duty; it is good for the maintenance of law and order, and for the political, social and economic well-being of the state; thus it helps to keep the ruler in power.

It is obvious that the art of government must be mastered by both caliph and emir, and that the political and moral obligations and aims are practically identical in both the *khilāfa* and the *mulk*. But although the *malik*, like every Muslim, has to perform religious duties, he is not charged with the defence of the faith, the punishment of heretics and the waging of *jihād*. These are the duties of the caliph alone, whose sovereignty the Emir of Mosul recognizes by a contract and by naming him in the Friday prayer. What orthodox theory never admitted is here acknowledged by a neutral observer of the political scene: the caliph is confined to the realm of "religion" for which he alone is responsible. The emir considers the inhabitants of his *mulk* as his subjects rather than as the community of the faithful, even though as Muslims they belong to that community by their recognition of the Abbasid caliph. Ibn al-Ṭiqṭaqa likens the relation between ruler and subjects to that between physician and patients.[4] This may imply a criticism of absolutist rule. But whether the ruler be a despot or more like a physician, good (that is, successful) government depends on his moral excellence and his practical ability as a military leader and administrator. In all his actions, he must be guided by the best interests of the state. As a Muslim he must be guided by "the fear of God as a quality which is the root of all good and the key to every blessing, for if the king fears Allah the servants of Allah have confidence in him".[5] Yet politics, the art of government (*siyāsa*), "is the capital of the ruler.... On it he relies in order to maintain ⟨sound⟩ finances, to preserve morals, to prevent evil, to subjugate wrong-doers and to forestall injustice, which leads to civil war and rebellion."[6] He must be held in that "fear and respect through which the order of the state is maintained and guarded against the ambition of the subjects".[7]

Ibn al-Ṭiqṭaqa is well aware of the qualities needed to obtain and remain in power and, through his reading and his observation of Islamic history, he shows an understanding of the realities of power and the state built upon it. But, being more concerned about the ruler than about the state as a political institution, he did not develop a political theory like that of Ibn Khaldūn in the context of Islamic civilization or of Machiavelli in that of Renaissance-Christian civilization. Thus, when Ibn al-Ṭiqṭaqa lists ten qualities required in the ruler, he thinks that he who possesses them all is fit for the highest office, that of *imām*, and that the theologians and jurists should pay due attention to them.[8] But he thinks of the *imām* as a ruler in the first place, and although most of the ten qualities are identical with those enumerated by Al-Māwardī, they are not derived by Ibn al-Ṭiqṭaqa from the *Sharīʿa* but are the result of political and moral considerations and are conditioned by the interest of the state. The ruler must have intelligence (*ʿaql*) "with the help of which empires are governed"; justice (*ʿadl*) to ensure prosperity and good conduct; knowledge (*ʿilm*) which enables him to engage scholars and poets in conversation at his court, since it is important for him to gain their confidence and obtain their advice.[9] To gain the confidence of all his subjects is no less essential for the ruler. "Among those who aspire to power he is the best who is naturally intelligent and discerning; who has acquired a knowledge of what happens in the world of changing times and tumbling empires; who is adroit in negotiating with the enemy and who can keep a secret; for he is the pillar of politics. He must form his judgement with the support of men of intelligence because isolated intelligence alone is not sufficient. He must be able to penetrate to the thought of opposing parties ⟨so that he can, at a given moment, make use of every one of them⟩. Firm resolve is the basis on which to build in ⟨the task of⟩ safeguarding the state."[10]

Just as it is his duty to protect his subjects, it is their duty to obey him. The safety of the country through security on the roads and fortified frontiers is his concern no less than the protection of the weak and humble by impartial justice. He is responsible for the welfare of all his subjects, who are bound by their allegiance to give him good advice. He must reward the good and punish the wicked in order to gain the confidence and service of his subjects, and by stamping out evil he should inspire them with the fear of punishment.[11] How strongly the author's ethics are influenced by political considerations and how utilitarian his outlook accordingly is we can gather from his advice to the ruler on the treatment of his subjects. Social status and influence are the deciding factors. The higher ranks of society should be treated with benevolence and consideration in order to gain their support, and use made of their influence to his own advantage. The middle class can best be kept in its place by judiciously balancing fear and interest, but the lower orders must be governed in the fear of the wielder of power. Yet he must show favour and kindness to all alike, otherwise the evil inclination in human nature will cause rebellion and endanger his throne.[12]

The parallel with Machiavelli is obvious in spite of the entirely different purpose of both writers and of their different milieu. They have in common an appreciation of power and a concern for the good, that is the successful, ruler. Ibn al-Ṭiqṭaqa, it seems, merely observed the political scene, relating his observations to his reading of Muslim historians like Ṭabarī, Ibn al-Athīr, Mas'ūdī and others, and produced his *History of Dynasties*. Machiavelli rationalized his experiences, relating them to the intellectual currents of his time, and evolved a political philosophy centred on the concept of the "reason of state" as the guiding principle of politics. The similarities between him and Ibn Khaldūn are much more real and significant. Yet Ibn al-Ṭiqṭaqa's interest in politics as such, notwithstanding his stress on the religious and ethical duties of a Muslim ruler, points in the direction of the power-state.

The *khilāfa* represented the ideal, the best state. But his real interest lay in the effective ruler and his state, within and theoretically under the authority of the Abbasid empire. Though his description of the reigns and administrations of caliphs, sultans, emirs, viziers and governors follows the pattern of the histories which served him as sources, he shows such keen interest in their political ability and success that a certain individuality and colour cannot be denied him. Were they capable of maintaining or even extending the realm, were they good generals, was their administration good and efficient? These are the questions which are uppermost in his mind. Moral virtues are considered valuable, not so much in themselves and for the happiness and perfection of their possessors, as for political purposes; they are useful in the state, which is observed as it actually is and not as the *Sharī'a* demands it. This is evident in Ibn al-Ṭiqṭaqa's judgement on the Umayyads (especially Mu'āwiya, who is generally credited with having transformed the *imāma* into a *mulk* and is condemned for this) and on the Abbasids. He stresses the other-worldly, saintly character of the first "dynasty", that of the first four caliphs, nicely balancing their piety, saintliness and austerity against their military success as empire-builders. The Umayyads are praised for their skilful blending of the spiritual heritage of their predecessors with political ability, so that the best people followed them for religious reasons, the more worldly minded out of fear of their power, and others again for their own personal advantage.[13] This interpretation clearly shows that effective government is the standard by which Ibn al-Ṭiqṭaqa measures dynasties and individual rulers; and effective government is successful government. By contrast the Abbasids are roundly condemned for their opportunism and stratagems, and their lack of forcefulness and power is stressed. At the same time as he acknowledges their interest in letters and the sciences, and their concern for religious observances, he deprecates their inability to maintain their authority in the later period of their reign.[14]

In short, we find in Ibn al-Ṭiqṭaqa a political consciousness born of observation and a historical sense which leads straight on to Ibn Khaldūn, although no influence, direct or indirect, can be traced. Ibn al-Ṭiqṭaqa's attitude is likewise different from the authors of "Mirrors for Princes" with whose views on the practical art of government he has much in common. They are concerned exclusively with the sovereign, and the interest of the state is understood in terms of the ruler's personal advantage and power.

Ibn al-Ṭiqṭaqa is the first to think of the state as an entity in its own right, yet not independent of the ruler, who at that period of Islamic history was still an essential part of the state. The state exists as an object of study, and a ruler is judged only by the performance of his duties in relation to its best interests.

2. THE VIEWS OF PRINCES, PRIME MINISTERS AND MEN OF LETTERS

A few of the "Mirrors for Princes" may be briefly summarized as characteristic of a whole class of literature, part of the Persian heritage now adapted to the peculiar character of Islam. But because of their origin their importance in relation to our main theme should not be over-estimated.

They were introduced into Arabic literature by Ibn Al-Muqaffa' in the 8th century C.E.[15] through his translation from the Pahlavi (Middle Persian) of the famous *Kalīla wa-Dimna* (of Indian origin) and other works of an edifying, moralizing nature, and also through his original writings. These two groups of books exerted a dominating influence on what is called *Adab* literature in Arabic. The Sassanian kings of Persia are set up as model rulers, based on Ibn Al-Muqaffa''s Arabic translations of Persian "Mirrors for Princes", by Ibn Qutaiba, Jāḥiẓ and Al-Baihaqī right down to Al-Ghazālī and the Spanish Muslim writer Ibn 'Abd Rabbīhi.

While their importance for the study of the art of government is considerable—and they have yet to be subjected to a detailed investigation covering a vast amount of largely unpublished texts—their value for the theory of government is much smaller. The examples here briefly discussed are among the best representatives of their kind and must suffice for this introductory survey. They take as their pattern the conduct of the great Persian kings and of their court and administration. The king's absolutism is mitigated and rendered more acceptable by being built into the structure of Islam, with its commandments, its concern for the hereafter and its insistence on the equality of all Muslims as members of "the community of the faithful".

These "Mirrors" were mostly written by men of affairs and of letters who had learnt in the school of experience. They are eager to advise rulers and their ministers, present and future, how best to conduct the affairs of state. The ruler is the centre of interest and the principal figure of the political scene. His own interest and that of the state are identical in actual fact if not in theory. The great stress laid on justice and equity in conformity with the tenets of Islam must not mislead us into overlooking a strong element of expediency which, in certain circumstances, condones political murder "in the interests of the state". Justice and equity are not conceived as absolute moral values and demands, but rather as politically useful and necessary in the interests of state and ruler.

These "Mirrors" are less concerned with the principles than with the art of government. This does not mean that their practical advice is not based on religious and moral principles, but rather that it is not the outcome of a political philosophy, a philosopher's or a statesman's theory of government. That is the second reason why only a summary treatment can be accorded them. Limited as is their significance for political thought in Islam, they are relevant as a background to the political realism of the utilitarian Ibn al-Ṭiqṭaqa, and as a contrast to the empiricist Ibn Khaldūn. Their method is to introduce traditions and anecdotes by a general statement or a political aphorism which sums up, by anticipation, what the subsequent story teaches. Their aim is to teach by example. Ibn Khaldūn, as will be apparent from the next chapter, deduces laws of history and politics from his own observations and his reading of Islamic history. If he comes to the same conclusions as the authors of the "Mirrors", or even to the same or similar formulations, his aim is different, and for that reason alone, apart from other and more important considerations, his *Muqaddima* or introduction to his universal history contrasts with the "Mirrors".

There is another respect in which they are of some interest; they are a good example of that genius for adaptation and transformation which characterizes Islam. But because they are concerned with the art of government, with political reality, the blending of Persian and Islamic ideas and concepts is less harmonious, less skilful and more superficial; or so, at least, it appears to me from some of the treatises under discussion.

Since Ibn al-Muqaffa' set the fashion in Islamic literature of writing about the *mores* of rulers and courtiers, a few remarks may serve to illustrate the pattern. Of the two *Adab* works, the "small" one is by far the more interesting and original. For it provides the theoretical basis for the practical advice on the right behaviour of princes and their servants which is the theme of the "great" *Adab* book. Its tenor is Islamic, and so is its tendency, with its stress on religious concepts and duties and its negative attitude to worldly politics. He says: "the aim of man is good order in this world and in the future life (*salāḥ al- ma'āsh wa-l-ma'ād*). The way ⟨to this goal⟩ is by sound reason (*'aql saḥīḥ*), acquired through knowledge coming from Omniscient God."[16] As a good Muslim, Ibn al-Muqaffa' stresses that the hereafter is the principal concern of rational man, who takes his religious duties seriously for this very reason.[17] Knowledge is all-important, and to teach oneself is more important than teaching others, especially if one wants to lead men and have authority over them.[18] His rationalism is, no doubt, a legacy from his pre-conversion period, successfully blended with fervour for his Muslim faith.

He has no illusions about politics and political leadership: "Ruling of men is a mighty misfortune".[19] The ruler must fulfil four conditions if the state is to be well founded and secure. He must exercise great care and circumspection in the choice of his ministers and officials. He must be firmly in command and control the affairs of state by strict supervision of his servants and their official actions. He must be just in punishing offenders and in rewarding those who serve the state loyally by good deeds. The first condition is the most important, because without capable and trustworthy functionaries no sultan can govern a vast empire efficiently. It is, therefore, essential that he should be well informed at all times by trusted persons everywhere about the activities of his governors.[20]

Religion, he avers, is God's greatest gift to man; of supreme advantage, it is the crown of all wisdom. Men of knowledge and wisdom are entitled to rule, and the *'ulamā* are the right people to guide and to advise.[21] This claim on behalf of the legal experts of Islam is a recurring feature in the "Mirrors" as in the treatises of the jurists on constitutional law. The way in which it is presented by Ibn al-Muqaffa', coupled with his religious interpretation of knowledge and wisdom, whose possession is the highest qualification for political authority, clearly shows his desire to adapt his Sassanian model to the leading exponents and institutions of Islam.

Ibn al-Muqaffa''s clear distinction between religion and man's opinion (*ra'y*), that is independent reasoning, is also interesting. Religion draws its support from faith (*īmān*); reasoning derives its certainty from argument in debate (*khuṣūma*). He who uses religion to debate and argue makes of it a matter of reasoning; he who raises reason to a religion, becomes an innovating lawgiver—in opposition to the revealed law—and has no religion, since he denies the validity of revelation. Religion and reason do not mix, though the boundary between them is often indistinct.[22]

That he extols the virtue of justice goes without saying, but it is noteworthy that, in his view, only just rulers can claim the loyalty and submission of their subjects.[23]

These general ideas are supplemented by advice and by reflections on the qualities and duties of the rulers, their servants, functionaries and subjects. These topics occupy the larger part of both the *K. adab al-ṣaghīr* and the *K. adab al-kabīr*; they form the principal contents of all "Mirrors". Since the "great" *Adab* book is altogether more practical and concrete, a few illustrations may be taken from it. He advises the *wālī*, governor or ruler, to give satisfaction to his master (*rabb*), that is, God; to his sovereign (*sulṭān*), if there is one above him; and to the good, decent men among his subjects (*ṣāliḥ*), since it is impossible to please everybody.[24] Next, he urges care in the selection not only of governors and functionaries, as in the "small" treatise, but also of friends and comrades, who should be godfearing men (*ahl al-dīn*). Then the ruler is advised to seek and accept the counsel of wise and expert men and to listen carefully and especially patiently to the views of men of merit and insight, even if their opinions and their advice run counter to his own views and intentions.[25] The ruler should attend to important affairs of state in person in order to preserve his authority, and he is warned not to misuse his power.[26]

In counselling obedience to religion, Ibn al-Muqaffa' is by no means unaware of the existence of power and of its role in politics. Consequently he differentiates between three kinds of dominion (*mulk*). The first is based on religion, and is by far the best and most secure, since it gives the subjects their due and they in turn fulfil their duties towards the state in obedience to the demands of religion. The second results from the will to power[27] and is well established and of stable authority; but it will have to contend with opposition.[28] The third, arbitrary rule,[29] is no more than the play of an hour and will soon collapse.[30]

Discussing the rules of conduct to be observed by a ruler, Ibn al-Muqaffa' concludes with the observation that to be successful the man in authority must blend power with popularity, so that he can count on the willing submission and support of his subjects.[31]

His views on politics as we have just culled them from his "Mirrors" do not offer a considered theory or a systematic whole. They are isolated reflections of a religious mind interested in the art of government; of a secretary to governors and notables who has an eye for the conduct of affairs of state, and with clear views on its efficient administration. Here he clothed his thoughts in a literary form, taken over and adapted from another civilization. He has also left us yet another treatise of a different kind, his *R. al-ṣaḥāba*.[32] It deals with subjects given exceptional interest by that unity of political and religious concerns in Islam which I have stressed before. These subjects are the education of the army—a novel feature—and the caliph's responsibility for the formulation and application of one law for the whole state. For reasons of security and efficiency, Ibn al-Muqaffa' suggests to the caliph—not so far as we know at his request—"that he should write a clear, concise and effective charter (*amān*) comprising everything they ought to do or refrain from doing. It should provide demonstrative proof ⟨and guidance⟩ within the bounds set ⟨by Islam⟩, and their officers should learn it so that they could rule their men with its help. If God wills, this charter will be good for their sound judgement and opinion (*ra'y*)."[33] This advice is born of Ibn al-Muqaffa''s keen perception of the need of the Abbasid dynasty, so recently established, for a disciplined, efficient army of good Muslims. The Khurasanians had taken the place of the Syrians of Umayyad times, and it is clear from Ibn al-Muqaffa''s description of their blind unquestioning obedience that guidance was needed to harmonize their conduct and their views with the best interests of the dynasty and the state, in conformity with the demands of the *Sharī'a* in peace and war. They must learn the Qur'ān and study the Sunna, show loyalty, virtue...resolution and modesty.... Their pay, provisions and share in the spoils of war must always be provided, and, since the commander of the faithful is responsible for their welfare, nothing of their history, circumstances and secrets in Khurasan must be hidden from him.[34]

Ibn al-Muqaffa''s suggestion that the caliph should write a comprehensive book of laws for his realm is of greater significance than his plea for such an *amān* for the army. His insistence on the caliph's independent decision where Qur'ān and Sunna have made no provision and where guidance cannot be obtained from precedents must be seen against the controversies of the time and against Ibn al-Muqaffa''s attitude to them.

There is, to begin with, his principal pronouncement: that God has placed the preservation of mankind and the good order of this life and of the hereafter in the co-existence of religion and reason (*dīn wa-'aql*), and of these two, the first place goes to *dīn* because it is revealed. Therefore strong religious convictions must be the basis of every exercise of man's intellect, expressed in *ra'y*. This is restricted to those in authority,[35] who govern. The caliph is enjoined to exercise the *ra'y* with which God has inspired him.[36] Hence he only is invested with the authority of using his own judgement in deciding questions and enacting laws in conformity with the Qur'ān and the Sunna when authoritative tradition (*athar*) is lacking.[37] Ibn al-Muqaffa' is very critical of the use of analogy (*qiyās*) and restricts it to cases where it results in good actions; but even so the caliph must carefully investigate precedents established with its help.

Ibn al-Muqaffa' is particularly perturbed about the great differences in the application of the law between regions like Iraq and Syria, cities like Basra and Kufa, and even between the centre and the outlying districts of Kufa. For nothing but chaos results if one permits what the other forbids. It is for this reason that he advises the caliph to supplement the charter for the army with one for the judges. For this is the meaning of "book" rather than "code", when our author expresses the hope "that God may make these ⟨divergent⟩ laws which combine what is proper with what is erroneous into one just law...."[38] It is here that the caliph's own judgement is needed most, especially when, through lack of agreement among the *salaf*, the early Muslims, different authorities applied different decisions.

It is not easy to decide whether practical considerations alone or concern for Islam and its religious law, or possibly both prompted Ibn al-Muqaffa' to advise the caliph to use his authority and act as legislator, as was Persian administrative practice.[39] The Islamic motive is suggested when one remembers that what Ibn al-Muqaffa' proposes is exactly what the Sunnī jurists postulated centuries later as one of the principal qualifications of the caliph: the quality of *ijtihād*. Ibn al-Muqaffa''s insistence that the caliph should comply with the *Sharī'a* as it was in his day, points in the same direction, and so does his opinion on the limits set to the obedience which Muslims owe to the *Amīr al-mu'minīn*. Supreme as the latter's authority is, he must never be obeyed if he demands rebellion against God and tries to impose penalties which are not prescribed by law. But the caliph is enjoined to fulfil the basic duties of every Muslim (such as prayer, fast and pilgrimage), to impose the legally prescribed penalties and not to permit what is forbidden, or to prohibit what is permitted by the Law of Allah.[40] His overriding consideration in his legislative activity should always be "the approved good",[41] and he should aim at restoring the Sunna of the Prophet and of the "right-guided" caliphs[42] in matters of criminal and private law. In all this, the sovereign has to rely on trusted advisers, those learned in the law, the *fuqahā*.

In this respect the *R. al-ṣaḥāba* agrees with the two *Adab*-books, as it does in advising the ruler to choose the right kind of companion, friend, adviser and public functionary, as the title of the treatise suggests. This theme is naturally taken up at length in the "Mirrors" as well, with stories and anecdotes to drive the lesson home. But only in this treatise is there recommended to the ruler a definite group or type of person from which he may choose his intimate friends and collaborators. For Ibn al-Muqaffa' was strongly in favour of the close association of the Arab nobility with the throne and the government, and recommended that relatives of the sovereign be given offices of state (in particular the 'Alids, whom he served). Such advocacy cannot have won him any friends, and it is quite likely that the *R. al ṣaḥāba* contributed to his discomfiture and murder.[43]

A generation later, Abū Yūsuf composed, at the command of the caliph Hārūn al-Rashīd, a manual on land-tax, a technical-legal treatise which he prefaced, in a kind of dedicatory epistle, with a grand exhortation. He reminds the sovereign at the height of his absolute power that his august office requires him to be a good shepherd of the flock entrusted to his care. He should choose the world to come rather than the one he now administers; he should rule in justice with the power granted him by God. It is his duty to guard and protect what God has given him on trust, and to obey God's commands so that his subjects will obey him; and just as he must obey God's commands, so he must watch over their fulfilment by the believers whose commander he is.[44] A long chain of Hadiths illustrates the qualities required in a pious, good caliph. In contrast to the authors of the "Mirrors for Princes", Abū Yūsuf does not go outside Muslim tradition.

Returning to the "Mirrors", we have a good example of the *genre* in the letter which the author of the *K. Baghdād*, Aḥmad b.

Abī Ṭāhir Ṭaifūr,[45] addressed to his son, who was appointed prefect of Diyār Rabī'a in Mesopotamia, in the reign of the caliph Al-Ma'mūn. He must observe the law, he must be just towards those whom he governs, he must fulfil punctiliously the religious duties, such as the five daily prayers, he must know the Book, that is the Qur'ān, and rule in accordance with its commands and with the Sunna of the Prophet. The man in authority is in the first place a Muslim, and as a believer his aim should be to draw near to God in knowledge and obedience. To help others to increase their knowledge of God and to gain the future life, at once enhances his position and strengthens his authority. This is a curious mixture of concern for the blessings and duties of religion and of utilitarian regard for the esteem and honour of the man in authority.

The father advocates the golden mean, moderation (*iqtiṣād*), as important for the maintenance of religion and of the laws which guide us aright (*sunan hādiya*). But as far as piety and the other world are concerned there is no limit, nor is there for drawing near to God.[46] "Seek access to God and his grace will be upon you" and "Know that the *mulk* belongs to God, who gives it to whom he likes and takes it away from whom he likes" are two sentences from the letter which show the extent of the writer's piety and the religious depth of the concept of rule which he tries to impart to his son.[47] Quite in line with this attitude is his by now familiar advice "take frequent counsel with the jurisconsults".[48] He again recommends generous and mild treatment of the flock whose shepherd and protector his son is and offers good advice about poll- and land-tax.[49] The letter ends with a repetition of the advice tendered at the beginning: "Hold fast to the *Sharī'a* and its laws (*sunan*)", and with the request to read the letter carefully and to act upon it as a true Muslim.[50]

Our next author is Jāḥiẓ, or whoever else was author of the *K. al-tāj*, the "Book of the Crown".[51] This ninth century "Mirror" is perhaps the most celebrated and typical of its kind. Although it is mainly devoted to etiquette at court, the *mores* of the king, of his son and of his courtiers, it contains here and there some general observations of principle bearing on the purpose and meaning of government. The treatise abounds in stories and anecdotes, mainly reflecting Sassanian rule and court life.[52] But on this the author superimposes Muslim concepts; he stresses the great value of Islam and its guiding principles, and he adds many examples from Arab history, taken from biographers, poets, the "historian" Abū 'Ubaida, and from the Hadith. As a result, in spite of the large space given to Sassanian royal practice, the author also mirrors life at the Abbasid court; and his advice is that of a Muslim tendered to the caliph and his entourage. With this aspect alone we are concerned here. Thus we find after a certain anecdote the remark that the king should admonish his subjects to hold fast to their tradition and to keep their laws, while he himself must govern them perfectly, giving the necessary orders.[53] He should reward in public any deed which strengthened the king's power, in order to encourage the people to consolidate the *mulk* and to reinforce its foundations.[54]

The author's concern for the unimpaired authority of the ruler is clear from his exposition of the son's duties towards his father, the sovereign. The son has no right to shed blood, even if the *Sharī'a* demands it, unless he has first obtained the consent and authority of the king. For if he were to assume this right he would be in authority as *ḥākim*, governor. This would be contempt of the king (*malik*) and would weaken the realm (*mamlaka*).[55] This applies also to the son who is, as heir presumptive (*walī 'ahdi-l-mulk*), already invested as his father's successor.[56]

In a king the qualities of generosity and modesty (*ḥayā'*), explained as a kind of compassion (*raḥma*), are essential. In his capacity of pastor the king should have compassion on his flock; in that of *imām* he should have pity on the faithful who follow him; in that of master he should be merciful towards his servants.[57] It goes without saying that Jāḥiẓ stresses the necessity of justice in the royal master. In this connection he speaks only of Persian kings dealing with complaints.[58]

Like the letter of Aḥmad b. Abī Ṭāhir Ṭaifūr to his son, the *K. al-tāj* has a good deal to say about the capital importance of knowing not only what goes on in the state, but also the secret thoughts in the minds of the courtiers, and even of the sovereign's own family. A network of spies must cover the court and the realm. It is of the essence of the pastor to know his flock and all their affairs, otherwise he has nothing but the name of pastor and the appearance of power. Without the secret information which his spies supply he cannot properly attend to the affairs of state, his principal concern. In fact, Jāḥiẓ chiefly attributes Mu'āwiya's organization of a strong government and his long successful reign to his having followed the example of the caliph 'Omar, who was most feared. This is followed by many examples from the history of the caliphs, Umayyad as well as Abbasid. The foremost reason for a sovereign's long reign is his knowledge of the people's secrets.[59]

Jāḥiẓ began his "Mirrors" with the Persian kings since they were the first in statecraft.[60] That is why he introduces so many stories of Persian etiquette and customs generally, and also holds up Persian kings as a shining example to the Muslim kings when in danger.[61]

Finally, a special trait of his character, his humanism, in the sense of humane concern for the worth and dignity of man, is sometimes clearly shown in the book. For example, he recommends the employment of ruse in warfare since it is imperative to avoid the unnecessary sacrifice of human lives. Money may be freely spent for everything else, but war demands human lives.[62]

This completes the survey of the more important of the early "Mirrors for Princes", which are as much part of the literary *genre* called *Adab* as of the *Akhlāq*- or ethical literature. But before summarizing two of the later "Mirrors", from a time when the Abbasids were no longer masters in their own house, and no longer absolute monarchs as Hārūn al-Rashīd, Al-Ma'mūn and Al-Mutawakkil had been, reference must be made to a *Risāla* of Jāḥiẓ which concerns political theory proper. It is his *K. istiḥqāq al-imāma.*[63] Stating that men need an *imām*, he goes on to distinguish three kinds of *imām*: *rasūl* (apostle), *nabī* (prophet) and *imām* (chief). The *rasūl* is *nabī* and *imām*; the *nabī* is *imām*, but not *rasūl*; and the *imām* is neither *nabī* nor *rasūl*. The *rasūl* is that most excellent of men who has promulgated the *Sharī'a* and inaugurated the religious community (*milla*). Next comes the *nabī* and last the *imām*.[64] Jaḥīẓ is bold enough to suggest that the *Sharī'a* changes with the changing times. But *ḥukm* and *ḥākim*, government and ruler, are always needed,[65] hence the *imāma* as the Muslims' government is necessary.[66] He justifies the need for prophets and their vicegerents (*khulafā*) with the assertion that man's intellect is not powerful enough to guarantee his welfare,[67] and finally proves that in the interests of the Muslims there should be only one *imām* in charge of their worldly and spiritual-religious welfare.[68] It is to be expected that a man with the intellectual attainment and prominent position of Jāḥiẓ should pronounce on the most characteristic institution and the principal instrument of the unity of Islam. He defines the purpose of the *imāma* exactly as the propounders of the classical theory were to do a century and a half later; his threefold distinction allows for the existence of non-Arab prophets but upholds the superiority of Islam, both in its founder and in his successors, thanks to his superiority as *rasūl.* But prophecy and *khilāfa* (*imāma*) are evidently not demanded by the *Shar*ʿ, but by reason, seeing that he postulates both by an appeal to man's needs.[69]

The *Qābūs-nāma* of Kai Kā'ūs and the *Siyāsat-nāma* of Niẓām al-Mulk, which both belong to the end of the eleventh century, when all power was firmly held by the sultan and when the caliph's authority largely existed in theory only, are chosen as representative of their kind because they originated in the same milieu, the Seljuq dominion within the Abbasid caliphate. The Seljuq Turks had only recently come under the influence of Islam; they had been converted after having conquered large parts of the Abbasid empire. Though politically independent of the caliph, they acknowledged his spiritual authority as "Commander of the Faithful" and, with the zeal of converts, vigorously defended Sunnī orthodoxy against sectarians and heretics. Both authors strongly champion Sunnī Islam, and Niẓām al-Mulk in particular describes in the last chapters of his "Treatise on Government" the schismatic rebellions of which he disapproves. The influence of their masters on the two writers may here be detected; it may account for the emphasis they place on the religious and ethical duties which the ruler must perform for his own salvation and for the welfare of his state.

The author of the *Qābūs-nāma*[70] was a prince of the Ziyarid dynasty which ruled part of the southern Caspian region as vassals of the Seljuq sultans. He wrote down his own experiences for the guidance of his son. Significantly, he begins with theology, with God and his apostles, and only after inculcating piety and gratitude to the Creator does he proceed to the mundane duties of a prince. It is essential that the king should be God-fearing and his religion spotless. The next requirement is wisdom ("for wisdom is the king's prime minister") followed by justice and truthfulness.[71] His practical advice about the king's vizier and other officers of state is born of experience and insight into human nature, especially of those in authority. Some of the author's maxims are the result of his political shrewdness and are worth quoting: "...the king...must realize that the welfare of his kingdom lies in the effectiveness of his authority. If there is no effective authority, ruin overwhelms the state, and effective authority cannot be maintained except by strict control...it is inexpedient for the king to place soldiery in authority over the people, else the realm will fail to retain its population. The welfare of the people must be as carefully guarded by him as that of the bodyguard, for the king resembles the sun in that he cannot shine upon one man and not upon another...it is through the people that the country is made prosperous, for the revenues are earned by the people, who remain settled and prosperous if given what is rightfully theirs. Therefore let there be no place in your heart for extortion; the dynasty of kings who recognize rights endures long and becomes old, but the dynasty of extortioners swiftly perishes, because fair treatment means prosperity and extortion means a depopulated land....The sages say that the well-spring of thriving conditions and of gladness in the world is a just king, while the source of desolation and misery is a king who is an oppressor."[72]

He recommends a bodyguard of many races. "If a prince's bodyguard is all from one race, he is ever the prisoner of his bodyguard....If they are of all races, one is held in check by another, and no single group, through apprehension of the other, is able to show disaffection. Thus your control of your army will remain effective."[73] He sums up the qualities of a king as follows: "Strive against becoming intoxicated with the wine of kingship and permit no shortcoming in your fostering of these six qualities: awesomeness, justice, generosity, respect for the law, gravity and truthfulness. If any one of these is lacking in a king, he is near intoxication with kingship, and no king who becomes intoxicated with kingship regains sobriety except with its disappearance."[74] "...it is your duty not to be ignorant of conditions in your realm, of the circumstances of your people or those of your soldiers. More particularly you must be vigilant concerning the doings of your vizier. He should not be able to swallow a drink of water without your knowing it, for you have entrusted your life and possessions to him."[75]

The remark about the vizier is not mere hyperbole but the natural consequence of absolutist rule; it is, like the advice to have a multi-racial body guard, matched by similar statements in Niẓām al-Mulk's *Siyāsat-nāma*, as we shall see presently. Of the vizier's duties Kai Kā'ūs says: "Urge your master ⟨the king⟩, therefore, to be well-disposed towards the bodyguard and the people; the king's continuance is dependent on his forces, and the prosperity of the countryside on the peasantry. Make it your constant endeavour to improve cultivation and to govern well; for, understand this truth: good government is secured by armed troops, armed troops are maintained with gold, gold is acquired through cultivation, and cultivation sustained through payment of what is due to the peasantry, by just dealing and fairness. Be just and equitable therefore. Yet even if you are incorruptible and without any taint of dishonesty, stand in awe of your master, there being no one who has greater need than a vizier to fear his master."[76]

The aphorism of Kai Kā'ūs expressing the interdependence of authority, army, finance and prosperity reads like a text upon which Ibn Khaldūn might have based his systematic exposition of the development and decline of the power-state. He states in his *Muqaddima*: "the edifice of the state rests on two indispensable foundations. The first, understood as army, is power and *'Aṣabīya* (driving force), the second is money, which sustains the army and creates the conditions necessary for the ruler. If the state is seized by disorder it is through ⟨a disturbance of⟩ these two foundations."[77] Ibn Khaldūn is not a dispenser of advice to rulers and administrators but a political scientist who probes into the causes underlying the historical and political process within that human civilization which is the subject of his inquiry. He therefore considers at length that interdependence of military power, finance, prosperity and security which is implied in the aphorism of Kai Kā'ūs. Finance is a composite element in the political fabric, and Ibn Khaldūn examines its several components, such as army pay, the taxation out of which it is paid, and goods sold in the market, whose prices fluctuate with demand and supply, and which yield the ruler's income. He sees all this in relation to an expanding economy which is not confined to agriculture, but comprises trade, commerce and arts and crafts as well. This economy expands with the growth of urban civilization, leading to luxury, ease and the ever-increasing difficulty of satisfying the demands of the ruler's mercenaries. Increased taxation stifles enterprise and reduces profits and the ruler's receipts in dues. The economy contracts, production, and with it trade and commerce, decline. Ruin threatens the population, the ruler lacks the means to pay his army and is no longer able to maintain security within and adequate defence against external enemies. The inevitable result is the fall of the dynasty from power. How Ibn Khaldūn develops this causal interdependence will occupy us in the next chapter. It is briefly mentioned here to explain how the "Mirrors" contrast with Ibn Khaldūn's method and exposition because of their different attitudes and aims.

The *Qābūs-nāma* was composed in 1082; ten years later Niẓām al-Mulk wrote his *Treatise on Government* for his master Malik Shah, the son and successor of the Seljuq sultan Alp Arslan. Niẓām al-Mulk had served both rulers for thirty years as prime minister (vizier). His actual advice is principally contained in introductory remarks at the head of each of the fifty chapters making up the *Siyāsat-nāma*,[78] the bulk of which consists of anecdotes (whose heroes are as often the great kings of pre-Islamic Persia as Muslim caliphs, emirs and sultans), and of traditions attributed to the Prophet Muḥammad adorned with suitable verses from the Qur'ān. The whole is permeated with Islam, and its specific religious colour is much more marked than in the *Qābūs-nāma*. As I have suggested, this may be largely due to the zeal for Sunnī Islam of the recently converted Turkish warriors which their famous vizier took fully into account. Its scope is much larger in that it includes, like the *K. al-tāj* but in less detail, general maxims on good government, and also rules for the various functionaries at court, in the capital, in the cities and towns and in the country. Niẓām al-Mulk writes as the chief government executive, and draws on the store of his thirty years' experience, and on historical sources and *belles lettres* which have the conduct and exploits of rulers, statesmen and savants as their theme. It is an open question whether much of his pious advice is based on strong religious conviction or simply on compliance with established canons and conventions. A story well told need not always reflect an actual occurrence; sometimes his good advice may be based on contrary practice. But he certainly sets out coherently and, which is not unimportant, entertainingly, what good government should be like. The Islamic setting offers a suitable background to the practice of good government.

A Muslim sovereign must have physical beauty, good character, justice, courage, warlike qualities, a taste for the arts and sciences; he must have solid faith and obedience to the duties imposed by God; he must observe prayer and fasting, care for the wellbeing of his people, show respect to saints, scholars and sages, give alms to the poor and be of a generous disposition; in all no mean achievement.[79] Equally significant is his contention that the good ruler disappears when the people rebel in defiance of the divine law, leaving them to their well-deserved punishment.[80] Justice is the most important quality of all. Since the ruler has to give account on the day of resurrection he must govern his people himself and not entrust another person with the government.[81] This means absolute monarchy, but clearly within the confines of the *Sharī'a*; justice and charity are prescribed as a check on arbitrary rule; they should transform the despot into a Muslim monarch bound by the religious law. He is responsible for the judges, who must combine knowledge with piety and integrity.[82] The redress of injustice becomes an important element in government since it is commanded by God in his law.[83] Hence Niẓām's insistence on the ruler's duty towards the doctors of the law. He must provide for their maintenance, hold them in respect, draw them to his court and consult them. Once or twice a week, he must listen to their exposition of the law and to their interpretation of the Qur'ān and the traditions of Muḥammad, until his ignorance is replaced by a sound knowledge of the commandments. This knowledge he must retain in his memory so that he is able to administer the affairs of this world and to prepare himself for the next. By concourse with the learned he will acquire sound judgement; and justice and equity must for ever be the basis for all the orders he issues to his ministers and to the people of his realm.[84]

It is interesting to note that the vizier devotes a special chapter to the need to maintain a network of spies to enable the ruler to keep all officers of state under close observation and control.[85] These spies must visit the provinces of his state and also find out what is going on in neighbouring states. The interests of the state could not be pushed further; the *Sharī'a* hardly prescribes a secret service!

Niẓām al-Mulk is also concerned with the right life at court. Ceremonial is described that it may be observed; the ruler must choose the right companions at table and the right counsellors for the business of state.[86] Pay must always be ready for the army, which must be composed, as we have already noted, of various races in order to secure loyalty and efficiency.[87] Slaves must be treated well,[88] and entertainment and distractions in moderation are the courtiers' duty.[89] The sovereign must liberally distribute food among his subjects[90] and discuss all affairs of state with his vizier,[91] a natural demand from such an outstanding vizier as the author. But he does not add a caution similar to that of Kai Kā'ūs, that the ruler should never accept his vizier's advice at once but should consider it carefully before giving his decision. Niẓām warns against charging an official with more than one office and openly criticizes the contemporary statecraft which employed non-Muslims, like Jews and Christians, and heretics, like Qarmatians and adherents of the Bāṭinīya.[92] Zeal for Islam and compassion for the people when collecting taxes and dues are essential for a flourishing state; their absence, through employment of non-Muslims who lack both, leads to the ruin of the state. He is strongly opposed to the Bāṭinīya sect, the principal enemies of Islam and of his master, the Seljuq sultan, and this is an interesting example of identifying an enemy of the state with an enemy of religion.[93] Niẓām advocates moderation, the golden mean in all acts of government, and again and again asserts that justice is the chief requirement. The shedding of innocent blood must never be allowed or condoned. "That will be a happy day which sees a just ruler (*pādishāh*)". "Justice", says a tradition, "is the might of the world and the power of sovereignty, in which the well-being of the common people as well as of the elect consists."[94] Therefore, the sovereign must devote his efforts to the good of religion so that God Most High may grant him the necessary ability to conduct temporal and spiritual affairs well. Of temporal affairs Nizām singles out the army and finance, of spiritual ones the sovereign's duty to defend pure, Sunnī Islam and the example of a life of piety and devotion. In his eyes, the Seljuq sultan, not the Abbasid caliph, is the defender of the faith as well as of the realm.

CHAPTER IV

THE THEORY OF THE POWER-STATE: IBN KHALDŪN'S STUDY OF CIVILIZATION

IN a world in which everything is related to God and his plan we can hardly expect an independent political theory. Yet a North African Muslim of the fourteenth century, Ibn Khaldūn (1332–1406),[1] did in fact propound a theory of the power-state which transcends the opinions generally held in the Middle Ages. Not only is the state an end in itself with a life of its own, governed by the law of causality, a natural and necessary human institution; it is also the political and social unit which alone makes human civilization possible. It is this human civilization which is the object of his inquiry and the subject of his "new science of history". In the *Muqaddima* (Introduction) to his *Universal History* (*kitāb al-'ibar*) he composed a *Summa*, not of theology but of civilization, founded on that Islamic civilization with all of whose aspects he was thoroughly familiar. His political theory is part of his description of *'umrān*, in the specific sense of "civilization". The close connection between civilization and politics as the art of government is apparent from Ibn Khaldūn's terminology; for *'umrān* is synonymous with *madanīya*[2] and *ḥaḍāra*, settled urban life (as distinct from *badāwa*, rural life). *Ḥaḍāra* in turn is equivalent to *tamaddun*, to live or become organized in a city (*madīna*) in the sense of the Greek *polis*.

Ibn Khaldūn's empiricism, manifest in his "new science", is matched by his traditionalism. This means that he is deeply rooted in the traditional beliefs and convictions of Islam and steeped in the traditional sciences. Chief among them are *Fiqh*, the science of law, and *Tafsīr*, that of the exegesis of the Qur'ān. Both his empiricism and his traditionalism—the former as a scientific method and the latter as an educational background and as an attitude to God and man, to culture and civilization—were formed and developed in his active career as judge (*qāḍī*) of the Mālikī rite and as statesman in the service of several Muslim rulers of North African principalities.

IV. THE THEORY OF THE POWER-STATE

The vicissitudes of fortune and his varied experience in and out of favour with his masters gave his penetrating, scholarly mind a rare insight into the motives of human action. His realistic approach to man in the state made him recognize the will to power and domination as the principal driving force; but he was convinced that the higher aspirations of rational man could only develop in a society efficiently organized in an effective political organization, and only the state could provide it. Hence his interest in politics springs from his Islamic heritage, with its stress on the "community of the faithful", the *umma* or *jamāʿa* of orthodox Islam. Together with his impartial observation, this living heritage enabled him to deduce a general law which he applied to the whole of human civilization.

It is true that his concept of universal civilization is derived exclusively from a dispassionate study of the Islamic empire of his day, with its variety of political entities and cultural levels. But this does not seriously affect his generalizations, nor impair the validity of most of them in the realm of human culture and civilization. It is no exaggeration to say that Ibn Khaldūn's "new science of history" represents a medieval witness to the premature birth of modern scientific inquiry into the human *group*,[3] transcending the bounds of Islam, and it is no coincidence that he speaks of *insānīya*, *humanitas*, of the citizens of the state, a concept which we usually associate with the Renaissance and the humanism of the West. (The parallel with Dante and his Christian humanism is an interesting sidelight on the ground common to leading thinkers of Judaism, Christianity and Islam, despite the differences, which are chiefly doctrinal.)[4] But while Ibn Khaldūn's approach, method and results are significant in the history of the human mind, we must not forget that his ideas are unique in fourteenth-century Islam, and bore no fruit for centuries. They are not the organic growth of the modern age. He lived in a time of transition, when the medieval order was gradually giving way to a new grouping of political, economic and spiritual forces. This may have helped him to formulate his ideas on the inevitable birth, growth, peak, decline and fall of society and culture in accordance with the unalterable law of causality.

Having made this claim, I must emphasize that for Ibn Khaldūn, Islam, in the form of the *khilāfa*, is the choicest fruit of a God-guided and God-centred human association. It is the ideal, the best way to the fulfilment of man's destiny, to the attainment of happiness in this world *and* in the world to come. In writing his *Summa* of civilization he was not concerned with the individual believer but with the human group; he saw it as the creator of culture and civilization in the natural and necessary framework of the state built on power and maintained by the force of law and arms under a single sovereign ruler. Monarchy already typifies an advanced stage in the development of political authority and organization.

It is necessary briefly to sketch the cycle of political life within which the several elements of human association, political, economic, legal (both religious and secular) and cultural, influence each other to the advantage or disadvantage of the state.

Ibn Khaldūn distinguishes three kinds of state according to their government and purpose: *siyāsa dīnīya*, government based on the divinely revealed law (*Shar*ʿ), the ideal Islamic theocracy; *siyāsa* ʿ*aqlīya*, government based on a law established by human reason; and *siyāsa madanīya*, government of the ideal state of the philosophers, *madīna fāḍila*, Plato's *Republic*.[5]

The state as such is the natural result of human life which requires association (*ijtimā*ʿ) and organization: "human association is necessary; the philosophers express this in the saying: 'man is a citizen by nature'. This means that association is indispensable; it is civilization (*madanīya*), in their terminology synonymous with ʿ*umrān*."[6] Mutual help is necessary to satisfy man's need for food, clothing and housing, and man must unite with many of his kind to assure his protection and defence. Experience forces men to associate with others and experience, together with reflection, enables man to live.[7] In addition to this rational explanation Ibn Khaldūn states that "this association is necessary for mankind, otherwise their existence and God's will to make the world habitable with them would not be perfect".[8]

The provision of the necessities of life is followed by a desire for its comforts, and so the stages of food-gathering and cattle-raising are supplemented by the arts and crafts which provide better and more varied food, more comfortable houses and elegant clothes in the cities. Both rural and city life (*badāwa* and *ḥaḍāra*) are necessary for the growth and development of civilization, the former being the natural foundation of the latter. But only a life of ease and leisure, the consequence of a well-functioning, differentiated economy, stimulates the will to power.

To translate the will into reality requires the effective support of like-minded men, held together by a common bond; in the first place, the ties of blood and family tradition which create a sense of solidarity and mutual responsibility, or a common outlook which shows itself in united action and serves as an important driving force in the formation of states and dynasties. Ibn Khaldūn calls it *'Aṣabīya*[9] and gives as its aim *mulk*, dominion, rule. It is as necessary as association itself, for the latter alone is not sufficient to protect man's life and property.

The evil inclination in man would inevitably lead to mutual destruction if there were not a universally recognized restraining authority in society which is given force by the *'Aṣabīya*. This restraining authority is called *wāzi'* or *wāzi' wa-ḥākim* (governor, ruler), or *ḥukm wāzi'*; it has power to prevent men from killing or injuring each other, "for hostility and violence are dominant in their animal nature. . . . This *wāzi'* is therefore the one among them who has power and authority and can exercise constraint over them. This is the meaning of dominion (*mulk*), and it is clear to you from this that it is specific and natural to man and indispensable for him."[10]

Power is thus the basis of the state and the necessary instrument of that restraining authority without which man cannot exist. At first, the man who exercises authority is the *ra'īs* or chief who is, like the *shaikh*, *primus inter pares*; his rule, *ri'āsa*, is a principate. In the opinion of Ibn Khaldūn, this rule represents a political organization prior to the state properly so-called. For he believed that the state as the frame of civilization is an urban institution ruled over by a sovereign monarch, *mustabidd*, exercising *istibdād*, that is, a kind of absolute monarchy. He relies on *'Aṣabīya*, but uses it independently for his own ends. The same idea is expressed in the term *infirād bi-l-majd*, "claiming exclusive authority, on the strength of a pre-eminence acquired by personal effort and achievement". This autocracy is achieved sometimes by the first ruler and founder of a dynasty, sometimes by the second and sometimes by the third.[11] The state goes through five phases: conquest, the building up of the dynasty, the attainment of the peak, decline and fall, within four generations of a dynasty; it reaches its greatest power in the second generation, in which autocracy is usually achieved.

Ibn Khaldūn describes this process of dynastic development in the chapter "The dynasty has a natural term of life like an individual...":

...the term of life of a dynasty does not normally exceed three generations [of 40 years each]. For in the *first* generation are still preserved the characteristic features of rough, uncivilized rural life (*badāwa*), such as hard conditions of life, courage, ferocity and partnership in authority (*majd*). Therefore the strength of the '*Aṣabīya* is maintained...and men submit to their domination. In the *second* generation their condition has changed, under the influence of the rule (*mulk*)...from rural to city-life, from a hard struggle to ease and abundance, from partnership in authority to autocracy...wherefore the strength of the '*Aṣabīya* is partly broken....The *third* generation has forgotten the time of *badāwa*...as if it had never existed—unlike the second generation which lives on the memory of the first—and loses the sweetness of force and '*Aṣabīya* because they are in possession of power. Ease reaches its peak under them because they become used to a pleasant and abundant life....The '*Aṣabīya* collapses completely, and they forget about defence, attack and pursuit ⟨of the enemy⟩....[12]

Incapable of resisting attack from without, they are obliged to hire supporters. He barely mentions the fourth generation because it no longer commands respect and authority.

The four generations of a dynasty are thus distributed over five phases of the state, which determine the character of the citizens. This character, therefore, varies with each successive phase. "The *first* phase is that in which ⟨the new group bent on dominion⟩ gains its objective and is victorious over its enemies, seizes ⟨the reins of⟩ power (*mulk*) and wrests it from the ⟨ruling⟩ dynasty. In this phase ⟨the ruler⟩ is the exemplary leader of his men to gain authority, acquire property and defend and protect the ⟨newly gained⟩ territory." In accordance with the demands of the '*Aṣabīya*, by means of which victory has been won, he does not set himself apart from his citizens.

"In the *second* phase he becomes sovereign and alone exercises rule without his followers; he thwarts their endeavour to share the rule with him...the master of the dynasty strives to hire men, acquire clients (*mawālī*) and supporters in order to break the self-reliance of those who make up his *'Aṣabīya*, and of his kinsmen who claim an equal share in the rule with him...until finally he consolidates the rule in his own family to whom alone he reserves the authority which he builds up...."

"The *third* phase is one of quiet ease and leisure to gather the fruits of rule and dominion, since human nature tends to acquire wealth and to leave behind...fame."

He regulates taxes and dues, is moderate in his expenditure, but at the same time erects monuments and palaces, is generous towards his family and supporters and pays his troops regularly and well in order to impress his allies and to put fear into the hearts of his enemies.

In the *fourth* phase "the ruler is satisfied with what his predecessors have built up, lives at peace with friendly and hostile rulers of his kind and imitates his precursors...as well as he can...".

"The *fifth* phase is one of extravagance and waste. In this phase the ruler destroys what his ancestors have brought together, for the sake of lust and pleasure. For he is generous towards his intimates and liberal at his banquets in order to win...the scum of the people, whom he entrusts with great tasks which they are unable to undertake....In this way he spoils ⟨his chances⟩ with the noble and distinguished among his people and with the followers of his predecessors, so that they are filled with hatred against him and agree among themselves to desert him. Moreover, he loses part of his troops because he spends their pay on his pleasures and prevents them from getting to know him personally....In this phase the natural ageing of the dynasty [that is, the decay] sets in; a chronic disease gets hold of it without remedy or release until it collapses."[13]

It appears that the generations of a dynasty and the phases of the state it rules do not tally unless we assume that in one generation, the third, a transition of the third to the fourth phase takes place. More important, however, is Ibn Khaldūn's recognition of the cyclical movement of states and generations of rulers, and of their interdependence, even if this was facilitated by the absolutist character of rule and the identification of the monarch with the state.

Moreover, he saw a connection between the upward and downward development of the state, the character of rulers and ruled, conditioned by psychological and economic factors, and the stability of the political order in its dependence on defence and security. There is no upward surge towards the millennium. The state is, like a natural organism, subject to growth, maturity and decline.[14]

His whole theory is based on the fundamental distinction between *badāwa*, a life of simplicity, courage, violence and striking power, and *ḥaḍāra*, a life of urban civilization in which these natural qualities are gradually submerged by the desire for peace and security, ease, luxury and pleasure in the wake of autocratic rule.[15] It is significant that Ibn Khaldūn's theory is based on his reading of the history of the Almoravids and Almohads, composed of war-like Berber tribes whose transition from rural to urban life was marked by the stages of political development sketched by him in the *Muqaddima* and described in great detail in his *kitab al-'ibar*.

The absolute monarch can maintain his independent rule only through the weakening of that *'Aṣabīya* by whose help he came to power. Since he must rely on an army to preserve order within and to protect his state against attack from without, the weakening of his supporters, originally animated by a strong *'Aṣabīya*, forces him to replace them by mercenaries. This requires considerable sums of money which he must raise by taxation and often by active participation in trade and industry. After a period of expansion and wealth leading to luxury and ease of living, the inevitable decline sets in, forcing him to take measures for self-preservation which alienate his subjects, harm them in their economic activities, and bring about the ruin and destruction of his dynasty and eventually of the state itself.

The political significance of economics is evident from these summary remarks. To my knowledge Ibn Khaldūn was the first medieval thinker to see the importance of economics for politics and for the whole life of any society organized in a state. A few instances may be quoted in which he stresses their interdependence.[16]

The chapter on "The decrease in pay means a decrease in revenue" begins:

> The reason is that state and ruler are the largest market in the world.... If therefore the ruler keeps back the goods or revenue, or if

they are not there so that he cannot spend them, the possessions of his trusted friends and defenders will ⟨also⟩ be few;...their expenditure decreases—and they form the majority ⟨of buyers⟩...the markets are deserted and the profits from the products decline so that the dues diminish; for dues and taxes come from agriculture, trade, well-frequented markets and from men's desire for profit and gain. The bad effect of all this recoils on the state through the decrease, because the paucity of dues results in diminishing the wealth of the ruler....Money must flow between ruler and subjects, from him to them and from them to him. If, therefore, he holds it back his subjects suffer loss.[17]

This means that a balanced budget is essential for a sound economy and is the key to the stability of the political order. The important place of revenue in political economy is also clear from this quotation:

In the beginning of the state taxes are light in their distribution ⟨on the individual⟩ but considerable in their total, and vice versa. The reason is that the state, which follows the way of religion, only demands the obligations imposed by the *Sharī'a*, namely, *zakāt* (poor-tax), *kharāj* (land-tax), and *jizya* (poll-tax), which are light in their distribution...and these are the limits beyond which one must not go.[18]

A rural economy based on agriculture, with a simple standard of living and light taxes, provides an incentive to work hard, with prosperity as the prize. But as soon as autocrats assume power and urban life, with a much higher standard of living, makes greater and greater demands, heavier taxes are levied from farmers, craftsmen and merchants. Production and profits decline, since the incentive has been taken away from all those engaged in the economic life of the state.

Economic and political development go hand in hand: "The wealth of the ruler and his entourage is ⟨greatest⟩ in the middle stage of the dynasty" is the title of a chapter dealing with the strengthening of the ruler's authority at the expense of the '*Aṣabīya* which once supported him, and consequently his need of mercenaries and auxiliaries and of the means to pay for their services becomes greater. This leads inevitably to increased taxation, a luxurious life at court, the decline of the former supporters of the ruler and finally to the ruin of the dynasty and the state.[19] For

only taxes and their collection increase the wealth of the ruler...and this is possible because he is just and considerate towards the propertied classes, and they are full of hope and begin to increase their possessions so that the revenue of the ruler increases greatly. The other kind, that the ruler engages in trade or agriculture, is of immediate detriment to the subjects and disastrous for the revenue....[20]

The vices in the wake of ease, luxury, and the loss of courage, manliness and professional pride spread in the population because of the bad example set by the ruling dynasty and its servants and hangers-on.[21]

It is clear from Ibn Khaldūn's statement that we are dealing not with a state based on the *Sharī'a*, but an autocracy dependent on a mercenary army for the maintenance of power. It is in this power-state that the political and economic egotism of the ruler and his associates leads to abuses much more easily and frequently than in the state based on the moral law founded in revelation.

Ibn Khaldūn, far from moralizing, does not criticize moral offences and shortcomings as an open flouting of moral precepts, or as a sin deserving divine punishment; he sets them in relation to the state, registers their political significance and implications and dispassionately states their disastrous effect on good government and public welfare. Nor does he condone political crimes. Here he stands out as a political scientist who diagnosed the ill-health of the state as an organism comparable to the human body, subject to the same law of cause and effect. Although he observed Islamic states, he deduced this general law for the state as such, and for human civilization as a whole, quite independently of the ideal *khilāfa*. But his remark that the taxes and imposts levied by the autocrat are far in excess of, and at variance with, those demanded by the *Shar'*, the prophetically revealed law of Islam, shows beyond question that it is precisely this ideal law which serves him as the norm and measure. The *Sharī'a* prescribes *zakāt*, *kharāj* and *jizya*, levied on the *Dhimmīs*, the protected non-Muslim "people of the Book" (that is, Jews, Christians and Zoroastrians). It guarantees private property as an inalienable right. If the ruler seizes the property of his subjects or forces them to sell it because he has destroyed their livelihood by monopolizing certain crafts or trades, the Muslim Ibn Khaldūn simply states that such an act offends against the *Shar'*. But he comments explicitly that it is detrimental to the interests of the dynasty and does great, even irreparable, harm to the state.

He devotes a chapter to the relationship between ruler and ruled which has the revealing title: "Exaggerated severity harms and mostly ruins the state (*mulk*)." The welfare of the subjects and of the state rests on good relations between the ruler—be he *malik* (king) or *sulṭān*—and his subjects.

The essence of the ruler is that he rules over subjects and cares for their affairs. . . . If his dominion over them, with all that it entails, is good, the purpose of the rule is fulfilled to perfection. For if it is good and well ordered, it is an advantage for them, but if it is bad and unjust, it is harmful to them and leads to their destruction. . . . Kindliness towards them belongs to good government, together with their protection, for through protection ⟨of his subjects⟩ the character of the ruler becomes perfect. Kindliness and good treatment also consist in . . . care for their livelihood, and it is a basic principle to be friendly towards the subjects.[22]

We note that the overriding consideration is public welfare and the interests of the state. All depends on the right kind of government, *siyāsa*, to which Ibn Khaldūn devotes a chapter entitled "Human civilization certainly needs political government by which its affairs are arranged in proper order". In it he says:

We have already stated in another place that association is necessary for man and is the meaning of civilization, of which we treat, and that men, in their association, must needs have a restraining authority (*wāzi'*) and a governor (*ḥākim*) to whom they entrust themselves. His authority over them is based at one time on the law sent down by Allah demanding their obedience, in their belief in reward and punishment . . .; and at another time ⟨it is based⟩ on rational government [that is, on a law devised by human reason] demanding their obedience to it in the expectation of a reward from the ruler. . . . The advantage of the first [that is, the *siyāsa dīnīya*] comes to pass in this world and the next because the law-giver knows what is best for them in the end, and because he looks after the salvation of the servants ⟨of Allah, *'ibād*⟩ in the hereafter. But the advantage of the second accrues in this world only. What you hear of the *siyāsa madanīya* (*politeia*) [the third of the kinds of government mentioned above] does not belong to this chapter; the philosophers mean by it what is incumbent upon every one of the citizens of this community in his own nature, so that they have no need of governors (rulers) altogether. Such a community is called *madīna fāḍila*, the ideal state [that is, Plato's *Republic*], and the statutes for its government are called *siyāsa madanīya*. Their intention is not a *siyāsa* by which the citizens of ⟨this⟩ association are to pursue the public good, for this is not ⟨the same as⟩ the other ⟨*siyāsa*⟩. This *madīna fāḍila* is in their opinion rare or unlikely to come into being, and they discuss it only hypothetically.[23]

We must here interrupt Ibn Khaldūn's account to consider his cursory treatment of the ideal state of the philosophers and his opposition to their views on politics. His realism, based on experience, made him dismiss their hypothesis as mere theory. He strongly objects to their concept of prophecy and the prophetically revealed law, at least as far as Al-Fārābī and Ibn Sīnā are concerned. He refutes as unproven their contention that prophecy is a necessary requirement of human nature and that the *wāzi*ʿ is demanded by the *Shar*ʿ. He simply points to the existence of human organization, both before prophets appeared and since; for a large part of mankind lives without prophets and prophetic laws. Their rulers exercise authority over them by their power or by means of the ʿ*Aṣabīya* which unites their supporters.[24] In his support he adduces the opinion of the *salaf*, the early followers of Muḥammad. The *Shar*ʿ, not reason, is the authority for prophecy. As we saw earlier, the prophetic lawgiver provides in the *Shar*ʿ—and we may add, there alone—for man's welfare in this world and salvation in the next. The believer who obeys this law has the *wāzi*ʿ in himself, for it is inherent in the very nature of revelation. It was only when religion (*dīn*) lost its influence over man and when the *Shar*ʿ became a science[25] that man needed restraining statutes (*aḥkām wāzi*ʿ*a*). For Ibn Khaldūn the *wāzi*ʿ is thus not an external authority prescribed by the revealed law of Islam, and the prophet is not a ruler. This is most probably a rejection of the political interpretation of prophecy advanced by the *Falāsifa*, with which we shall deal later.

The prophet is primarily a lawgiver; the caliph, his vicegerent and successor, is the ruler under the *Shar*ʿ which bound together the *umma*, the people of Muḥammad, in the *jamā*ʿ*a*, the community of ⟨right⟩ believers. It ruled supreme as the law of Muslim theocracy in the time of the first four caliphs, the *khulafā rāshidūn*, and of Muḥammad's companions generally. The decline of religion coincided with the transformation of the *khilāfa* of that time into the *mulk* of Muʿāwiya and the Umayyads. This was also the time of the transition from *badāwa* to *ḥaḍāra* and the expansion of Islam into a vast empire. Urban life, guided by the restraining statutes of the *mulk*, led to the gradual loss of courage and self-reliance due to the replacement of the *wāzi'* inherent in the *Shar'* by the *wāzi'* of the state built on the power and conquest of a sovereign ruler. Ibn Khaldūn therefore defines the political system of the Muslim *malik* or *sulṭān* as *siyāsa 'aqlīya*, even though the primary source of the statutes by which they rule their subjects is the *Sharī'a*. He says:

> Politics based on reason can take two forms. In the first care is taken of welfare in general, and of the advantage of the sultan in respect of the maintenance of his rule in particular.... Allah has dispensed with it for us in ⟨our⟩ religious community (*milla*) and for the time of the *khilāfa* [that is, of the first four caliphs], because the statutes of the *Sharī'a* dispense with it in respect of the general and the particular welfare. The statutes of the *mulk* are included in it [that is, the *Sharī'a*].
> In the second form care is taken of the advantage of the ruler and that the *mulk* should be firmly established for him by force and superior power; the general welfare ⟨of the subjects⟩ takes second place. Such a government (*siyāsa*) is that of ⟨all⟩ the other kings in the world, Muslim and non-Muslim, except that the Muslim kings act in accordance with the requirements of the Islamic *Sharī'a*, as far as they can. Hence their laws are composed of statutes of the *Sharī'a*, rules of right conduct, regulations which are natural for ⟨political⟩ association, and necessary things concerning power and *'Aṣabīya*. The requirements of the *Shar'* come first, then the philosophers with their rules of conduct and ⟨after that⟩ the kings in their way of life.[26]

We note the interplay of factors and forces of different provenance in Ibn Khaldūn's argument: on the one hand Islam as a collective as well as a personal factor, and on the other power and its maintenance.

The distinction between *siyāsa dīnīya*, based on the divinely revealed prophetic law and represented by the *khilāfa*, and *siyāsa 'aqlīya*, founded by conquest, based on laws devised by reason and realized in the *mulk*, the power-state, is fundamental;[27] it underlies Ibn Khaldūn's historical inquiry into existing society and its civilization. He is bent on discovering the principles of political organization, on finding out how the state runs its course and how it works. His point of reference in this analysis is the *Sharī'a* of Islam, the constitution of a theocracy founded by the lawgiver.

Like Al-Māwardī and the other jurists he defines the *khilāfa* as the lieutenancy of the lawgiver to guard religion and administer the world in the chapters "On the meaning of *khilāfa* and *imāma*" and "On the religious concerns of the *khilāfa*".

His own contribution to political thought consists in two important findings. They are the result of the blending, in his searching mind, of empiricism and traditionalism, and they are: (*a*) that the *khilāfa* has survived in the *mulk* of the Islamic empire, and (*b*) that religion, if not the determining factor as it is in the *khilāfa*, still remains an important factor in the *mulk*. He applies his own experience in Islam to society and civilization in general. He thus combines a primarily theological with a power-political concept of the state, without in any way abandoning the accepted Muslim position, since the spiritual and the temporal power are united in the caliph or *imām*. This does not mean, however, that there is simply a difference of degree: religion being either the sovereign ruling factor, a *primus inter pares*, or only one factor among many, though a very important one. For Ibn Khaldūn maintains again and again that dominion is as necessary as the will to power and domination is natural, and that power can be gained and dominion established without the call of religion, so long as '*Aṣabīya* unites a large enough group of like-minded enthusiasts to supply the man aspiring to political leadership with sufficient backing. But he would not be a Muslim if he did not stress the support, often decisive, which religion lends to the '*Aṣabīya*, transforming a driving force originally based on descent or common material interests into an irresistible spiritual influence reinforced by the energy and striking power of a closely knit group of activists. This applies in particular to Islam in its period of expansion and consolidation into a world power.

Ibn Khaldūn has correctly deduced that a weakening of the religious *élan* must strengthen the temporal component of the *khilāfa* and inevitably lead to its transformation into absolute monarchy in the form of the *mulk*. On the other hand, religion, whether by prophecy or by a call (*da'wa*) to ⟨its⟩ truth, is the source from which great empires spring. For where otherwise rivalry and discord might threaten to disrupt the '*Aṣabīya*, religion unites all hearts, replaces the desire for the vanity of the world with its rejection and turns men to God, seeking right and truth in unison.[28] In support of his claim that "the call to religion increases the force of the '*Aṣabīya*...",[29] he cites the Lamṭūna and the Almoravids in the Maghreb, whose religious zeal made their '*Aṣabīya* irresistible in spite of the numerical superiority of their opponents, and tells how the decline of this zeal led to their destruction at the hands of those whom they had previously subdued. In other words, religious enthusiasm provides a strong incentive for the will to power, and thus sublimates what was originally part of man's baser nature, which he shares with the animals. This is expressed in *taghallub*, subjugation, and *qahr*, force, which stem from *ghaḍab*—equivalent to the irascible part of the soul—and from *ḥayawānīya*, the concupiscent part. Ibn Khaldūn borrows these terms from the psychology of the *Falāsifa* where they had a Platonic-Aristotelian meaning.

These natural forces spend themselves after an initial effort—the conquest of power and the foundation of the state. As long as religion unites ruler and ruled by stressing the higher purpose of man and his salvation, the life of the state is guaranteed. Ibn Khaldūn is concerned more with the political relevance of religion than with its moral and civilizing aspects. Conversely, he is realist enough to know and to emphasize in the chapter entitled "The religious call (*da'wa*) is not complete ⟨and effective⟩ without '*Aṣabīya*", that force and power are necessary for the realization of an ideal and for the effective implementation of religious ideas in practical life. He quotes in his support the Hadith: "Allah did not send a prophet without the protection of his tribe." If this applies to prophets, how much more to others. Ibn Khaldūn extends this principle to the rebellion against tyranny which is demanded by God of those only who have the power to overthrow it. He cites again a suitable prophetic utterance in his support: "He among you who sees something displeasing to Allah, must change it by force, if he is unable by his word; but if not even that, then at least in his heart." For "only a strong attack, backed by the '*Aṣabīya* of tribes and clans, can remove rulers and destroy the edifice of their states which are firmly established".[30]

It is this combination of religious conviction with political power which determines the nature and purpose of the *khilāfa* which Ibn Khaldūn so clearly recognized. The observer of the state as it is has drawn the conclusion from this knowledge that the transformation of the *khilāfa* into the *mulk* is natural and inevitable. At the same time he is convinced that, although the *mulk* is capable of looking after the welfare of man in this world, even this is achieved more perfectly with the aid of the laws of the *Sharī'a*, since the prophetic lawgiver knows best what is to man's advantage in both mundane and religious matters. "Therefore if the *mulk* is Islamic it comes second in rank after the *khilāfa*, and they are linked together. But the *mulk* is isolated if it is outside the religious community (*milla*)."[31] Since political association in Islam originally took the form of the *khilāfa*, its significance and character were preserved after its transformation into the *mulk*,

> namely, to choose religion and its ways and rites and to follow the paths of right without a visible change, except that the restraining authority (*wāzi'*) which had been religion (*dīn*), was replaced by the *'Aṣabīya* and the sword. This was the case in the time of Mu'āwiya, Merwān and his son 'Abd-al-Malik as well as in the early days of the Abbasid caliphs up to the period of (Hārūn al-)Rashīd and some of his sons. Then the characteristics of the *khilāfa* disappeared, nothing but its name remained and the state became a *mulk* pure and simple. The condition of subjugation reached its peak and was used for purposes of force, a variety of desires and sensual pleasures. Such was the case under the sons of 'Abd-al-Malik and the successors of Hārūn al-Rashīd among the Abbasids. The name *khilāfa* remained, thanks to the continuance of the *'Aṣabīya* of the Arabs. *Khilāfa* and *mulk* intermingled with each other in the two phases, but then the characteristics of the *khilāfa* disappeared with the disappearance of the Arabs, the destruction of their tribes and the ruin of their affairs.... It is, therefore, evident that the *khilāfa* at first existed without *mulk*, then their character became intermixed and finally the *mulk* alone remained, isolated ⟨from the *khilāfa*⟩ at the moment when its *'Aṣabīya* became separated from that of the *khilāfa*.[32]

The transference of power from the Arab aristocracy to autocratic rulers in the Persian style, governing after the Persian model, is here explained in terms of the decline of Arab solidarity and striking power (*'Aṣabīya*) and of Islam as a political driving force.

Ibn Khaldūn, as a Muslim observer of history, expresses this transformation as the natural result of psychological conditions which largely determine political developments. He does not condemn it as long as the ruler fulfils his obligations towards his subjects; to protect their life and property and to show concern for their welfare. In return his authority is recognized and his rule accepted. Ibn Khaldūn is at pains to point out that the prophetic lawgiver pays due attention to human nature in his law (*Shar'*) and condemns only excess:

> Know that the whole world...is for the law-giver but a way[33] to the hereafter, for he who has no animal to ride on does not reach his goal. His [the law-giver's] intention is not to forbid or blame man's deeds... or to destroy the forces altogether which produce them, but rather to change their direction towards the aims of truth as far as possible, so that all intentions become right and the direction ⟨of man's desires and plans⟩ a single one ⟨namely, to Allah and the hereafter⟩.[34]

In this spirit Ibn Khaldūn examines the criticism of '*Aṣabīya* that it consists of descent and pride of descent. He finds that '*Aṣabīya* properly applied and understood is desirable, provided it is directed towards truth and the cause of Allah. For

> if he [the lawgiver] eliminated it, the laws would become inoperative, since they can only fully function with the help of the '*Aṣabīya*....The same applies to the *malik* (king). When the lawgiver reprimanded him he did not mean rightful authority, sufficient compulsion of religion and concern for the ⟨general⟩ welfare, but he blamed useless subjugation.... For if the king were sincere that his dominion over men were in the cause of God, and would charge them with service of God and holy war (*jihād*) against his enemies, it would not be blameworthy.[35]

There can be no doubt that Ibn Khaldūn gives religion (that is, in practice, the *Sharī'a* of Islam) if not the first at least a very important place in the existing state. His inquiry into Islamic history and his experience of the contemporary Muslim states in the Maghreb taught him that there is always a gap between the ideal demands of the ideal *Sharī'a* and political reality. But even if considerations of power politics have at times set aside the *Sharī'a*, its theoretical validity and overruling authority have never been questioned. Jurists, like Al-Māwardī, Ibn Jamā'a and Ibn Taymīya, strove to maintain the purity of the law and showed what government ought to be in accordance with its provisions—despite their far-reaching and often compromising concessions. Ibn Khaldūn, no less ready to acknowledge the theoretical authority of the *Sharī'a*, turned his attention to the state as it actually was, and showed why it had to be so. Restricting his observation to the

Islamic states whose law was in theory the *Sharīʿa* of Muḥammad, the Prophet of Islam, he does not devote special chapters to the discussion of law as a political factor, though he discusses other factors, stressing their interaction and interdependence. It is the more noteworthy that he emphasized the composite nature of the *mulk* precisely on account of the laws which regulate the life of the state. For whatever the source of the law of the state—whether God through a prophetic lawgiver, or human reason through the leading men of action and sages—a state cannot be established except on a foundation of law. In the chapter "On the meaning of *khilāfa* and *imāma*", referred to above, Ibn Khaldūn justifies the promulgation of *qawānīn siyāsīya*, political laws—that is, laws regulating the administration of the polity and the relations between the ruler, who has seized power by force, and his subjects—by the need to curb the selfishness and arbitrariness of the ruler. In the absence of such laws the ruler would impose burdens on his subjects which would be too heavy for them to bear, and they would rebel.

If the state is Islamic the government will be a religious one—the *siyāsa dīnīya*—based on God's revealed law, the *Sharīʿa*. The government will be a *siyāsa ʿaqlīya* if it is based on political laws made by rational man. Such was the case in pre-Islamic Persia.[36] The different kinds of government have already been discussed, and I refer to them here for another reason: to stress the political aspect of law. This is implicit in the term used by Ibn Khaldūn, *qawānīn siyāsīya*, and from his comment: "If the state is without such a *siyāsa*—government on the basis of legally binding rules and regulations—its affairs are not in good order and its authority is not complete."[37]

It cannot be over-emphasized that Ibn Khaldūn leaves no doubt that the law of the prophetic lawgiver is best and is superior to that of the human lawgiver, who is guided only by his reason. The former implies that

> this world alone is not man's goal, for it is altogether useless and vain, since its end is death and destruction. God says: Do you think that we created you for sport? (*Sūra* XXIII, 117.) What is intended for man is his religion, which lets him attain happiness in the hereafter as the way of God.... The laws came which placed an obligation upon him in all his

affairs, like service of God, trade and commerce, including rule (*mulk*) which is natural for human association, so that they ⟨the laws⟩ lead the rule towards the ways of God and everything is within the reach and range of the *Shar*ʿ.[38]

Together with the earlier exposition of the respective spheres of *siyāsa dīnīya* and *siyāsa ʿaqlīya* this passage shows that the state based on the religious law of Islam has a duty to care for the individual, who has to give account of his earthly life in the hereafter, as the creature of God, whereas the state based on the law of reason is concerned with the good order of society and the earthly well-being of its members. As a Muslim writing of the Islamic state, Ibn Khaldūn discusses only those aspects of religious law which have a bearing on politics. In the main he follows Al-Māwardī, and expressly quotes him as his source. In writing of the conditions which the caliph must satisfy, he insists—as we saw in chapter II—on descent from the Quraish because of their powerful ʿ*Aṣabīya*, with the help of which they can guarantee and maintain the unity of the Muslim community. This is not surprising, for Ibn Khaldūn proudly traces his own descent from the early Muslims, because the Arabs attach the greatest value to noble descent and have developed the science of genealogy to a fine art. That Ibn Khaldūn considers power based on ʿ*Aṣabīya* to be indispensable follows naturally from his theory of the state. Since it is the caliph's job to look after the temporal and spiritual interests of "the community of the faithful" God must give him the necessary force. "Nobody is charged with a task except he has the power to ⟨fulfil⟩ it."[39]

In yet another respect the difference between religious and temporal law is stressed in a manner typical of Ibn Khaldūn. Mild and just rule encourages self-reliance and personal courage; force and severity instil fear and timidity in the subjects. Therefore the Arabs living in the country are manly, but the urban population, living under restrictive statutes and being educated from childhood to obey for fear of punishment, loses its manliness. Urban life includes an education in the religious sciences, such as reading the Qur'ān and studying under shaikhs and Imams. He says:

Do not try to refute this by ⟨pointing out⟩ that the companions of the Prophet in fact accepted the statutes of religion and of the *Sharīʿa* without a decline in manliness. On the contrary, they were the most manly ⟨of all⟩. For when the Muslims accepted their religion from the lawgiver, a restraining authority (*wāzi'*) ⟨developed⟩ in their own self from the promises and threats which were recited to them out of the Qur'ān. It did not consist of instruction in the arts and education in the sciences, but they absorbed spontaneously the statutes and *mores* of religion which they received by tradition, because beliefs and convictions were firmly established in them. Therefore the force of their manliness remained as strong as before and the claws of education and authority did not scratch them. . . . But when religion slowly declined among men they accepted restrictive statutes; the *Shar'* became a science and an art which was acquired by education and instruction, and they went over to a settled, civilized life (*ḥaḍāra*) and ⟨acquired⟩ the character-trait of obeying the statutes. Then the force of manliness declined among them. It is thus clear that the statutes of the government and instruction corrupt manliness, because in them the *wāzi'* is external. Yet the *Sharī'a* has no deleterious effect because the *wāzi'* is in it as belonging to its essence. Therefore the statutes of the (temporal) government and instruction impress the urban dwellers ⟨adversely⟩ by weakening their souls and breaking their strength.[40]

In conclusion, it can be said that the kind of law governing the state depends on the political and historical situation at any given time in its development and on the power of the ruler to enforce the law. Ibn Khaldūn wished to demonstrate this interconnection between law and politics.

We have seen that for Ibn Khaldūn the state, the object of his empirical inquiry, is the cradle of human civilization. The ideal pattern of political organization is the *Sharī'a*-state of the formative period of Islam, the time of the first four caliphs. The field of his observation is the Islamic empire of his own day, and in particular in the Maghreb, the scene of his own political and legal activities. His insight into human nature, born of a religious humanism, enabled him to generalize from the facts of Islamic history, as he discovered them in themselves and in their mutual relations.[41] The state as it is, built on force and conquest and maintained by power supported by an adequate army, aroused his historical interest; he set his realistic assessment of social life in the state against his ideal pattern. For his roots are deeply embedded in Islamic civilization, and the spiritual values of Islam are set as the goal of human endeavour.

Something must be said of the causal relation between the state and the higher cultural values to which the arts and sciences point, and to which their pursuit leads. We have considered urban civilization in relation to the origin, growth and decline of the power-state. We have seen the importance of the ruler and his court for the development of arts and crafts, caused by the growing demands of a life of leisure, ease and luxury; and how the close dependence of this life on finance and security eventually curbs the production of luxury goods, and causes its rapid decline. Increased taxation removes the incentive from the craftsmen and reduces the profits of the traders, at the same time reducing the spending power of a diminishing clientele for such goods.

Ibn Khaldūn expresses this relationship thus:

> All this comes from state and dynasty, for the state collects the money from the subjects and spends it on the court and its dependants.... Thus this money comes in from the subjects and goes out to the supporters of the dynasty ⟨ruling the state⟩, and then to the citizens who join themselves to them—and these are in the majority.[42]

Well-being and wealth increase, especially in the centre of the state, the capital.

> This is so only because the ruler is in their midst and his money flows among them, like water which makes the ground in the vicinity green, but what is far away remains dry. We have already said that ruler and state are the market for the world, for all goods are on the markets and in their vicinity, and if you go away from the markets the goods are wanting altogether.[43]

Civilization is thus the direct result of the establishment of the state and depends on its consolidation for growth and stability.

> Reflect, [says Ibn Khaldūn] on the deep significance of this (for it is hidden from men) and know that these are matters which stand in a relationship with each other, namely the position of the state as to strength and weakness, the numerical strength of the state or tribe, the size of the city or region, the degree of ease and wealth in life; this is that state and rule are the *form* of the creation, and civilization and everything else ⟨namely⟩ the subjects, the cities and the other phenomena provide the *matter* for them....[44]

This shows that Ibn Khaldūn recognized the inevitable correlation between the political situation and the standard of living, the state of civilization of rulers and ruled.[45] Significantly, man's humanity (*insānīya*) is, in his view, profoundly affected by the degree of culture and civilization; it declines with them, and is at its lowest when his moral qualities and his religion have been corrupted.[46]

To turn to the sciences in the strict sense, it must be borne in mind that Ibn Khaldūn was himself versed both in the philosophical and in the traditional sciences. His account of the Muslim sciences is an authoritative summary of their scope, content and meaning. But his attitude to the philosophical sciences is determined by his traditionalism and by his empiricism. For him, the rational sciences are natural to man and are found among all civilized nations.[47] They derive from man's power of reflection, which distinguishes him from the animals. But food and its provision are connected with his animal nature; therefore the sciences and arts take second place after the necessities of life.[48] In the chapter "The sciences only increase where...civilization increases"[49] he speaks of man's quest for what is specific to him, the sciences and the arts and crafts. The third phase of the state[50] is particularly favourable to the development of the sciences, thanks to the liberality of the ruler and the prevailing peace and prosperity. The capital as seat of the ruler becomes a centre of culture; scholars, poets and singers vie with each other at his court. But the more luxury, and with it moral laxity, increase, the less interest there is in spiritual values or the inner life and the less respect for scholars and their work. Here is an invaluable illustration of Ibn Khaldūn's important differentiation between urban civilization and spiritual culture, and the interrelation of the two.

Quite apart from the natural decline of the sciences in the wake of political, social and economic deterioration, Ibn Khaldūn stresses the grave danger of philosophy to religion. And because religion is important for the state, there is a consequent danger to society. It is true, he says, that the philosophical sciences form an integral part of *'umrān* and are useful to everybody. But since philosophy propounds doctrines in opposition to the *Sharī'a* and its teachings as they are literally interpreted, speculation is to be discouraged, unless the student has first mastered the religious sciences. On the other hand, he stresses the importance of speculation for the historian and, on the whole, shares the view of Al-Ghazālī, who accepts logic and mathematics, and sees no harm in physics as long as the teachings of the Qur'ān are not contradicted, but warns against metaphysics. His sustained attack upon the *Falāsifa* must remain outside the present summary of his views.[51] It is sufficient here to underline the importance of philosophy and of his emphatic refutation of some of the views of the *Falāsifa* "because these sciences are ⟨natural⟩ concomitants of civilization, occur frequently in the cities, and do much damage to religion".[52] Since decline in religion is harmful to the state, whose good order is essential for man and his destiny in this world and in the hereafter, it is clear that Ibn Khaldūn must oppose the views of the *Falāsifa*. He does so as a convinced Muslim, for whom the prophetic law is perfect and alone adequate to lead man to his happiness. This happiness transcends that joy resulting from the perception of all "existing things", which the *Falāsifa* held to be the happiness peculiar to the speculative philosopher. Ibn Rushd would agree with him here, despite his spirited defence of philosophy (*falsafa*).[53]

Ibn Khaldūn doubts whether this happiness is the blessedness in the hereafter promised by the prophetic lawgiver to the obedient believer. But as a political scientist he is equally at variance with the *Falāsifa*, since his method is empirical, not speculative. Observation of reality and experience determine his views, whereas the *Falāsifa* rely on "hypothesis and supposition" in politics.[54]

In one respect he is right, though. The ruler of the state is not the metaphysician—Plato's philosopher-king equated by the *Falāsifa* with the Muslim prophetic lawgiver and *imām*—but the sovereign ruler of the power-state, supported by '*Aṣabīya* and religion.

Ibn Khaldūn's importance was not recognized in his own time, and not until the seventeenth century did Muslim writers take any notice of him, while European scholars discovered him only in the last century. His importance consists in a number of novel insights of permanent value and significance: (1) in his distinction between rural and urban life, and the necessity of the latter for the emergence of civilization and a state in the strict sense of the term; (2) in his postulating the '*Aṣabīya* as the principal driving force of political action; (3) in his projection of Islam into a universal human civilization, thus standing on the soil and in the climate of Islam and looking out towards humanity at large; (4) in his realization of the causal interdependence of the several factors of social life in the power-state: economic, military, cultural and religious; (5) in the concept of the parallel existence of the state founded by a prophetic lawgiver, as distinct from the state built on power in response to the human need for political association, and the desire of strong personalities for domination; (6) arising from the last point, in his definition and analysis of the Islamic *mulk*, as a composite structure whose law is a mixture of *Sharī'a* and rational, i.e. political, law; (7) in his fundamental recognition of the vital part which religion should play in the life of the state, especially if it transforms the *'Aṣabīya* into a durable, cohesive spiritual motive power; and (8) in that he postulates a causal law for the state which determines its development in a cycle of origin, growth, peak, decline and fall.

It is only natural that a man living in an age of transition should stress now one aspect and now another. Consistency can be as little expected as a complete integration of revolutionary ideas, almost modern in their tendency, and traditional Muslim thinking, into a new coherent philosophy. But, though prematurely, he broke new ground, not least in his insight into the workings of power politics, in his discovery of the importance of the human group animated by *'Aṣabīya*, and in his momentous recognition of the necessity of a healthy economy for a smoothly functioning state, a flourishing society, and a highly developed civilization. Some of the points enumerated constitute a signal contribution to political thought in general, far transcending medieval Islam.

It is not, therefore, out of place to compare some aspects of Ibn Khaldūn's thought with the strikingly similar views of Machiavelli, although there is certainly no connection between the two thinkers, direct or indirect. This similarity concerns points 2, 4 and 7. *'Aṣabīya* is a term which Ibn Khaldūn coined to express the corporate will of a group. It enables that group, and especially its leader, to realize their united will in political action; and specifically to found and to maintain the state. There is at first sight no comparable term in Machiavelli. But a consideration of his concept of *virtù* makes a comparison with it plausible. *Virtù* originally expressed the personal courage, skill and determination of an individual, but was ultimately used to denote the force inherent in all citizens of the state, particularly in the ruler, and it finds its expression in decisive action in the political and social life. It is the determining factor of political action. In contrast with the collective nature of the *'Aṣabīya*, however, *virtù* remains a personal driving force confined to its possessor, and it is in its origin more a spiritual force. Yet in combination with the *virtù* of others, its place in the state and its effective influence on politics make it serve the same purpose as *'Aṣabīya*; this may help the Western reader to understand better the significance of the Arab's concept. Fr. Meinecke defines *virtù* in the Introduction to his German edition of the *Principe* as "heroism and capacity for great historical achievement, and the founding of flourishing and powerful states".[55]

In general, there is in Machiavelli the same appreciation of the role of power and of the will to power to establish, develop and consolidate the state, as, for example, in the third chapter of the *Principe*. Ibn Khaldūn's chapter called "The goal at which the *'Aṣabīya* aims is dominion (*mulk*)" forcefully makes the point that the state is conditioned by the will to power of strong personalities and groups which must be able to rely on a powerful *'Aṣabīya*.[56]

We have seen that in the power-state (*mulk*), in contrast to the *khilāfa* in the strict sense under the first four caliphs, the interest of the state is the overriding consideration. The ruler is responsible for the state, its safety, good order and welfare. To discharge his responsibilities he must have sufficient power. Machiavelli's attitude to the state is basically the same: the interests of the state are paramount. But Machiavelli would go much further than Ibn Khaldūn, who held to Muslim ethics, was prepared to go. *Necessità*, political necessity in the interests of the state, demanded by "Reason of State", made Machiavelli condone morally reprehensible actions, such as violence, treason, breach of faith and even murder. For Ibn Khaldūn these are evil and bound to recoil not only on the perpetrators but on the state as a whole; they must prove injurious in the end. Machiavelli recognizes that they are bad, but he deems them useful for the state and for that reason justifiable.[57] There are other differences between the two. Ibn Khaldūn, as we have seen, observes and diagnoses and draws conclusions as a historian of civilization. Machiavelli is himself a political activist and reformer. He gives advice in the hope that it may lead to the unification of Italy. He is part of the Renaissance.

Both he and Ibn Khaldūn share an impartial empiricism, both seek the truth in examining political reality. But Ibn Khaldūn inquires into the origin and development of the state in order to find and formulate an underlying law. Machiavelli also recognizes the causality of history and development in cycles. He is influenced by Polybius in his concept of the cyclical change of constitutions. Whether Ibn Khaldūn, or any other Muslim author, knew Polybius is, as far as I know, uncertain and indeed doubtful. Unlike Ibn Khaldūn, Machiavelli is not satisfied with discovering cause and effect in historical and political phenomena; he wants to learn a lesson from the past in order to apply it to the present.

In one respect both men came to practically identical conclusions quite independently. Both stress the importance of religion for the state and the connection between religion and power. In his *Discorsi* Machiavelli says: "If we read Roman history attentively we will always find how much religion contributed to obedience in the army, to courage among the people, to the preservation of morality and to shaming the wicked....As the worship of God is the cause for the greatness of republics, so is its neglect the cause of their ruin...."[58] Religion consolidates the state. Ibn Khaldūn stated that religion without '*Aṣabīya* is unable to impress people, impose its law on them and secure their obedience. Only authority backed by effective power can bring success, in religious matters no less than in political affairs. Machiavelli says: "Only he should set out to conquer who has also ability and force...."[59] In the sixth chapter of his *Principe* he speaks of the difficulty of preserving newly won power and says: "...but when he must rely on himself and can use coercion, he rarely runs a risk. It is for this reason that all armed prophets have been victorious, and all unarmed ones have perished." This agrees with the quotation from the earlier chapter: "The religious call (*da'wa*) is not complete without '*Aṣabīya*",[60] to which this further passage may be added: "The situation of the prophets was the same when they called men to God with the help of clans and groups, and they were fortified by God...."

Machiavelli also resembles Ibn Khaldūn in his evaluation of religion in relation to the state when he claims (*Discorsi* II, 2) that Christianity makes man humble and submissive. From the passage quoted above[61] it is clear that Ibn Khaldūn exempts pure Islam from such a charge, at any rate when the *khilāfa* corresponded in reality to its theory as laid down in the *Sharī'a*. It is true this formulation happened long after the *khilāfa* had been transformed into the *mulk*, and for this reason Ibn Khaldūn avers that once the *Shar'* had become a science to be studied at a time when religion had lost its impetus, the deference of the students towards their teachers resulted in a decline in manliness and self-reliance. But while he safeguards Islam as a religion and the *khilāfa* as the ideal state he would agree with Machiavelli as far as the *mulk* is concerned, that is, the *mulk* which is based on a mixed government, and whose law contains both the ordinances of the *Sharī'a*, and political statutes promulgated by the autocratic ruler.[62]

Machiavelli is at one with him in stressing that the fear of God which religion inspires in man makes him obedient to orders and laws, reliable in keeping an oath or a promise, and easy to rule. In his view, religion is also conducive to the formation of a good army; indeed, he summed up those things which preserve the state in the words: "Religion, laws and army."

It is their insight into human nature and their realization of the importance of force and power, supported by indispensable authority, which links the Muslim historian of human civilization to the man of the Renaissance, who had studied the history of Rome and of Christian Italy.

PART TWO

THE PLATONIC LEGACY

CHAPTER V

POLITICAL PHILOSOPHY IN ISLAM

So far we have considered the views of the jurists on the theory and principles of the *khilāfa* as an institution required by the *Sharī'a*, and the views of moralists and men of affairs on *siyāsa*, the art of government. Both groups started with and concentrated on the Islamic state; the first took their stand upon constitutional law as part of *Fiqh* and, in an attempt to vindicate this law in the face of divergent practice in political reality, stated what the *khilāfa* should be.

The second group accepted political reality, the state as it was, and pronounced on good government in general conformity with the religious and ethical teachings of Islam rather than with the exact provisions of its constitutional law. Their realism had a strong element of expediency, especially when they wrote as men of affairs, and their form and style largely depended on their Persian literary models. Sometimes these models were only superficially adapted to Islamic conditions.

Ibn Khaldūn is in a class by himself and stands out as an independent political thinker firmly rooted in Islam and sharing the historical and political approach of the second group without being content with their didactic aim and literary expository forms. He surveyed the political scene dispassionately, and deduced the laws of political life in its various mutually dependent aspects. He was interested in the reasons for the existence of a state and in the causes of its development and decline. Preoccupied with the real state as he observed it, he never lost sight of the original ideal Muslim state out of which it had inevitably grown, though falling more and more short of its requirements.

We now turn to the views of a separate group, the *Falāsifa* or religious philosophers of Islam. They are distinguished in approach, method and aim alike from the representatives of political thought in Islam discussed in the previous chapters. Their political philosophy is as much a part of their own general philosophy as was that of their masters, Plato and Aristotle. The title of this chapter is meant to suggest that it was the study of Platonic political philosophy which gave their own philosophy its character and its form: that of a commentary on Plato's political treatises. In other respects it is a modification or adaptation of his ideas in the light of Aristotle and to some extent of his commentators.[1] The Alexandrian summaries of Plato's *Republic* and *Laws* which presumably form the basis of Al-Fārābī's and Ibn Rushd's works are of course no longer pure Plato. Plotinus (whose *Enneads* were known to the *Falāsifa* as the *Theology* of Aristotle), Porphyry and Proclus had a large share in shaping Islamic philosophy, especially in metaphysics. But despite Neoplatonic revision and its tendency to harmonize the views of Plato and Aristotle, it is permissible to speak of the predominant influence of Plato in political philosophy, although Aristotle's *Nicomachean Ethics* was commented and drawn upon by Al-Fārābī and Ibn Rushd, and by Ibn Bājja who can be considered as the link between them in important details.

In confining ourselves to the political philosophy of the *Falāsifa* we must remember that it is only a part of a whole philosophy and cannot be fully appreciated in isolation from metaphysics, ethics and psychology. It was in these branches of philosophy that Aristotle exerted a greater influence than Plato, as is clear from Ibn Rushd's commentary on the *Republic*.

This is not the place to enter into even a brief description of Islamic philosophy as a whole.[2] But it is obvious that metaphysics presented a formidable challenge to Muslim theology, especially in such vital questions as the creation from nothing, the eternity of matter and the immortality of the soul. Even the concept of the Deity itself is affected. For the One of Neoplatonic theology, Aristotle's highest God or First Cause, became known to Muslim theologians and philosophers through the *Theology* of Aristotle and through the summary of the *Elements of Theology* by Proclus, wrongly attributed to Aristotle,[3] under the name of *Liber de Causis*. Writings like these, together with Aristotle's *De Anima*, *Physics* and especially his *Metaphysics*, embodied rational concepts of God, man and the universe which were at variance with the crude description of the nature and attributes of God in the Qur'ān. Among religious thinkers in Islam the Mu'tazilites were the first to concern themselves with the conflict between revelation and reason.

They sought to defend revelation against Aristotle by discarding anthropomorphism and opposing a purified concept of the God of revelation to the god bound to the eternity of matter of Aristotle. They devised a figurative interpretation of scripture to demonstrate that scripture did not contradict reason. This inner meaning of scripture could be ascertained by reason only; it was additional to the literal, external meaning. Al-Ash'arī, in his opposition to the Mu'tazilites from whom he stemmed, had to admit reason as a source of religious knowledge. *Kalām*, or dialectic theology, was the result, and this was Islam's official answer to the challenge of Greek-Hellenistic philosophy.

The *Falāsifa* became the recipients and transmitters of that philosophy while remaining Muslims for whom the absolute truth of revelation was established. I have already said (in chapter I) that they saw the problem of revelation and reason as a contrast between the divinely revealed law, mediated by a prophet, and the human laws devised by reason.[4] I need only add here that in their attempt to reconcile revelation with philosophy they insisted that, since truth was one and indivisible, the intention of revelation and philosophy must be identical.[5] Religion (in this case Islam) teaches this through the revelation contained in the Qur'ān, the "precious Book", the greatest miracle. Accepting the concept of the twofold meaning of scripture, they taught that religion speaks in metaphors and parables for the masses, who are capable of understanding them only literally. The inner, hidden meaning is accessible only to the philosopher, and by demonstrative argument. Truth thus arrived at is the same as that taught by philosophy. All *Falāsifa* are agreed on this, except that Ibn Rushd, no doubt under the influence of Al-Ghazālī whom he combated, insisted on the inadequacy of human reason to grasp the full truth of revelation, which for him was embedded in the prophetic revealed law. Consequently this law contains statements about God, and certain commandments addressed to the believer, which human reason is incapable of understanding by means of demonstration.[6] They must be accepted in their literal meaning. But those other concepts that are capable of rational understanding must be so explained by the philosopher, whose duty it is to attain to as perfect a knowledge of God as is possible for a fallible rational being. The superiority of prophetic revealed law over human law was stressed in the first chapter and illustrated with a quotation from Maimonides which could be paralleled from Ibn Rushd.[7]

It is important to realize that, at any rate for Ibn Rushd, the apparent conflict between revelation and reason was resolved by his definition of revelation as prophetic revealed law. Al-Fārābī is less explicit, but can, like Ibn Sīnā, be associated with this formulation, except for their psychological theory of prophecy. The Prophet's law is free from error because it comes from God. This applies in particular to those features which it has in common with the general human law based on reason. Hence the claim can be made that it is in the field of political philosophy that harmony between revelation and philosophy was established. This is due to the common ground, which I have several times mentioned,[8] between Greek political philosophy and the *Falāsifa*, chief among them Ibn Rushd. This common ground is provided by the law, which has a central place in the political thought of Plato and Aristotle as well as in that of Al-Fārābī, Ibn Sīnā and Ibn Rushd. This means that the study of the *Republic*, the *Laws* and the *Nicomachean Ethics* led the Muslim philosophers to grasp more fully the political character implied in the *Sharī'a* of Islam (as in the *Torah* of Judaism). Hence revelation is for them not simply a direct communication between God and man, not only a transmission of right beliefs and convictions, a dialogue between a personal God of love, of justice and of mercy and man whom he has created in his image; it is also and above all a valid and binding code for man, who must live in society and be politically organized in a state in order to fulfil his destiny. In short, it is the law of the ideal state. As such it includes regulations about worship and charity just as Greek law dealt with temple sacrifices. It provides for man's welfare in this world and prepares him for the hereafter, and thus alone guarantees his perfection and happiness as a religious being. In so doing it goes beyond the *nomos*, the man-made law of Greek philosophy, which knew of no twofold happiness, though it was equally designed to enable man to reach his goal, intellectual perfection.

Superficially considered, complete identity of purpose seems established between *Sharī'a* and *Nomos*. For the latter also was meant to educate man towards a "following of the gods" from whom ultimately the law derives. But we must remember that "god" did not mean the same for Plato as it does for the Muslim philosophers. It is clear that despite the central place of the law in the thought of both, the Muslims were fully conscious of the fundamental difference between the law revealed by God to the Prophet for the happiness of mankind as a whole (including elect intellects *and* the masses alike), and Plato's law, which, though laid down for the whole state, was designed to enable only the philosophers to reach the highest perfection. Granted that the Plato of the *Laws* had a lofty idea of God and that he held, as did Ibn Rushd, that right beliefs and convictions alone promote the justice and happiness for whose sake the state exists, there is still a difference between the two conceptions. It is due to the different character of the two civilizations to which the two men belonged: the one based on revelation and centred in God, and the other based on a myth and centred in rational man. Naturally, this contrast is based on a literal interpretation of Ibn Rushd's writings, and the possibility cannot be excluded that a figurative interpretation might produce some approximation in religious concepts. But there still remains the conscious realization in the Muslim's mind that the sphere of the *Sharī'a* with its "Know and love God in willing obedience to his commandments" is wider than the sphere of the *Nomos* with its "Know thyself". But Greek and Muslim philosophers are agreed that without law there can be no state and that unlawful behaviour is damaging to the state. Every departure from the law is bound to have serious consequences for public safety and for morale and right beliefs and convictions. In the state under the *Sharī'a* such deviations will cause error, heresy and schism, and prove the undoing of the state. In Plato's ideal state under the *Nomos* it will lead to a transformation of the best, or the perfect constitution, into a bad or imperfect constitution, and so also of their respective citizens.

When law is so considered, the constitutional form of the state is secondary, since it depends directly on the rule of law. Islam, we have seen, is ideally a theocracy, and the caliphate is its earthly political form. The *Sharī'a* rules supreme. Once the authority of the *Sharī'a* is impaired, the *mulk* or power-state comes into being. In it secular laws compete with and often submerge the rule of the *Sharī'a*. In Plato's *Republic* the philosopher-king rules by means of the *Nomos*, the best law reason can devise. If the authority of this *Nomos* is flouted, rule passes into other hands and the state takes the form of one or other of Plato's imperfect constitutions.

It is thus clear that as far as life in the state is concerned the *Falāsifa* found in the *Republic* and the *Laws* of Plato and in Aristotle's *Nicomachean Ethics* a kindred concept in the rule of law as the guarantor of human welfare. Seeing this, they applied Greek political philosophy to their own civilization. But while they realized the close parallel between the respective laws, they yet discovered the fundamental difference between prophetically revealed and philosophical human law. The *Sharī'a*-state was for them the ideal state of Islam, as the *Republic* was for Plato the ideal state of the philosopher. At the same time the Prophet was superior to the philosopher, at least for Ibn Sīnā and Ibn Rushd.

In order to understand the political thought of the *Falāsifa* as a blending with Islamic notions of Platonic political ideas, modified by Aristotle and the Neoplatonists, we must turn from the principal problem of political philosophy in Islam—prophetic revealed law against human law—to a definition of the purpose and scope of political science.

We recall Aristotle's definition of politics as "the most authoritative of the sciences", which determines what man's "happiness" as the "supreme good" is and teaches the means to its attainment. This is but an elaboration of Plato's statement in the *Politikos*: "there is one science of all of them: and this science may be called royal or political or economical".[9] Politics is a practical science like ethics and economics. Both Ibn Sīnā and Al-Ghazālī follow Aristotle in this, while Al-Fārābī and Ibn Bājja (Avempace) agree with Plato in seeing the household merely as a part of the state.[10] However, the dividing line between ethics and politics is not rigid, since they stand to each other as theory to practice. Political science deals with man's volitional actions and behaviour. They spring from his choice, which is conditioned by his knowledge of good and evil, right and wrong, virtue and vice. According to Ibn Rushd (Averroes), political science, like medicine, has two parts, the first theoretical, and contained in Aristotle's *Nicomachean Ethics*, and the second practical, and contained in his *Politics* and in Plato's *Republic*. "The first and second parts of this science stand in the same relationship to each other as do the books of *Health and*

Illness and the *Preservation of Health and the Removal of Illness* in medicine."[11] This is only an echo of Al-Fārābī's definition in his *Iḥṣā al-'ulūm*. A summary of it shows Ibn Rushd's indebtedness to his predecessor, and (more importantly) Al-Fārābī's introduction of Platonic views into Muslim thought in their Greek and Hellenistic meaning. Al-Fārābī laid the foundations of Islamic political philosophy by his acceptance and transformation of the Platonic legacy, whose first inheritor and creative continuator had been Aristotle.

"Political science", Al Fārābī says, in the fifth chapter "On Political Science, Jurisprudence and Theology", "inquires into the ⟨various⟩ kinds of actions, and conscious volitional ways of life (*siyar*), and into the habits, *mores*, and natural dispositions which produce these actions and ways of life...."[12] But politics does more in that its inquiry into man's volitional behaviour aims at leading him to true happiness (*sa'āda*) through right actions. Significantly, the Muslim Al-Fārābī qualifies this by maintaining that true happiness is obtainable only in the world to come. Moreover, true happiness is to be distinguished from supposed happiness,[13] which consists in wealth, honour or pleasure. Virtue and good deeds promote true happiness in city-states and nations, by promoting orderly co-operation between citizens under authority.[14] Authority is represented by "the royal office and dignity (*mahna malakīya wa-l-mulk*)", and government (*siyāsa*) is the performance of this office. Al-Fārābī distinguishes two kinds of authority: the excellent (ideal) authority through which true happiness is attained, and the ignorant authority[15] under which assumed happiness is attained. Excellent (ideal) city-states and nations obey the first kind of authority, whereas the latter is divided into as many kinds as there are aims. If the aim is wealth the rule is a vile one,[16] if honour we have a timocracy.[16] Al-Fārābī here clearly follows Plato's *Republic*, but it is significant that the Greek city-state is supplemented by "nations". This is probably due to the Hellenistic summary (presumably Galen's) which Al-Fārābī used, and to some extent perhaps to the Islamic empire of his own day.

In his summary exposition of the philosophy of Plato[17] Al-Fārābī defines politics in similar terms as "the royal, political art" assigning to it the task of leading man to happiness by having a philosopher-king as ruler.[18]

Two practices must combine to make the government "royal and excellent (ideal)": to follow general rules, and to rule with practical wisdom and experience—as is the case in medicine—so that political (or civic) acts encourage virtue and good behaviour among the citizens.[19] The practitioner of the art of government acquires the general rules from the study of political philosophy.[20] The science has two parts: the one extends to the knowledge of happiness and the distinction between true and assumed happiness, and comprises the general rules. Ibn Rushd called this the theoretical part of politics. The other is concerned with the actions and morals of the citizens in the excellent as well as the non-excellent city-states and nations and leads to the attainment of their respective happiness, true or alleged. "This is ⟨found⟩ in the book *Būlīṭīqī*, that is, in the book *Siyāsa* of Aristotle, and also in the book *Siyāsa* of Plato and in ⟨other⟩ books of Plato and others."[21] Following Plato's *Republic*, Al-Fārābī further assigns to the practical part of politics the discussion of the transformation of the excellent (ideal) into the ignorant states.[22] In "the excellent (ideal) royal office (*mahna*)" the study of the theoretical and practical sciences is necessary because here the king must be a philosopher.[23] Actions and ways of life vary with every city-state and nation. But the ideal state (*madīna fāḍila*, the Muslim equivalent of Plato's *Republic*) will enjoy continued existence only so long as its kings follow each other without interruption and observe the same conditions of good government. The cultivation of philosophy, both theoretical and practical, guarantees these conditions and through them the maintenance of the ideal state. The absence of philosophy is identical with ignorance; hence we have ignorant or imperfect states. They reach their goal through the experience and innate ability of their rulers.[24]

We have seen that politics is devoted to the investigation of the highest good in its theoretical part and of the actions and volitional habits leading to its attainment in its practice. This short general introduction to political philosophy in Islam, seen as the legacy of Plato's political philosophy, may therefore be rounded off with a few remarks about "the quest for happiness", as understood by Al-Fārābī in his *K. taḥṣīl al-sa'āda*[25] and accepted by all his successors among the *Falāsifa*. This leads us back to the first chapter of this book and at the same time forward to the more detailed discussion of the political thought of the principal *Falāsifa*, in the first place of Al-Fārābī himself.

In his *K. taḥṣīl* Al-Fārābī asserts that it is natural for man to strive for perfection (*kamāl*). Man is guided and helped in this endeavour by the successive study of physical science (*'ilm ṭabī'ī*),[26] metaphysics and politics. Physical science furnishes him with rational principles.[27] The highest perfection is unobtainable without the help of many men; therefore another science is needed to examine these rational principles in the light of human necessities in association, namely, "the human or political science". Man, when able to satisfy his physical wants as a *ḥayawān insī* or *madanī* —Aristotle's *zoon politikon*—turns to metaphysical speculation. That is, he begins to speculate on "existing things" (that is, reality, *mawjūdāt*) beyond the natural things (*ba'da-l-ṭabī'īyāt*). This speculation leads to the perception of the first principle (*mabda' awwal*), that is, God. Then man enters upon the human science (politics) and asks about the end of human existence: that is, the perfection which man must needs reach. He investigates everything which helps man to reach this perfection, such as virtues and good deeds, and distinguishes them from that which is an obstacle, such as vices and evil deeds. He collects knowledge of the nature of these things, their modes and relationships with each other until he gains a rational understanding of their working. This is political science; it is the science of the things through which every citizen attains, by political association, the happiness to which his natural disposition conditions him.[28] As there are degrees of happiness, so there are degrees of perfection. The highest perfection is speculative perfection, which man can reach only in a political association, be it a city-state or a nation. It is final happiness.[29]

CHAPTER VI

AL-FĀRĀBĪ: THE FOUNDATION

IT is clear from the last chapter how important it is to see political science in the context of philosophy as a whole; it becomes abundantly evident when we examine in greater detail the works of Abū Naṣr al-Fārābī,[1] in particular those concerned with politics. Though preceded by Al-Kindī, as initiator of Islamic philosophy, Al-Fārābī is the first Muslim thinker to have left political writings, either in the form of commentaries or in treatises of his own, based upon Plato. That he was more than a pioneer can be deduced from the habit of later writers of calling him "the second teacher", with Aristotle as the first. In fact, he profoundly influenced all subsequent Muslim philosophers, in particular Ibn Bājja and Ibn Rushd in Spain, and Ibn Sīnā in the East, where he himself lived. He showed the way to, and gave an authoritative beginning to, the integration of Greek-Hellenistic philosophy in all its branches with Islam. In this preliminary sketch of political thought in medieval Islam we are concerned only with his contribution to political philosophy.[2]

Under Neoplatonic influence he wrote his *Book of Agreement between the ideas of the two philosophers, the divine Plato and Aristotle.*[3] This treatise—as the title suggests—attempts to establish a harmony between the two Greek philosophers where their views are apparently at variance, but it also seeks to reconcile philosophy and revelation, a necessary pre-condition of the integration of philosophy with Islam. His summary of *Plato's Philosophy*[4] stresses its political character, and although this may be found in his Greek source (in Arabic translation) it shows that Al-Fārābī realized the importance of politics in the philosopher's search for truth about God, the universe, reality and man. Philosophy aims at the perception of the creator, and the philosopher must strive "to become in his actions like God" as far as this is humanly possible. For man, the way to this end is first to improve himself and then to improve others in his house or state.[5] This idea originated with Plato, who says in his *Theaetetus*: "to become like

God so far as this is possible; and to become like God is to become righteous and holy and wise".[6] But it is perhaps even more likely that Plotinus is Al-Fārābī's immediate source.[7] This *imitatio Dei* constitutes the highest perfection and ultimate happiness. It is Al-Fārābī's principal concern in his political philosophy which has its source in Plato as much as in the tenets of Islam. For as a Muslim he believes in the Creator-God, in reward and punishment, and in a hereafter. The end of man is happiness; but happiness for a Muslim, if he is a disciple of Plato and Aristotle, is a blending of that promised in the *Sharī'a* (and guaranteed by it to the believer who fulfils its commandments) with the reward of the study of philosophy. Or, differently expressed, the philosopher's happiness is included in that promised by the prophetic lawgiver, which also transcends the philosopher's in that it is twofold: well-being in this world and bliss in the next. It is true that in his political treatises Al-Fārābī, as a *failasūf*, a philosopher leaning on Plato and Aristotle, expounds this happiness (as his Greek masters had done) as intellectual perfection combined with the moral perfection which precedes it. But as a Muslim he is bound to accept the teachings of the *Sharī'a* about God, the angels and reality. His significance as a metaphysician lies in his drawing on Greek metaphysics, physics and psychology for the explanation of such religious doctrines as the creation out of nothing, divine providence extending to particulars, and the Creator-God's domination over the whole world. He says that these doctrines would confuse men if Plato and Aristotle had not shown sure proofs of their truth and thus given Muslims "a way by which these statements of the *Sharī'a* become clear, and that the law (*Sharī'a*) is perfectly correct and true".[8]

To balance philosophy and revelation is not easy, and we cannot therefore expect always to find complete harmony between them, or rather consistency in the way in which Al-Fārābī applies his basic assertion, the genuineness of which I see no reason to question. I respect Al-Fārābī's desire to vindicate the absolute truth of revelation through philosophy and do not therefore interpret his statements as giving reason supremacy over revelation. This is not the place to enter into an argument about the relative place of both in Al-Fārābī's thought, the more so since I have tried to do this elsewhere.[9] But I would repeat that to my mind he was a Muslim first and a disciple of Plato, Aristotle and their Hellenistic successors and commentators second. For I interpret the passage just quoted, and its continuation, in the sense that philosophy shows the metaphysician the way to faith. Starting from physics, we proceed to problems of metaphysics, politics and finally religious law. Men of insight and intelligence deal with demonstrative questions, men of judgement with political problems, and men of spiritual inspiration with those of the religious law, which are the most comprehensive of all.[10] Since Al-Fārābī draws a clear distinction between the metaphysician and the inspired teacher of the *Sharī'a*, whose problems are the most comprehensive and universal ones, transcending human reason, I feel justified in my assessment. The difference in method between the demonstrative and intuitive became an important element in all subsequent religious philosophy in Islam.[11]

It is against this background that we must see his political thought. His interest is predominantly metaphysical and theoretical; he was not interested in the art of government, nor was he a critic of contemporary politics or even a reformer. He was concerned about man's ultimate goal and how to achieve it. Only under this aspect do questions about the best state and the various constitutions, as Plato treats of them, enter his mind for discussion. He was convinced that only a philosopher-king, or at least an association of philosophy with government, could secure complete happiness to man, but this does not imply that he was actively concerned to bring such a philosophical rule into existence. As far as we know, he lived a retired life of study and writing.

Of his political writings three are of special relevance; their proper evaluation is hampered by the lack of critical editions of the Arabic text, in spite of Dieterici's edition of at least one of them, the *Ideal State* (*Al-madīna al-fāḍila*).[12] This treatise, based in its political part on Plato's *Republic* and to a lesser extent on Aristotle's *Nicomachean Ethics*, has a theological and metaphysical superstructure which draws on Plato's *Timaios* and on the pseudo-Aristotelian *Theology* mentioned in the preceding chapter. The full title, *Treatise on the Opinions of the Citizens of the Ideal State*, indicates Al-Fārābī's theoretical interest and explains why the first twenty-five chapters are taken up with a lengthy disquisition on the One, God, followed by a cosmology, and continued with an exposition of the philosophical sciences, and why only the last nine chapters deal with political matters in the strict sense of the term. Similarly, the first half of the second treatise, *Book on Political Government* or *On the Government of the City-State* (*K. siyāsa madanīya*), expounds Al-Fārābī's theory of the soul and especially of the intellect; the second half is devoted to a discussion of man and his perfection in the state. Plato's ideal and imperfect states serve Al-Fārābī as the model for the "political" sections of these two treatises. The third work, *Book on attaining Happiness* (*K. taḥṣīl al-sa'āda*), is the most important, independent and mature of the three. It begins with a statement on the twofold happiness of man, which he can only attain in association with others in a nation or city-state. Happiness is the highest good, which is desired for its own sake; and political science teaches how man as a citizen of a state can attain his happiness in accordance with his natural disposition. This definition is borrowed from Aristotle, who says in his *Nicomachean Ethics*:[13] "The Good of man must be the end of the science of politics." For this reason certain knowledge (*ḥaqq yaqīnī*) is opposed to opinion (*ẓann*) and persuasion (*iqnā'*). This is reserved for the metaphysician, as Ibn Rushd stressed in his fight against *Kalam*.[14] Instruction and education are recommended, and epistemology rather than psychology is used to describe man's nature and existence, since intellectual perfection is the aim.[15]

Of Al-Fārābī's other political writings I must at least mention his commentary in the form of a summary of Plato's *Laws*, now available in F. Gabrieli's critical edition, and of his *Political Aphorisms*.[16]

In spite of the fragmentary state of our knowledge, there is enough material to enable us to summarize tentatively Al-Fārābī's political ideas against the background of these general remarks, as far as his style and diction permit.

Why must there be a state? As we have seen, this question was answered later by Ibn Khaldūn, in the same way as by the *Falāsifa*: because man cannot live by himself, he cannot provide himself with the necessities of life, such as housing, food and clothing, let alone with everything needed for the attainment of his perfection. He is dependent on the help of many others of his kind, since his needs are also many. He must therefore combine with others in communities. There are complete or perfect communities, and incomplete ones; their degree of perfection or imperfection depends on their size. The smallest perfect political unit is the city, which is part of the territory of a middle-sized association, the nation. The largest organization covers the whole inhabited earth under cultivation, which Al-Fārābī called *ma'mūra*, from the same root as Ibn Khaldūn's *'umrān*, civilization. The need for political association is described in the *Madīna fāḍila* and in the *Siyāsa madanīya* in similar terms;[17] but in the *K. taḥṣīl al-sa'āda* the author simply states that it is man's natural disposition to require the help of others, and that he must form a political association with them because he cannot attain his goal, perfection, in isolation.[18] He is therefore called *ḥayawān insī* or *ḥ. madanī*—Aristotle's *zoon politikon*—and the science that inquires into the human actions and habits necessary for the attainment of perfection is consequently the *human* or *political* science.[19]

Plato's view that a person should have only one occupation can be traced in Al-Fārābī's emphasis on the need of many persons, who must co-operate in order to satisfy one another's many requirements. Al-Fārābī's distinction of perfect states according to size is also probably influenced by Greek and Hellenistic political thought. *Madīna*, as the smallest political unit in which man can attain happiness, corresponds to Plato's *polis*. The large association, comprising the whole civilized world, and the middle-sized nation (*umma*), may well be due to Al-Fārābī's Islamic environment; it accords with the universalism of Islam as a way of life and with the claim of the Islamic empire, the *dār al-Islam*, to win by *jihād* (holy war) the *dār al-ḥarb* (the realm of war), and thus to extend the power of Islam over the whole world. But I am inclined to attribute it rather to a blend of this Islamic idea and the concept of the *Oikoumene* of Hellenism.[20]

"Perfect" in size is, however, not the same as "perfect" in quality. For Al-Fārābī defines the ideal state as one whose citizens help each other to obtain those things by means of which true happiness is gained.[21] This true happiness is a state of the soul, in which it exists free from matter and tends towards pure substances entirely free from corporeality.[22] Political science, with the help of metaphysics, shows man the way of a gradual ascent from a perception of the physical world and its *Intelligibles* to that of the spiritual world, in search of the principles of "existing things", that is, of reality. It teaches man to distinguish what is good in that it helps him to his end, from what is evil.[23] Ethical virtues must be joined by intellectual virtues and practical arts, in order to prepare man to acquire the speculative virtues by means of the speculative sciences. They alone enable him to perceive reality, and thus to reach the highest perfection and ultimate happiness.[24] Since man must live in a state in order to attain happiness, these virtues and arts are political or civic. What applies to the individual also applies to "cities" and nations: another Platonic idea from the *Republic*.[25] The way to virtue and the arts is by teaching and education. Teaching is by word of mouth only and leads to the speculative virtues; education uses both speech and example[26] and produces ethical virtues and practical arts.[27] Al-Fārābī's detailed description of the virtues and arts served later as a basis for Ibn Bājja and Ibn Rushd in relation to politics. Like him, they also adopted Aristotle's distinction between rulers and ruled, and between master arts and subordinate or subsidiary arts and crafts.[28] Al-Fārābī illustrates this by an analogy between the state and the human body. The members of the body are designed and arranged in a hierarchy; the highest is the chief (*ra'īs*), that is, the heart; the rank of the lower members is determined by their nearness or remoteness from the heart. Those members nearest to the heart both rule and are ruled, those farthest removed from the head only serve, but all are united in serving the purpose of the heart. It is the same with the state; when all parts of the state serve the purpose of the chief or ruler, we have the ideal state, *madīna fāḍila*. But whereas the members of the body are naturally disposed to fulfil their functions, the citizens of the state are guided by will and choice. Leadership or rule is possible on two conditions only: fitness by natural disposition, and willpower and habit.

Similarly, some arts both rule and serve, others are merely subordinate, while the highest art rules only. This is the art of government, practised by the ruler whom nobody must dominate.[29] So far we are on Greek ground. But in his attempt to understand the state of his own civilization, Al-Fārābī had not only to transfer Greek notions to Islamic concepts and conditions, and to apply Platonic and Aristotelian ideas and criteria to his own surroundings, for the Islamic state had existed for a long time and had a character of its own. What was needed, therefore, was a synthesis, a blending of Islamic and Greek notions; in this synthesis lies Al-Fārābī's importance as a political thinker, in himself and as a formative influence on all subsequent *Falāsifa*.

To appreciate this synthesis between the ideal ruler of Plato, the philosopher-king, and the ideal ruler of Islam—the prophet/lawgiver/*imām*—a brief explanation of Al-Fārābī's theory of prophecy is necessary. For the ruler of his *Madīna fāḍila* is neither the caliph—the successor and vicegerent of the prophetic lawgiver Muḥammad—simply transformed into the philosopher-king of the *Republic*, nor yet the philosopher-king transformed into the caliph. The qualities and functions of the first ruler are the result of adjustments and combinations; in short, they represent a synthesis between Platonic and Muslim requirements.

The prophetic qualification of the first ruler is discussed by Al-Fārābī only in the *Madina fāḍila* and the *Siyāsa madanīya*. It is based on his own theory of prophecy, for which I have so far been unable to find a Greek or Hellenistic source, apart from the theory of emanation evolved by Plotinus in the *Enneads* and transmitted to the Arabs in the so-called *Theology* of Aristotle. It may be summarized by saying that Al-Fārābī distinguishes a theoretical and a practical reason in man, who is thereby naturally endowed with imaginative and rational faculties. These are only potentially in him, and must be brought to actuality by the emanation of the Active Intellect, the *nous poietikos* of Aristotle, called by Al-Fārābī "angel (*malak*) after the ancient philosophers", that is, the angel Gabriel, or "Holy Spirit".[30] He calls this emanation a revelation (*waḥy*). Through the Active Intellect God mediates to the first ruler's theoretical reason a revelation which first makes him a philosopher, and then affects his imaginative faculty, that is, his practical reason, making him into a prophet, a "warner" capable of directing men to their happiness. Such a man has reached the highest degree of perfection and the utmost happiness which a human being can attain; his soul is united with the Active Intellect.

He is the *imām*, the first ruler over the ideal city-state, over the ideal nation and over the whole inhabited earth.[31] These are the three possible perfect states, and it is obvious that only the ruler endowed with the gift of prophecy can rule any or all of them. The philosopher-prophet, in the opinion of Al-Fārābī, is alone qualified to help man as a citizen to reach his true human destiny, where his moral and intellectual perfection permit him to perceive God, under the guidance of the divinely revealed *Sharīʿa*. Those ruled by the first ruler are the "excellent, best and happy citizens".[32]

To the combined first ruler-philosopher and prophet-*imām* of the *Madīna fāḍila* Al-Fārābī adds in the *Taḥṣīl* the lawgiver and king without mentioning the designation "prophet" any more than does the *Siyāsa*. It speaks, however, of revelation as contact of the soul with the Active Intellect by the intermediacy of the passive and acquired intellects. We thus see that the imaginative faculty is not acted upon, and so the gift of prophecy cannot be granted. We must therefore rely on the full account in the *Madīna fāḍila* and assume that in equating the first ruler with philosopher, king, *imām* and lawgiver, the last named is to be understood as the prophetic lawgiver. This seems clear from the meaning Al-Fārābī[33] gives to the terms "philosopher" and "*imām*".

On the other hand, we find in the *Taḥṣīl* the most comprehensive and thorough exposition of the qualities demanded of the ideal ruler. The *imām*-king must study the speculative sciences. As king he is compared to the master of the household or to the leader of young people who are taught with or without their consent. Without education no citizen can attain perfection and happiness. Al-Fārābī again distinguishes between education by certain proof (the method appropriate to the speculative virtues to be inculcated in the king) and education by persuasion, which is suitable for acquiring the other virtues and arts. The king must possess persuasion and imagination to perfection, as well as be a philosopher skilled in the speculative sciences. The masses, on the other hand, who serve the state by their arts and crafts, can be taught by means of persuasion and imagination only. Political leadership is the prerogative of the elect.[34] This distinction between the elect few and the masses ultimately goes back to Plato's views on education and on the three classes, in the *Republic*.[35] Al-Fārābī himself refers to Plato in presenting his own ideas on education for citizenship.

The distinction is usually associated with the Stoa, but there is no need to go beyond Plato, at least as far as the *Falāsifa* are concerned. They all adopted it as an argument in favour of their own position and their superiority over the theologians, and in justification of the twofold interpretation of the Qur'ān. They reserved for themselves the right and the duty to investigate the hidden, inner meaning, thanks to their superior intellect and training in the speculative sciences, which enabled them to use demonstrative arguments. They owe the distinction to Al-Fārābī, who in the Introduction to his *Summary* of Plato's *Laws* praises Plato for not disclosing and explaining the sciences to the people in general. Instead, he had used the method of allegory and enigma in order to withhold knowledge from the uninitiated.[36] Knowledge is understood in the sense of "knowledge of the inner meaning", which is only accessible to the metaphysician by means of demonstrative proof. We shall take up this point once more when dealing with Ibn Rushd.[37] Al-Fārābī says accordingly of the first ruler that he is, as philosopher-king, "the most elect of the elect...who aim at the complete fulfilment of his aim and purpose. He possesses knowledge of the *Intelligibles* by means of certain proofs and thereby perceives reality. As far as ruling is concerned, this is the first and most perfect science, and the other master-sciences are under the authority of this science...its aim is the utmost happiness and ultimate perfection which man can reach."[38]

This science is called wisdom or philosophy; it originated with the Chaldeans (Iraq), migrated from there to Egypt, then to the Greeks and Syrians until it came to the Arabs. Since the first ruler must master philosophy "there is no difference between the philosopher and the first ruler".[39] In possession of all the theoretical and practical virtues, he has the power to establish them in nations and city-states in proportion to the natural dispositions of their citizens. The political significance of philosophy is thus evident. It is further borne out by Al-Fārābī's insistence that the lawgiver must be a philosopher first and foremost.[40] He is, moreover, identified in the *Taḥṣīl* with the *imām*.[41] Al-Fārābī refers to the lawgiver by the term *wāḍi'u-l-nawāmīs*, which corresponds to Plato's *nomothetes*, whereas Ibn Rushd uses the term *wāḍi'u-l-sharā'i'*. The comparison between the *Taḥṣīl* and the other two treatises appears to show that a revealed law, brought by a prophetic messenger to mankind (Muḥammad), is implied in spite of the use of *nāmūs* rather than *Sharī'a*. This lawgiver "has the power, by the excellence of his reflection, to create conditions by which the laws actually exist ⟨and effectively function⟩, and thus utmost happiness is attained".[42] But before he can lay down laws he must be masterful and not servile by nature, and skilled in philosophy. He must possess the fourfold perfection in speculative, ethical, intellectual and practical virtues and also a capacity for excellent persuasion and imagination.[43] "Philosophy is for the lawgiver what habit (*hexis*) is for the masses; what in his knowledge is certain insight, is with them persuasion and imagination."[44] Al-Fārābī has so far established that "the meaning of *imām*, philosopher and lawgiver is one ⟨and the same⟩",[45] and he now proceeds to a definition of "king": "king indicates dominion and power with utmost knowledge...he is in his essence a philosopher and lawgiver."[46] When Al-Fārābī asserts that "the meaning of philosopher, first ruler, king, lawgiver and *imām* is the same",[47] the synthesis between Plato's philosopher-king with the ideal Islamic ruler is complete. It has been achieved by the blending of Greek and Islamic qualifications. This synthesis represents Al-Fārābī's outstanding contribution to political thought in Islam, and it may be added, in Maimonides (who accepted the theory of prophecy and the prophet/philosopher/lawgiver as the ideal ruler) but not in Judaism generally.

As we have seen, it was the common ground provided by the central place of law in both civilizations that enabled Al-Fārābī to arrive at this synthesis, in which the later *Falāsifa* followed him. But this common ground must not blind us to the decisive difference between the *Sharī'a*, divinely revealed to the prophetic lawgiver, and the *Nomos* of the philosophers of Hellas. Because the *Sharī'a* alone guaranteed twofold happiness, in this world and in the next life, the *Falāsifa* placed it in the centre of their political philosophy. All the same, for them philosophy alone enabled man to understand the hidden, deeper meaning of that law.[48]

At the same time it must be admitted that Al-Fārābī concentrates, at least in the *Taḥṣīl*, on the philosophical qualifications of the first ruler, and contents himself in the *Madīna fāḍila* with a simple assertion of the dominant position of the *Sharī'a* as the sole guarantor of the twofold happiness and perfection, without giving a detailed account of its teachings and regulations. This is perhaps not surprising in a philosopher writing on political science. Moreover, he was to some extent bound by Plato's arrangement in the *Republic*, though this applies much more to the *Madīna fāḍila* and

Siyāsa than to the *Taḥṣīl*, which is exclusively concerned with the nature and meaning of the citizen's happiness. Since it stresses the part which the ruler has to play in furthering the citizen's attainment of happiness as the highest good in the ideal Muslim state, it is only natural that Al-Fārābī should devote considerable space to the qualities necessary in the ideal ruler.

In the last pages of the *Taḥṣīl*, as it is at present available to us, he discusses the nature of true and false philosophers in connection with the ideal Muslim ruler (the philosopher/lawgiver/*imām*/king). The discussion takes the form of a summary of *Republic* 484a–487a, giving, as he himself says, "the conditions which Plato mentions in his book on *Politics*".[49] Similarly, *Republic* 487b–497b serves him as a model for his description of the false philosophers. His summary of the qualities of the true philosophers agrees in all essential details with those laid down for the first ruler of the *Madīna fāḍila*. It is to be noted that they are Platonic and do not reflect the qualifications demanded of the *imām* according to Al-Māwardī. That some qualifications like justice (*'adāla*), knowledge (*'ilm*) and physical fitness (*salāma*) occur in both groups is probably due more to political realism in the interests of good government than to a blending of Islamic and Platonic qualifications.[50] Al-Fārābī simply follows Plato's description of the philosopher-king; but he does so after having first identified the philosopher-king with the prophet-*imām*.[51] In the *Taḥṣīl*, a much more original composition, a further condition is of great importance: the true philosopher must have sound religious convictions: "he shall have perfect faith in the opinions of the religion in which he was reared and seize the virtuous actions which ⟨are enjoined⟩ in his religion."[52] Plato also demands right beliefs and convictions, but more especially knowledge of reality, which is superior to belief.[53] Conversely, philosophy is the best guide to the understanding of the deeper meaning of the *Sharī'a* for Al-Fārābī, Ibn Sīnā and Ibn Rushd. Nor was Al-Qiftī (who knew only Al-Fārābī's *Siyāsa madanīya* and *Sīrā* (for *Madīna*) *fāḍila* wrong when he stated that in them Al Fārābī "described the ⟨various⟩ kinds of perfect and imperfect states and the need of the state for royal ways of life and prophetic laws".[54]

Al-Fārābī knew, both as a disciple of Plato and Aristotle, and as a citizen of the Abbasid caliphate, that the ideal state was very difficult to realize, even if he would not have agreed with Ibn Khaldūn's verdict that the *Falāsifa* looked at the ideal state as a "hypothesis and supposition". Like Plato, Al Fārābī starts from the ideal state, whose first ruler must possess twelve qualifications which are all derived from Plato.[55] Aware of the near-impossibility of finding such a perfect man Al-Fārābī is satisfied if the ruler has six or even five of these qualities. He is succeeded by the second ruler who must fulfil six conditions. He must be a philosopher, must know and keep the laws and ordinances of the first ruler and observe them all in his own actions as an obligation on himself and an example to others. Next, he must be able to decide points of law which have not arisen before, guided by the example set by the first *imāms*. He needs insight and knowledge to grapple with new problems unforeseen by the first ruler;[56] in their solution he must be guided by the best interests of the state. He must be able to make deductions from the laws laid down by the first *imāms* and guide and direct his people in their application. Lastly, he must master the principal and subordinate arts of war.

It is at once clear that this second ruler has a good deal in common with the caliph; the affinity between their respective qualifications is much more than one of terminology, it extends to the substance. That Al-Fārābī uses the term *ḥarb* for war and not *jihād*, holy war, as in the corresponding passage in the *Fuṣūl*, may be explained by the different purpose and public for which the two treatises were written. The *Madīna fāḍila* is addressed to a wider circle interested in philosophy and not necessarily confined to Muslims, though they are no doubt uppermost in Al-Fārābī's mind. The *Fuṣūl al-madanī*, as it is called by its editor and translator, may have been designed for a Muslim public, even for Al-Fārābī's patron Saif al-Dawla, the ruler of Aleppo, assuming that this tract falls in that period of Al-Fārābī's life and work.[56a] The ruler described in the *Fuṣūl* certainly appears to be modelled more on the Islamic than on the Platonic pattern, since the man who corresponds to the second ruler of the *Madīna fāḍila* is in the *Fuṣūl* stripped of his philosophical qualification. Again, the *Fuṣūl* is silent about the rule of two men, who in the *Madīna fāḍila* share authority if one is a philosopher and the other combines the remaining legal and military qualifications. Both treatises have a rule of "the most excellent men", Plato's *aristoi*, if each of a group possesses one of the necessary qualifications, of which there are six in the *Madīna fāḍila* and four in the *Fuṣūl*.[57]

The absence of the philosophical qualification in the *Fuṣūl* is the more surprising in that Al-Fārābī explicitly states in the *Madīna fāḍila* that the state is without a king if wisdom (that is philosophy) is absent from the government, even if the other conditions are fulfilled. The state will gradually go to ruin unless a philosopher is attached to the man in authority over it.[58] That means that the ideal state cannot survive without a philosopher sharing its government, at least in an advisory capacity. That Al-Fārābī makes no such demand in the *Fuṣūl* strengthens the possibility that this treatise was meant for Muslims; it may also suggest a more realistic attitude to the existing, as opposed to the ideal, state. His insistence on the ruler's ability to wage holy war (*jihād*) points in the same direction.[59] Saif al-Dawla's preoccupation with *jihād* is well attested.

Consonant with his main interest, Al-Fārābī discusses the states opposed to the ideal state ruled over by the Prophet, who is at the same time philosopher-king, lawgiver and *imām*, from the point of view of the human end, happiness. All these states are imperfect, not in the sense in which this term was used before, but in the qualitative sense: they lack certain essential features of the perfect state and show characteristics which make the attainment of the highest good impossible. These states are discussed more fully in the *Siyāsa* than in the *Madīna fāḍila*, and not at all in the *Taḥṣīl*, which concentrates on true happiness in the ideal state. Since Plato classified these states in accordance with their political constitution, Al-Fārābī uses the terms he found in the Arabic version of the Alexandrian summary of the *Republic*, made by Galen, without showing much interest in the constitutions from the political point of view. In addition, he uses terms which, because they occur in the Qur'ān, have a definite Islamic meaning; they characterize the nature of the states they designate, according to the views and actions of their citizens, and not the political constitutions. The result is that we meet in Al-Fārābī with greater variety and differentiation than in Plato. This may or may not be due to Al-Fārābī's Arabic source, as far as the subdivision of Plato's four imperfect states—into timocracy, oligarchy, democracy and tyranny—is concerned.[60] All imperfect states together are termed "ignorant states" (*jāhilīya*).[61] Although "ignorance" is used by Al-Fārābī in the same sense as by Plato[62] (as the opposite to knowledge), it may well have the additional meaning which *jāhilīya* has in Islam: pagan idolatry, ignorance and an evil way of life. The inhabitants of the ignorant states do not know happiness as it is understood in the ideal state. Their aim in life, individual as well as social, is material, and consists in such things as health, wealth, the pleasures of the senses, power or honour. Like Plato, Al-Fārābī divides this collective state into an association of states according to the aim pursued, but distinguishes more kinds than Plato.

The first is the State of Necessity (*ḍarūrīya*); its inhabitants aim at the necessities of life, like food, drink, clothing, a place to live and carnal gratification; and they assist each other in securing their object. The Arabic term used goes back to *Republic* 369c, but is not employed by Plato as a designation of a constitution. While the description is brief in the *Madīna fāḍila*, we are given precise details in the *Siyāsa*[63] about the means of acquiring the necessities of life.

Next comes the Vile State (*nadhāla*); its citizens strive for wealth and riches for their own sake. The account in the *Siyāsa*[64] includes a description of its ruler.

In the Base and Despicable State the citizens concentrate on the pleasures of the senses, games and other pastimes.[65]

Timocracy (*madīna karāma*) contains a variety of honours.[66] Since the Arabic source of Al-Fārābī is lost we cannot determine whether this lengthy and diffuse description goes back to it or represents Al-Fārābī's own amplification. The latter seems more likely. The citizens of these honour-loving states assist each other in gaining honour, glory and fame. The honours fall into two groups. The first is a personal relationship between one who is worthy to be honoured because of some virtue in him, and the other who accords him honour and respect because he recognizes him as his superior. The second kind of honour is shown to men because of their wealth, or because they have been victorious, exercise authority or enjoy other distinctions. This state is in Al-Fārābī's opinion the best of the "ignorant states". In this view, like Ibn Rushd after him, he may be influenced by Aristotle.[67]

Tyranny (*taghallub*) receives its name from the aim of its

citizens; they co-operate to gain victory over others, but refuse to be vanquished by them. Their efforts are crowned with success once absolute mastery is reached, and the pleasures of victory have been enjoyed.[68] Tyranny has even more variations for Al-Fārābī than timocracy; in fact, as many as the tyrant has desires, for his despotism expresses itself in imposing his will on his subjects and making them work for his personal ends. Al-Fārābī knows of two kinds of tyranny within which these variations occur, internal and external tyranny. The first consists in the absolute mastery of the tyrant and his helpers over the citizens of the state, and the second is the enslavement of another state or people.

From his detailed description it is clear that tyranny is actually a mixed imperfect state, since it contains elements of timocracy, to which he accords an equally loose combination of aims, and of oligarchy, as we see from Ibn Rushd's treatment which is based to some extent upon Al-Fārābī.

Democracy (*madīna jamā'īya*) is marked by the freedom of its citizens to do as they please. They are all equal and nobody has mastery over another. Their governor only governs with the explicit consent of the governed. It contains good and bad features "and it is therefore not impossible that at some time the most excellent men (*afāḍil*) grow up there, so that philosophers, orators and poets...come into being. It is thus possible to choose from it elements of the ideal state...⟨therefore⟩ out of democracy most of the ignorant states, good and bad ones together, arise."[69]

The states enumerated so far all go back to Plato's *Republic*[70] and correspond to its four imperfect states.

The Arabic terms used for timocracy, tyranny and democracy have Greek equivalents. That oligarchy is meant by the "Vile State" is clear from its definition and from Ibn Rushd's *Commentary on Plato's Republic*, which exists only in a Hebrew version. The "Base and Despicable State" is simply a more specific kind of oligarchy, which Ibn Rushd calls plutocracy—a term going back to Xenophon—or hedonistic rule. That is, *nadhāla* is used for oligarchy, and *khissa* (or *khasīsa*) and *shahwa* for plutocracy and hedonistic, or pleasure-seeking, government. Al-Fārābī may have found this subdivision of oligarchy in his source, but it is strange that he should not have used the designation "state of the few", as does Ibn Rushd, who uses Al-Fārābī's three terms to characterize the viciousness of the "rule of the few" or "the plutocratic association", also called the "government of the pleasure-seeker".[71]

To these four Platonic states Al-Fārābī adds three more "ignorant states", namely, the vicious (*fāsiqa*), the transformed (*mubaddala* or *mutabaddala*) and the erring (*ḍālla*) states. In the *Madīna fāḍila*, *sāqiṭa* is in one passage used for *fāsiqa*.[72]

The citizens of the Vicious State have right beliefs and convictions like those of the ideal state, but their actions are like those of the "ignorant states". Although they know what true happiness is, they cannot gain it.[73]

The Transformed State has, as the name suggests, undergone a change. Originally it was an ideal state in opinions and actions, but different opinions later gained entry, ousted the right opinions, and also caused a change in the actions of its citizens.[74]

The State in Error is seemingly like the ideal state, but its inhabitants hold corrupt beliefs, though they imagine that their views on God, the Active Intellect and happiness are correct. Similarly, their first ruler fancied that he had received a revelation; but it was not genuine. True happiness cannot be theirs, since wrong opinions and bad actions were commanded by their ruler; he, himself in error, led his people astray as well.[75]

That Ibn Rushd does not treat of these three states makes me suppose that they represent an addition of Al-Fārābī's to his source, which no doubt Ibn Rushd also used in conjunction with Al-Fārābī's political treatises.[76] This supposition gains in importance when we consider that all three terms (and *sāqiṭa*) occur in the Qur'ān and had, therefore, a definite meaning for a Muslim. It seems plausible to assume that Al-Fārābī introduced them deliberately, in order by this amplification to effect an assimilation of Plato's imperfect states to Islamic notions. It is also probable that the Muslim thinker understood "right beliefs and convictions" and their opposite in both their Platonic and Islamic meaning.

For he follows his description of the ignorant states with an exposition of the knowledge required of the citizens of the ideal state. It is prompted, no doubt, by Plato, and is in terms similar to the detailed discussion in the *Taḥṣīl*, which was summarized earlier in this chapter.[77] The philosophers of the ideal state gain their knowledge through their insight and by means of demonstration, and teach their followers by the same means. All others must be taught by allegories. It would lead us too far if we were to summarize here Al-Fārābī's theory of knowledge. Suffice it to say that he uses as illustration Plato's allegory of the cave:[78] the philosophers see the sun with the naked eye, the masses indirectly through reflection in water. It is a difference between direct perception and imagination.

The aim of the ideal state is true happiness in intellectual perfection; the aim of the various ignorant states is that of their kings. The vicious states arise because their religion is false and their opinions are corrupt.[79] This is a Platonic notion, but applied and adapted to Islamic tenets.

The inclusion by Al-Fārābī of "individuals from the 'Excellent' States" among the ignorant states calls for comment. It can only be understood in the context of Al-Fārābī's preoccupation with happiness, which is attainable only in the ideal state. Individuals living in isolation forfeit their chance of true happiness, which they can attain only as citizens performing their civic duties. Averroes is in full agreement with this view, which is that of the Greek masters Plato and Aristotle. Al-Fārābī calls such men *nawābit*, "plants". On the one hand they are completely negative and a danger like weeds and thorns;[80] on the other hand, there is one kind among the six, distinguished by Al-Fārābī in a long discussion towards the end of the same treatise, which is "not opposed to the ideal state but follows the right road and seeks after truth".[81] From this description Ibn Bājja must have derived his entirely positive evaluation of these isolated men.[82]

Al-Fārābī characterizes the five other kinds by varying degrees of error and imperfection, the worst kind being truly heretics. Jāḥiẓ devoted a little treatise to a sect called *nābita*, the singular of *nawābit*, from which Al-Fārābī might have taken the term.

Ibn Bājja identifies the *nawābit* with the *ghurabā* (strangers). Al-Fārābī, however, speaks of those who live in a state ruled by the prophetic first ruler as "happy and excellent"; if there is no such ideal state and they have to live in places whose inhabitants are imperfectly governed, they are only "excellent and are strangers in those places".[83] Ibn Bājja traced the *strangers* to the Sufis, and thus a clear link is established between Al-Fārābī and Sufism. The concept of *ghurabā* plays an important part in the thought of mystics like Al-Hallāj and Al-Suhrawardī.[84] Ibn Bājja's definition allows us to see why Al-Fārābī denied them ultimate happiness, even while he admitted that they were excellent men: "though they live in their own countries and among friends and neighbours they are strangers in their opinions, they travel in their thoughts to other planes which are for them like homelands."[85]

A consideration of the *Political Aphorisms* and especially the qualifications it requires of the ruler will complete the treatment of the imperfect states and bring out once more the Muslim component in al-Fārābī's political thought.[86] We recall that the philosophical qualification is indispensable in the second ruler of the *Madīna fāḍila*, but not in the *Fuṣūl*.[87] We have noted further that the qualifications demanded of the "king of the law(s)"[88] in fact constitute important and necessary qualifications of the caliph. I refer to the legal qualification, in particular his ability to make independent decisions (*ijtihād*) thanks to his expert knowledge of *Fiqh*, and to his ability to wage holy war (*jihād*). In the *Fuṣūl* and in the *Madīna fāḍila*, the combination of the two determines the Islamic character of the state and its ruler except that—as we have seen—in the *Madīna fāḍila* the absence of a philosopher takes perfection (in Plato's meaning of the term) away from state and ruler and leads to the ruin of the state. *Ijtihād* and *jihād* as requirements of Muslim law establish beyond question how deeply rooted Al-Fārābī and Ibn Rushd were in Islamic tradition. This suggests that they were first and foremost educated Muslims, since *Fiqh* is a primary element of traditional education. It shaped their outlook. They approached Greek-Hellenistic philosophy as Muslims, at any rate where politics were concerned, and took what was akin to their own way of life and thought from Plato and Aristotle, as they came across their ideas in their writings, summaries and commentators, and had to adapt them to Islamic concepts. In the case of the "king of the laws"[88] we have, indeed, a Platonic source as well: *Laws* 710, and especially 710d, a passage, moreover, upon which Al-Fārābī commented in his summary of the *Laws*.[89] There we have the combination of legislator and autocrat.

It is this common ground, based on the concept of law, which is so essential to the proper understanding of the attitude of the *Falāsifa* to Plato and Aristotle. It is the conviction that good government depends on just laws, and that man can reach true happiness only if he believes, thinks and acts as a responsible citizen[90] of such an ideal state.

In his blending of certain Platonic and Islamic qualifications of the ruler, Al-Fārābī is more inclined towards Plato in the *Madīna fāḍila* and more towards Islam in the *Fuṣūl.* One qualification in particular gives a clear indication that he did not hesitate to take a stand against Plato: he insists on "good persuasion" and "imagination"; that is, the ruler must be a good orator, which runs counter to Plato's objection to rhetoric.[91] Al-Fārābī obviously did not share Plato's view that the orator was a serious rival to the statesman.

Yet this is of much less significance than Al-Fārābī's equation of the Platonic philosopher-king with the Islamic prophetic lawgiver and *imām.*[92] But it must be frankly admitted that the claim made for this synthesis between Hellas and Islam cannot be established beyond reasonable doubt by a demonstrative argument. I have said that consistency is not to be expected if two systems starting from divergent premisses are to be harmonized. Apart from the particular purpose which a Muslim philosopher has in mind when writing a treatise he must consider the kind of reading public to which he is addressing himself. This will determine his argument and emphasis. Next, shifts in emphasis, or even developments in his own thought, must be taken into account in attempting to evaluate his specific contribution. Nor can we be certain of the exact meaning of the terms he uses. This is of great importance when we consider Al-Fārābī's equation of philosopher-king with lawgiver and *imām.* Is the lawgiver promulgating a *nāmūs* or a *shar'*? It was suggested earlier that Al-Fārābī had the prophetic lawgiver in mind even though he used the term *nawāmīs.*[93] The same applies to the use of "*imām*". Can we be certain that he means the caliph behind whom the community of the faithful prays or is *imām* simply a "chief"? As far as this last example is concerned I see no reason to doubt that Al-Fārābī has the caliph-*imām* in mind, unless we are to suspect a hidden meaning in his definition of the *imām*, who is to be imitated in his actions, virtues and accomplishments.[94]

There can be no doubt about the political significance of philosophy; and the philosophical qualification of the ideal ruler of the ideal state is as necessary as his ability to exercise authority and wield effective power. Another point cannot be settled so easily and definitely. We saw that the prophetic quality is not mentioned in the *Siyāsa* though "the first cause is the revealer to man...".[95] When we turn to the *Taḥṣīl* we find that neither prophecy nor revelation is mentioned at all. Does this mean that Al-Fārābī, as metaphysician, freed himself from his Muslim environment? Can we assert this in face of the insistence on the *imām*? What conclusions can be drawn from these changes and omissions in his political treatises? I am convinced that it would be unsafe to dogmatize; I would rather content myself with registering these discrepancies and inconsistencies. I should explain them as due to the tension in the mind of a Muslim disciple of Plato and Aristotle and their Neoplatonic interpreters, and to the immediate purpose of the various treatises. Inconsistencies there are, but we do not know whether Al-Fārābī was aware of them. By and large, he is consistent in his preoccupation in his whole philosophy with the central problem of politics: the highest good or happiness. But he emphasizes different aspects in different treatises. Whether this shift in emphasis and in subject-matter (and reading public) can be traced to different times of composition, and can help us to establish a chronology of his writings cannot be answered with certainty. But I would like to repeat a tentative suggestion which I made in a recent study of Al-Fārābī's political thought.[96] I assume that Al-Fārābī wrote the *Madīna fāḍila* first, next the *Siyāsa madanīya* and last the *K. taḥṣīl al-sa'āda*, if we confine ourselves to these three treatises. I am led to this assumption because the *Madīna fāḍila* contains the most detailed and comprehensive superstructure, physical and metaphysical, to politics proper. Much less space is given to revelation in the *Siyāsa*, where it is confined to man's theoretical reason; but his practical reason, imagination, is not acted upon in the process of emanation. I would conclude from this that Al-Fārābī considered a full explanation unnecessary since he had already given it in the *Madīna fāḍila*. It is, however, possible that the text of the *Siyāsa* is incomplete, although there does not seem to be a break in that particular passage. One might object to this interpretation by assuming that the shorter version comes first and the elaboration later. The *Taḥṣīl* might support such a view since it represents, at least in my opinion, the most mature and concise statement of happiness and how to attain it in the ideal state. But I draw the opposite conclusion, because the "first ruler" is not defined, as he was in the *Madīna fāḍila* and yet he is introduced in the *Siyāsa*, and prophecy and revelation are not mentioned. In contrast great emphasis and much space are given to the philosophical training of the philosopher/king/lawgiver/*imām*, and attention is focused on the lawgiver, who does not appear in the other two treatises at all. Though I do not wish to press the parallel, this reminds us of the relationship between the earlier *Republic* and the later *Laws* of the mature, aged Plato. Al-Fārābī was concerned, it seems to me, with the philosophical nature of the lawgiver in the first place, and not with the revelation of the law as such. For the lawgiver could only be an effective ruler if he was qualified to interpret the law, and in particular its theoretical teaching about God, man, the universe, reward and punishment, and providence. Hence Al-Fārābī stresses the fourfold perfection based on a thorough training in the theoretical sciences and culminating in the speculative virtues. This law is the common ground between Greek and Islamic philosophy, at least as far as politics is concerned.[97]

CHAPTER VII

IBN SĪNĀ[1]: THE SYNTHESIS

LAW and lawgiver are of the greatest importance in political life. We saw this in the discussion which Al-Fārābī devotes to this question in relation to prophecy and to philosophy, the two primary qualifications demanded of the first ruler. The *Mu'tazila* had already stressed the necessity of a divinely revealed law to ensure the common weal (*maṣlaḥa*) of the Muslim state. The *Falāsifa* similarly insist on the political necessity and significance of the divine law. Al-Ghazālī attacks them as heretics and unbelievers because they reduced revelation to an act of emanation. The Active Intellect or Holy Spirit influences the human mind, conditioning its imaginative and intellectual faculties to receive a revelation in form of a law. This is the position of Al-Fārābī.[2] It is also that of the Ikhwān al-ṣafā' ("Brethren of Purity") and of Ibn Sīnā. The first simply reproduce almost word for word Al-Fārābī's 28th chapter of the *Madīna fāḍila* in their *Encyclopedia*,[3] and their dependence on Al-Fārābī must therefore be assumed.

Ibn Sīnā, known to the West as Avicenna, did not write any political treatises of the kind we have discussed in the last chapter. He is concerned with human happiness and perfection, the highest stage of which consists in the contemplation of God, or Truth, and in mystical union with Him. It is in this context that man as a political being, a citizen, is considered. This gives Ibn Sīnā's philosophy a definite political orientation, and so we find important pronouncements on politics in his principal philosophical writings, including those belonging to the so-called "Eastern Philosophy", which is mystical.[4] I have observed[5] that in his *Aqsām al-'ulūm* (*Divisions of the Sciences*) he distinguished between three practical sciences: Ethics, as taught by Aristotle in his *Nicomachean Ethics*; Economics, as set out in *Bryson* and dealing with the household and its management; and Politics, which is taught by Plato and Aristotle. His *K. al-siyāsa* is devoted to ethics and to economics, the "regimen of the household", which comprises the master of the family, his wife, children and servants.

His summary of politics shows that Ibn Sīnā was interested in all aspects of Plato's *Republic*, including the transformation from one constitution to another, as was Ibn Rushd in his detailed commentary on it. In addition, he draws a distinction between secular kingship (*mulk*), which is the subject of the *Republic* and of Aristotle's *Politics*, and another kind of politics, concerned with prophecy and the *Sharī'a*, which is the subject of Plato's *Laws*. Like Al-Fārābī he thus links the ideal state of Islam with the ideal state of Plato's philosopher-king. In the last part of his *Metaphysics*[6] he speaks of the ideal state and the *khilāfa*, and in his treatise on *Prophecy* (*R. fī ithbāt al-nubuwwa*) he assigns the prophet a double task: he must ensure the good order of the physical world through political government, and that of the spiritual world by means of philosophy.[7] In his psychological explanation of prophecy he follows Al-Fārābī only in part: its possession is a gift transcending ordinary human qualities since it is the outcome of the emanation of the Holy Spirit. Prophetic man can perform miracles and is capable of spontaneous and immediate perception; this calls for no training like that of the philosopher, who attains to knowledge of the intelligible world by means of syllogism and demonstration. The prophet has thus reached a stage higher than the philosopher and is ready to hear the word of God and to see his angels. This appears to be in marked contrast to Al-Fārābī, who had required of the prophet skill in philosophy acquired by study and training in the use of demonstrative argument. If we supplement Ibn Sīnā's definition of prophecy in his *Psychology*[8] with his description of the stages on the road to bliss in his last work, the mystical *K. al-ishārāt wa-l-tanbīhāt* (*Book of Indications and Admonitions*),[9] we see how far beyond Al-Fārābī he has gone.

For Ibn Sīnā differentiates between three types of seekers after God, or Truth. The first is the *zāhid*, or Sufi ascetic; the second is the *'ābid*, who worships God by the external means of ritual and prayer; and the third and highest is the *'ārif*, who *knows* God and bends all his energies towards the kingdom of God. By overcoming the world of the senses, he frees his mind for divine inspiration. All three types can go their way through life to God only if that life is guaranteed them; this is possible only in society, where men help each other to obtain the necessities of life. The same idea is stated in his *Metaphysics*. Such a society must be based not only on particular laws (that is, on laws laid down by human authority to secure material well-being), but on a comprehensive, general law which takes account of man's spirituality. Such a law is the divine law (*Sharī'a*), which is the revelation of God through his messenger, the prophetic lawgiver. He must teach the masses the unity and oneness of God, and retribution in the hereafter, since the masses will obey God's commandments only by the promise of reward and the threat of punishment. Those who obey his law are assured of God's reward in this and in the next world. The true service of him who knows God (the *'ārif*) consists in his earnest striving to perceive God's being; his reward will be perfection in contemplation of God's essence (for Ibn Sīnā essence and existence are one in God, the necessary being). God created man and wishes mankind to survive; therefore he sent his law through his Prophet.[10]

We remember that Ibn Khaldūn rejected the claim put forward by the *Falāsifa* that prophecy is necessary for man and his existence in political association. He has in mind the chapter in Ibn Sīnā's *K. al-najāt*, headed, exactly as the separate treatise on prophecy, *Fī ithbāt al-nubbuwa*. Appropriately, Ibn Sīnā stakes the same claim in the *Aqsām al-'ulūm*, already referred to. The passage is important enough to be quoted in full. After mentioning the *Laws* he continues:

> The *Falāsifa* mean by law (*nāmūs*) not what the masses think, namely, that it is trickery and cunning ruse, but rather that it is the *Sunna*, the permanent, certain pattern and the revelation sent down ⟨from Heaven⟩. The Arabs also call the angel, who brings down a revelation, law (*nāmūs*). Through this part of practical philosophy we know the existence of prophecy ⟨as something necessary⟩ and that the human race needs the *Sharī'a* for its existence, preservation and future life.

He goes on to point out that such a law varies with every nation and time, and ends with the significant sentence: "through it we know the difference between the divine prophecy and all the false pretensions to it."[11]

He thus affirms that prophecy is necessary, and that political science, as part of practical philosophy, teaches its divine origin and truth by its superior character and usefulness. All three divisions of practical philosophy (ethics, economics and especially politics) are necessary to ensure man's happiness in this and the other life.

It is clear that the Prophet is above the *'ārif*, though he includes the accomplishments of the *'ārif* in his own nature. This nature is apt and worthy to receive a divine revelation in the form of the law that guarantees the twofold perfection and happiness. Intuitive rational mysticism is very different from the conviction that one is the chosen vessel of a revelation designed to guarantee man's welfare in political organization and his salvation in the hereafter. Ibn Sīnā agrees with Al-Fārābī in assigning to the prophet the principal task of bringing mankind the divine law for its guidance, preservation and salvation. At the same time he elevates the prophet by granting him spontaneous perception of the same kind as that attained by the *'ārif* who has stripped himself of his corporeality. It may be noted in passing that Ibn Khaldūn is profoundly influenced by the *K. al-ishārāt* in his exposition of knowledge and its stages, unless he and Ibn Sīnā both draw on a common earlier source.[12]

Ibn Sīnā clearly establishes the political significance of prophecy. In the interests of the state the prophet must prevent false opinions; but Ibn Sīnā does not proceed to identify the prophet with the philosopher-king, the *imām* and the first ruler, as Al-Fārābī had done. This is perhaps due to his mystical tendencies, which made him concentrate on the secrets of Eastern philosophy. In his treatise on *Prophecy* he refers to Plato's *Laws* and credits Plato with the saying that only he who pays attention to the allegories of the prophets, and perceives their ⟨inner⟩ meaning, will enter the divine kingdom. By prophets here he does not mean Muḥammad, but the Greek "prophets" Pythagoras, Socrates and Plato, who hide their secrets in their books in the form of allegories.[13] He excepts Muḥammad explicitly as different from the other prophets.

The "Eastern philosophy" centres in *ishrāq*, illumination, and Plato is considered as the chief of the *ishrāqīyūn*. The foremost representative in Islam of the philosophy of *ishrāq* is Al-Suhrawardī, whose mystical philosophy falls outside our presentation of political thought. It is sufficient to refer to H. Corbin's analysis of the sources of his philosophy in the Introduction to Al-Suhrawardī's *Opera Metaphysica et Mystica*, I and II, and to relate this analysis to Ibn Sīnā, who was attacked by Al-Suhrawardī as a quite inadequate adept of *ishrāq*. Ibn Sīnā's remark about Greek "prophets" applies not only to Neoplatonic and Neo-Pythagorean sources, but also to Zoroastrian, Manichaean and Hermetic writings, as well as Ismailian gnostic texts. In Al-Suhrawardī's view, the "strangers" whom Al-Fārābī discussed are exiled from their true source, to which they must return.[14]

We can now understand why practical philosophy (ethics, economics and politics) should be included in Ibn Sīnā's *Metaphysics*. It is because prophecy alone provides the law for the good society in the ideal state. Prophecy and *Sharī'a* are not only indispensable to the life and preservation of mankind. The divinely revealed law contains also the truth about God, his universe, his angels, the hereafter, reward and punishment, and providence. This truth is the object of the metaphysician's study. Moreover, the philosopher must live in society, and only the society whose political organization is that of the ideal state can provide the basis for the attainment of his ultimate perfection, the highest good, the knowledge and love of God.

The Muslim's God of revelation, of love and mercy is not Plato's God, though the attribute of justice is common to both and although both care for the world through providence. But granted the fundamental difference in the concept of God, it is undeniable that Plato's God as portrayed in Book x of the *Laws* impressed Ibn Sīnā because of his qualities of justice and providence. We have seen that in his view politics, based on prophecy and the *Sharī'a*, is the subject of the *Laws*. A. E. Taylor stresses, in the Introduction to his English translation of *The Laws of Plato*, that "the true statesman must think rightly about the ultimate things, God, man, and their relation to one another". He describes Book x as "the foundation of all subsequent 'natural' theology, the first attempt in the literature of the world to *demonstrate* God's existence and moral government of the world from the known facts of the visible order".[15] Passages such as I quote below cannot fail to appeal to a religious mind. Together with the philosophy of law enshrined in the *Laws*, and the detailed provision for the regulated, moral life of the individual in the community, they provide that "common ground" between the *Falāsifa* and Plato which is at the root of their political thought, and which enabled the *Falāsifa* to accept Platonic political ideas, adapting and transforming them in the spirit of Islam, as was claimed in a previous chapter.

Plato says in Book IV: "God eternally pursues the even tenor of his way." He stresses that happiness is contingent on justice, and that to follow God means to be like God. In Book VIII Plato provides a detailed mode of worship for the daily life of the political community. The religion of the rulers, as distinct from the citizens, for whom the authority of the state is sufficient warrant for belief, must be based on knowledge of God and reality. The nature of God and the purpose he has in mind for the world are clearly expressed in Book x: "He who provides for the world has disposed all things with a view to the preservation and perfection of the whole...the purpose of all that happens is what we have said, to win bliss for the life of the whole; it is not made for thee, but thou for it."[16]

"Common ground" presupposes an area of agreement large enough to enable a thinker reared in one religious tradition, which has both universal and specific features, to accommodate ideas from another tradition. This is the case with Al-Fārābī, Ibn Sīnā and Ibn Rushd. The Islamic element in the ensuing synthesis is less articulate, but by no means less implicit, in Al-Fārābī than in Ibn Sīnā. The wider range of Ibn Sīnā's encyclopaedic mind, his mystical bent, and the knowledge of the world which he gained as a physician and man of affairs, combined to give him a more original blend of traditional education and philosophical and theosophical knowledge. Steeped in Muslim law at an early age, as we learn from his autobiography,[17] he discovered a kindred mind in the Plato of the *Laws* as the following passage shows: "God, who, as the old saw has it, holds in his hands beginning, end, and middle of all that is, moves through the cycle of nature, straight to his end, and ever at his side walks right, the justicer of them that forsake God's law. He that would be happy follows close in her train with lowly and chastened mien."[18]

Ibn Sīnā states the same need for law and justice in man's life. Such a life is possible only by means of mutual help. He says in his *K. al-ishārāt*:

it is necessary that there exist between men commercial transactions (or social relations) and justice, that a ⟨divine⟩ law guards what a ⟨prophetic⟩ law-giver imposes as an obligation. ⟨This law⟩ is distinguished ⟨from others⟩ in that he [the Prophet] demands obedience on the strength of his possessing exclusive signs which point to their provenance from his Master (or Lord). It is necessary that there be retribution for the doers of good and evil from the ⟨All⟩-knowing and ⟨All⟩-powerful. It is also necessary to have a knowledge of him who recompenses and gives his divine law and, together with this knowledge, to have reasons for guarding it. Therefore they are under an obligation to worship ⟨him⟩ and to remember by repetition ⟨of prayer⟩ him who is worshipped, so that the appeal to justice, which preserves the life of mankind constantly, remains ⟨with them⟩. Then he who is ⟨always⟩ occupied with prayer will have added to the great advantage in this world abundant recompense in the hereafter.[19]

If we accept this passage as it stands, without mental reservations concerning its author's sincerity (and there does not seem to be any compelling reason to doubt it), it is at once clear that there is a strong affinity between Plato and Ibn Sīnā and between the law of Plato's God and the revealed law of Ibn Sīnā's God. Yet, and this is all-important, the realm of the *Sharī'a* includes the hereafter, but the *Nomos* of Plato does not. As the laws are different, so are the states which they serve. We know that words can have different meanings if used by different people in different contexts. Plato's phrase "to win bliss for the life of the whole" means one thing, and Ibn Sīnā's use of "abundant recompense in the hereafter" something different; at least as long as we have no documentary evidence that he put another, more philosophical, interpretation on the word "hereafter", thus giving it an inner meaning emptying it of its plain religious sense.

Yet the matter is further complicated by the well-known fact that the works of Plato and Aristotle were not available to the *Falāsifa* in their original form, but in summaries made by Neoplatonists and in a revised form. Among them, Galen, Plotinus, Porphyry and Proclus modified Plato to accord with Aristotle and vice versa. Plotinus and Porphyry in particular gave Plato's thought a definite turn towards religious monism. Their harmonizing tendencies are reflected in the treatises of Al-Fārābī, as we saw. This, in turn, made Platonism acceptable in this modified form, to Christians like Augustine, and to Muslims like Al-Kindī, Al-Fārābī, Miskawaih, Ibn Sīnā, Ibn Bājja, Ibn Ṭufail and Ibn Rushd, not to speak of Rāzī and Ṭūsī. Such concepts as prophecy and the hereafter in particular may well have undergone a change in meaning between the time of the *salaf*, the early Muslims, and the *Mu'tazila* and *Falāsifa*, as mentioned a little earlier. In the absence of clear evidence from texts we cannot be sure whether Al-Fārābī and Ibn Sīnā and Ibn Rushd meant by prophecy what the Muslim theologians meant, or rather what Plotinus and Porphyry meant. But I am inclined to think that their use of the concept of *tanzīl*—that is, of a revelation sent down by Allah through the angel Gabriel, and the designation of Muḥammad as the *rasūl Allah*, the messenger of Allah, the warner, as distinct from the *nabī* (used of the other prophets)—suggests that they accepted the Muslim meaning. Admittedly, they may have interpreted these words, which denote specific religious concepts, in a Neoplatonic sense, but there is no evidence that they actually did so, except for the identification of *malak* and *'aql fa''āl*, angel and Active Intellect, by Al-Fārābī and Ibn Sīnā. Until such evidence is forthcoming I continue to maintain that they were Muslims first.

The case of the hereafter is perhaps different. It is not easy, if at all possible, to decide whether Al-Fārābī and Ibn Sīnā, for example, understood *al-ākhira* and *al-ḥayāt al-ukhrā* in the accepted Muslim sense or in a transferred sense, denoting the survival of the soul, Immortality.[20] Did they believe in the reward of an after-life in Paradise, and in the punishment of hell, when they maintained that the *Sharī'a* alone teaches us about reward and punishment? Again, there is no evidence to the contrary, nor can we affirm or deny that they had in mind the survival of the soul, of the soul as an entity, or of its rational part only. Did the hereafter mean the return of the soul, imprisoned temporarily in the body, to its original, natural state of pure spirituality, freed from matter? I must leave the decision of these questions to the experts in philosophy. I mention the difficulty because it must be faced in any ultimate assessment of the real meaning of perfection and happiness, which are the concern of political philosophy.

Its bearing on the wider problem of revelation and reason cannot concern us in the context of politics. It is sufficient to repeat a view I have expressed before;[21] the starting-point for the *Falāsifa* was their faith in God and his revelation through his apostle Muḥammad. This placed a certain limitation upon the freedom of their philosophical speculation. They tried to make it less irksome by the axiom that since there was only one truth, revelation can and does teach nothing which is contrary to reason. It must, naturally, remain an open question whether at times they overstepped the boundary by appealing to a hidden, inner meaning at which their speculative reason had arrived. In that process at least Ibn Bājja, in the example quoted in the next chapter concerning the hereafter, did violence to the plain meaning of scripture and set it aside. The psychological interpretation of prophecy advanced by Al-Fārābī and developed by Ibn Sīnā did not, as far as I can judge, impair God's absolute free will and choice. He is entirely master of himself, and of his will and action; his self-revelation to his chosen prophets is not *caused* by a natural disposition in them which forces him to reveal his will to them in form of a law, although such a disposition must exist in order that they may receive his law. This law teaches true and right convictions and opinions about God, the angels, nature and man—and the emphasis is on true as "provable by demonstrative arguments"; it also lays down rules of behaviour in the form of duties to God and one's fellow-men, at which reason would arrive only after a long time. This law is therefore superior to the human law devised by the philosopher-lawgiver. In addition prophetic revealed law contains commandments such as prayer, fasting, alms, pilgrimage and holy war, which enable man to draw near to God in order to know him. At the same time they ease and improve social relations and the general welfare of man in this life and, by promising reward and threatening punishment, make man look to a future world and upon his earthly life as a preparation for the next.

The distinction between the elect metaphysicians and the masses maintains religious equality and a concern for the happiness of all in accordance with the intellectual capacity of each individual, despite its claim that only the philosopher can penetrate to the inner, hidden meaning of these concepts, whereas the masses must be content with a metaphorical explanation. Ibn Rushd explicitly exempts certain religious teachings from interpretation.

We now return from the rarefied air, which the few elect who reach the highest good breathe, to the earth-bound generality of citizens. We follow Ibn Sīnā's exposition of economics and politics which forms the last two chapters of the final section of his *Shifā'* at the end of the treatment of metaphysics.[22] He assigns to the lawgiver (*sānin*) the primary task of ordering the life of society organized in the state, by dividing the citizens (as Plato had done) into three estates: the rulers, the artisans and the guardians. Each group is administered by a master (*ra'īs*) who, in turn, appoints masters of lesser authority over smaller units. We are reminded of Al-Fārābī's division, based on Aristotle, into rulers and ruled in hierarchical order, from the first ruler over secondary rulers who partly rule and are ruled, down to those who only accept rule, the masses. Every citizen executes his allotted task, so that there is not one person who does not benefit the state by his work. Idleness is not to be tolerated: if it is due to illness the sick person must be isolated; if there is no reason for it other than laziness, such a person must be destroyed.

The care of the sick and infirm, together with the explicit provision for those who become impoverished and are unable to earn their own living, may be due to Ibn Sīnā's Muslim ethical standards and to his activity as a physician. It is in contrast to Plato's teaching.[23] Ibn Sīnā calls ignominious (*qabīḥ*) the killing of those who can no longer fulfil their civic duties through no fault of their own.

Next he stresses the need for capital in order to guarantee the general welfare and in particular to provide for the guardians. It is to be made up of taxes, fines and legal booty (*fay'*). This last, a concept peculiar to the Islamic state, is to be used equitably in the general interest (*maṣāliḥ mushtaraka*). The lawgiver must forbid games of chance, for gain ought to be the result of work, which is also of advantage to others. Theft, robbery and usury are also forbidden since they are detrimental to society.[24]

So far Ibn Sīnā has dealt with public finance and the gainful occupation of the citizens. Next, he discusses marriage and family life. His account is based on Muslim law, with classical tradition in the background, such as is reflected in *Bryson*,[25] one version of which we owe to Ibn Sīnā; it is identical with his *K. al-siyāsa*. Marriage guarantees the propagation and perpetuation of the human race; the family is the foundation upon which the state is built; it forges a bond between parents and children which should serve as a pattern for social life. Hence, Ibn Sīnā discusses at length measures necessary to safeguard the purity of married life and the health of the family. He adds a long statement about divorce, which he allows as a last resort if reconciliation proves impossible, in spite of the danger to the children if the home is broken up. In this, as in the matter of the status of women and the care of children, he is in full accord with the relevant injunctions and regulations of Muslim law, especially with the law of inheritance.

In the last chapter he deals with certain aspects of the ideal Muslim state, concentrating on the *khalīfa* and *imām*. Above all, it is the duty of the lawgiver to impress upon the citizens their obligation to obey the *khalīfa*, who takes the place of Muḥammad. He then summarizes the duties of the *imām*, entirely in accord with the orthodox legal theory. In doing so he accommodates the Islamic qualifications within the four cardinal virtues of Plato. The caliph must possess noble virtues like courage, temperance and "right conduct" (*ḥusn tadbīr*).[26] This last seems to correspond to Plato's justice, since Ibn Sīnā uses the terms *fāḍila*, *'ādila* and *ḥasana* interchangeably for the ideal Muslim state. He must also have a high intelligence which will enable him to acquire practical wisdom (as distinct from theoretical wisdom), and also an expert knowledge of the *Sharī'a* in which nobody must surpass him.

The election of the caliph must proceed on the lines prescribed by the law and outlined in chapter II. Ibn Sīnā adds, however, that the electors become unbelievers (*faqad kafaru bi-llah*) if they are guilty of a wrong choice. He roundly condemns usurpation, and actually demands the death of a tyrant (*mutaghallib*) and the punishment of those who fail to carry out such a tyrannicide if they have the means to do it. This seems to go beyond the orthodox theory, which only demands removal from office, not death, if the people have sufficient power to force the caliph's abdication. Ibn Sīnā goes so far as to claim that, next to belief in the Prophet Muḥammad, tyrannicide is most pleasing to Allah and draws man near to him.

If the lawfully elected caliph is unworthy to hold office and is challenged by a worthy rebel (*khārijī*), the citizens are advised to recognize the claimant, if he is intellectually and physically fit to be caliph, even if he should lag behind in virtue. This can only mean that the legal requirements are partly waived in favour of an authority based on power and intelligence. This is preferable to a weak authority exercised by a virtuous, pious caliph who lacks the two basic requirements of a ruler. This view comes near to the expediency which swayed the jurists whose theories we considered in chapter II. Such realism appears inconsistent with Ibn Sīnā's denunciation of tyrannous rule and with his call to end it by murdering the tyrant.

Next, he stresses the importance and value for the political, social and personal life of the citizens of the ideal Muslim state of religious duties in the narrow sense (*'ibādāt*), like the public Friday prayer and festivals, fast and pilgrimage. These observances "bind those who fulfil them closely together, they strengthen their desire for the defence of their state by imbuing them with courage ⟨and devotion⟩, and finally lead them to virtues. Communal prayer calls down God's blessing upon the affairs ⟨of the state⟩." He is convinced that the lawgiver arranged all this best in the *khilāfa*. The regulations must be neither too rigid nor too lax; Ibn Sīnā often stresses the golden mean.

'Ibādāt thus comprise man's duties to God, and at the same time benefit society. We saw earlier that both Muslim and Greek law agree in recognizing the political value of religious observances.

Mu'āmalāt, commercial transactions, cover the whole range of man's duties towards his fellow-men, his social duties. These inter-human relations must be the concern of the *imām*. He must regulate them in such a way that "they promote the construction of the two pillars of the state, namely, family life (*munākaḥāt*) and the generality of things men share in common (*mushārakāt*). He must promulgate laws concerning mutual help and the protection of property and of personal life."

Next he turns his attention to the opponents of the *Sunna* within and to the enemies without, which brings him to a discussion of one of the principal duties of the caliph, *jihād*, or holy war.

This is the complement to the positive duty of co-operation in defence of life and property. Hence he advocates war first against the opponents of the prophetic law. Their property is to be confiscated and administered in the interests of the common weal. They themselves are to serve the citizens of the just state (*madīna 'ādila*). Since he says that "those who are far removed from acquiring virtues are slaves (*'abīd*) by nature like the Turks and negroes and in general people living in an unfavourable climate" he obviously wants them reduced to the status of serfs. "For there must be masters and slaves."

He distinguishes between the prophetically revealed constitution, which he calls "our *Sunna* which was sent down ⟨from heaven⟩", and "a good *Sunna* (*jamīla*)" which has come into being in another state after a long time, and "nations and states" for which, if they are in error (*'idhā ḍallat*), a *Sunna* has to be laid down. Such a constitution must needs be the *Sunna* of the prophetic lawgiver which is "the most perfect and excellent (*'atammu wa-'afḍalu*)". If the ideal state (*madīna ḥasana*) is of the opinion that the affairs of the corrupt states (*mudun fāsida*) can be restored to a good and just order (*ṣalāḥ*) it may impose on them its own constitution. If there is opposition "and they refuse to accept it and accuse the lawgiver of lying when he claimed that it was sent down for all states, then they must be punished. For refusal to obey the *Sharī'a* which Allah sent down" cannot remain unpunished.[27]

It is to be noted that Ibn Sīnā emphasizes the paramount need for law as the regulator of earthly life in the state. He explicitly remarks that not everybody is concerned with the hereafter (*al-ākhira*). Therefore, "the lawgiver must legislate for this life, and most regulations are directed against actions which run counter to the *Sunna*, actions which are apt to corrupt order and harmony in the state. Individuals may suffer" in the process of law enforcement. But this is inevitable and has, moreover, "educative value". He thinks, no doubt, of punishment as a deterrent.

So far Ibn Sīnā has been concerned with the prophetic revealed law, its excellence and validity. He now returns to the stipulation that the Prophet's vicegerent, the *khalīfa*, must possess an expert knowledge of the law. For the lawgiver did not provide for the particular cases which are bound to arise as the result of changes in time and circumstances. It is, therefore, the duty of the governor (*sā'is*, the man in charge of the *siyāsa madanīya*, the political administration) to issue regulations (*aḥkām*) to cover every single contingency as it arises. The application of the general principles laid down by the lawgiver to individual cases, which are subject to change in course of time, must be entrusted to counsellors (*ahl al-mashwara*). This last condition seems to mean that the caliph is entitled to good advice, but the decision (in the form of regulations) is his prerogative and duty. In all this Ibn Sīnā is entirely within the orthodox theory of the *khilāfa*.

Lastly, he turns to ethics. The lawgiver must be equally concerned with personal character and habits (*akhlāq wa-'ādāt*). These character traits and moral habits must lead to justice (*'adāla*) which is the (golden) mean (*wasāṭa*).[28] Its object is to overcome the lower forces and tendencies and to make the soul supreme and free from corporeality. The pleasures of the senses exist to preserve the body; courage is needed to defend and protect the state. Justice as the mean includes equity and balance. It is concerned with individual and social welfare and the avoidance of excess and injustice. Thus *'adāla* is the sum total (*majmū'*) of the three others, wisdom, temperance and courage. Ibn Sīnā thus returns to Plato's four cardinal virtues. Wisdom, as we saw, consists of practical wisdom or prudence (*ḥikma 'amalīya*), concerned with actions in this world (*af'āl dunyawīya*), and of theoretical wisdom (*ḥikma naẓarīya*), acquired by the study of philosophy. The man who combines with the four "political" virtues this metaphysical virtue, which Al-Fārābī called speculative virtue, is happy (*faqad su'ida*).[29] This is the moral and intellectual perfection of the *Falāsifa*. Ibn Sīnā excludes the character of a mean from theoretical wisdom and ends the *Shifā'* significantly with man's crowning achievement, the prophetic gift; the man distinguished by possession of it as well as the practical (or political) and theoretical virtues "is on the point of becoming the human lord, *rabb insānī*, and he is the ruler (*sulṭān*) of the terrestrial world (*'ālam arḍī*) and the vicar of God in it (*khalīfat-Allah*). He may be worshipped after Allah."

This conclusion of the *'ilāhīyāt* (metaphysics) of the *Shifā'* shows us why Ibn Sīnā included politics, which though a royal or master art was still a practical art, in metaphysics. The ideal ruler is the Prophet; he is in this above the happy man who combines to perfection the practical and the theoretical virtues.

But this conclusion of the *Shifā'*, important as it is for the Islamic character of Ibn Sīnā's political philosophy and as an indication of his own personality, does not entitle us to draw the obvious conclusion that this is the essence of his whole religious philosophy.

For there is another work with another concluding section, the witness to his Eastern philosophy, the *K. al-ishārāt*, already quoted. The last chapters of this profound treatise leave no doubt that the *'ārif*, the speculative mystic, is removed—at least in his mind—from the plane of law and politics. His soul soars above and beyond this earthly world, when, in his supreme moment of bliss, he has effected an intellectual union with God in pure knowledge. It is this mystical intellectualism which found expression in his allegory *Ḥay ibn Yaqẓān*, which has left its mark on Ibn Bājja and especially on Ibn Ṭufail. Ibn Rushd, on the other hand, has more in common with the Ibn Sīnā of the last chapters of the *Shifā'*. The Islamic ideal state legislates for all its citizens. Obedience to its law guarantees their well-being in this world and prepares them for the utmost happiness in the next.

CHAPTER VIII

IBN BĀJJA: INDIVIDUALIST DEVIATION

In Abū Bakr ibn al-Sa'igh ibn Bājja,[1] the first Muslim philosopher in the West, we meet with a different approach to Plato and his political philosophy. For Avempace, to give him the name by which he was known to the Scholastics and to modern students of philosophy, is exclusively interested in the individual thinker's perfection and happiness. He sees this in the union (or, more correctly translated, the contact) of the human with the Active Intellect, which is the highest stage before the mystical contemplation of God.[2] Political science concerns him only as it affects the philosopher; the qualities of the ruler, law as the basis of government, the happiness of the community, the various political constitutions and their transformation are not the object of his study. He knows of Plato's ideal state and that it helps the individual seeker after Truth to attain his goal, whereas the imperfect states hinder him. But, unlike his predecessors Al-Fārābī and Ibn Sīnā, and unlike Ibn Rushd after him, he does not admit that the highest human perfection and ultimate happiness are possible only in the ideal state. The quest for happiness has precedence over state and society. If necessary, man must isolate himself from society and concentrate on the self-knowledge which will lead him to the perception of God, unaided by society and the prophetic law which guides it.

The other *Falāsifa* mentioned above acknowledged Plato and Aristotle as their masters in political philosophy and followed their authority with such modifications and adaptations as their Islamic environment required. Hence their political interpretation of prophecy and their insistence on the *Sharī'a*, the prophetic revealed law, as the constitution of the ideal state. For them man is a political being; he must therefore live in a political association which guarantees his life and makes possible his perfection in accordance with his natural disposition. He is a part of the state and this is the true essence of his humanity. If he separates himself from the community he forfeits his right to and his chance of perfection.

It is not that Ibn Bājja did not know his Plato and Aristotle. Every line of his difficult and often obscure writings, which in their present form we probably owe to a pupil, betrays a precise knowledge of their philosophy, a fine understanding and the independent judgement of an original mind. But though the writings of Plato and Aristotle contained basic political teachings for other Muslim philosophers, Ibn Bājja was not afraid to depart from them. The Hellenic legacy did not supply the centre round which he built his own philosophy, which can be characterized in the words of the title of his treatise as "the self-government of the ⟨metaphysician⟩ in isolation" (*Tadbīr al-mutawaḥḥid*). This assertion must be qualified in that it is correct only with reference to Plato's political philosophy. It does not apply to Plato's theory of knowledge, in particular to the doctrine of the Ideas.

Since we are concerned with political thought it is essential to grasp the difference in outlook on politics between Ibn Bājja and Al-Fārābī, despite their agreement on the ultimate human end. Moreover, if the interpretation of Ibn Bājja which I have attempted elsewhere[3] is correct, we can discern a development of his thought away from Plato and from Al-Fārābī's presentation of Platonic political philosophy. But although we will not find any acceptance of this political thought as authoritative or even formative, there is still sufficient Platonic material embodied in Ibn Bājja's "way of life" to justify a detailed exposition.

This exposition is based on the three treatises edited by M. Asín Palacios: the *Risālat-al-wadā'*, aptly titled by the Latin translator of its Hebrew version, Jacob Mantinus, "Epistola de Perfectione"; the *K. tadbīr al-mutawaḥḥid*, and the *K. ittiṣāl-al-'aql bi-l-insān.*[4]

In the first of these treatises Ibn Bājja adopts a position which is nearest to that of the ideal state in contrast to the imperfect states. His picture of these Platonic states is largely that with which we are familiar from Al-Fārābī's political treatises. He leaves no doubt that Plato's ideal state is the one in which the philosopher can best pursue his aim. But in this treatise it is already evident that Plato's questions when dealing with the individual are not those of Ibn Bājja. Whereas Plato asks "What is justice? What is the best government and how do we achieve it?",

Ibn Bājja asks only "How can the metaphysician best reach his goal?" In the *Tadbīr* the emphasis is naturally on the "philosopher in isolation", the *mutawaḥḥid*. The term *mutawaḥḥid* is probably borrowed from Al-Fārābī. Moses Narbōnī, who incorporated a Hebrew summary of this treatise in his commentary on Ibn Ṭufail's *Ḥay ibn Yaqẓān*,[5] adds the qualification "whether he is a part of the state or not" to the word *mutawaḥḥid*. This is a good pointer to the discussion, in the course of the treatise, of how the philosopher should conduct himself if he has to live in one of the imperfect states. It is clear to Ibn Bājja that only self-government, based on laws similar to those devised for the ideal state, will enable the philosopher to satisfy his desire for knowledge of the Spiritual Forms and through them of God. This knowledge, or rather vision of the Spiritual Forms, also termed Separate Intelligences, is tantamount to a mastery of the speculative sciences. When this is achieved, the philosopher proceeds to contact or union with the Active Intellect before he can hope to draw ever nearer to God himself. The third treatise is devoted to this penultimate stage. It contains many references to the first two.[6]

When we turn first to the *Risālat-al-wadā'* it is important to remember that Ibn Bājja inquires into the highest human perfection and utmost blessedness (or happiness) within the framework of the state as the central problem of his philosophy. We can, therefore, expect references to those political concepts and institutions with which Al-Fārābī's treatment of Plato's *Republic* has made us familiar. Just as Plato argues from the correspondence between the individual, especially the ruler, and the constitution, so Ibn Bājja assumes an interaction between the perfection of the individual and that of the state. Consequently the highest perfection is possible only in the *madīna fāḍila*, the ideal or perfect state. If he calls the ruler of this state *ra'īs*, he means by this term him whom Al-Fārābī calls, in his *Madīna fāḍila*, *al-ra'īs al-awwal*, the first ruler. He takes over from Al-Fārābī the Aristotelian distinction between ruler and ruled and defines their proper relationship as that "between master and pupil". It is for the ruler to assign to the subject such tasks as will enable him to reach the goal for which he is qualified, provided he does them well. The "ruler" of the other, imperfect states is termed *mudabbir*, regent; he resembles the king only in certain respects, and can therefore be called *ra'īs* only figuratively, because he is really like a horseman who "rules over the bridle". This means he is a secondary ruler, since the art of horsemanship is a subordinate art, whereas the art of kingship is a master art.[7] This example shows, especially when compared with its source, Al-Fārābī's *Siyāsa*,[8] the striking difference in approach, attitude and interest despite the clear literary dependence. Ibn Bājja agrees with Al-Fārābī that the attainment of the goal depends on the character of the rule under which the subjects live. He is not concerned with the different kinds of happiness which Al-Fārābī noted, seeing in them the distinguishing characteristics of the various kinds of states, since the kind of aim pursued by the rulers (honour, wealth or pleasure) determined their conduct.

Ibn Bājja believes that virtuous men living in imperfect states by cultivating their virtues are "like the guardians in the state who have authority over the people. With their help the affairs of state are perfected since the ethical virtues promote social relations through which the state becomes perfect."[9]

Like Al-Fārābī in the *Taḥṣīl*[10] Ibn Bājja is concerned with man's destiny and how to reach it. He discusses human faculties and virtues as they affect the master-servant relationship (as distinct from those of animals, which share some of them with man). "Medicine, navigation, agriculture, rhetoric and generalship are evidently all subordinate faculties. For generalship is only ⟨directed⟩ to the welfare of the state....Rhetoric is intended to furnish persuasion by which philosophy is illumined. For, if philosophy did not exist, rhetoric would be useless and vain."[11] Although Ibn Bājja, like Al-Fārābī, was aware of Plato's low opinion of rhetoric, he was not perturbed by the political danger oratory can present if used by sophists.

He is interested rather in the fact that these subordinate arts cannot be the final goal for man. This is because of the intellect, a unique faculty peculiar to man. By its possession we become divine beings capable of coming as near to God as possible. Like Al-Fārābī, Ibn Bājja uses Plato's allegory of the cave. The goal is immediate perception, though most people come no nearer to it than the perception of the *Intelligibles* which is like the reflection of the sun in water. He says: "It is clear that this goal is intended for us in our nature. But it is possible only in political association.

Men were fashioned opposite to each other in their stations so that through them the state should be perfected. Then this intention can be fulfilled."[12]

While he thus still agrees with Al-Fārābī and the other *Falāsifa* that political association is necessary, we note that his reasons differ significantly from theirs, which come from their Greek masters. For it is not to secure the necessities of life and to live in peace with justice that men must join in political association; it is to gain intellectual perfection that men of varying natural disposition must associate in a state. The perfection of the state guarantees their individual perfection. It is equally noteworthy that Ibn Bājja does not require a divine law to guide the community and guarantee life and property, to regulate social relations and to enable man to achieve his higher purpose as a rational human being in this world and the next. He concentrates on the intellect, and speaks of two methods by which the union between the human and the Active Intellect may be effected. There is the natural way: man's own unaided effort by means of the study of the speculative sciences or philosophy. The other is the divine way: God helps man through his messengers and prophets. The knowledge they provide, for example, in the Qur'ān, is God's most precious gift to man, and it is demanded by the *Sharī'a*. God desires man to draw near to him, by a knowledge of his essence. To this end God has endowed man with reason, his dearest creation. By its possession man has become God's dearest creature. Knowledge alone leads to God, but ignorance removes man from him.[13] Ibn Rushd makes the same statement in his *Faṣl al-maqāl*.[14]

Ibn Bājja underlines the metaphysical purpose of politics by asserting that "political human contact for mutual help, such as contact for instruction and perception, is intellectual encounter".[15] The union of the intellects is the ultimate aim; in order to effect it, political association is essential for the philosopher, according to the *Risālat al-wadā'*, in my opinion[16] the first of the three treatises. The other *Falāsifa* and Ibn Khaldūn agree that the state is necessary to guarantee man's physical and spiritual existence, and that the *Sharī'a* best secures man's happiness in this life and the next. Such a state cares for all its citizens, it ministers to the needs and aspirations of all. Ibn Bājja is only interested in the philosopher.

The *K. ittiṣāl* never speaks of the state, and seems to express the culmination of Ibn Bājja's thought, first reached in the later chapters of the *Tadbīr*. Although in the *Tadbīr* his literary dependence on Al-Fārābī is still strong, he appears to have freed himself largely from the hold which Al-Fārābī's political consciousness and sense of civic responsibility had hitherto exercised over him. For we know how strongly Al-Fārābī had insisted on the need for mutual help and co-operation and therefore for political association. Happiness, he said, is impossible in isolation from the community, which must be organized in a state; the highest perfection cannot be attained except in the ideal state.

Ibn Bājja inquires in the *Tadbīr* into the possibility of gaining perfection in imperfect states. For, like Al-Fārābī, he is convinced that the citizens can reach their goal in the ideal state which is ruled in justice and mutual love. Thus, he must assume the existence of the ideal state when he says: "Speculation in this respect ⟨that is, leading to the perception of the universal spiritual forms—Reality—⟩ is the future life; it is the utmost happiness, peculiar to man alone."[17] It would appear from this definition of the Muslim's *ḥayāt ākhira* (after- (or next) life) that Ibn Bājja has here drawn the full logical consequences of the method of rational interpretation of scripture which aims at the esoteric, hidden meaning. His definition has certainly nothing in common with the plain meaning, with the accepted theological interpretation of the future life, of the hereafter, in Islam. If in the case of Al-Fārābī or Ibn Sīnā doubt may perhaps be entertained as to the precise meaning which they gave to this concept, Ibn Bājja is so bold and outspoken that only one conclusion is possible: by his statement he places himself outside Islam. If the attitude of the other *Falāsifa* can rightly be termed intellectualism, his is undiluted rationalism. This is the more evident if we place his definition alongside his attitude to the *Sharī'a*. He had discussed, we remember, the divine method of achieving union between the human and the Active Intellects, and speaks of *rusul* (messengers) in the plural, not of the one *rasūl*, Muḥammad, as distinct from the *anbiyā'* (prophets); this is certainly a significant departure from linguistic usage and Muslim conviction. For him "our law" merely legitimizes rational speculation by the divine command to acquire knowledge and understanding. It is true that the other

Falāsifa identify the angel Gabriel (who brought "the precious book", the Qur'ān, from Heaven to the *rasūl* Muḥammad) with the Active Intellect and thus rationalize revelation. But neither Ibn Sīnā nor Ibn Rushd denied or even doubted the spontaneity or the freedom of God's will in sending his revelation to whom he pleased, whatever the natural disposition of the recipient. Natural disposition is necessary, but it cannot force God to mediate his revelation through the angel. Moreover, though they distinguished between the few elect superior intellects and the masses, they did not question the unique capacity of the divinely revealed prophetic law to bring happiness to all believers who obey it, and obey God's will through it. But Ibn Bājja is only interested in the happiness of the exceptional man, the metaphysician. He acknowledges God as the giver of reason to man. That is the beginning, but also, it seems, the end. Once in possession of this most precious divine gift, man is sovereign through his intellect. He takes the divine command to know God seriously; hence his ceaseless striving for intellectual perfection, considered as the union of his human intellect with the Active Intellect as the indispensable prelude to the knowledge of God. But while not despising divine help in this upward progression, Ibn Bājja concentrates on the natural method, man's unaided intellectual effort. Thus, he distinguishes three grades of ascent: the first, natural stage is achieved through the practice of the arts; the second by the acquisition of speculative knowledge—this grade is compared to seeing the sun through its reflection in water; the third and highest degree is reached when rational man sees reality in its essence. This is the stage of the happy or blest, the *su'adā*, who are capable of immediate intuitive perception.[18] He then asks the question: how can such an ascent of the human soul be effected in existing, imperfect states? The difficulty is that right beliefs and opinions are absent from these states, and, as a result, they lack the good administration of the ideal state which is favourable to the philosopher. Ibn Bājja met this difficulty by isolating the seeker after God.

The *Tadbīr* shows how such an individual must conduct himself if he is to achieve his purpose.[19] In justification of the use of the term *tadbīr* for the "government" of the self, Ibn Bājja says that its proper application is to city-states and households. It is also applied to God's rule over the world, the noblest of all rules, because of its connection with the creation, a statement strongly reminiscent of Al-Fārābī's designation of God as "the creator... the governor (*mudabbir*) of the whole world".[20] Ibn Bājja distinguishes between the *Falāsifa* who use this and all terms in their "pure association", and the masses (*al-jumhūr*) who use them in an "ambiguous", that is, equivocal, sense.[21]

In connection with the government of city-states Ibn Bājja describes Plato's *Republic* as explaining "the government of states, the meaning of right [or justice] therein, wherefrom error affects it", and states that "he ⟨Plato⟩ pronounced on merit, ignorance and vice".[22] Al-Fārābī in his description of the *Republic* stresses that corruption and decay are the result of man's abandoning political society.[23] Unlike Ibn Sīnā and Al-Ghazālī, Ibn Bājja denies to economics the character of an independent science since, in the view of Plato, the household is only part of the city-state. Its perfection is intended for the perfection of the state and for man's natural goal;[24] consequently, for him it is on the same level as rhetoric, strategy or medicine.[25] It is a partial or subordinate art and belongs to man's government of himself, or politics.

Plato's ideal state knows neither physicians nor judges; its citizens are united in mutual love and never quarrel among themselves; all the actions in the state are just; its citizens live on a simple sensible diet which saves them from illness and makes doctors superfluous.[26] By contrast, the four simple states need both judges and physicians; their need is in direct proportion to the degree of their remoteness from the ideal state.[27] Ibn Bājja must have read the *Republic* himself, for he could not have found any reference to judges and physicians in Al-Fārābī. Ibn Rushd, who commented on the *Republic*, speaks of both categories.[28] It is important to note how Ibn Bājja, though not interested in government and political questions as such, sees a connection between these two professions and the character of the states. His concern for individual perfection made him concentrate on the ideal state and refrain from discussing the imperfect states to which he merely refers as "the four simple states (*basīṭa*)". Only once does he mention them by names such as Plato or Al-Fārābī give them. Usually he speaks of simple or composite imperfect states, echoing the *Laws* and possibly the *Politikos*.[29] We only need think of the normal constitution in the *Laws* as a mixture of monarchy and democracy, or of Plato's advocacy of a combination of a tyrant with a philosopher as suggested by his own experience at Syracuse.

The passage in the *Tadbīr*[30] which names four states unfortunately contains a blank. This makes it impossible to determine one of them with certainty. But Asín's guess at "oligarchy" may well be correct, since Narbōnī, though in a different place, speaks of a "moneyed" state, that is, plutocracy, the other designation for oligarchy. Democracy and tyranny are beyond doubt, and what Asín read as "*iqāmiya*" must be understood as *imāmiya*. This is because it is the Arabic equivalent of *kōhanīth* in Narbōnī, which literally means "priestly", and also because we find such a state discussed in Ibn Rushd's commentary and there linked with the ancient Persians[31] (as Ibn Bājja and Al-Fārābi had done). In a Hebrew source the "priestly" state is said to be excellent in actions and opinions and thus equated with aristocracy.[32] But since aristocracy is for Plato, together with monarchy, the best state, it would perhaps be more correct to think of timocracy. This would, moreover, complete Plato's four vicious constitutions of which timocracy is the least bad, as we have seen in the chapter on Al-Fārābī. Against this interpretation an objection must, however, be raised. Ibn Bājja speaks of the corruption which must befall the state if children, in whom prudence and counsel cannot be expected, are made rulers, as had happened in his time. He says: "This is the gravest and most powerful reason for corruption in it, whichever of the four states it is. It is in no way possible in an *imām*-state. It happens most often in an oligarchy(?), then in a democracy, then in a tyranny."[33]

We now turn to a more detailed consideration of the "political" references in the *Tadbīr* in their proper sequence. For they are used chiefly as illustrations and analogies, and must therefore be understood in their context, difficult as Ibn Bājja's mode of expression and style are. Whether they take the form of general observations or of references to actual situations and events, like the example just quoted, they seem to give the *mutawaḥḥid* the right to withdraw into himself, to isolate himself from the community in whose midst he lives, in order the better to prepare himself by the study of metaphysics for the perception of the Spiritual Forms. This leads him to union with the Active Intellect and subsequently to God. Ibn Bājja, though aware that the *highest* perfection is unattainable for his philosopher in isolation in the imperfect states, nevertheless advocates his withdrawal in order to attain as near to perfection as is possible.[34] Bent on ruling himself, he does not acknowledge any obligation to serve the community: the duty on which Plato insists, since the philosopher ought to rule. Only if the people reject him as useless and deny him that honour and esteem which are due to a ruler, is Plato's philosopher barred from the government of the city-state. Nor does Ibn Bājja share Plato's anxiety that the very virtues of the philosopher may turn into defects.[35]

The ideal state is characterized by just actions and true opinions.[36] Opposition in actions and opinions cannot arise in it, but "this is possible in the four states".[37]

From this possibility Ibn Bājja draws an interesting and, from the point of view of the *mutawaḥḥid*, positive conclusion. Not only false opinions may arise, but also true and right ones. The same applies to actions. Thanks to the self-government of the *mutawaḥḥid*, there can therefore exist in these four imperfect states a man or a group of men possessed of true opinions and of faultless conduct. Such individuals are equated by Ibn Bājja with the *nawābit* of Al-Fārābī, but in an entirely positive meaning.

> Those who fasten on a true opinion which did not exist in that state or ⟨where⟩ there exists the opposite of what they believe, are called *al-nawābit*.... This term is transferred to them from the plants which grow spontaneously in a cultivated field. Now, we would attribute this term exclusively to those who hold true opinions. It is evident that it is of the essence of the ideal state that there are no *nawābit* in it... because there are no false opinions represented therein.... But in the four ⟨imperfect⟩ ways of life *nawābit* are to be found, and their existence is even a reason for the coming into being of the perfect state.[38]

Apart from the fact that this formulation is possibly the outcome of his personal experience and reflects the actual contemporary situation in the Spain of the Almoravids, this assertion certainly runs counter to the teaching of Plato and of the *Falāsifa*. This is borne out by the continuation in the *Tadbīr*:

> But the three classes which either exist or can exist ⟨in these four states⟩ are the *nawābit*, the judges and the physicians. The blessed ones [or happy ones, *su'adā*] in so far as they can exist at all in these states,

enjoy an isolated blessedness. For the just government is only the government of the isolated, be he one or be they more, while neither nation nor city-state is in agreement with their opinion.[39]

This isolated existence in an uncongenial world where they live as "strangers" is a deliberate turning aside from political activity and civic duty, and represents an individualistic mystical attitude which is fully developed in Ibn Ṭufail's *Ḥay ibn Yaqẓān*, a kind of contemplative *Robinson Crusoe*.[40]

Another conclusion is equally important. The *Falāsifa*, Al-Fārābī and Ibn Sīnā as much as Ibn Rushd, agree that normally the ideal state can only be brought into being by a prophetic lawgiver, and not by one or more men of mere moral and intellectual perfection, Ibn Bājja's *nawābit*. Besides, the other Muslim philosophers follow Plato in assuming a corruption of the ideal state and a downward transformation from one imperfect state to the next. Ibn Bājja is not concerned with such a deterioration; indeed, he asserts the very opposite, the possible emergence of the ideal out of an imperfect state through his *nawābit*, who are identical with the "strangers".[41]

At the same time he is conscious that the *mutawaḥḥid* is subjected to extraneous influences, and so his nature must be protected. His "government" must be carefully studied and planned, on the analogy of the regimen which the physician prescribes for the patient. This holds good for the isolated *nābit* (*mufarrad*), and it must be considered "how he can reach blessedness [or happiness] if it does not exist, or how he can remove from himself the accidents that hinder him from ⟨gaining⟩ happiness, or what is possible of it.... But it is not possible in the three ways of life or a mixture of them."[42] The "three ways of life" apparently are the oligarchy, tyranny and democracy of the passage previously quoted. If this assumption is correct, the single *nābit* would be able to reach blessedness, wholly or in part, only in the *imām*-state. It is less likely that Ibn Bājja has in mind the three states which Al-Fārābī opposes to the ideal state in his *Siyāsa*.[43]

A discussion of Ibn Bājja's epistemology and psychology—in itself of the greatest importance for the *mutawaḥḥid*—would lead us too far from our immediate subject, his attitude to politics. Suffice it, therefore, to state that man shares with the animals the faculties of sense, imagination and memory, but the cogitative faculty is exclusively his own. This enables him to perceive the spiritual forms or *Intelligibles*. In conformity with Aristotle's *Nicomachean Ethics*, he sees the origin of human action in man's free will (*ikhtiyār*) by which he means "the will arising from reflection". In his view

> the majority of human actions in the four ways of life...consists of animal and human elements. It is rare to find the animal element isolated from the human...but the man who acts ⟨solely⟩ on the basis of ⟨right⟩ opinion and judgement without any regard for his animal soul... is more worthy that his action be ⟨considered⟩ divine than human. Therefore he is necessarily excellently endowed with the ethical virtues.[44]

From here Ibn Bājja goes on to a lengthy discussion of the spiritual forms, distinguishing universal, that is, superior and pure spiritual forms from individual, that is, inferior spiritual forms mixed with matter.[45] In this context he speaks of the errors which man is liable to make in his judgement, thereby affecting the state. Having no intention of discussing the various kinds of government, he stresses his exclusive concern with "the true government, because it is the most excellent *tadbīr* and because by it the *mutawaḥḥid* may perhaps be able to attain essential blessedness". Hypocrisy and ruse are found in the existing, imperfect states, and the use of sophistry is detrimental not only to the masses, but also to the principal citizens who imagine it to be that prudence of which Aristotle speaks "in the sixth ⟨Book of the *Nicomachean Ethics*⟩".[46] He then makes the claim that by nature man loves the spiritual forms and states: "The end of all human actions—provided man is a part of the state—is the state. But this is the case only in the ideal state." In the four simple or mixed imperfect states, the inhabitants consider all these forms from the point of view of the pleasure they derive from them as an end in itself. What are introductions, that is, means to a higher end, in the ideal state, are ends in the other four.[47]

This suggests that Ibn Bājja considered man as a part, or rather a citizen, of the state only in the ideal state. Here man contributes his share to the common weal and here only can he attain his highest perfection. The state is an institution which enables man to reach his human goal; its purpose is ultimately metaphysical.

Finally, Ibn Bājja examines the ends which the *mutawaḥḥid* pursues: corporeal-individual and universal spiritual forms. "If he is a part of the *imām*-state his ends have already been discussed in political science."[48] Which end it will be in each of the imperfect states depends on its character and on his actions as a *mutawaḥḥid*. The case of the ideal state has similarly been expounded in political science. In it, he will naturally exercise his powers of reason and reflection in investigation and judgement in order to attain all his ends. But when his rational faculty is not functioning, his actions are no higher than those of an animal, without any connection with his human nature. In this case, he cannot become a part of the state and must live in isolation.[49] This is reminiscent of what Ibn Bājja had said about the "*isolated nābit*". It is actually based on a passage in Al-Fārābī's *Siyāsa*,[50] immediately following the discussion of the various kinds of *nawābit*. There Al-Fārābī spoke of men who are like domesticated or even wild animals. If they are domesticated they are just good enough to be servants, but not to be citizens living in political associations.

Ibn Bājja's purely metaphysical object is clear from his definition of the philosopher as the virtuous divine man, who, perceiving the simple substantial intelligences, becomes himself an intelligence and reaches his ultimate end (by the union of his intellect with the Active Intellect). In explanation of the meaning of "intelligences" he refers to Aristotle's *De Anima*, *De Sensu et Sensibili* and *Metaphysica*.[51]

It is clear that the *mutawaḥḥid* ⟨this philosopher living in isolation outside the ideal state⟩ ought not to associate with mere corporeal beings, nor with anybody whose end is a spirituality mixed with corporeality. He should rather seek the company of those skilled in the sciences. Such men are now more numerous, now less, or even non-existent in some ways of life. Therefore the *mutawaḥḥid* is obliged, in some ways of life, to withdraw altogether from the society of men in so far as it is possible for him to do so. He should not mix with them, except to the extent required by necessity. Or he should emigrate to ways of life in which the sciences are ⟨cultivated⟩—if such ⟨ways of life⟩ exist. This is not in opposition to what is said in political science nor to what is made clear in physics. For it is made plain there that man is a political being [citizen] by nature, and in political science that retreat is wholly bad. But this is only so in principle; it is good in certain circumstances.[52]

It is clear from Ibn Bājja's subjective interpretation of the *zoon politikon* and from his disregard of the teachings of political science that he is not thinking of the ideal state of the *Republic* with its "pattern set up in the heavens", but rather of imperfect states, including those of his own time. Political reality forced him, concerned as he was with the individual soul and its perfection, to acknowledge the imperfection of existing states and to search for a means to save the divine element in man. His remedy is the retreat of the mystic, as expressed in the terms used by Ibn Sīnā, not the *zāhid*, the ordinary Sufi, but the *'ārif*, the speculative mystic.[53] Retreat is the only way to avoid contamination with the materialism, impurity and evil of imperfect society. This is the real meaning of his *mutawaḥḥid*, who sets himself apart in his *tadbīr*, self-government, and if necessary cuts himself off completely from social life and thus becomes the very negation of the *zoon politikon*.

The complement of this retreat is Ibn Bājja's interpretation of Plato's metaphorical description of the state of the blessed as "gazing into the sun".[54] This means, he says, that man perceives "existing things", or reality. This is the highest degree of that ascent to union with the Active Intellect which assures blessedness. Unlike Al-Fārābī and Ibn Rushd, Ibn Bājja thus rejects the Platonic demand of service to the community in terms of the civic obligation of the philosopher. Plato expresses this in the *Republic* in these words:

> Then when they are fifty, those who have come safely through and proved the best at all points in action and in study must be brought at last to the goal. They must lift up the eye of the soul to gaze on that which sheds light on all things, and when they have seen the Good itself, take it as a pattern for the right ordering of the state and of the individual, themselves included. For the rest of their lives, most of their time will be spent in study; but they will all take their turn at the troublesome duties of public life and act as rulers for their country's sake, not regarding it as a distinction, but as an unavoidable task. And so, when each generation has educated others like themselves to take their place as guardians of the commonwealth, they will depart to dwell in the Islands of the Blest.[55]

Ibn Bājja's self-rule of the philosopher in isolation from the community is in direct contrast with Plato's insistence on the contribution of all to the welfare of the community. He demands this in particular of the philosopher, whose duty it is to govern so as to ensure the best rule:

It is for us, then, as founders of a commonwealth to bring compulsion to bear on the noblest natures. They must be made to climb the ascent to the vision of Goodness, which we called the highest object of knowledge, and, when they have looked upon it long enough, they must not be allowed, as they now are, to remain on the heights, refusing to come down again to the prisoners or to take any part in their labours and rewards, however much or little these may be worth....

The law is not concerned to make any one class specially happy, but to ensure the welfare of the commonwealth as a whole. By persuasion or constraint it will unite the citizens in harmony, making them share whatever benefits each class can contribute to the common good; and its purpose in forming men of that spirit was not that each should be left to go his own way, but that they should be instrumental in binding the community into one.[56]

Ibn Bājja wants to leave his philosopher on the summit of his beatific vision and would not bring him down into the cave of civic duty, of social obligation. He does not acknowledge a law that binds all citizens alike in harmonious co-operation for the welfare of the whole community, each according to his natural disposition and acquired skill. He seems to hold with the philosophers' "compeers in other states" who "may quite reasonably refuse to collaborate: there they have sprung up, like a self-sown plant, in spite of their country's institutions; no one has fostered their growth, and they cannot be expected to show gratitude for a care they have never received".[57]

If I am not mistaken, we have here the source for the *nawābit* in Al-Fārābī and Ibn Bājja. The latter is nearer to Plato than the former who, as we have seen, distinguishes between various kinds of *nawābit*. Ibn Bājja only accepted the positive kind and, in agreement with the passage from the *Republic* quoted above, identified his *mutawaḥḥid* with this "stranger".

Ibn Bājja, though ever mindful of the pattern of the ideal state, turned his back on it and searched for a way to attain blessedness in the existing imperfect states, or as much blessedness as circumstances would permit. The outcome of his reflection is the self-government of the speculative thinker, who retreats into his own self and strives for perfection and happiness, if necessary by complete withdrawal from the society in which, unless it be the ideal state, he is inevitably a stranger. In his self-imposed solitude he spends his time in study and contemplation and is a law unto himself. His egotism is only justified on the grounds that in perceiving reality he draws near to God the creator and lord of the universe, who desires man to know himself and through his self-knowledge to proceed to the knowledge of God. He thus resembles Plato's "compeers in other states".

Yet Plato was determined to realize the ideal state, based on justice through a law which ultimately derives from the gods, as he states in the *Laws*. For this reason he addresses the philosophers in the ideal state of his dream (in contrast to "their compeers in other states") in these words:

But, ...it is not so with you. We have brought you into existence for your country's sake as well as for your own, to be like leaders and king-bees in a hive; you have been better and more thoroughly educated than those others and hence you are more capable of playing your part both as men of thought and as men of action. You must go down, then, each in his turn, to live with the rest and let your eyes grow accustomed to the darkness. You will then see a thousand times better than those who live there always; you will recognize every image for what it is and know what it represents because you have seen justice, beauty, and goodness in their reality; and so you and we shall find life in our commonwealth no mere dream, as it is in most existing states, where men live fighting one another about shadows and quarrelling for power, as if that were a great prize; whereas in truth government can be at its best and free from dissension only where the destined rulers are least desirous of holding office.[58]

Ibn Bājja not only rejected Plato's demand that the philosopher as citizen of the ideal state has a duty to this state. In his passionate concern for the individual's happiness and perfection he sought and found a way in an imperfect and uncongenial world, by his advocacy of isolation and retreat. In so doing he turned his back on Plato and Aristotle as well as on Islam, and its definite social obligations and observances. This asocial or even anti-social behaviour is matched by his one-sided application of the *Sharī'a* as a means merely to bring about with divine help what man's natural ability can achieve unaided: the knowledge and understanding of reality. If ever there was a rationalist in medieval Islam, it was Ibn Bājja, as his bold definition of "the other life" unmistakably shows. In this extreme rationalism and in his denial of social responsibility and civic duty he stands alone among the *Falāsifa*, in spite of his quest for the *amor Dei intellectualis*.

CHAPTER IX

IBN RUSHD: THE CONSUMMATION

WITH Ibn Rushd[1] (Averroes to the Schoolmen) we return to the main stream of Platonic tradition in political philosophy. His high regard for his compatriot Ibn Bājja did not hinder him from being critical of some of his opinions. He gave him full credit for his attempt to solve the intricate problem of the union between the human and the Active Intellect. In spite of Ibn Bājja's incomplete and often obscure treatment Ibn Rushd considers the *K. ittiṣāl* worthy of a commentary by himself,[2] as I mentioned in the last chapter. In the context of our exposition of political thought in Islam two criticisms are relevant. In the epilogue to his commentary on Aristotle's *Nicomachean Ethics*, Ibn Rushd expresses surprise that Ibn Bājja believed that Plato's *Republic* offered a complete discussion of the ideal state, and he is sure that Ibn Bājja would not have made such a statement if he had been familiar with the completeness and perfection of Aristotle's treatment.[3] This seems to reflect a different attitude to Plato on the part of Ibn Rushd, who almost always sides with Aristotle if he is at variance with Plato. For Ibn Rushd must have known from his study of Ibn Bājja's writings that Ibn Bājja knew both the *Nicomachean Ethics* and Al-Fārābī's commentary on it. Ibn Rushd is thinking in the first place of Aristotle's discussion of the imperfect states and of Plato's omission to speak of the third category of citizens in the same way as he had discussed the other two, the philosophers and the Guardians. Next, he noticed that Plato did not deal with the laws which should be common to the imperfect states, a topic which Aristotle treats in his *Politica*.

Of far greater significance is Ibn Rushd's strong disagreement with Ibn Bājja's assertion that man must if necessary isolate himself from the community in order to gain perfection. Commenting on Aristotle's statement that man is "a political being by nature" Ibn Rushd says: "This means that it is impossible for him to live without the state...."[4] He is equally emphatic in his detailed commentary on the *Republic*. While he is convinced that man can reach his highest perfection only in the ideal state, he insists that no man can live, let alone reach happiness and perfection, outside any kind of political association.

To understand and evaluate Ibn Rushd's political thought, we must include, in addition to his commentaries on the *Republic* and the *Nicomachean Ethics*, his spirited defence of philosophy (*Tahāfut al-tahāfut*) against Al-Ghazālī's attack, and his other polemical treatises on the philosophy of religion (*Faṣl al-maqāl*, *Ḍamīma* and *Manāhij*).

For Ibn Rushd is more conscious than Al-Fārābī of the supremacy of the *Sharī'a* as the ideal revealed law, and of its political function as the ideal constitution of the ideal state. This consciousness expresses itself in clear formulations and explicit assertions which leave no doubt about his importance, next to Ibn Sīnā, as *the* religious philosopher of Islam, a title he deserves as much as the one by which he is better known, namely as *the* medieval commentator of Aristotle.

But the vindication of the *Sharī'a* as the supreme authority in the ideal state—which he provides as a philosopher, not as a Muslim jurist (which he was as well)—is not his only claim to consideration as a political thinker. He takes Plato's political philosophy seriously, accepts his basic conclusions as valid and only subject to occasional modification in the light of Aristotle's thought, and considers them as applicable to his own civilization and state. Consequently he applies Plato's ideas on politics as general principles to Islam, past and present (especially present). In this way, his commentary on the *Republic* becomes at the same time a philosopher's comment on and critique of contemporary Muslim political institutions, especially those in the Maghreb. Frequent references to the history of the Muslim West (Spain and North Africa) in the eleventh and twelfth centuries form an integral and valuable part of his *Commentary*. His position as physician at the court of two Almohad rulers, Abū Ya'qūb Yūsuf and Abū Yūsuf Ya'qūb Al-Manṣūr, with both of whom he had often engaged in philosophical argument, gave him first-hand knowledge of affairs of state. Moreover, as *qāḍī* of Cordoba he took an active part in the civil administration. Under the Almoravids, the predecessors of the Almohads, this office involved applying Muslim law in the law courts, and also extended to the whole civil administration, as we know from the activities of Ibn Rushd's grandfather Abū Walīd, Grand Qāḍī of Cordoba.[5]

But before we can deal with this novel side of Ibn Rushd's commentary on the *Republic* we must touch at least briefly on his vindication of the *Sharī'a* as applied to the problem of revealed law and reason. At the present stage of our knowledge of the entire work of Ibn Rushd, our conclusions are bound to be provisional. In view of the widely assumed extreme rationalism of Ibn Rushd and of the claim that in his mind philosophy was superior to "religion", such a reservation is necessary and important. Any evaluation of his thought will perhaps always remain controversial since a certain subjectivity can never be entirely excluded from the mind of the student of Averroes' philosophy as a whole. To my mind, other obstacles are more serious, such as the apparent loss of much of Ibn Rushd's theological and legal writings and the fact that his commentary on the *Republic* and that on the *Nicomachean Ethics* are both extant only in a Hebrew version which leaves much to be desired. While the commentary on the *Republic* is now available in my critical edition of the Hebrew version,[6] that on the *Nicomachean Ethics* is still in manuscript and as yet largely unexplored.

Since I have dealt fully with this problem elsewhere[7] I shall confine myself here to a summary. I begin with the assertion that Ibn Rushd was a Muslim philosopher, and more pronouncedly so than Al-Fārābī or even Ibn Sīnā, on whose writings his own philosophy is dependent, both in what he accepted and in what he rejected. That means that he was a Muslim first and a disciple of Plato, Aristotle and their commentators second, but I do not deny that Ibn Rushd is not always consistent and unambiguous. But consistency is a rare intellectual virtue and not only medieval thinkers sinned against it. Due allowance should also be made for the fundamental difference in approach to revelation, and to the problem of revelation and reason, which separates us from the Middle Ages. Moreover, Islam was not encumbered by so elaborate and rigid a body of dogma as was the Church, though the cry of unbelief and heresy was raised in Islam no less often and to no less devastating effect.

In the case of Ibn Rushd, it must be remembered that he lived under the Almohads, champions of orthodoxy and defenders of the purity of Sunnī Islam. The two caliphs whom he served were enlightened, and what is more, students of philosophy. But the state was under the dominant influence of the doctors of theology and of law, the *'ulamā* and the *fuqahā*, who were strongly opposed to philosophy. While, therefore, a certain caution and circumspection was called for on the part of Ibn Rushd, it does not seem necessary to doubt that he meant what he wrote. Until clear evidence can be produced to show that his "religious" statements are merely lip-service, and that his own writings must be examined in the way which he claimed to be a right and a duty in reading the Qur'ān and the other sources of religious law (namely, that an inner meaning must be found, in addition to the plain, external meaning), I accept his statements at their face value. The interpretation offered here is provisional, for the reasons suggested, and assumes that there is no compelling reason to look for such a hidden meaning contradicting the plain sense. Moreover, his spirited defence of philosophy (*ḥikma* or *falsafa*) and philosophers (*Falāsifa*) against Al-Ghazālī, and in particular against the *Mutakallimūn*,[8] the dialectic theologians, is clear evidence that he was serious in his claim that the intention of philosophy is identical with that of the *Sharī'a*.[9] His forceful plea that the metaphysician alone—as opposed to the *faqīh* and the *mutakallim* (the jurist and the theologian)—has the right and duty to supply a rational interpretation of revelation by means of demonstrative argument, and his rejection of the dialectical arguments of theology as inadequate, misleading and dangerous, point in the same direction.[10]

In this spirit and for this practical reason he wrote his three polemical treatises on the philosophy of religion: in defence of the superiority of the *Sharī'a* as the ultimate arbiter of faith and practice, doctrine and observance, and in order to stake a claim that only the metaphysician was qualified correctly to interpret those beliefs and convictions of the *Sharī'a* which would lend themselves to rational explanation.

This claim represents the positive side of his defensive position, which is the result of Al-Ghazālī's attack on philosophy. For, subsequent to this attack, Muslim philosophers had to be more cautious and accommodating to traditional concepts. The very success of Ibn Rushd's defence of philosophy bears this out and thereby acknowledges Al-Ghazālī's authority.

It is surely significant that Ibn Rushd states in the *Faṣl* that "philosophy is the companion and foster-sister of the *Sharī'a*",[11] and in his commentary on the *Republic* which has a different purpose and is addressed to a different public:

> ...the only way to know what it is that God wills...is ⟨through⟩ prophecy. If you investigate the laws, this knowledge is divided into abstract knowledge alone—such as our religious law commands regarding the perception of God—and into practice, such as the ethical virtues it enjoins. Its intention in this respect is essentially the same as that of philosophy in respect of class and purpose.[12]

Once the identity of intention and purpose between revealed law and philosophy is established, the claim of the philosopher to interpret the "abstract knowledge" contained in the *Sharī'a* is justified. For Ibn Rushd says in the *Faṣl*:

> the aim of the law is only to teach true knowledge and true practice, and true knowledge is the knowledge of God and the other "Existing Things" in their reality, in particular the *Sharī'a*, and the knowledge of happiness and misery in the future world. True practice consists in adopting the actions which promote happiness and in avoiding those which promote misery.[13]

True knowledge is philosophical knowledge arrived at by demonstrative argument only. Revealed law, as the essence of religion, teaches the same truth as that which the metaphysician seeks to find by rational inquiry into the cause and nature of reality. There is thus only one truth, and it is incorrect to suppose that Ibn Rushd entertained the concept of double truth, a concept which must be attributed to the Averroists, but not to their master. Philosophy teaches the few elect, religion the masses; this is how the distinction between the two is attributed to the *Falāsifa*. But it is not quite correct, at least in the case of Ibn Rushd. We have already encountered the distinction between the elect philosophers and the masses of the people in Al-Fārābī and have seen that he attributed it to Plato. It would be more correct to formulate it, in respect of the *Sharī'a*, thus: philosophy is the province of the philosopher; religion is for all, philosophers and masses alike. The "abstract knowledge" contained in the law can be fully acquired and understood only by the philosopher who applies demonstrative proof; the masses have to accept the apparent or literal sense of its metaphors and parables, that is, as poetical and rhetorical statements. But the law contains the whole truth which is not distinct from the philosopher's truth, but is superior, whether it can be grasped rationally or not, because it springs from God's infallible wisdom and not from man's fallible reason.

Ibn Rushd insists on the inadequacy of human reason to fathom the hidden truth completely; therefore certain statements of the law must be accepted in their literal meaning. It is forbidden to speculate, for example, on such concepts as God's providence, which for him extended to the smallest particulars, or reward and punishment in the hereafter and such commandments as the ceremonial laws. In other words, he excludes the practical beliefs and observances which are obligatory for all.[14] It is thus clear that revelation sets reason certain limits. But outside these limits man has a duty, imposed upon him by the law, to seek a rational explanation, if he is capable of demonstrative argument. By this limitation medieval philosophy forfeits sovereign independence, since it is *under* the law, and it becomes religious philosophy.

One problem remains, however, though it is more limited in application, and it is this: How can the findings of human reason be harmonized with the perfectly true and absolutely binding teachings of a law which is divinely revealed through prophecy and enshrined in the *Sharī'a*? The philosopher answers: not by dialectical arguments (*jadal*) of the theologians, the representatives of *Kalam*, but by certain demonstrative argument (*burhān yaqīnī*). Principles (*uṣūl*) like the existence of God, his sending of prophets, and reward and punishment in the hereafter, are accessible to all three classes of men and all three types of argument; therefore their external meaning must be accepted by all Muslims.[15] But apart from these, there remains a residue of teachings which are inaccessible to demonstration, e.g. the ceremonial laws.

This is, I believe, the position of Ibn Rushd in his defence of philosophy and in his insistence on the perfect nature of revealed truth. It also explains why he confined himself to the theoretical statements in the *Republic* and ignored the mythical element, and why with the help of Aristotle he sometimes turned a dialectical statement in Plato into a demonstrative one. The quotation from his commentary on the *Republic* (p. 179) shows how by his recognition of the supreme authority of the *Sharī'a* he adapted to the requirements of Islam Plato's demand that the philosopher must have the right beliefs and convictions. The *Sharī'a*, as the divinely revealed prophetic law, is thus the Islamic equivalent of the constitution of the ideal state. The philosopher, who alone can penetrate to the inner meaning of this law by means of demonstrative arguments, has thus the most important political function in the Muslim state. Hence Ibn Rushd's opposition to the *Mutakallimūn* who use dialectical arguments which are insufficient, liable to be false and therefore damaging to the faith of the masses; hence also his insistence that the philosophers—whose claim to be the only legitimate interpreters of the theoretical teachings of the *Sharī'a* by means of *certain* demonstrative arguments he had put forward in the *Faṣl*—must on no account divulge the inner meaning, the hidden truth, to the masses who cannot rise to demonstrative arguments. For as a Muslim he is concerned for the purity of Islam and for the orthodoxy of the masses. He even invokes the "secular" power of the Almohad government in his appeal to the caliph to forbid the *Mutakallimūn* to divulge the "inner" meaning, arrived at by dialectic, to the masses, lest they become confused, and fall into schism and heresy.[16] For dialectical arguments are insufficient to penetrate to the truth of revelation, and divisions result among those using them; only demonstrative arguments can, with certain reservations, reach that goal. The *Sharī'a* contains all three classes of arguments, which correspond with the intellectual capacity of the three classes of the Muslim community; so each class can gain the religious truth appropriate to it, by demonstrative, or dialectical, or rhetorical and poetical arguments.[17] It is the philosopher's task to reveal the identity of the infallible truth of revealed law and the same truth of speculation arrived at by demonstration.

This attitude shows Ibn Rushd in full agreement with Almohad doctrine. This had been formulated by Ibn Tūmart and made the basis of the Almohad state by his disciple 'Abd al-Mu'min, the founder and first caliph of the Almohad dynasty. Some Almohad principles are relevant to the understanding of Ibn Rushd's position and must therefore be briefly stated. Ibn Tūmart demanded faith in the unity of God, supplemented by knowledge of the *Sharī'a* and its teachings. He excluded subjective opinion from interpretation, but commended the use of *qiyās shar'ī* (legal deduction by analogy). So far Ibn Rushd in his endeavour to explain the *Sharī'a* would agree. But as a philosopher he insisted on *qiyās 'aqlī* (logical deduction by analogy) which Ibn Tūmart had excluded from the *uṣūl al-fiqh*, the principles of jurisprudence. Being opposed to *Kalam* as developed by Al-Ash'arī and his school, Ibn Rushd was also opposed to Ibn Tūmart in matters of theology. But here he was on safe ground, since his two masters, the second and third caliphs, in their preoccupation with *Fiqh* had moved away from Ibn Tūmart's theology. Ibn Rushd was opposed to *ta'wīl*, allegorical interpretation, and to *taqlīd*, the interpretation of *Fiqh* based on the authority of an independent jurist (*mujtahid*). We know from the historian Al-Marrākushī that the Caliph Abū Yūsuf Ya'qūb ordered Mālikī *Fiqh*-books to be burned because he objected to *taqlīd*.[18] In his *Faṣl* Ibn Rushd acknowledged the reform of the Almohads in these words:

> Allah has removed many of these evils (e.g. hatred and enmity through sects), follies and erroneous ways through this ruling power, and has made a path for many good things, and in particular for those who follow the way of speculation and are eager for a knowledge of the truth....He has called the masses—in respect of the knowledge of God—to a middle way which is far above the low level of the *muqallidūn* ⟨who practise *taqlīd*⟩, but below the disputatiousness of the *mutakallimūn*. He has awakened the elect to the need for a complete theoretical inquiry into the root-principle of the *Sharī'a*.[19]

Allowing for a possible tendency to flatter the Almohad rulers, this passage suggests that the Almohads did something to acquaint the masses with the plain meaning of the *Sharī'a*, contrary to the practice prevailing under the Almoravids, their predecessors, who kept the masses ignorant. It must also mean that they raised no objection to the activity of men like Ibn Ṭufail and Ibn Rushd in expounding the inner meaning of the *Sharī'a* by means of demonstrative arguments.

In this respect it is, however, rather Ibn Ḥazm than Ibn Tūmart to whom Ibn Rushd could appeal for support, for it is Ibn Ḥazm who allows a departure from *ẓāhir*, the clear, external meaning, when sense-perception and experience demand a different interpretation.[20] In the *Faṣl* Ibn Rushd contrasts the method of the philosopher with that of the jurist and the dialectic theologian: the former has certain knowledge on the basis of demonstrative proof, "syllogism of certainty", whereas the latter lack certainty since they rely on "syllogism of (subjective) opinion".[21] The philosopher alone possesses the knowledge and the means to interpret the *Sharī'a*.

In this connection Ibn Rushd's concept of prophecy is of great importance and deserves notice. We recall that only prophecy can declare and elucidate the will of God, and it does so in a revelation which takes the form of law. This law tells man what his highest good is and how to attain it.

Prophecy is the source of the *Sharī'a*. How do we know that it is true? The answer is that the Qur'ān, "the precious Book", is the true warranty of prophecy. The Qur'ān is the miracle that confirms the prophetic character of Muḥammad who is the seal (that is, the last) of the prophets. Prophecy ceased with Muḥammad, and the wise—the philosophers—are heirs to the prophets in knowledge of God.

We do not, to my knowledge, find in any of Ibn Rushd's extant writings any trace of the psychological explanation of prophecy as we have it in Al-Fārābī and Ibn Sīnā. He stresses the legislative function of the prophet by means of divine revelation (*waḥy*). The prophet promulgates laws (*sharā'i'*) which enable man to reach perfect happiness, mediate knowledge (*'ilm*) of God, the angels, reality, reward and punishment and of the hereafter, teach good actions and forbid vicious religious convictions (*i'tiqādāt fāsida*) and evil actions.[22]

Miracles take second place with Ibn Rushd; it is more important that the prophet performing them is virtuous and truthful—we know that Plato permits his philosopher-kings to lie. It was the bringing down of the Qur'ān to Muḥammad that made him a prophet, and the giving of the law on Sinai that made Moses a prophet, not the dividing of the Red Sea at the Exodus from Egypt. That this is really Ibn Rushd's view of prophecy is clear from a statement by him in a strictly philosophical work (his *Tahāfut al-tahāfut*): his defence of the *Falāsifa* against Al-Ghazālī's attack. He affirms that the prophets lay down "religious laws which conform to the truth and impart a knowledge of those actions by which the happiness of the whole creation is guaranteed".[23]

Naturally, since men are diverse in their natural aptitude and capabilities, happiness is relative to their disposition; but each individual is guaranteed his share of happiness and perfection by the Prophet's law. This law enables man to acquire the practical arts without which he could not live in this world; the speculative virtues needed in this world and in the hereafter; and the ethical virtues, whose possession alone provides the basis for man's perfection in the speculative virtues.

There is thus no difference between the *Tahāfut al-tahāfut* and the *Manāhij*, though in the latter Ibn Rushd clearly differentiates between the knowledge of the philosopher and that of the prophet. The claim that the *Sharī'a* provides for the happiness of all raises in his mind the natural question: how does the prophetic lawgiver know what this happiness is, and by what means can the individual reach it? The prophet possesses certain knowledge through the mastery of speculative sciences and in particular through the promulgation of religious laws with precise regulations and statements about the circumstances of the hereafter.[24] The speculative philosopher, on the other hand, has only knowledge acquired by the study of the speculative sciences, unaided by revelation; hence he cannot lay down laws derived from the Qur'ān and, as a result, he cannot provide for the happiness of the masses. This statement, of the utmost importance in itself, is further clarified in the *Tahāfut al-tahāfut*, to the effect that philosophy explains the happiness of some elect intellects and the study of philosophy is a sign of man's humanity. The religious laws, by contrast, teach the masses and lead them to happiness.[25]

Taken by itself, this looks like the familiar division into the few elect philosophers and the masses, and has given rise to the assumption that religion is something inferior, good enough for the masses, but not the proper sphere for metaphysicians. Against this interpretation there stands the passage already quoted from the same book about the "happiness of the whole of creation". This must include the philosophers, whom Ibn Rushd explicitly admonishes to choose the best religion, which in his time is Islam, just as it was Judaism for Israel and Christianity for Rome. He speaks as a Muslim political philosopher and not primarily as a metaphysician.

His vindication of the *Sharī'a* goes far beyond anything the earlier *Falāsifa* had attempted, who were content with asserting its superiority because of its provision for the hereafter. For he not only boldly insists on its absolute truth, but also emphasizes its universal character. If we add to this, in the absence of a contrary theory, his traditional interpretation or rather definition of prophecy, we realize that among the *Falāsifa* he is in a class apart.

In yet another respect he goes beyond his predecessors: in his realization of the political character and significance of the prophetic law. In his commentary on the *Republic* he frequently compares and contrasts religious and human laws, a topic that will be considered more fully later on. The aim of the *Sharī'a* is the same as that of political science, a branch of practical philosophy, as set out by Aristotle in his *Nicomachean Ethics*, taken over by Al-Fārābī, as we have seen, and repeated by Ibn Rushd in his commentaries on the *Republic* and the *Nicomachean Ethics*. Thus prophecy, metaphysics and politics all have the same aim: man's happiness. He is here at one with Al-Fārābī and Ibn Sīnā.

The purpose of the state is to lead its citizens to their goal by the observance of a law. But only the prophetic lawgiver who is also a philosopher can lay down a law which guarantees the twofold happiness in the ideal *Sharī'a*-state, ruled by the *imām*. The Islamic state *is* the ideal polity; it is the highest expression of Islamic civilization, just as the *Republic*, the Greek polity, is the political ideal of Greek civilization. But the *khilāfa* is not simply the *Politeia* of Plato transferred and adapted to Islamic conditions. Although both are based on law, the *Sharī'a*, as revealed prophetic law, is superior to the *nomos*, as revelation is superior to myth.

The commentator of the *Republic* is aware of the common ground that exists between the religious law which he applies as judge, and the general, human law "the adoption of which no nation can escape". Jewish medieval thinkers expressed this same idea when they affirmed that all men would eventually arrive at the same ethical laws after a long time of trial and error. But the revealed law stipulates them, in absolute perfection, from the beginning. Such a law, therefore, is the foundation of the perfect state. But not all nations have a revelation, and Ibn Rushd asserts that of the "secular" states Plato's is the best.[26] The close link between politics and law, though implied in the teaching and practice of Islam, became clear to the *Falāsifa* through their study of Plato and Aristotle. This explains Ibn Rushd's interest in the *Republic* and his application of Platonic ideas to the Muslim state, as we shall see later.

It is also characteristic of his commentary on Aristotle's *Nicomachean Ethics*. Reproducing one of Aristotle's statements, he says of the *mudabbir* (the regent or ruler), whose principal concern is for Virtue, that he strives to make the citizens "good, excellent and submissively bent under the laws".[27] He agrees with Aristotle when he stresses that the chief function of the ruler is his guardianship of justice: "when he guards justice, he guards equality". He accepts Aristotle's definition: "political justice is partly natural, partly legal, that is, conventional", distinguishing with Aristotle between "justice in the absolute sense" and "political justice". Of the latter he says, again with Aristotle, "it exists when there is naturally a law between them [the citizens]. Justice then consists in that some are rulers and others accept rule; this means that true justice only exists between men who are either rulers or ruled."[28] There is a similar tendency in his commentary on the *Republic*, especially where he makes Plato's preoccupation with justice his own. The just state is based on law.

Ibn Rushd also uses Aristotle's distinction between natural and conventional rules of justice in respect of Plato's *Republic*.[29] He differentiates between general and particular laws. The former are common to all nations and necessary to their political organization; they correspond to Aristotle's natural laws. The latter vary from nation to nation. This applies in particular to ceremonial laws, that is, regulations governing prayer, fasts, festivals, sacrifices, ritual cleanliness and the glorification of God. In his commentary on the *Nicomachean Ethics* he makes them vary, as Ibn Sīnā had done, with every nation, religion, time and place. In this he followed the lead of Aristotle himself.[30] He calls these laws "necessary political institutions" in his *Tahāfut al-tahāfut*,[31] in accordance with his adaptation of Plato's demands in the *Republic* to Islam. Here he also includes the teaching of right beliefs and convictions, again accepting Plato's requirements. It must be stressed that in this vital point Islamic and Platonic teaching are at one, notwithstanding their different concepts of God, angels and prophets. I am inclined to think that the use of the term *madanīya*, "political", usually indicates that the writer is a disciple of Plato and Aristotle, and that the Greek philosophers have helped him to see the political implications and significance of the ceremonial laws of Islam. For we must remember that Ibn Rushd studied Plato not only as a Muslim but also as a commentator of Aristotle. This is clear from this statement at the beginning of his commentary on the *Republic*:

The first part of this art ⟨of Politics⟩ is contained in Aristotle's... *Nicomachea*, and the second part in his...*Politica*, and in Plato's book also upon which we intend to comment. For Aristotle's *Politica* has not yet come into our hands. But before we begin with a detailed commentary on these treatises, it is fitting that we should mention what was explained in the first part and may be laid down as a root-principle for what we should first like to say here:....[32]

While this should not be taken to mean that the *Republic* is merely a substitute for the *Politica*, it is clear that Ibn Rushd attached the greatest importance to the first, theoretical part—the *Nicomachean Ethics*—and looked upon it as the foundation of the second, practical part—the *Politica* and the *Republic*. Both are complementary parts of a whole—political science—just as wisdom and prudence are both needed to achieve absolute justice in the ideal state.

In the epilogue to his commentary on the *Nicomachean Ethics* Ibn Rushd refers to Aristotle's *Politica* as "the book in which ⟨is contained⟩ the perfection of wisdom", since, in the words of Aristotle ("the philosopher"), "that which is ⟨contained⟩ in Plato's *Politeia* is not complete". After a brief account of the contents of the *Republic* (transformation of the simple states into one another, etc.), Ibn Rushd points out that Plato did not speak of the laws which should apply to the simple states in common, but that Aristotle intended to do so, "and it was something which was not achieved in the books of Plato".[33] Commenting on *Republic* 424f., Ibn Rushd stresses the importance of general laws and the danger to them and to the state which any departure is bound to present. He says:

This is evident from the case of those men who, if they grow up under such general laws and statutes, arrive by their own effort at many particular laws and good disciplines, such as honouring their parents, remaining silent before their elders and similar practical laws. It is therefore not right to lay down such particular matters as laws. If the general laws are firmly established, they lead the citizens by their own initiative easily towards those particular laws. . . . Anyone seeking to lay down these particular laws without having laid down the general ones—as has happened to many lawgivers—is, indeed, on the same level as a man treating sick persons who, because of their excessive desire for food, drink and sexual intercourse, are unable to receive any advantage from the remedies with which they are treated. . . .[34]

These examples show how Ibn Rushd blended Platonic with Aristotelian ideas and both with the teachings and regulations of Islamic law. Equally instructive is his treatment of wisdom as a political virtue, closely linked to law. For he introduces Plato's discussion of wisdom thus:

He began with wisdom and said it was manifest that this state was wise and possessed knowledge and wisdom. This means that it has a sound understanding of all the laws and ordinances which it advises and which we are going to mention. Good government and good counsel are without doubt a kind of knowledge, only we cannot say that this state possesses good government and good counsel on account of knowledge in the practical arts, like agriculture, carpentry and others. This being so, it possesses wisdom only in that knowledge which we are setting forth. It is evident that this wisdom can only be perfected through knowledge of the ⟨ultimate⟩ human aim, since this polity tends that way. It is also evident that we only perceive this human aim through the speculative sciences. Thus this state is necessarily spoken of as wise in two ⟨kinds of⟩ knowledge simultaneously, practical and theoretical.[35]

Citing *Republic* 428c–e Ibn Rushd gives wisdom a markedly Aristotelian meaning, as we find it defined in the *Nicomachean Ethics*.[36] Al-Fārābī had already anticipated Ibn Rushd's concept of the human aim and its attainment. Thanks to Ibn Rushd's more penetrating understanding of Plato and Aristotle his formulation is more precise, and his diction is much more terse.[37]

He deals similarly with the two remaining cardinal virtues, courage and temperance, and then returns once more to justice, paraphrasing *Republic* 433, 434, thus:

We say: in this state fairness and self-control which is the business of justice are simply what we said before regarding the government of this state. For we have already said that it was proper for every single man in this state to adhere to ⟨only⟩ one of the activities of the state, namely, the activity for which he is fitted by nature. This is the fairness (or equity) that bestows upon the state preservation and continuity, as long as it continues to exist in it. . . . This will result when the rulers and the masses are agreed by conviction to keep that which the laws demand. . . . So this state will be just by reason of the communities ⟨of just men?⟩ in it. For in it justice consists in every one of its citizens doing only that for which he is destined. This is civic (or, political) justice. . . .[38]

This quotation again shows that Ibn Rushd often makes Plato's discussion more explicit by the use of Aristotle. The term "political justice" comes from the *Nicomachean Ethics*, as we saw a little earlier.[39]

When discussing injustice as consisting in "every one of its citizens growing up with more than one occupation . . .", he points to "what happens in ⟨these⟩ states". Thus he clearly indicates the relevance and validity of Plato's views for the contemporary Muslim states in the Maghreb.

This application to the contemporary scene of Platonic ideas on government, and the duties of the rulers and the ruled, especially of the philosophers and Guardians, is a remarkable and novel feature of Ibn Rushd's commentary on the *Republic*. It is particularly so since he himself says that he commented on the *Republic* because Aristotle's *Politica* was not available. This Aristotelian treatise is considered as the second, practical part of political science, the *Nicomachean Ethics* being the first, theoretical part. Besides, this feature is absent from all his other extant commentaries, including that on the *Nicomachean Ethics*,[40] and is not to be met with in his great predecessor Al-Fārābī. These references are far more than mere illustrations of a point made by Plato. They must be understood as the reasoned critique of a Muslim philosopher trained in political philosophy by Plato and Aristotle. He could not rule, therefore he had to serve the state in other ways. It is significant that he combined in himself the two offices of physician and judge which are necessary only in imperfect states. It is hard to say whether he hoped to influence policy for the better by his sustained criticism of political and social groups and institutions of the contemporary state in the Maghreb (and of the past century as well). We only know from a few personal remarks that his official duties occupied most of his time, and that he found it hard to gain the necessities of life.[41] On the other hand, these official duties permitted him an insight into men and affairs which a philosopher would rarely enjoy. He used his experience to test Plato's theories, developed in different circumstances, against his own state and civilization.

In doing so, he was conscious not only of the authority of Plato and Aristotle in general philosophy, and especially in political science, but also of that of the ideal *Sharī'a*-state of early Islam. This was the Golden Age of the first four caliphs, treasured in Muslim memory as the ideal theocracy following and developing the Prophet's legacy and laying the spiritual and temporal foundations of the Islamic empire. There are thus two focal points to which contemporary Islam is related in Ibn Rushd's mind: the ideal *Khilāfa* and the ideal *Politeia.* The *mulk* that partly transformed the legacy of early, pure Islam and yet preserved the ideal structure in theory and partly also in constitutional practice is for Ibn Rushd the Islamic counterpart of Plato's imperfect states. Accordingly, contemporary Muslim states in the Maghreb are compared either with the ideal *Khilāfa* and the ideal *Politeia*, or with timocracy, oligarchy, democracy and tyranny as understood by Plato; but they are also seen in relation to the *Sharī'a*, as approaching or receding from it. All this gives the commentary its specific character and lends it importance and value. For here an integration has been attempted between two different cultural and political patterns. This is immediately apparent if we compare Ibn Rushd's attitude to Plato with that of Al-Fārābī, from whose description of the imperfect states Ibn Rushd accepted so many features.[42] Or a comparison with Ibn Bājja's use of Platonic material,[43] or with Ibn Rushd's own strictly theoretical commentary on Aristotle's *Nicomachean Ethics* brings out more clearly the topicality of that on the *Republic.*

We consider first the ideal state. Ibn Rushd applies Plato's strictures on poetry (because it describes and imitates base and blameworthy actions and emotions) to the contemporary states:

I said: those poems should be eliminated which follow the Arab custom of describing these matters and of imitating things which are akin to them. For all these reasons, it is not proper on several counts to allow the poets in this state to imitate everything. Among them is that the activity of one imitator is only excellent if one man imitates in one kind, as is the case in the arts....[44]

While this is in keeping with the general attitude in Islam on religious and moral grounds to pre-Islamic poetry, there is also a political element in Ibn Rushd's thought, since he accepts Plato's view of the danger to the state arising out of the bad effect of such poetry on the character of the citizens.

The same applies to painters, and Ibn Rushd also agrees with Plato in his views on education in music,[45] which he considers relevant to his own time. He defends Plato against Galen's attack in connection with the right size of the state and the number of Guardians needed to protect it. Galen, he says, "indicated the power of the empire that existed in his time. But it can be seen from Plato that he did not make that statement ⟨about 1,000 Guardians⟩ wishing it to be unalterable....He said this only in relation to his time and nation, that is, the Greeks."[46]

Ibn Rushd's application to contemporary states of Plato's ideas about the equality of women in respect of civic duties is a mark of political realism and shows a courageous willingness to go against established Muslim thought and practice. After reproducing Plato's arguments he draws this conclusion:

In these states, however, the ability of women is not known, because they are only taken for procreation there. They are therefore placed at the service of their husbands and ⟨relegated⟩ to the business of procreation, for rearing and breast-feeding. But this undoes their ⟨other⟩ activities. Because women in these states are not being fitted for any of the human virtues it often happens that they resemble plants. That they are a burden on the men in these states is one of the reasons for the poverty of these states. They are found there in twice the number of men, while at the same time they do not, through training, support any of the necessary activities; except for a few which they undertake mostly at a time when they are obliged to make up their want of funds, like spinning and weaving. All this is self-evident.[47]

This outspoken criticism of the structure of Islamic society is the more astonishing in that it comes from an adherent of Almohad orthodoxy and from a man well versed in *Fiqh*. It shows that he boldly applied to Islamic civilization and life Platonic notions derived from an entirely different outlook and social organization. Plato's political principles, born of his philosophy, and based upon his experience of the Greek city-states, are considered valid, generally and in detail, and applicable to Muslim concepts and institutions. We cannot understand in any other sense his critical attitude to the Almoravid and Almohad states of the Maghreb, and his use of arguments against "false" philosophers (and especially against the *Mutakallimūn*) taken from Plato's attack on the Sophists. In the rule of the *Mutakallimūn* he saw the greatest danger to the state of his time. No doubt Ibn Rushd also had some personal stake in this matter; Berber fanaticism was not congenial to the flowering of philosophy, which could survive only under the personal protection of the Almohad caliphs.[48]

We have seen that Ibn Rushd considered Plato's method of bringing the ideal state into being as the best after the *Sharī'a*-state. He answers the objection that its coming into being is impossible, since nobody could possess all the qualities demanded of the philosopher-king, thus:

> The answer is that it is possible for men to grow up with these natural qualities, as we have described them, and at the same time to develop by choosing the general law, whose adoption no nation can escape. In addition, their own particular (religious) law should not be far from the human laws. Philosophy should already be perfected in their time. This is like the situation that prevails in our time and in our religious law. If it happens that such men are rulers...then it is possible....[49]

We note the connection between religious and general law and the opportunity which the *Sharī'a* gives for the emergence of the ideal state. Like Plato, Ibn Rushd was aware of the difficulties of such a state and of the imperfections of man and consequently of states. Convinced Muslim as he was, as a disciple of Plato and an acute observer of the contemporary scene he envisaged a secular or at least a mixed state as well. Though the manner described by Plato is the best

> it is also possible for it to come into being in a different manner, though then after a long time.[50] This is after a long succession of excellent kings ⟨ruling⟩ over these states; they will continue to influence these states gradually, until in time the best government will come into existence. Their influence will work in two ways at once, that is, by their activities and actions, and by their convictions. This will be easy or not easy according to the laws in existence at a given time, and to their being near

to this state or far ⟨from it⟩. In general, their influence is more likely to lead to excellent deeds than to sound convictions in the present time.[51]

The continuation of this passage and other references to contemporary states leave little doubt that Ibn Rushd measures existing states by the two ideal states of his experience as a Muslim and a disciple of Plato and Aristotle; hence a mixed state, composed of elements of the *Sharī'a*-state and of a secular state based on the laws of its kings. He continues:

You can test this in respect of these states. But on the whole it will not be difficult for him who has completed the study of ⟨all⟩ the parts of philosophy, as well as their manner of deviation from his ⟨Plato's⟩ opinion ⟨to realize⟩ that they will not improve by convictions ⟨alone⟩.

States that are excellent in their actions alone are called "priestly". It has already been stated that this state, namely the "priestly" state, existed among the ancient Persians.[52]

We have here Ibn Bājja's *imām*-state. In his discussion of Plato's imperfect states Ibn Rushd spoke of an *imām*-state of his own time which he connects with Plato's tyrannical constitution. This is in direct opposition to the democratic state. The transformation of democracy into tyranny arose over property which was at first public, but was later concentrated in the hands of the ruling families. "For this reason the 'priestly' part in them is today completely tyrannical."[53]

This means that the purpose of the ruling dynasty dictates the direction in which the subjects must bend their energies. They serve the ruler's ends, but he is not interested in their happiness, as is the ruler in the ideal state. Aristotle makes the same distinction between the king and the tyrant.

But this is not the case in the tyrannical state, for in it the masters seek no other aim in respect of the masses but their own. Therefore, the similarity between the "priestly" and the tyrannical states often leads the "priestly" parts that exist in these states to be transformed into tyrannical ones, thus bringing into disrepute him whose aim is "priestly". This is the case with the "priestly" parts that exist in the states to be found in our time.[54]

I take this passage to refer to the administration of the Almohad state with the Caliph Abū Ya'qūb Yūsuf as *imām* in succession to his father 'Abd al-Mu'min, who had restored pure Sunnī Islam as the disciple of Ibn Tūmart. Ibn Rushd, following Al-Fārābī, defines the *imām* as he "whom one follows ⟨as chief⟩ in his actions",[55] and identifies him with the philosopher-king and law-giver. The *imām*-state is based on the *Sharī'a*, and the *imām* tries to implement it, but is obviously hampered by political and economic circumstances which "bring him into disrepute". This may be an attempt on the part of Ibn Rushd to exculpate the caliph while incriminating the administration.

These passages must be read in conjunction with further critical references to the Almoravids and Almohads, whose states had undergone the same transformation as Plato's ideal state.

> You may understand what Plato states concerning the transformation of the ideal constitution into the timocratic, and that of the excellent into the timocratic man, from the case of the government of the Arabs in the earliest period. For they used to imitate the ideal constitution, and then were transformed in the days of Mu'āwiya into timocratic men. It seems to be the case with the constitution that exists now in these islands.[56]

This is quite in keeping with the orthodox interpretation of the Islamic state: first the four model caliphs, vicegerents of the Prophet Muḥammad, and then Mu'āwiya, the founder of the *mulk* and perverter of pure theocracy, whom Ibn Rushd sees as a timocratic ruler. By implication the ideal *khilāfa* is likened to the ideal *Politeia*, and the rule of Mu'āwiya to that of the Almohad rulers of his own time. He could hardly go further in criticizing the state of the patrons whom he served as judge and physician.

How completely Ibn Rushd correlated Muslim and Platonic states is clear from his characterization of the Almoravids:

> In general, the transformation of the timocratic into the hedonistic man is obvious, whether he takes delight in money or in the other remaining pleasures. The same seems to apply to the timocratic and the hedonistic state. For the plutocratic and the hedonistic state belong to the same category.[57]

These two constitutions are Ibn Rushd's addition to Al-Fārābī's "ignorant states in error". As I have said before, they represent a more specific exemplification of Plato's oligarchy.

> We often see kings becoming corrupted into such men. Similarly there is in our time the kingdom of men known as the Almoravids. At

first they imitated the constitution based on the law [that is, the *Sharī'a* of the *Khilāfa*]—this under the first of them [Yūsuf ibn Tāshfīn]—then they changed ⟨it⟩ under his son into the timocratic ⟨constitution⟩, while there was in him also an admixture of the love of money. Further it changed under his grandson into the hedonistic ⟨constitution⟩ with all the paraphernalia of the hedonists, and it perished in his time. The reason was that the constitution ⟨of the Almohads⟩ which was opposed to it at that time resembled the constitution based on the law.[58]

In other words, Ibn Rushd acknowledges the religious enthusiasm and the noble intentions of the founder of the Almoravid dynasty. We note that not lust for conquest and power moves the founder of a dynasty, but concern for the purity of Islam and the rule of its prophetic revealed law. This view implies that the weakening of the enthusiasm for pure Islam and consequently of the hold of the *Sharī'a* over the heirs and successors of the founder goes hand in hand with the growing assertion of the human desires for money, pleasures and luxury as the generations succeed each other. At the same time Ibn Rushd sees the decline and fall of a Muslim dynasty in terms of Plato's transformation of constitutions. By contrast, Ibn Khaldūn, as we saw in chapter IV, formulated the law of cyclical growth and decay of dynasties from observation of the states of his time, and from a study of the use of power in Islamic history, without being in any way influenced by Plato. He attributed decline and fall in part at least to a weakening of the *'Aṣabīya*, in this particular case of an *'Aṣabīya* strongly reinforced by and blended with religious zeal. But both Ibn Khaldūn and Ibn Rushd would agree that a declining dynasty inevitably brings on the scene a vigorous leader who can seize power and found a new dynasty.

Ibn Rushd gives a similar illustration of the transition from democracy into tyranny, where the year 540 A.H. marks the turning point in the Platonic sense.[59] His summing up of tyranny is equally significant and shows considerable courage in a man who was in the service of the ruling family.[60] He well illustrates the effect of constitutional changes on human character:

You can discern this in the qualities and morals that have sprung up among us since the year 540 ⟨A.H.⟩ among the rulers and dignitaries. For because the timocratic constitution in which they had grown up was weakened, they came by those vile character-traits which they now

⟨exhibit⟩. He only among them perseveres in the excellent virtue who is excellent in accordance with the religious laws, and this is rare with them.[61]

Such passages stand out as a sustained and outspoken criticism of the contemporary Muslim state in Spain, and are notable for their positive attitude to and evaluation of the *Sharī'a* and its moral power. Another interesting feature is Ibn Rushd's repeated reference to the year 540 A.H. as the climactic point in the inevitable process of change and deterioration in the character of the state. The decline coincides with a lessening of the authority of Islam and thus with a weakening of the rule of law. Therefore, the last passage and others similar to it must be seen against Aristotle's definitions and illustrations of law, equity and equality in the fifth book of his *Nicomachean Ethics*, especially v, vi, vii and x, which are reproduced and commented upon in Ibn Rushd's commentary. A few examples were given earlier in this chapter; a further illustration will show how Ibn Rushd applied Aristotle's principles and definitions even to Muslim law. That he replaces Greek notions by Islamic ones can often be observed in his commentary on the *Republic*; that he replaces Greek persons and proper names, meaningless to Muslim readers, is not surprising.[62] But here he explains Aristotle by an example taken from one of the principal institutions of Islam, namely, *jihād*, holy war, which is, as we know, one of the basic duties of every Muslim. He discusses Aristotle's definition and exposition of equity as a rectification of legal justice. Replacing Aristotle's example of the Lesbian builders' rule by the rules of war in Islam, Ibn Rushd tries to explain the character of a special ordinance as a rectification of a defective general law. The command, in the form of a general law, utterly to destroy the enemy proved injurious to the interests of the Muslim community, especially in view of the impossibility of fulfilling it. Therefore God took this into consideration and ruled that sometimes peace was preferable to war. It was thus the intention of the lawgiver to counteract the absolute obligation by commending peace and leaving the decision to those in authority.[63] This example illustrates two things: it shows the relevance of Greek concepts (here of law) to Islam; and also the importance of Aristotle's *Nicomachean Ethics* as the first theoretical part of political science.

To return to Ibn Rushd's point about the *Sharīʿa* as the guarantor of a ruler's excellence in virtue: it is clear that the superiority of the religious law could not be expressed more plainly, since only loyal observance of the *Sharīʿa* guarantees the continuity and permanence of the ideal state and its excellent citizens. Despite the relevance of the thought of his Greek masters, for Ibn Rushd first place and centre are ultimately claimed by the *Sharīʿa* and not by Plato's *Nomos* as it had been defined by Aristotle. The *khilāfa* and not the *Politeia* serves as the ideal pattern, as his example of the Almoravids and their inevitable replacement by the Almohads clearly shows. This means that Islamic values are, in the last resort, paramount, and that in a concrete historical and political situation Ibn Rushd's living Muslim legacy is stronger than his Platonic-Aristotelian theory. However, an element of realism is added by his remark about the rarity of the strict observance of the religious law.

Apart from this very important reservation concerning the *Sharīʿa*, Ibn Rushd recognizes in Plato's *Republic* and *Laws* and in Aristotle's *Nicomachean Ethics* an authority second to no other. There can be no doubt that the *Summary* of the *Laws* was available to him, as his threefold division of the laws, based on *Laws* 697, shows, as well as other passages.[64] Yet he is a critical commentator; he tests Plato's ideas not only by his own experience and with independent judgement, but also by the authority of Aristotle, whose theoretical and practical philosophy he applies to the *Republic*.

This concerns the theoretical parts in the first place. He is exclusively interested in them in conformity with his preference for demonstrative as against dialectical or rhetorical arguments. Thus, he does not comment on Books I and X, notably the myth of Er. He often supplements Plato's exposition with ideas and formulations taken from Aristotle, especially the *Nicomachean Ethics*. A notable feature of his commentary on the *Republic* are frequent introductions, which summarize the subsequent detailed commentary on Plato's discussion or supply a link between various sections. He also makes theoretical digressions, particularly in psychology and epistemology, based on Aristotle's *De Anima*, *De Physica* and *Metaphysica*. This usually involves a modification of Platonic doctrines in the light of Aristotle's thought and systematic formulation. On the whole, Ibn Rushd follows Plato in ethical and political questions (here there is substantial agreement between Plato and Aristotle in any case). Only rarely do we meet with statements like: "if this is not the opinion of Plato, it is, however, the opinion of Aristotle, and is undoubtedly the truth."[65]

Whereas Ibn Rushd when commenting on the *Republic* does not criticize the order in which Plato sets out the transformation of constitutions, he does so in his commentary on the *Nicomachean Ethics*.[66] He sides with Aristotle, in whose opinion monarchy deteriorates into tyranny, followed by timocracy and finally by democracy. He realized that Plato's thought was conditioned by the life of his own time. We saw this in his defence against Galen, and it is clear from his recognition that the education of the philosophers could not have begun with logic in Plato's time since it was Aristotle who later introduced it as a discipline. In his commentary on Plato's *Republic* he deems logic an indispensable element of the education for statesmen. Logic takes first place and mathematics—with which Plato lets their education begin—second.[67] The political significance of logic is thus clear. Ibn Rushd himself used Aristotle's *Analytica Posteriora* to good purpose, together with Aristotle's systematic presentation of physics and metaphysics, to convert many a persuasive or dialectical argument used by Plato into a demonstrative one. We have seen how Ibn Rushd's full use of the *Nicomachean Ethics* resulted in a clarification and amplification of Platonic statements about law and justice, and also economics.

If we add Ibn Bājja and especially Al-Fārābī as important contributors to Ibn Rushd's political philosophy, it will be apparent how complicated the affiliation of sources is, and how difficult it must remain to determine, in the absence of the Arabic version of the summaries of Plato's *Republic* and *Laws*, what can be attributed direct to Ibn Rushd and what must be assigned to Al-Fārābī as intermediary. But this difficulty cannot diminish the high degree of originality usually achieved by Ibn Rushd in his harmonious and systematic blending of Platonic and Aristotelian thought with Muslim notions. His division of political science into theoretical and practical parts[68] did not prevent his mind from blending the *Republic* with the *Nicomachean Ethics* so skilfully that the essential unity of both parts is at once apparent.

Some of the credit should go, no doubt, to Al-Fārābī, but exactly how much is difficult to decide. For though the origin is unmistakable Ibn Rushd compresses whatever of Al-Fārābī's discussions he incorporates in his comment and theoretical digressions. It must, however, be remembered that identity of terminology may go back to the common source of both: the Arabic versions of the *Republic*—most likely in the shape of Galen's *Summary*—and of the *Nicomachean Ethics* in political matters, and the aforementioned works of Aristotle in the theoretical digressions. There can be little doubt that much of the adaptation of Greek to Islamic notions goes back, as far as the *Republic* is concerned, to Ḥunain ibn Isḥāq's Arabic version of Galen's *Summary*, which is unfortunately lost. He may have turned Plato's gods into angels or demons, but we cannot be sure who replaced the Delphian Apollo by "what the Most High commanded through prophecy"—whether it was he or Ibn Rushd, who probably substituted Arab for Greek poetry.

Despite all the similarity and a good deal of actual borrowing by Ibn Rushd from Al-Fārābī, there is a fundamental difference in approach, purpose, interest and method between the two. Al-Fārābī worked Platonic ideas and material into his own treatises. But though they are based on Plato's dialogues the treatises are quite different in conception, form and content. Ibn Rushd wrote a detailed commentary on Books II–IX of the *Republic*. Al-Fārābī had a purely theoretical interest in politics as a part of practical philosophy. He concentrated on the qualifications of the prophet/philosopher/lawgiver/king/*imām*, his intellectual perfection and happiness. He described the imperfect states without going into detail about the reasons for and the means of their transformation one into the other. Nor is he interested in the correspondence between the individual and the state. He was a metaphysician, not a statesman, notwithstanding the greater realism of his *Fuṣūl al-madanīya*.[69] For him Plato's theories remained in the realm of speculation; the only adaptation is his synthesis between the ideal ruler of Islam and of Plato's *Republic*. But he never applied Platonic political ideas to contemporary Muslim states, not even by analogy.

Ibn Rushd's interest in Plato is a double one, theoretical as regards the perfection and happiness of rulers and ruled alike; and practical in the relevance and validity of Plato's ideas, analyses and judgements for his own state. And yet he took over, mostly without acknowledgement, considerable parts of Al-Fārābī's theoretical discussions and descriptions of the bad constitutions. This is due to the identical outlook of both as Muslim religious philosophers: they are agreed on the human end and how to attain it. Ibn Rushd took over the concept of the fourfold perfection (in the speculative, intellectual and ethical virtues and the practical arts) from the *K. taḥṣīl al-saʿāda*, although they go back to the *Nicomachean Ethics* where, however, they do not occur all together in any one passage.[70] Ibn Rushd is usually more concise and systematic. He apparently refers only once to Al-Fārābī's lost commentary on the *Nicomachean Ethics*[71] and in one other instance to his *K. al-siyāsa al-madanīya*,[72] but his indebtedness to his precursor is considerable, as I have shown elsewhere.[73] A few examples, in addition to those adduced in chapter VI, may illustrate this.

That the city-state is the smallest political unit wherein man can reach happiness goes back to the *Madīna fāḍila*;[74] Ibn Rushd's discussion of the intellectual virtues is a terse summary of Al-Fārābī's treatment in the *Taḥṣīl*.[75] He never simply copies his source, but modifies and condenses Al-Fārābī's usually long-winded description in the light of his own deeper understanding of Aristotle and of the political significance and relevance of Plato's argument. This is particularly the case in his treatment of the imperfect states, where he follows Plato much more closely, but at the same time makes use of Al-Fārābī's description.[76] In the chapter on Al-Fārābī I noted the curious fact that Al-Fārābī does not use the term for "oligarchy", but Ibn Rushd does, employing at the same time Al-Fārābī's terms for specific variants of oligarchy.

Our comprehension of several passages of Ibn Rushd's commentary on the *Republic* depends on Al-Fārābī, since the Hebrew translator either misread or misunderstood his Arabic original. In some instances, such borrowing is more likely to have taken place since it seems improbable that Galen would have raised terms used by Plato to characterize states to the rank of constitutions. For example, Al-Fārābī speaks of "states of necessity"; so does Ibn Rushd, but not Plato.[77] Again, Al-Fārābī, and after him Ibn Rushd, speak of "ignorant states" and of "states in error".[78]

In this connection it is worth remembering that Ibn Bājja used the terms "simple" and "mixed" of the imperfect states. Ibn Rushd has either taken over the term "simple" from Ibn Bājja or from the *Politikos* or more likely from the *Laws* of Plato.[79] It is certain that one of his *imām*-states goes back to Ibn Bājja, whereas the other may perhaps be found in Al-Fārābī's lost commentary on the *Nicomachean Ethics*; for both Ibn Bājja and he refer to Al-Fārābī, and Aristotle mentions the Persians there, though as parental tyrants.[80] It is probable that out of a combination of both Ibn Rushd developed his idea of the transformation of the "priestly" into the tyrannical part.

How Ibn Rushd used the material derived from Al-Fārābī may be seen from his deviation from Al-Fārābī in the matter of constitutions. Al-Fārābī looks upon tyranny as a mixed form, since it contains elements of timocracy and oligarchy. He also combines honour and pleasure, including wealth, but includes in the tyrannical state those who look upon wealth, games or the pleasures of the senses as a kind of honour to be aimed at. Ibn Rushd on the other hand follows Plato; he lets timocracy be transformed into oligarchy, only adding the hedonistic man to the kinds of ruler, and plutocracy and the hedonistic state to the kinds of constitution, thus increasing the number of constitutions to eight. Six are Plato's: monarchy, aristocracy (in Plato, both are alternatives of the ideal state), timocracy, oligarchy, democracy, tyranny; to these Ibn Rushd adds the "state of necessity", adopted from Al-Fārābī, and "the government of the pleasure-seeker", his own addition. His treatment of tyranny is clear and concise, closely following Plato's discussion, and in striking contrast to Al-Fārābī's involved description of a hybrid state.[81] His dependence on Al-Fārābī sometimes involves him in inconsistency, and he does not always succeed in blending Platonic, Aristotelian and Islamic political ideas.[82]

We have seen that Ibn Rushd accepted Al-Fārābī's synthesis between the caliph and Plato's philosopher-king. But he left undecided the question whether the ideal ruler must also be a prophet.[83] A possible explanation for this indecision may be found in Ibn Rushd's conviction of the extinction of prophecy with the death of Muḥammad. Moreover, the ideal Islamic state no longer needed to be founded; it had once existed, and the *imām*-state of his day came, at least in intention, as near to it as an imperfect state ever could come. An objection may at once be raised: why does he then retain the qualification of lawgiver? If the *Sharīʿa* is to be the law of the ideal polity no new law or lawgiver seems called for. This objection can be met, I believe, by reference to the emphasis given in his Greek sources to the law, without which no state can exist, and to the rule of one "expert in the laws which the first ⟨lawgiver⟩ laid down...."[84]

Since we have here an example of adaptation typical of Ibn Rushd, the whole passage may be quoted and compared with his source, Al-Fārābī's *Fuṣūl al-madanī*.[85] Ibn Rushd introduces the third treatise of his commentary on the *Republic* with a summary of the imperfect states, combining Plato's dialogue with Al-Fārābī's description. The Hebrew text is difficult and obscure; but by a comparison with the *Fuṣūl*, his unquestioned source, it can be understood quite accurately.[86] It demonstrates one striking feature of the commentary: Ibn Rushd's power of adapting and modifying his borrowed material with the help of a judicious restriction to the essential elements, on which he then comments in detail, closely following Plato's text.

Ibn Rushd says:

For if there is placed over this administration one in whom five conditions are combined, namely, wisdom, perfect intelligence, good persuasion, good imagination, capacity for ⟨waging⟩ holy war[87] (*jihād*), and no physical impediment to the performance of actions *in connection with holy war*,[87] then he is absolutely king, and his government will be a truly royal government.

But when these qualities exist only separately in a group ⟨of people⟩..., but they help each other to bring about and preserve this constitution, then they will be called the elect princes [that is, Plato's *aristoi*], and their rule will be called the exalted and choice rule [that is, aristocracy].

It also happens sometimes that the prince of this state will be one who does not attain this status, that is, the dignity of king, yet he is expert in the laws which the first ⟨lawgiver⟩ laid down, and possesses a good ⟨power of⟩ conjecture so as to deduce from them what the first did not expound, for every single legal decision (?) and every single lawsuit. To this category of knowledge belongs the science called among us the art of jurisprudence. In addition he has the capacity for ⟨waging⟩ *holy war*,[87] and he is called king of the laws.[88]

This means that he is capable of *ijtihād*, independent legal decision, on the basis of the existing *Sharī'a*. In that sense he is a lawgiver, without at the same time being a prophet.

Ibn Rushd reproduces *Fuṣūl* § 54 A–C in his own concise, clear manner, with a significant and very important variation in the "king of the laws". For this ruler combines with those of § C of the *Fuṣūl* the conditions of Al-Fārābī's second ruler of the *Madīna fāḍila*, without possessing the first, philosophical qualification. He adds an explanation concerning jurisprudence and altogether clarifies Al-Fārābī's wording. Al-Fārābī envisaged in his *Madīna fāḍila* the joint rule of two men, a kind of intermediate stage between monarchy and aristocracy. One is a philosopher, the other possesses all the other qualifications of the second ruler. This is, to some extent, paralleled in the *Fuṣūl*, § 54 D, again without the philosophical qualification, and with a distribution of the other qualifications over a number of people, similar, it seems, to aristocracy without philosophy. Characteristically, Ibn Rushd combines the idea of dual rule in the *Madīna fāḍila* and the joint rule of a group in the *Fuṣūl* into a dual rule of the legal expert and the man capable of waging holy war: "However, it may not happen that both these ⟨qualifications⟩ are found in one man, rather the one ⟨capable of⟩ waging *holy war*[87] being another than the *legal expert*.[87] Yet of necessity both will share in the rule, as is the case with many of the Muslim kings."[89]

This statement is important for two reasons: in the first place, it constitutes a deliberate approximation to Islam by adapting Al-Fārābī's rule of two men in the *Madīna fāḍila* (though not insisting on a philosopher) to Muslim rule based on the *Sharī'a*, which demands expert knowledge of *Fiqh*, the power of independent judgement and decision, and the duty of *jihād*, on the part of the caliph. Undoubtedly Al-Fārābī had this in mind in the *Fuṣūl*, but in a manner that was hardly practicable, since he would vest power in a group of people of whom each has some but not all of the necessary qualifications. Secondly, by pointing to a parallel situation in his own time, among "many of the Muslim kings", Ibn Rushd establishes the Islamic character of such a joint two-man rule. We know from Al-Marrākushī's *History of the Almohads* that the Almohad caliph, Abū Ya'qūb Yūsuf, ordered his legal experts to collect all the traditions concerning *jihād* which he combined into a *Kitāb al-jihād* for his guidance in the wars which he waged against the Christians and those Almoravids who still defied Almohad rule. Ibn Rushd may have had him in mind. One is also reminded of the same caliph's struggle against *taqlīd*, the reliance on authority as against exercising one's own judgement and arriving at independent legal decisions (*ijtihād*: the very qualification demanded of the "king of the laws").

It is clear from all this that Ibn Rushd built on strong Al-Fārābian foundations. He brought a systematic, clear mind and considerable practical political experience to bear on the theories of Al-Fārābī, which he scrutinized with greater understanding of Plato and Aristotle. This penetrating knowledge and political realism enabled him to transform borrowed material critically and systematically and so to build up a political philosophy which was at the same time Islamic and Platonic. No doubt the different climate of Almohad Islam is at least in part responsible for Ibn Rushd's clearer realization of and greater emphasis on the superiority of the *Sharī'a* over the *Nomos* and of its political significance. At the same time, he studied and commented on the *Republic* and the *Nicomachean Ethics* in order to gain a deeper understanding not only of the Muslim states, but also of a secular state. This may perhaps have provided additional grounds for his doubt whether the prophetic quality was required in the ideal ruler. These elements in his political philosophy, together with his critique of existing Muslim states, point to some extent towards Ibn Khaldūn.

But he did not advance to the concept of the power-state as conceived by Ibn Khaldūn, nor even so far as Ibn al-Ṭiqṭaqa.[90] For "Reason of State" is not the foundation and centre of his political thought; the interests of the state are not the determining factor in policy. The happiness of all the citizens, philosophers and workers alike, under the law of God is his ultimate purpose. He saw more clearly than the other *Falāsifa* the difference between the divinely revealed law (the *Sharī'a* of Islam) and the *Nomos*, human law, despite their common features and strong affinity. But it must be remembered that the range of his mind and his comments are to some extent determined and limited by the material he commented on. Unlike his original, "theoretical" polemical treatises, his political writings are primarily commentaries.

Another difference—of which he was acutely aware—further

emphasizes the superior nature of the *Sharī'a*. He is opposed to the use of myths and fables in education designed to promote the virtues, and he stresses the fact that many have attained those virtues guided only by their religious laws.[91] This means that the *Sharī'a* is all-comprehensive, and teaches everything a man should know for the attainment of moral and intellectual perfection—so far as this is possible.

Here the distinction between the elect and the masses receives added significance. For Ibn Rushd, like Plato, knew that the masses cannot see the truth with the naked eye; that they are amenable to persuasion only, not to demonstration. But while he would withhold the hidden, inner meaning of revelation from the masses as something beyond their capacity to understand and even likely to undermine their faith, he insists that the *Sharī'a* contains the whole truth in a way that is accessible to all three classes of men.[92] The basic teachings about God and the hereafter are clear for all and must be accepted by all. He who denies them is an unbeliever. Right beliefs and convictions and moral conduct secure the happiness of all, philosophers and masses alike. Herein lies the fundamental difference between the law of Islam and the law of Plato. The truth of revelation was never questioned by the *Falāsifa*. But Ibn Rushd questioned the truth of Plato's fables and myths. They represent a rhetorical or dialectical argument, and so he does not comment on them. For example, he says at the end of his commentary about Plato's views on the immortality of the soul:

> What the tenth treatise comprises is not necessary for this science. For at its beginning he explains that the art of poetry has no ⟨ultimate⟩ purpose; and the knowledge which results from it is not true knowledge. . . . After that he also produces a rhetorical or dialectical argument in which he explains that the soul is immortal. Then after this there is a tale in which he describes the bliss and delight which the happy, just souls attain, and also what the tormented souls attain. But we have made known more than once that these tales are of no consequence. For the virtues that result from them are not true virtues. . . .[93]

In direct contrast, he continues: "However, we see here many men who hold fast to their statutes and religious laws and at the same time lack these tales, yet are not inferior to those who possess the⟨se⟩ tales."[92]

Plato's tales and myths, especially the myth of Er of Book x, cannot be proved, but the proof of revelation is in the "precious book", the Qur'ān, which is accessible to all and is a guide to happiness and perfection to those who believe in its truth. The masses believe it in its plain, literal sense; its inner, hidden meaning is reserved for the philosophers. The *Falāsifa* may have differed in the degree to which they resorted to a philosophical or esoteric interpretation of basic Islamic theological concepts. As I stated in an earlier chapter, it is often difficult, in the absence of clear documentary evidence, to know how they understood such important doctrines as a future life, or reward and punishment in it. Ibn Bājja is explicit about the hereafter, but others are not. Ibn Rushd would need to have been a very cunning hypocrite if we are to doubt his sincerity in the three polemical treatises and in his commentary on the *Republic*. A case in point is his use of identical terminology in the passage just quoted about the happy and the tormented souls in his commentary and in the *Faṣl*—"the knowledge of happiness and misery [or 'torment'] in the hereafter"—as far as we can judge from the Hebrew translation of the commentary. What is a "tale" in Plato is "true knowledge" in the *Sharī'a*.

The constitution and the life of the Greek state—as the *Falāsifa* knew them from the *Republic*, the *Laws* and the *Nicomachean Ethics*—are devised and arranged according to the *Nomos* in such a way that the philosopher-rulers alone attain the highest perfection and happiness, the Guardians are appropriately educated and respected, and the masses have to ensure that these two superior groups reach their goal. That is Plato's view, at any rate; though we have to remember that the *Falāsifa* saw Plato and Aristotle at least partly through the eyes of their ancient interpreters. Plotinus, Proclus and Porphyry were nearer to the *Falāsifa* in their religious outlook.

To sum up: we have in the *khilāfa* the ideal Muslim state in which all Muslims are united and equal in faith and observance, no matter what interpretation they put on vital doctrines. Under the prophetic revealed law, philosophers are in no better position than the masses of believers to reach the goal of happiness in this world and in the next. It is true that the attainment of this twofold happiness is affected by their natural disposition and aptitude, and depends on the use which the individual makes of his natural gifts and opportunities and on the fulfilment of his duties to God and to his fellow-Muslims. Though the *Falāsifa* may have thought that as wide a gulf separated them intellectually from the Muslim masses as the Greek philosophers from the bulk of their own people, they never denied that in the sight of Allah all Muslims were equal and all entitled to their appropriate share of happiness.

When Ibn Rushd insisted on the obligation of all three classes of men to accept the basic Muslim tenets in their plain sense, and when he based his claim of the superiority of the *Sharī'a* over the *Nomos* on that obligation, I see no reason to doubt his relative "orthodoxy". It goes much further than that of any other Muslim religious philosopher, with the exception of the rationalistic mystic Ibn Bājja, who placed himself outside tradition. On this point disagreement is strong and widespread among modern students of Ibn Sīnā and Ibn Rushd. As far as political thought in Islam is concerned, it is not as relevant as the practical conclusions which Ibn Rushd drew from his study of Plato's political philosophy, or his realistic application of Plato's teaching to political affairs in contemporary Islam. This feature of his Commentary, even more than his traditionalist attitude to the *Sharī'a* and especially to prophecy, undoubtedly sets him apart from his predecessors. The seriousness with which he applied Platonic notions to his own civilization, which differed entirely in many important aspects, establishes his originality. It is more important for the history of political thought in Islam than his evident dependence on Al-Fārābī. However much Al-Fārābī's treatment of Plato influenced Ibn Rushd's own exposition—and it was a considerable influence—it was his remarkable insight into the administration of the Almohad state and its Almoravid predecessor which helped him to realize the validity and topicality of Plato's political ideas. The deeper understanding of Plato and Aristotle in turn enabled him better to understand the Muslim state and to analyse more accurately its structure and transformation. To this we must add his profound and acute appreciation of the political character and significance of the *Sharī'a* against the background of law, and of law in relation to politics. His study of Plato and Aristotle taught him this, as has been stressed repeatedly in the course of this chapter. His defence of *falsafa*, coupled with his claim that the *Falāsifa* are the exclusive guardians and interpreters of the *Sharīʿa* through their ability to give demonstrative proof, assumes a political significance in view of his identification of the theologians (who made the same claim) with Plato's Sophists who are a danger and a menace to the ideal state. From this point of view the unity of Ibn Rushd's political philosophy is apparent: it links his commentaries on the *Republic* and the *Nicomachean Ethics* and his three polemical treatises, the *Faṣl-Ḍamīma*, *Manāhij* and the *Tahāfut al-tahāfut.* His reasoned critique of the contemporary Muslim state and society in terms of the *Republic* is the philosopher's contribution to political life; it is an important fulfilment of his civic duties, over and above his function as judge and physician.[94]

The vote of thanks to his patron and master at the end of his commentary on the *Republic*, and the prayer for his preservation which is identical with the opening words of the *Ḍamīma* may be more than flattery and a sense of favours to come. For the two Almohad caliphs whom Ibn Rushd served were noted for their keen interest in philosophy and were no doubt in his mind when he discussed the *imām*-state. We recall in this connection the passage quoted from the *Faṣl* earlier in this chapter, in which Ibn Rushd commends "this ruling power" for its encouragement of philosophy and of popular instruction in the basic teachings of Islam. We know from Plato that right convictions and beliefs are as indispensable as justice to the welfare of the state, and Ibn Rushd simply adapts these Platonic ideas to the Muslim state. They are even more important there since the *Sharīʿa* provides in its theoretical and practical knowledge for the welfare of the citizens in this life and for their happiness in the next. In short, the aim of the *Sharīʿa* is identical with that of philosophy, including political science as defined by Aristotle and repeated by Al-Fārābī and all the later *Falāsifa*.

Ibn Rushd's preoccupation with political science and political virtue (as a combination of prudence with moral virtue) is clear from his lengthy comment on Aristotle's statement that as prudence is no more in authority over wisdom than medicine over health, so political science does not govern the gods simply because it regulates everything in the state. "Everything" clearly includes observances. The mere fact that Aristotle mentioned political science was reason enough for Ibn Rushd to paraphrase Aristotle's definition of politics—at the beginning of the *Nicomachean Ethics*—thus: "General political government, that is, the art of governing states, is the ruling disposition over all dispositions in the state, I mean the arts which are under this art because it commands its subordinate arts what they should do."[95] Wherever the term "political" occurs, Ibn Rushd explains its significance for the community of men as partners in a common endeavour for the common good, echoing the ideas which Aristotle expounded.[96] The religious observances of Islam promote fellowship since they represent duties incumbent on the individual in association with his fellow-Muslims. Ibn Rushd must have felt a certain affinity with Aristotle when he stressed the "civic" character and social influence of thanksgiving for harvests and assemblies for sacrifices.[97]

In conclusion, it may once more be pointed out that the concern for law and justice provided that common ground between the Muslim philosopher and his Greek masters which enabled him to apply Greek practical philosophy to Islam and the Muslim state of his time, and to underline the political character of the *Sharīʿa* with its unrivalled opportunity of securing for the Muslim what philosophy was to obtain for the Greek: the highest good.

CHAPTER X

AL-DAWWĀNĪ[1]: APPLICATION AND INTEGRATION

THE *Falāsifa* as a group did not exert much influence on political thought in traditionalist circles. To some extent this was because their political philosophy was only a part of their general philosophy, which aroused hostility and opposition. We have discussed Ibn Khaldūn's criticism of their political thought, but we must bear in mind that his acquaintance with their writings was inadequate and rather superficial and, moreover, influenced by Al-Ghazālī's opposition to *falsafa*.

On the other hand, the discussion by jurists like Al-Māwardī and Ibn Taymīya of the reasons for the existence of the *khilāfa* or *imāma* betrays some influence by them. It is not wholly negative—at least in the case of Ibn Taymīya—and shows at any rate that writers on constitutional theory felt the need to take account of the *Falāsifa*. The chief obstacle was, no doubt, the theory of prophecy propounded by Al-Fārābī and Ibn Sīnā. Those *Falāsifa* like Ibn Sīnā and especially Ibn Rushd, who built their political philosophy round the law of the prophetic lawgiver, established an area of agreement which enabled some traditionalist Muslim thinkers like Ibn Taymīya[2] and Al-Dawwānī to incorporate some of their political ideas in their own thought. This seems to bear out my claim that in the realm of political philosophy it is the central position of law which provides the common ground between Plato and Aristotle on the one hand and the *Falāsifa*, Ibn Taymīya and Al-Dawwānī on the other.

I have tried to show in the previous chapters how Al-Fārābī, Ibn Sīnā and Ibn Rushd dealt with the question of law in the context of the central problem of Islamic philosophy—the "agreement between philosophy and prophetic revealed law"; how Ibn Sīnā took the decisive step towards a synthesis, and how Ibn Rushd almost succeeded in integrating the two ways to the one Truth. From his theological premiss, which was a traditional view of prophecy, he proceeded to a philosophical interpretation of revelation in the form of law. To my mind, he achieved as nearly as possible that "agreement between philosophy and revealed law" which he set out to accomplish in the *Faṣl al-maqāl*. (I say "as nearly as possible" since an absolute harmony between faith and reason in complete logical consistency and intellectual honesty appears to me to be unattainable. Faith is an act of our free will; it requires a leap, after which the intellectual position is no longer what it was before, because the absolute sovereignty of reason is limited by our voluntary acceptance of doctrines which are beyond demonstrative proof.) Despite their common quest for happiness and perfection in the knowledge and love of God, there must always remain a distinction between the philosopher and the traditionalist in their attitude and approach to revelation. Hence inconsistency, which should not be confused with insincerity.

This recapitulation is necessary if we are to assign to Al-Dawwānī his place in this great intellectual struggle, which is by no means confined to medieval Islam. If a claim were made that he achieved a complete integration of Greek-Hellenistic philosophy with Muslim theology and jurisprudence it would only be superficially true. For his *Akhlāq-i-Jalālī*, called by its translator W. F. Thompson, *Practical Philosophy of the Muhammadan People*,[3] is not the work of an original thinker, but is only a well-written, eclectic popularization of "practical philosophy" as propounded by Naṣīr al-Dīn Ṭūsī. But it is not simply an "edition" of Ṭūsī's *Akhlāq-i-Nāṣirī*,[4] which itself was strongly influenced by earlier Muslim writers on ethics, economics and politics. Al-Dawwānī's contribution is the skilful adaptation to Muslim doctrine of Ṭūsī's strictly philosophical treatise. Naturally, Ṭūsī assimilates Platonic and Aristotelian ideas and opinions to his Islamic environment, especially the concept of law. Al-Dawwānī summarizes Ṭūsī's treatise and, in so doing, acclimatizes it to traditional Islam in his capacity as theologian and jurist. This would at any rate give him a claim to be considered in a study of political thought in Islam. Moreover, he has a claim to consideration as a writer in his own right. This is clear from a comparison of his adaptation with his original. His style is simple, fluent and lucid; consequently he often makes Ṭūsī's thought superficially clear while sacrificing precision and fulness of argument. The relevance to Muslim life is apparent throughout; it shows itself in the compression of Ṭūsī's exposition, omitting matter belonging to Greek surroundings, and in a loosening of the philosophical discussion by illustrations culled from Hadith, "Mirror"-literature and Muslim history and naturally in quotations from the Qur'ān. It shows itself most significantly in a deliberate modification of Ṭūsī's terminology and thought. It may well be that Ibn Rushd's stress on the *Sharī'a* in his *Faṣl* and in his commentary on Plato's *Republic*, as well as Ibn Taymīya's *Siyāsa shar'īya*, partly account for Al-Dawwānī's insistence on the supreme authority of the divinely revealed law as the guarantor of just government, equity and man's happiness and perfection.

A few examples may illustrate his adaptation of Ṭūsī to traditionalist Muslim thought and at the same time the accommodation of Platonic and Aristotelian ideas to Islam.

He follows the arrangement of Ṭūsī's treatise, with its division into ethics, economics and politics. Ṭūsī's first part is based on Miskawaih's *K. al-Ṭahāra*;[4] the second part is his version of *Bryson*, dependent on Ibn Sīnā's;[5] and the third part on politics, with which we are mainly concerned, is greatly indebted to Al-Fārābī's *Madīna fāḍila* and *K. al-siyāsa al-madanīya*. But Ṭūsī was no mere copyist, and there are many indications that he knew Plato's *Republic* and Aristotle's *Nicomachean Ethics* independently.

Al-Dawwānī, following Ṭūsī, adapts Aristotle's definition of justice in his *Nicomachean Ethics* to Islam in a manner both interesting and characteristic. Accepting the derivation of money (*nomisma*) from custom (*nomos*), he gives *Nomos* the meaning of a *divine law* which provides the standard, since it is difficult to maintain equity by ascertaining the necessary mean in any other way.[6] Such a mean is necessary because man is a political being by nature and must co-operate with others in order to obtain the necessities of life. We are familiar with this justification of political association from Al-Fārābī on, and Ṭūsī and Al-Dawwānī use it again at the beginning of the third part. No other among the *Falāsifa* seems to have regarded political association as the reason for the introduction of money as a means of exchange in order to establish equity. Justice is preserved, according to Al-Dawwānī, by three things: the "holy divine" *Sharī'a*, the just ruler, and money. In Ṭūsī they are the divine law (*nāmūs ilāhī*), the human ruler, and money. "The philosophers laid it down that the greatest *nāmūs* is the *Sharī'a*, the second is the *sulṭān* who obeys the *Sharī'a*—for *dīn* and *mulk* are twins—and the third *nāmūs* is money."[7] Ṭūsī's text shows interesting and significant variants, compared to Al-Dawwānī's. In the first place, where Al-Dawwānī speaks of "the philosophers", Ṭūsī refers to Aristotle in these words: "the greatest *nāmūs* is from God's presence, according to the *Book Nīkūmachīa*". This is characteristically changed by Al-Dawwānī into "...the *Sharī'a*", thus effecting a complete assimilation to Islam. He does the same with the "second *nāmūs*". Here his source simply said: "the second *nāmūs* is of the same kind as the greatest." Ṭūsī does not mention a *sulṭān* nor obedience to the *Sharī'a*. But in the third part he calls the second *nāmūs* "governor" (*ḥākim*). It is possible that Al-Dawwānī changed the text of Ṭūsī here to agree with the later passage; interpreting Ṭūsī, he gave his words at the same time a distinct Islamic colouring and meaning. Al-Dawwānī then explains that the philosophers mean by *nāmūs* "rule and government" (*tadbīr wa-siyāsa*).[8] He quotes the Qur'ān in support: "The Book" alludes to the *Sharī'a*; "the balance" alludes to money; and "steel" alludes to the sword of the ruler.[9] Three kinds of transgressors correspond to the three guarantors of justice; they are the unbeliever and sinner who disobeys the law of God; the rebel who opposes the ruler; and the thief who desires more than his due. Obedience to the divine law is paramount.[10] The story of Malik Shah and the Shāfi'ī *imām* Abū-l-Ma'ālī 'Abdu-l-malik Juwaynī is used to illustrate the spheres of competence of the ruler and the jurist. Where duties towards God are concerned the *sulṭān* must consult the teacher and interpreter of the *Sharī'a*; in temporal matters the *sulṭān*'s orders must be obeyed.[11]

Al-Dawwānī applies Aristotle's threefold division of justice to Islam and the Muslim community. He does not specifically mention Aristotle's distinction between domestic and political justice, the latter being subdivided into natural and conventional or legal justice;[12] but he probably has them in mind, and Aristotle's discussion of them. In Muslim law (as we saw when discussing in the previous chapter Ibn Rushd's comments on Book V of the *Nicomachean Ethics*) a broad distinction is drawn between "duties to God" (*'ibādāt*) and "duties to our fellow-men" (*mu'āmalāt*). It seems that Al-Dawwānī subdivides the social duties rather as

Aristotle subdivided political justice, and understands the religious duties in the sense of Aristotle's domestic justice. God demands our obedience as of right: he is the creator and we are his creatures. Al-Dawwānī obviously looks upon this religious obedience as the equivalent of Aristotle's filial obedience and thus of the master-servant relationship. He divides the second Islamic group into duties towards our fellow-men as citizens, singling out on the one hand obedience to the rulers, the learned (*'ulamā*) and the "*imāms* of the Faith", and trust and honesty in commercial relations, and on the other respect for our predecessors as honouring their financial obligations.[13] The *Sharī'a* comprises all three kinds, based on the Qur'ān. Modern philosophers, examining the *Sharī'a*, observe that it contains the whole of practical philosophy and therefore turn their back on the ancient philosophers and their books.[14] The justice of the ruler is indispensable for that of his subjects. This is supported by a suitable Hadith and a saying of 'Abdu-llah b. al-mubārak to the effect that the righteousness of the ruler was the sure means to the advantage of all creation.[15]

These examples show how Al-Dawwānī combines philosophy, both ancient and modern, with Qur'ān, Hadith and tales as found in the "Mirrors". In this way he gives an interesting and colourful account of political thought which is intellectually satisfying and traditionally unobjectionable. It explains his popularity; but whether his combination of *falsafa* and *Sharī'a* produced a workable political theory in place of the discredited "classical" theory of the *khilāfa*, as one authority claims,[16] I am not prepared to accept or to challenge without a more detailed examination of the relevant literature. For the moment I am content with a brief description of Al-Dawwānī's discussion of political science as influenced by Ṭūsī, and with pointing out his more significant deviations from his source. The integration of philosophy with traditionalism was achieved by Al-Dawwānī's eclecticism, and holds good for certain opinions of the *Falāsifa* in the field of political philosophy. To my mind Al-Dawwānī is much closer to Ibn Taymīya and his advocacy of "government based on the *Sharī'a*" than to the *Falāsifa*, with the exception of Ibn Rushd. Although he equates Plato's "world-ruler" with the *khalīfa*, he is, like Ibn Taymīya, not interested in the *khilāfa*, but in government in accordance with the *Sharī'a*. When he speaks of the "ruler" in connection with justice he refers to him as *bādishah* or *sulṭān*. Let us now examine his political thought in more detail.

Like the *Falāsifa*, speaking of political association (*ijtimā'*), he follows Ṭūsī in calling it *tamaddun*, "civilization", derived from *madīna*, "city-state", as we find the same terms used by Ibn Khaldūn before him.[17] He defines *tadbīr*[18] as "supreme government", where Ṭūsī had only spoken of "government" (*siyāsa*); and he says that *nāmūs* (law), *ḥākim* (a governor) and *dīnār* (money) are needed to ensure "the supreme government".[19] After setting out the aims for which political association is effected, such as pleasures, wealth or honour, Ṭūsī discusses at length Aristotle's "simple" constitutions—monarchy, tyranny, timocracy and democracy. This is not to be found in Al-Dawwānī.[20] On the other hand, as compared with Ṭūsī, Al-Dawwānī makes significant changes in terminology and important additions. He says:

> the lawgiver is a person endowed with divine inspiration and revelation...to establish regulations governing man's duties to God (*'ibādāt*) and his social relations (*mu'āmalāt*)...for the good order of this life and the next (*ṣalāḥ ma'āsh wa-ma'ād*)....The ancient philosophers call him a lawgiver and ⟨his⟩ ordinances a law while the moderns [the *Falāsifa*] call him a prophet and ⟨divine⟩ lawgiver and the ordinances the *Sharī'a*.[21]

Ṭūsī leaves out "revelation" (*waḥy*), the description of the purpose and scope of the law, and more significantly still, he also omits "prophet" (*nabī*). He calls the law of the ancient philosophers "divine". It is clear that Al-Dawwānī used the terms *waḥy* and *nabī* deliberately so as to leave no doubt that he meant the Islamic law handed down by a prophet who had received it in the form of a revelation. Ṭūsī only implies this by his use of the term *nāmūs ilāhī*; he equates this with the *Sharī'a*, yet he also employs it when speaking of Aristotle. The inclusion by Al-Dawwānī of *'ibādāt*, *mu'āmalāt* and *ṣalāḥ ma'āsh wa-ma-'ād* not only corroborates his tendency to acclimatize *falsafa* to Islam and to conform to accepted Muslim opinion, but also brings him into line with the writers on constitutional law among the jurists. A further remarkable difference between the two writers consists in Al-Dawwānī's substitution of the term *muta'ākhirān* for Ṭūsī's *muḥaddithān*, which can only mean "traditionalists, orthodox, true believers". This may imply that, at this distance and no longer mindful of the battle against *falsafa*, he accepted the *Falāsifa* as "orthodox" Muslims who conformed, not only in observance but also in beliefs and convictions. But since terminology is not always unequivocally and consistently employed—at times intentionally—we cannot be quite certain whether Al-Dawwānī means the *Falāsifa* when he uses the term *muta'ākhirān* by itself, not preceded by *qudamā* or *ḥukamā qudamā*. This is despite its clear meaning—"later, modern thinkers" (in contrast to "first, earlier, ancient philosophers"). If he meant the early Muslims he would no doubt have used the common designation of *salaf*. A similar caution is advisable in the case of *ḥukamā*, which may sometimes mean the "wise" in general. As a rule the context is a reliable guide to the particular connotation intended, but not always. Applied to the present passage, there is hardly any doubt that the *Falāsifa* are intended; otherwise Al-Dawwānī would have retained Ṭūsī's *muḥaddithān*, if he had understood this term in the original meaning which Ṭūsī presumably intended it to bear. This seems to be further borne out by his use of the same term *muta'ākhirān* when he defines the "governor" or ruler in these terms:

> the governor is a person endowed with the divine support...in order to perfect individual men and to arrange ⟨and bring about⟩ the (general) welfare. The philosophers call this person "king absolutely speaking" and his ordinances the art of government.[22] The modern ⟨philosophers⟩ call him imam and his function imamate. Plato calls him "world ruler" and Aristotle "statesman" (*insān madanī* here equals *politikos*), that is the man who watches over the affairs of the city-state....[23]

His foremost concern is with the *Sharī'a*. He must guard its ordinances effectively, but he is free to take into consideration the circumstances of the time—provided he acts in harmony with the general principles of the *Sharī'a*, in the interests of the community. "Such a person is in reality the shadow of God, the *khalīfa* of God and the vicar of the Prophet."[24] This equation between Plato's ruler and the *imām*-caliph is the legacy of Al-Fārābī and the *Falāsifa*, but Al-Dawwānī has again modified what he found in his sources in the interests of traditionalist opinion. For here we have no identification between philosopher-king, lawgiver (prophetic lawgiver according to the *Falāsifa*) and *imām*. Al-Dawwānī distinguishes between lawgiver and ruler, and only equates them individually, that is, the *nomothetes* corresponds to the prophetic lawgiver in Islam while his "vicar" corresponds to Plato's "ruler of the world".[25] Al-Dawwānī's *imām* has the statutory qualification of *ijtihād*; although he does not use this term, it is clear from his description of his principal function.

With Al-Fārābī and Ibn Rushd he denounces isolation from society as an injustice to our fellow-men, since those who refuse co-operation rely on the support of the others. Justice demands mutual help; what justice is must be learned, and this knowledge can only be gained by the study of "the principles and rules of this science".[26] The rulers (*salāṭīn*) especially must acquire such knowledge. They are "physicians to the temperament of the world and rulers over the affairs of mankind".[27] It is interesting to note that Al-Dawwānī here identifies the *sulṭān* with the *imām-khalīfa* and the Platonic-Aristotelian ruler.[28]

Though based on Ṭūsī, the discussion of the ideal or perfect and the imperfect states follows Al-Fārābī in terminology, but adopts Platonic concepts in explaining their meaning.

The *madīna fāḍila* is one, according to the philosophers, the one kind of *tamaddun*, whereas there are three different imperfect states (*madīna ghayr fāḍila*). The reasoning faculty is paramount in the ideal state, and association aims at attaining happiness (*sa'āda*) and repulsing evil. Right opinions and convictions are held and good actions performed by all its citizens.[29] In place of Plato's three classes Al-Dawwānī enumerates five, which conform to four kinds of natural disposition, varying with individuals. The four individual psychological types correspond to Plato's as we know them from his allegory of the cave, but they are assimilated to Muslim types. Plato's philosophers thus enjoy divine support which enables them to see reality with their pure intellect freed from corporeality. Those unequal to pure intellectual perception, unlike the first class of saints and philosophers, can conjecture reality. They are the men of faith. The third class relies on imagination while the fourth can only grasp the world of the senses. Ṭūsī remains within Plato's concepts and terms.[30] The *Sharī'a* provides for all the four classes and ensures their happiness according to their mental capacity, since the Qur'ān is couched in such language that by literal or figurative interpretation all Muslims can be guided and enlightened. Under the authority of the ideal ruler (*mudabbir fāḍil*) they rise gradually through mutual help to perfection.[31] Al-Dawwānī has here achieved a harmonious blending of philosophy and tradition, presented in terms to which no exception could be taken. Ṭūsī does not go quite as far.

Turning now to "the five pillars of the ideal state", the first group whom he calls "the most distinguished" (*afāḍil*) are entrusted with the government of the state. They correspond to the first kind of individuals; they have mastered theoretical and practical philosophy and consequently possess a true knowledge of reality. The second "pillar" is composed of orators, who call the masses to human perfection by employing dialectical, rhetorical and poetical arguments. They are the practitioners of *Kalam*, *Fiqh*, rhetoric and poetry. Next come those who see to it that justice and equity prevail among the citizens; they are skilled in the arts of calculation, measurement, geometry, medicine and astronomy. Next the warriors, corresponding to Plato's Guardians, who defend the state against enemies. Lastly, there are those who provide food and clothing, which must be a lucrative trade since he calls them *arbāb amwāl*, the rich.[32] Like Plato he assigns one occupation to each person as a matter of justice.

In contrast to the "pillars" (useful citizens whose work benefits society), Al-Dawwānī mentions the *nawābit*, whom we know from Al-Fārābī and Ibn Bājja. Since Ṭūsī depends for much of this third part on Al-Fārābī it is natural that Ṭūsī and Al-Dawwānī should have reproduced Al-Fārābī's negative estimate of these "pests". The text closely follows Al-Fārābī's classification in his *Siyāsa*.[33]

The three imperfect states are the ignorant state (*madīna jāhila*) in which the irascible or appetitive faculty and not the ratiocinative (that is, truly human) faculty are responsible for political association; the vicious or wicked state (*madīna fāsiqa*) in which the ratiocinative faculty serves the two others; and the state in error (*madīna ḍālla*) which is the result of the citizens' agreement in wrong convictions. Al-Dawwānī concentrates on those states to which Al-Fārābī had given Islamic names,[34] yet he defines them in Platonic terms, as Ibn Rushd had done in his commentary on the *Republic*. Ṭūsī is much more explicit and discusses all the variations with which we are familiar from Al-Fārābī.

In Platonic fashion, Ṭūsī and Al-Dawwānī uphold the correspondence of state and individual. Just as there are ideal and imperfect states, so there are men in authority possessed of virtues and vices which make their rule perfect or imperfect. Platonic criteria are applied to Islam, but thoroughly adapted to the requirements laid down in constitutional law as qualifications for the caliph or *imām*. The ideal ruler corresponds to the ideal state, and his ideal government is called *imāma*, which is defined exactly as in the treatises of the jurists. Al-Dawwānī repeats the designation of this ideal ruler as "the *khalīfa* of Allah and the shadow of Allah who imitates the lawgiver in order to make his government perfect".[35] Strangely enough, Al-Dawwānī contents himself with these few generalities, unlike Ṭūsī, who distinguishes four phases of this "monarchy". The first is represented by the Prophet Muḥammad, the king "absolutely speaking" whose distinction consists in his combining in his person the four qualities of wisdom, perfect intellectual comprehension, liberality and ability to wage *jihād* (holy war). His is a reign of wisdom. But it is significant that at least one qualification is Islamic, and that apart from the first no other qualification can be equated with any of Plato's four cardinal virtues except after prior adaptation to Muslim conditions. Ṭūsī goes on to speak of what seems to correspond to Plato's aristocracy; in this case the four virtues are not found in one person, but are shared between four men who are "like one soul" and whose rule is "the reign of the pious". No doubt Ṭūsī has in mind the reign of the four first caliphs, treating it according to Muslim traditional opinion as one rule, the real caliphate in purity. It is extraordinary that his traditionalism led him to ignore the fact that, since these four caliphs ruled in succession and each possessed only one of the necessary qualities, the ideal character of their rule would not be accepted in any strict sense by Plato, whose *aristoi* rule at the same time. Al-Fārābī follows Plato. Ṭūsī's third phase is characterized by the absence of qualified persons but by the presence of a ruler (*ra'īs*) who has knowledge of the laws (*sunan*) of past rulers; his rule is the "reign of the Sunna". We have here Al-Fārābī's "king of the law(s)" (in his *Fuṣūl*). Finally, where these legal qualifications are not present in one person, but in a group who rule together, we have "the reign of the followers of the Sunna".[36] Historically, this could apply to the time after the fall of the Abbasid caliphate, but since Ṭūsī was a Shī'ī he may well have had his own time in mind, provided he wrote his *Akhlāq-i-Nāṣirī* before 1258. If it was written after that date, it is not difficult to see this fourth phase as a picture of his own times.

Al-Dawwānī defines as tyranny the defective government where the master strives to enslave the servants of God and to devastate the land of God.[37] This may be a reference to his own time, since Al-Dawwānī states that such injustice cannot endure and its perpetrators will be called to account in this world and the next. By contrasting the good government of the *imāma* with the tyranny of his own day he shows that his interest is centred in the Muslim state, and in particular in the rule of the *Sharī'a*. He stresses the need for unity through justice, otherwise the just ruler cannot govern, nor can his subjects prosper.

Corresponding to the four elements of the physical temperament there are four classes which together make up and preserve the equity of the body politic, "the political temperament". The first are the men of knowledge (*'ilm*); and this class is composed of doctors of theology and law, judges, secretaries, fiscal officials, geometricians, astronomers, physicians and poets, who guarantee the maintenance of religion and the world. Next come the warriors and defenders. The combination of pen and sword ensures stability and guarantees public welfare. The third class consists of traders, artisans and craftsmen who provide for the needs of all. Last come the farmers who produce our food. Only the equilibrium in mutual help of these four classes secures political life.

Al-Dawwānī then proceeds to another classification. Because equilibrium is only preserved by authority and discipline, he distinguishes five kinds of men: good with a good influence on others, good in themselves without influence, indifferent, bad without bad influence, and finally the opposite of the first group, the bad ones who exert a bad influence. The first class consists of the *'ulamā* of the *Sharī'a*, the "elders" and the mystics (*'urafā al-ḥaqīqa*), who should be near the ruler and in authority over the other classes, according to the philosophers.[38] It is interesting to note that Ṭūsī does not name the members of this class, that Al-Dawwānī includes the mystics in it on a par with the *'ulamā*, and that he cites the philosophers; we find that the jurists usually plead for a close association of the *'ulamā* with the government. The first class in both classifications is identical. In the first passage *'ilm* is interpreted not in the Platonic but in the Islamic sense of the term. But there can be no doubt that the four classes correspond to Plato's three estates, the second being identical in Plato and Al-Dawwānī, while Plato's third class is subdivided by Al-Dawwānī. If we compare the twofold grouping with the *Republic*, Al-Dawwānī's approximation to Islam becomes clear. But he is not always so fortunate in harmonizing philosophy and religion. This is apparent from the description of yet another first group, the rulers in the ideal state. In this passage the equality of philosopher with Muslim saint can only be considered convincing if we assume that the *awliyā* (saints) are identical with the *'urafā al-ḥaqīqa.*

This example shows how difficult it was even for Al-Dawwānī at the end of the fifteenth century to harmonize and integrate two different concepts stemming from two different civilizations, a point which seems to me of the greatest significance. Philosophy as an intellectual force was long spent in Al-Dawwānī's time and he falls far short of his source, Ṭūsī, who was still a philosopher of considerable stature (as his commentary on Ibn Sīnā's *K. al-ishārāt wa-l-tanbīhāt* demonstrates). Al-Dawwānī uses philosophy and the Muslim philosophers as an important element in his literary work, together with the traditions of Islam and the "Mirrors", and as a means to show the basic agreement between practical philosophy and the *Sharī'a* of Islam, particularly in the realm of ethics and politics. But the integration which he achieved is not, and in the nature of the problem cannot be, complete.

It now remains to illustrate his use of material from the "Mirrors". The ruler must keep his treasury and his dominions flourishing; he must show kindness and compassion to his subjects; and must not confer high office on small men. Although Al-Dawwānī states these three conditions on the authority of "the philosophers"[39] they belong to the kind of advice given in the "Mirrors". In fact, the continuation expressly refers to the Sassanians, who say that the edifice of justice must rest on ten foundations. These are moral rules which the ruler must observe; they can be paralleled from any "Mirror for Princes" such as we considered in chapter III. In the ruler sobriety, moderation, devotion to his subjects by close supervision of his administration and just decisions are essential, and all are based on the fear and service of God. The ruler must associate with the right people and accept their advice. Himself just, he must see that his subjects deal justly with each other, for he will be called to account at the resurrection.[40] The subjects must observe justice and acquire virtues. Wisdom is the fountainhead of the *Sharī'a*, and public affairs must follow the path of the *Sharī'a*.[41] Al-Dawwānī counsels the ruler to know his enemies, to use spies and informers and to engage in conversation with everybody. He warns against wars of conquest intended merely to enlarge his dominions, but advises the ruler to take up arms in the interests of Islam.[42] The subjects must obey the *sulṭān* and his governors and execute their orders provided they are not in opposition to the divine command.[43] Al-Dawwānī continues in this vein, stressing the importance of observing a strict etiquette at court, on the lines of the "Mirrors". He follows his source without adding anything material.

If one considers to what extent Al-Dawwānī chose to follow his pattern, Ṭūsī's *Akhlāq-i-Nāṣirī*, in structure as well as in content, it may well be asked why it was Al-Dawwānī who influenced later Sunnī jurists, and why it was his theory that underlay the use of the terms *khalīfa* and *imām* in the Ottoman and Mughal empires, as Sir Hamilton Gibb asserts.[44] I have no opinion on this claim. I have simply tried to describe Al-Dawwānī's views in the words he used and in the order he expressed them, and to analyse them in relation to Ṭūsī, to the *Falāsifa* and to the expositions of the theory of the *khilāfa* by earlier Sunnī jurists. I am not aware that Al-Dawwānī differs in any material point from the current opinion that the ideal *khilāfa* came to an end with the first four *khulafā rāshidūn*, or that he even introduced this basic distinction into the thought and literature of a subsequent age. To my mind *khilāfa* and *imāma* are synonymous, and he does not use these terms in any different sense from an Al-Māwardī, Al-Ghazālī, Ibn Jamā'a or Ibn Taymīya. Like the last two, especially Ibn Taymīya, he upheld the pure *khilāfa* as the ideal which, though long past, it was hoped to re-establish, if the rule of the *Sharī'a*, under whatever government, were to be reaffirmed and effectively realized. The supremacy of the *Sharī'a* and the unity of the *Jamā'a* as the *ummat al-Islam* was their concern as much as his. This is clear not only from his own formulations and repetitions in his *Akhlāq*, but also from his quotations from, or at least ascribed to,

Plato. It is surely significant that in support of the supreme authority of the *Sharī'a* he does not quote sayings from the Hadith or from the "doctors of theology and law" but a pronouncement which he puts in the mouth of Plato. Life must be regulated in accordance with the ordinances of the *Sharī'a*, for "Plato says, 'guard the law (*nāmūs*) and it will protect you' " which he paraphrases by substituting the term *sharī'a* for *nāmūs*.[45] Here—more than five hundred years after Al-Fārābī—is the link, still intact, that bound Muslim thinkers to the political philosophy of Plato and Aristotle, that common ground of the law which I have stressed so often in these chapters. Al-Dawwānī was no longer a philosopher like the *Falāsifa* from Kindī to Ibn Rushd, nor even like his source and model Ṭūsī. We no longer sense in his pages their passionate zeal for Truth, their inquiring mind, or their intellectual curiosity and striving. But he is nevertheless heir to a tradition in Muslim thought, conscious of the Platonic legacy: the perfect law, the gift of divine wisdom. He accepts that inheritance and hands it on, untrammelled by the demonstrative argument of the metaphysician, to a generation who would have rejected the *Falāsifa* and who would not have accepted it except in the lucid, pleasing, harmonizing form in which he presented it. He reduced the problem of revelation and reason, of law divine and human, to manageable proportions by ignoring the inherent difficulties and by simplifying, even over-simplifying, the issues. And yet he preserved the core in his equation of the ideal *Republic* with the ideal *khilāfa* by laying all the emphasis on the law of the Prophet. Like Ibn Taymīya, he was chiefly interested in the *siyāsa shar'īya*, the unchallenged rule of the perfect God-given law. To describe and to commend it as the only sure guide to happiness and perfection he drew on Qur'ān, Hadith, the sayings of pious Muslims and of men of affairs, and on Plato and Aristotle. Under his hands and in his words the two Greek political thinkers almost became Muslims. In this adaptation and acclimatization he must have expressed the spirit of his age, otherwise he could not have exerted the influence which is claimed for him. *If* his influence surpassed that of the earlier jurists, and of philosophers like Ṭūsī, it must be due to the spiritual climate, the political and social circumstances of his time and, not least, to his felicitous style.

APPENDIX

SOME TURKISH VIEWS ON POLITICS[1]

SINCE this book deals with political thought in medieval Islam, the Western student might expect that Al-Dawwānī's treatise discussed in chapter x would be the last to be considered. Even if we take the view that cultures and civilizations decline and, to all outward appearance, even die as a distinct and coherent spiritual force, we know that they survive and remain active and creative in varying degrees. Because this survival is a very real influence, there can be no doubt that Islam as a way of life, as a religious civilization, cannot be confined within the rigidly drawn frontiers of time implied in the terms "medieval" or "modern" history (wherever the division between the two is considered to fall). The basic tenets and attitudes of Islam have never ceased to be "medieval"; those who call themselves Muslims today can lay claim to this title only as long as they profess and try to realize these fundamental beliefs and convictions.

In this sense, the year 1500 in Islam was like any other year; it was no watershed, no demarcation line. The spiritual conflict in modern Islam is not, therefore, between believers and atheists, but between rigid upholders of the *Sharī'a* as formulated in the Middle Ages—and since that time static and unalterable—and those others who are bent on reform and modernization. To discuss modernism is outside the scope of this book, since much more is at stake than a revival of the caliphate and a modification of the classical theory of the *khilāfa*. The modernist attitude to the *khilāfa* is not uniform, but this would not be a reason for not discussing it. The real issue is between those countries, like Pakistan, which want to have the *Sharī'a* as the law of the state and those others, like Iraq, which want a modern national state based on a "political" law on the lines of Western law. This is why the problem falls outside the scope of this book and must be dealt with separately, quite apart from the question of faith and observance which Muslims—at least in principle—share with Jews and Christians. Our present spiritual malaise is world-wide;

but different historical backgrounds and social and economic conditions set the world-religions quite different additional problems in East and West. Different problems require different solutions, and there are usually alternatives and not just one solution.

The case is different, however, with the Ottoman empire. Built on military power and maintained by a professional army which exercised great influence on politics, it became at the same time the centre and an outpost of Sunnī Islam. The Abbasid caliphate came to an end in 1258, but members of the family lived on in Cairo until the last shadow-caliph was brought from there to Constantinople in 1519. From him the Ottoman dynasty usurped the caliphal title, which it retained until Kemal Ataturk abolished the caliphate. Culturally dependent on what the Arabs and Persians had created (and politically indebted to Mughal principles and practice) the Ottomans assumed the role of defenders of Sunnī Islam and of guardians of the *Sharī'a*. When we remember how Ibn Khaldūn described the *mulk* as a mixed constitution with the *Sharī'a* as its foundation, supplemented by the ordinances of the "king", we are not surprised to find similar conditions in the Ottoman caliphate. Ottoman law is a mixture of *Sharī'a* and *Qānūn*. That is, the law of Islam is supplemented by the "canons", or political and administrative ordinances, of the *sulṭān*; both together are intended to serve religion and the state. The *Sharī'a* is paramount; but some of the treatises of the seventeenth century also stress the need to restore the old *Qānūn* to its rightful position and recommend adherence to it. Three treatises in particular are relevant to our problem. They are occasioned by the bad state of public finance, and they try to diagnose it and to suggest effective remedies to cure the sickness. They have in common a deep concern for religion and the state and are interesting on that account. I can discuss only their general tendency, or the expression of their theoretical attitude to politics, and must largely leave out of account their detailed analysis of matters of administration and organization and the advice which they give as a result. It would not at any rate be profitable to discuss the practical measures without the background of political, social and economic life in the Ottoman empire at a time when it had passed the summit of its power and influence.

To name the treatises in their chronological order—and following W. F. A. Behrnauer[2]—they are: a memorandum on the decline of the Ottoman state by Kōja Beg, dating from 1630; the *Naṣīḥat-nāma* of an unknown author dated 1640, apparently a reply to the *sulṭān's* request for information about the state of affairs; and the important *Dustūr al-'amal* of the celebrated historian and biographer Hājjī Khalīfa which is of special interest by reason of its semi-philosophical superstructure, which links it with Al-Dawwānī and Ibn Khaldūn.

Kōja Beg stresses the need for the Muslim law as the basis of the existence and maintenance of empire and religion; its application is the necessary condition for the good order of both. He advises the sultan to consult the *'ulamā* because they are expert in the law and well acquainted with the position. In the course of a historical sketch of the ancestors of the sultan, who were all worthy rulers in the service of religion and state, he counsels his master to put the vizier in sole effective charge of the administration. This will ensure security and prosperity, whereas interference with the vizier will weaken authority and lead to disaster. He devotes special sections to an elaboration of these two points, in order to show that the vizier must be independent and that the sultan by showing favour to the *'ulamā* will restore the greatness of religion and state as they were in the time of the first sultans. Then the *'ulamā* were a tower of strength to the dynasty with the Shaikh al-Islam as Grand Mufti at the helm, and the *Qāḍī-l-'askar* of Anatolia next in rank. They were then intent upon maintaining the order of the realm and of Islam and they properly supervised the affairs of the subjects. The rot set in when the offices of state were sold to the highest bidder and the *'ulamā* fell into disrepute as the result.

Next Kōja Beg deals with the army. He discusses at length the status of those in possession of large and small fiefs and those who receive pay. He strongly advises the abandonment of payment, and a return to reward in the form of fiefs. This will help to improve the lot of the poor subjects (*ra'āyā*) who are at present oppressed by heavy taxation. His picture of the ideal state contains an army without foreigners, a full treasury, and just, benevolent treatment of the masses of subjects, and he concludes by saying: "the order and arrangement of affairs is dependent on the noble heart of the Padishah: the Padishahs are the heart of the world;

while the heart is in good health the body is healthy, too." His practical advice to the sultan includes these points: stop corruption, appoint to office worthy *'ulamā*, limit the number of officials in certain classes and grades, and observe a definite scale in giving large and small fiefs; in other words, a return to the state of affairs under the early Ottomans, when everybody acted in accord with the sublime *Sharī'a*.[3]

The author of the *Naṣīḥatnāma* also pleads for a lowering of the taxes and gives advice on the organization and pay of the army and the officials. He recommends the sultan to supervise the mint and improve the coinage so that it regains its purchasing power; otherwise the army and the subjects will suffer hardship and difficulties. The chapter on taxes is particularly interesting because it reveals an extraordinary state of affairs. The author deprecates the auctioning of tax-lists to the highest bidder, since the poor subjects are the principal victims. The successful "proprietor" of the tax-list must first see that he gets the actual amount to be collected—the house-tax is singled out—plus the bribe he had to pay for getting the list allotted to himself, plus naturally a reward in the form of profit. The sultan is therefore advised to appoint pious Muslims as tax-collectors and to fix a certain percentage per house. "The *ra'āya* are the treasure of the Padishahs. As long as they enjoy prosperity and are not oppressed the treasury is full... they must be protected against injustice and oppression." The Mufti and the Qāḍīs must be admonished to act justly in accordance with the law of Islam.[4]

These two treatises were written by men of affairs who were only interested in advising the ruler on the current parlous state of public affairs in the hope of improving them. Ḥājjī Khalīfa's *Dustūr al-'amal*, though equally occasioned by the immediate danger to the good order of the state which he served as an official in the fiscal administration, is of a different order altogether. Its learned author sets his practical advice in the larger context of the purpose and function of the state as such, and in particular of the Muslim state represented by the foremost Muslim power of his day. Though he is not an original thinker and has really nothing new to say, his presentation of politics is born of serious thought, and shows knowledge of the Platonic legacy and the living tradition of the jurists and theologians of Islam. He writes as a historian with a philosophical bent, and offers practical advice for the improvement of institutions which have their origin in human needs and aspirations and have a long history behind them. He does so, fully conscious (through his systematic reading of philosophers and historians, theologians and jurists) that political organization and administration are dependent on, and conditioned by, men of character as much as by men of ability. Human character is formed by beliefs, convictions and ideas, which are themselves the result of a definite concept of human destiny and divine purpose.

He writes as a Muslim who has studied the writings of previous generations of Muslim authors. If we speak of the "Platonic legacy" it is much less in his case than in that of Al-Dawwānī a living tradition maintained by a study of Plato and Aristotle in their own writings and in those of Stoic, Neoplatonic, Neopythagorean and gnostic Hellenistic interpreters, commentators and continuators. It is a literary tradition, permeated with Muslim thought, and in a much diluted form, as we met it in Al-Dawwānī. He does not mention the *Falāsifa*, nor even Plato and Aristotle. Behrnauer tells us that the author refers in a marginal note in the Leipzig MS. to the beginning of Ibn Khaldūn's *Muqaddima*, and there are, indeed, points of contact between Ḥājjī Khalīfa and the historian of civilization, precisely in the seventeenth-century author's concept of civilization and its meaning.

We now consider the *Dustūr al-'amal* as found in Behrnauer's German translation in the author's own arrangement.

There is nothing unusual in his opening with the praise of God, the ruler of the world, whose will determines the just management of human affairs, and in his blessing Muḥammad, whose *Sharī'a*-government is a sufficient moderator of the temperament of the state and a restorative of the equilibrium of the natural forces of religion. Speaking of signs of abnormality and disharmony in the affairs and forces of the Ottoman empire, he gives this as the reason for his treatise, written in response to an inquiry ordered by the sultan. What is interesting is the recognition of these signs not as something peculiar to the Ottoman state but as something natural in any political organism; "caused by the normal course of the world ordained by God and brought about by the nature of civilization and human society".[5]

In the Introduction to his treatise, a "Directive to the measures ⟨needed⟩ to heal the damage", he treats of "the periods of the state" (*dawla*). *Dawla* is defined as "human society (organized) in the state". Basing himself on both speculative and practical philosophy he is certain that social relations correspond to the life of the individual, the physical side of which proceeds in three stages: an age of growth, an age of stasis and an age of decline. The same applies to the body politic.[6] This is reminiscent of Ibn Khaldūn's five phases through which the state runs within four generations. "Stasis" no doubt implies a development to full stature which is maintained until a downward trend makes itself felt. The duration of these three stages varies from state to state.

The statesman, like the physician, knows the symptoms peculiar to each stage and can take the appropriate steps.[7] We know that this comparison goes back to Plato; we have met it in Al-Dawwānī as an echo from the *Falāsifa.* No doubt Ḥājjī Khalīfa chose the title for his treatise for this reason and looked upon himself as a statesman-physician.

The first chapter is devoted to "the affairs of the people". God entrusts the people to sultans and emirs. In the style of the "Mirrors" Ḥajjī Khalīfa states that there is no authority (*mulk*) without an army (*rijāl*),[8] no army without finance (*māl*),[9] and no finance without subjects.

His knowledge of the human body with its humours is, no doubt, derived from Ibn Sīnā's *Qānūn* and ultimately from Galen. Like his Muslim sources, he is fond of comparing social phenomena with the elements and functions of the body throughout this treatise.

Just as the body consists of four elements or humours, so human association is composed of four "pillars" (*arkān*). Political government is in the hands of the sultan, who represents the rational soul which rules individual life. The sultan is assisted by the dignitaries who correspond to the senses and natural forces of man. The four "pillars" are the scholars (*ʿulamā*), the army (*ʿaskar*), the traders (*tajjār*) and the subjects (*raʿāyā*). His model may have been Al-Dawwānī, whose fourth class, the farmers, are here replaced by the labouring masses as a whole. The *ʿulamā* resemble the blood, and are the heart, that is, the source of the spirit of life (*rūḥ ḥayawānī*); they are those learned in the *Sharīʿa*, and in the *haqīqa*, doctors of the law and mystical thinkers, the latter corresponding to Al-Dawwānī's *'urafā al-ḥaqīqa.*[10] They hand their knowledge on to the masses directly or indirectly; as "the spirit of life" is the cause of the existence and maintenance of the body, so science is the cause of the existence and maintenance of society.[11] But whereas Al-Dawwānī included the philosophers in his first class, Ḥājjī Khalīfa restricts it to the *'ulamā* and the mystics.

The four classes as "political beings by nature" act upon and with each other to their mutual advantage; hence the social organism and the "complexion" of the state remain healthy as long as they are in equilibrium.

The same analogy is applied to the other three classes; within this seemingly theoretical exercise Ḥājjī Khalīfa discusses the sickness of the present state and attributes it to the same causes as his two predecessors: too-heavy taxation with consequent oppression of the masses, and the sale and re-sale of offices in order to enrich the individual at the expense of the masses. This happens openly although such misuse and abuse is condemned both by natural[12] and by religious law; it goes against justice and reason.[13] Since even infidel kings oppose such practices as unjust it is incumbent on Muslims (who were given the divine law) to repent and to return to justice. Offices must no longer be sold and re-sold and taxes must be reduced, otherwise the curse for the transgression of the law and the guilt of injustice and oppression and violence will lead to the certain ruin of the empire.[14]

The second chapter is devoted to the army. An interesting gloss in the margin of the Leipzig MS. states that after the period of stasis the army increases its power. Mercenaries become more numerous, requiring a larger expenditure on pay, which demands a close watch lest damage befall the other classes. At the same time, the author thinks the army must be kept at its present strength, but pay must be reduced. There are ways and means of satisfying both sides, but they cannot be discussed in writing. The ruler must use his authority to achieve this end. Both religion and state demand such a measure.[15]

The third chapter discusses finance. He again uses the analogy of the human being: the rational soul equals the sultan, as he stated earlier; the reasoning faculty is represented by the vizier; the faculty of comprehension corresponds to the *mufti,* and so forth for all grades and degrees of the administrative hierarchy. Only this well-arranged hierarchy working in unison guarantees the even flow and distribution of public money. Officials must be absolutely incorruptible in order to preserve the population from oppression, injustice and poverty. Once these forces weaken, the circulation is disturbed and decline sets in. This decline—entirely in line with Ibn Khaldūn's teaching—is accompanied and characterized by luxury and ease. It first attacks the ruling circles, and then the middle classes, with the result that expenditure grows out of all proportion to income. Ḥājjī Khalīfa proves this by treasury returns of revenue and expenditure which show that in the third phase of the state, that of ageing and decline, expenses grow faster than income.

From this general observation he deduces that the necessary balance cannot easily be restored and, since the financial experts say it is altogether impossible, he suggests strong action by the wielder of power, the sultan. He advocates measures which might halt the downward trend, at least temporarily. In the first place a powerful ruler must force the people to obey the law. Since the dignitaries argue that God is the ruler of the world and the sultan merely his *khalīfa*, they set a good example by their behaviour and actions in justice. Of one mind and heart they administer the affairs of state to the honour and glory of God. By "dignitaries" he means not only the ministers and their subordinate officials, but also the *'ulamā* and mystics forming the first class from which the administrators are naturally chosen.

In the third place the leaders of the army—that is, those who have experience of affairs—band together to uphold right and justice. If need be, they will remove unjust officials by the use of troops, thus giving service to religion and state. Lastly, the ministers combine to enact justice and, with the help of the army, they keep down expenses. He deplores the difficulty of meeting this last requirement because the right men are not available and most people are out for pleasure. It reads like a counsel of despair when Ḥājjī Khalīfa says that at the moment of composition of the treatise the solution is a strong man. But he makes the following suggestions: restrict expenditure in high offices of state and appoint devout, unselfish and understanding men to key posts. This will cut excessive expenditure within a few years. Take off or at least reduce taxes and thus alleviate the financial straits of the people. Keep uncorrupt men in office for a long time and forbid the buying and selling of offices; punish severely those who oppress the people. In a few years the people will regain strength, and prosperity will return to the realm.

He consoles himself (and the sultan, if he thought this treatise would ever reach him!) with the remark that these troubles are nothing new, and that rivalry for office and power and rebellion were always resolved by appropriate measures in the past, with the help of God.[16]

Finally, he draws certain conclusions: there are several means to rectify the existing situation, which are partly possible, partly impossible, to apply. The first is again "the man of the sword" who will enforce obedience to the law. Next, the real Padishah is he who rules the world and to whom treasury, army and people belong; the human ruler is only his vicegerent. Those who think so will serve in justice, being of one heart and mind, and administer the affairs of state for the love and honour of God and will maintain the realm.[17] What follows is also a repetition of earlier suggestions. He ends with an appeal to the ministers and subordinate officials to act in accordance with the holy law so that God will help them to vanquish the enemies of the state. If they administer the state well in accordance with the regulations and precepts of the law and of reason they will bring it into harmony with the basic law of the realm.[18]

If we look at this mixture of pious hope and realistic appraisal of the political situation we may legitimately ask ourselves what the author had in mind. Did he expect to reach the ear of the sultan and to impress him sufficiently to act upon the advice tendered? Behrnauer quotes Ḥājjī Khalīfa as saying: "Since I knew that my final result would hardly be realized I did not trouble any further. But a Padishah will in time have his attention drawn to it and realize it; this will then bear the choicest fruits for him."[19] In fact, the work was shown to the sultan of his own day and the author was informed of it.

Was there any possibility that the conscience of the ruling class could be awakened to the danger that threatened the state? Would the appeal to obey the *Sharīʿa* find an echo in their hearts?

It seems that Ḥājjī Khalīfa thought and hoped so. But his appeal to force, to the sword of a strong man, should make us hesitate, and we should not perhaps rate the chances of success too high, if it were not for the fact that both appeals are made simultaneously. This combination reminds us of Ibn Khaldūn's dictum that a religious call without '*Aṣabīya* will not succeed, in other words that spiritual authority is only a real power if it is backed by military force and personal coercion, that only this combination ensures successful government in the interests of all.

If we compare his treatise with those of his two predecessors we see a noble double legacy applied to the problems of the day.[20]

NOTES

CHAPTER I

This chapter aims at setting the scene for the subsequent discussion. It is meant to illustrate the basic unity of the human aim in the Middle Ages and the "climate of opinion" in which men of all creeds shared and expressed their views. It serves, together with the Introduction, as a general introduction of the subject. It is taken up once more in Part II, chapter V, with special reference to the Muslim philosophers.

1 *Nicomachean Ethics*, I, II, 1094a, b (H. Rackham's edition and translation). For the political thought of Plato see Sir Ernest Barker, *Greek Political Theory*[3] (London, 1947).
2 *Ibid.* 1094b.
3 Quoted from Thomas Aquinas, *Philosophical Texts*, edited and translated by T. Gilby (Oxford University Press 1951), pp. 268 and 284.
4 *K. Taḥṣīl al-sa'āda* (Hyderabad, 1345 A.H.).
5 See ed. Cairo, 1322 A.H., p. 14.
6 See *Dalālat al-ḥā'irīn*, ed. S. Munk, vol. I, ch. 54; vol. III, chs. 28 and especially 51; and Erwin I. J. Rosenthal, (*a*) "Maimonides' Conception of State and Society" in *Moses Maimonides*, ed. I. Epstein (London, 1935), pp. 200f.; (*b*) "Medieval Judaism and the Law" in *Law and Religion* (*Judaism and Christianity*, vol. III, London, 1938), section "The Philosophers and Divine Revelation", pp. 196–206.
7 See *Wenn die Waffen schweigen* (Basel, 1945), p. 22.
8 *Il Convivio*, IV, 4.
9 *De Monarchia*, III, 16.
10 Thomas Aquinas expressed it in these words: "At the sight of God the mind cannot but delight" (Gilby, p. 273).
11 Cf. Erwin I. J. Rosenthal, "Avicenna's Influence on Jewish Thought", in *Avicenna: Scientist and Philosopher* (London, 1952), *s.v.* Philo.
12 See E. Barker, *op. cit.* pp. 304ff. and on the connection between law and religion, *ibid.* pp. 351ff.
13 He follows the first Arab philosopher Al-Kindī. See E.I.J.R., "Maimonides", etc., *loc. cit.* p. 193, and ch. V, below, n. 3.
14 In his *Reason and Revelation in the Middle Ages* (New York and London, 1939), pp. 72ff.
15 In his *God and Philosophy* (1941), p. 33.
16 *Ibid.* p. 41.
17 *Ibid.* p. 43.
18 *Ibid.* p. 47.
19 Quoted after Gilson, *ibid.* p. 90.
20 In his *Reason and Revelation in the Middle Ages*, pp. 81f.
21 *Dalālat al-ḥā'irīn*, vol. II, ch. 40, p. 86b. This is reminiscent of

Al-Fārābī's *Iḥṣā al-ʿulūm*, pp. 91 ff. See also ch. v, below, pp. 115 ff., and p. 119 with note 13.

22 *Ibid.* vol. III, ch. 27, pp. 59b, 60a.

23 *Ibid.* vol. III, ch. 28, pp. 60b, 61a.

24 *Ibid.* vol. II, ch. 39, p. 85a.

CHAPTER II

1 Or, as Professor D. H. Baneth has convincingly argued, Islam means absolute monotheism.

2 See, for the several roots of Muslim law, the relevant articles in *EI* Cf. D. Santillana, *Istituzioni di Diritto Musulmano* (Roma, 1926), vol. I, especially Libro Primo.

3 See the important study by Ilse Lichtenstaedter "From Particularism to Unity: Race, Nationality and Minorities in the early Islamic Empire" in *Islamic Culture*, vol. XXIII (1949), pp. 251–80.

4 See J. Wellhausen, *Skizzen und Vorarbeiten*, vol. IV (Berlin, 1889), "2. Muhammads Gemeindeordnung von Medina".

5 See Ilse Lichtenstaedter, *op. cit.* pp. 258, 263.

6 See Wellhausen, *op. cit.* p. 74.

7 *Ibid.* p. 76.

8 The Sunnī challenge came from certain Muʿtazilites. See I. Goldziher's "Hellenistischer Einfluss auf muʿtazilitische Chalifats-Theorien" in *Der Islam*, vol. VI, pp. 173 ff. According to Fūṭī the *imām* can be dispensed with at certain periods. Abū Bakr al-Aṣamm differs from Fūṭī in that he thinks that the *imām* can be spared in times of peace and tranquillity (precisely when Fūṭī considers him essential). He also makes the perfectionist demand that the installation of an *imām* be valid only if the agreement of every single member of the *umma* has first been obtained. This is, in fact, equivalent to the assumption that the institution of the caliphate is not necessary at all. Goldziher is of the opinion that the source for this view is Pseudo-Aristotle's *Peri Basileias*, which, according to Lippert, was translated into Arabic by Yaḥya b. Bitrīq.

Sectarian opposition also came from the Kharijites, who rejected the caliphate altogether, as well as from the *Shīʿa*, who owned allegiance to ʿAlī and his direct descendants only.

9 *Mawerdii Constitutiones politicae*, ed. M. Enger (Bonn, 1853); French translation by E. Fagnan under the title *Les status gouvernementaux* (Alger, 1915), based on Enger's edition and an Algiers MS., accompanied by valuable notes.

Abū-l-Ḥasan ʿAlī b. Muḥammad b. Ḥabīb al-Māwardī, a native of Basra, was a prominent representative of the school of al-Shāfiʿī, and as such his treatise on government is of special interest for our problem. Like other Muslims who received the traditional education, he wrote on many topics besides law, for example, a commentary on the Qurʾān, a treatise on prophecy and several works on ethics. As for his legal writings, it is noteworthy that government and administration at all levels were his principal concern.

As *qāḍī* under the Caliph Al-Kā'im, who entrusted him also with diplomatic missions, he was actively engaged in the application and administration of *Fiqh*. This, no doubt, helped him in his authoritative exposition of the principles of constitutional law as well. His *Al-Aḥkām al-sulṭānīya* are the result of blending reasoning derived from the traditional bases of law (Qur'ān, Sunna, Hadith, *Ijmā*' and *Qiyās*) with historical and political deductions from the formative period of Islam, supported by the views of the *salaf* (the early Muslims), and a realistic appraisal of the contemporary political scene. He also discusses objectively the views of other jurists, not necessarily belonging to his own *Shāfi'ī madhhab*.

10 "Al-Māwardī's Theory of the Khilāfah" in *Islamic Culture*, vol. XI (1937).

11 Although these terms must be used to describe the constitutional theory they are, strictly speaking, not applicable to Islam, as I have tried to show in the introductory chapter.

12 *Aḥkām*, p. 3. Cf. also Ibn Tūmart's statement that the *imāma* was "one of the pillars of religion and one of the props of the *Sharī'a*, and the maintenance of right in the world (*dunya*) was only guaranteed by the existence of the *imāma* (*i'tiqādu-l-imāma*, literally: 'affirmation, belief') at all times until the hour of judgement" (*K. Muḥammad b. Tūmart mahdī al-muwaḥḥidīn*, ed. Luciani (Alger, 1903), pp. 245 ff.). Ibn Tūmart traces the existence of the imamate from Adam through Noah to Abraham.

13 *Aḥkām*, pp. 7 f.

14 *Ibid.* p. 5: '*adāla*, to be equal to all the requirements (of the *imāma*), a moral quality, a sense of justice and equity; '*ilm*, understood in a legal sense, as explained in the text, and comprising a knowledge of the traditional Muslim sciences necessary for interpreting the law; *salāma*, soundness of the senses of hearing and sight, of speech, of the limbs, guaranteeing free movement (this is counted as two conditions); *ra'y* (sound) judgement enabling him to govern his subjects and to secure their welfare; *shajā'a wa-najda*, courage (prowess) and energy to wage holy war (*jihād*) and to defend the realm; *nasab*, descent from the Quraish.

15 He reduces them to five: '*ilm*, '*adāla*, *kifāya*, *salāma*, *nasab*. See *Muqaddima* (ed. Beyrouth, 1900), pp. 193 ff. Cf. also Erwin I. J. Rosenthal, *Ibn Khaldûns Gedanken über den Staat* (München/Berlin, 1932), pp. 64–8.

16 *Ibid.* Cf. also E.I.J.R., *op. cit.* the first chapter on "Aṣabīya", and F. Gabrieli, "Il concetto della 'aṣabīyyah nel pensiero storico di Ibn Khaldûn" in *Atti della Reale Academia delle Scienze di Torino*, vol. LXV (1930), pp. 473–512. The question is fully discussed in ch. IV below.

17 Three conditions must be fulfilled: '*adāla*, in respect of all the con-

ditions required of the candidate; *'ilm*, knowledge of those worthy of the *imāma*; and *ra'y wa-ḥikma*, judgement and wisdom to choose the one fittest in every respect for the caliphal dignity. (*Aḥkām*, p. 5.)

18 *Ibid.* p. 6. "Qualified elector" means, in theory, one who fulfils the three conditions (see last note). These electors have come to be identified with "those who have the power to bind and to loosen" (*ahl al-ḥall wa-l-'aqd*). The latter are represented by the *'ulamā* in every generation. Since they stand for the whole *jamā'a* or *umma* they are deemed sufficient for the required *ijmā'*. Cf. also Imām al-Ḥaramayn (Al-Juwaynī), *Irshād*, ed. and transl. J. D. Luciani (Paris, 1938), pp. 239–356 for the same view, stressing that one properly qualified elector can invest the caliph, no unanimous *ijmā'* by the *umma* being required, since there is neither a rational nor a traditional necessity for witnesses in public.

19 This can be seen from the high-sounding titles conferred upon the caliphs in the Abbasid period, especially at a time when their effective power had passed into the capable hands of emirs and sultans. The "Vicegerent of the Prophet" and "Commander of the Faithful" has become the "Vicegerent of Allah", "the Shadow of God", etc. When E. Tyan, in *Le Califat* (*Institutions du Droit Public Musulman*, vol. I, Paris, 1954) adduces poets as proof for the sacrosanct character of the caliphs (e.g. pp. 471, 473) with expressions like "the holy prophetic presence", the question may be put whether this is not poetic exaggeration rather than clear evidence of the growing tendency to stress the religious, indeed, the theocratic character of the office of caliph.

20 *Aḥkām*, pp. 6f. See also E. Tyan, *op. cit.* This important work is an excellent illustration of the thesis that the theory of the caliphate is based entirely on historical precedent; it adduces ample evidence from the Muslim historians, traditionists and men of letters and poets, which forms the material for constitutional theory and law. As for the two precedents set by the election of Abū Bakr and Uthmān, Tyan is of the opinion that Abū Bakr's election was not properly carried out; in the struggle, confusion and indecision among Aws and Ḥazrāj, 'Omar seized Abū Bakr's hand and declared for him. This led to the *bay'a* of the companions in private, followed by a second *bay'a* in public. Similarly, he agrees with Caetani and Levi della Vida who discount the testamentary designation by Abū Bakr of 'Omar as his successor; 'Omar simply seized power on the death of Abū Bakr. In fact, no account of 'Omar's accession left us by the historians mentions a *bay'a*.

Nevertheless, the results of modern historical research cannot affect the classical theory of the *khilāfa*, which is based on a legend conveniently publicized, because its truth has been accepted by generations of Muslim believers, learned as well as unlearned.

21 See above, p. 24.

22 See *Aḥkām*, pp. 8f. Two later *Shāfi'ī* jurists, Al-Ghazālī and Ibn Jamā'a, writing on constitutional law, faced this ugly political reality

and unashamedly declared accession by usurpation lawful, as we shall see later in this chapter, pp. 40ff., and 44ff.

23 Owing to the similarity of treatment, discussion of the vizierate and emirate will be reserved for Ibn Jamā'a (below pp. 47f.).

24 See *Uṣūl al-Dīn*, p. 274. Al-Juwaynī, *op. cit.* pp. 239–357, shares this view.

25 See *Aḥkām*, pp. 12f. for the following paragraph. Tyan, *op. cit.* pp. 267ff., sees in *'ahd* here not a specific contract, but only a juridical bond, being simply a formal promise of obedience to the order of the caliph who designates his successor to whom homage is paid. But there can be no doubt that this "bond" was legally and morally binding upon the *'ulamā* present, hence their *bay'a*. Tyan further claims that the person designated was not an "heir presumptive" but a "caliph *in potentia*" (*calife en puissance*). I do not see how the one could exclude the other. He is, however, right in emphasizing the religious character of the *bay'a*, since *bay'a* to caliph equals *bay'a* to God. It is the expression of a personal obligation to the caliph; homage signifies recognition and the duty of obedience (*ibid.* pp. 326ff.).

26 Tyan, *op. cit.* p. 203, thinks that the theocratic character of the caliph requires that he should designate his successor, since no human authority can hinder him who has been called to office by God.

27 See *Aḥkām*, pp. 13ff.

28 See *ibid.* p. 17.

29 See *ibid.* p. 19.

30 Consultation of the *'ulamā* is stressed by all writers on the *imāma*, especially the authors of "Mirrors", as an important obligation of the caliph, as we shall see later. See also n. 25, *re bay'a*. Cf. Tyan, *op. cit.* pp. 257–65, for examples from Mu'āwiya onwards, right through the Umayyad dynasty until towards its end the caliph was too weak, and the great men, especially the members of the ruling house, designate the next sovereign. In Tyan's opinion the succession was secure after the first five Umayyad caliphs; designation had come to stay and "had become the guiding principle of public law in Islam". The same applies to the Abbasid dynasty. The hereditary-dynastic principle underlying the designation of a successor seems to me capable of derivation as much from pre-Islamic tribal practice as from Byzantine and Sassanian examples, though the latter have undoubtedly accentuated the tendency, as they have furthered the trend towards absolutism and despotism concealed under the cloak of piety and by the pretence of fulfilling the demands of the *Sharī'a* on the part of the Abbasid caliphs.

31 See *Aḥkām*, pp. 20 ff., for details about the prerogatives and duties of heirs presumptive after their accession and about those of the electors.

32 See *ibid.* pp. 23f.

33 Tyan, *op. cit.*, brings many examples to show the divine origin of the office of caliph. Thus, he quotes from Ṭabarī 'Omar's claim when

calling the Arabs to war and conquest that "God has conferred upon me authority over you". Ibn 'Abd-Rabbīhi (d. 940) reports in his *'Iqd al-farīḍ*, belonging to the literary genre of "Mirrors", many a saying to this effect; for example, Uthmān exclaimed when facing his murderers: "I am the servant of God and his *khalīfa*" (vol. III, p. 88). Yazīd says of his deceased father Mu'āwiya, according to Ibn Qutayba's *Imāma*, vol. I, p. 186 (quoted by Tyan, p. 440), that he was installed by God as his vicegerent to rule his creatures. Abū Yūsuf, whose introduction to his *K. al-kharāj* (pp. 2ff.) will occupy us later on, tells Hārūn al-Rashīd that God has invested him with power. On the other hand, when Tyan quotes Hajjāj as addressing the caliph 'Abd al-Malik as *khalīfa rabb-al-'ālamīn* (quoted from *'Iqd*, vol. III, p. 240), it may be seriously doubted whether this studied exaggeration and obvious flattery can be accepted at its face value. The expression "*rabb-al-'ālamīn*" is one of the names and designations of God in the Qur'ān and hardly applicable to a human being even though he be the divinely appointed caliph. For the titles of caliphs see also I. Goldziher, *Muhamm. Studien*, vol. II, pp. 61f.

34 Abū Ḥāmid Muḥammad Al-Ghazālī was born in 1058 at Ṭūs and educated under the principal guidance of Al-Juwaynī. He was well received and highly respected at the court of Niẓām al-Mulk, the all-powerful vizier of the Abbasid caliph, and appointed to Niẓām's *madrasa* when he was 34. Having passed through several phases in his spiritual development (and consequently in his attitudes, outlook and opinions), he finally succeeded in harmonizing the intellectual, mystical and legalistic trends in Islam into an intensely personal faith based on strong religious experience. As Imām Abū Ḥāmid *hujjatu-l-Islām* he commands general respect and unchallenged authority among the faithful.

35 In his *Faṣl al-maqāl*, ed. L. Gauthier (Alger, 1948), p. 21, he accuses Al-Ghazālī of having no definite doctrine, but of being a philosopher with the *falāsifa*, an *Ash'arī* with the *Ash'arīs* and a Sufi with the Sufis.

36 See *K. al-iqtiṣād fī-l-'itiqād*[2] (1327 A.H.), p. 95.

37 See above, p. 28.

38 See *Maqāṣid al-falāsifa* (Cairo, 1355 A.H.), pp. 3f. His order is: politics, economics, ethics, whereas Ibn Sīnā lists them as ethics, economics, politics in his *Aqsām al-'ulūm* (*Tis' rasā'il*, Istanbul, 1298 A.H., pp. 73f.).

39 See I. Goldziher, *Streitschrift des Ġazālī gegen die Bāṭinijja Sekte* (Leiden, 1916). The following exposition is based on Goldziher's masterly analysis (pp. 80ff.) and extracts from the Arabic text. Cf. also Imām al-ḥaramayn (Al-Juwaynī), *Irshād* for the same view that the discourse on the *imāma* does not belong to the principles of the faith (*uṣūl al-'itiqād*), pp. 231–344, and that all questions connected with it are questions of (independent) legal decision (*min al-mujtahadāt*).

40 See *K. al-iqtiṣād*, p. 95.

41 See Goldziher, *op. cit.* pp. 81 f.

42 Or "harmony" (*niẓām*). L. Binder, "Al-Ghazālī's Theory of Islamic Government" (*The Muslim World*, vol. XLV, 3 (July 1955), pp. 229–41) speaks of Al-Ghazālī's insistence on the *ijmā'* as "the most important innovation". First of all, this is no new thing, but one of the *uṣūl al-fiqh*; secondly, Al-Ghazālī explicitly states that *ijmā'* is insufficient without an *imām* who is obeyed.

43 He may here be deliberately equivocal, however, and may mean *sulṭān* in both senses. In Al-Ghazālī's "Mirror", the *Tibr al-masbūk* (p. 48, l. 7) *mulk* stands in place of *sulṭān*, and in his *K. al-mustaẓhirī* the pair is *Islām* and *mulk*. See Prof. Lambton's article "The Theory of Kingship in the *Naṣīḥat ul Mulūk* of Ghazālī" in *Islamic Quarterly*, vol. I, i, for an analysis of Al-Ghazālī's "Mirror".

44 See *K. al-iqtiṣād*, p. 95. L. Binder, *loc. cit.*, stresses the co-operation between caliph and sultan; he probably has *Iḥyā*, vol. II, p. 124, in mind, where *sulṭān* clearly refers to the effective ruler.

45 See *K. al-mustaẓhirī* in Goldziher, *op. cit.* p. 91.

46 See *K. al-iqtiṣād*, p. 95 and cf. *K. al-mustaẓhirī* in Goldziher's quotation (*op. cit.* p. 93): "Divine religion and the law of the Prophet are the aim and object of everything."

47 Al-Juwaynī, *op. cit.* pp. 240–358, insists on the *imām* being one of the *ahl al-ijtihād*. Cf. also Al-Māwardī, above, p. 29 with n. 14. As for the question of deposition Al-Juwaynī is against it, but he gives the impious *imām* leave to resign (*ibid.*).

48 See *K. al-mustaẓhirī* in Goldziher, *op. cit.* pp. 83 ff. *Wara'* also figures as a necessary qualification for the *imām* with Al-Juwaynī, *op. cit.* pp. 240–358. In his view, descent from the Quraish is not necessary, but *kifāya* is demanded by the unanimous consent (*ijmā'*) of the *umma*.

49 See *K. al-iqtiṣād*, p. 97.

50 It is surprising to find Al-Ghazālī employing this title for the vicegerent of the Prophet ("God's caliph over all mankind", see Goldziher, *op. cit.* pp. 58 f.). See *K. al-iqtiṣād*, p. 95 and Goldziher, *op. cit.*, for a similar statement in the *K. al-mustaẓhirī*, p. 92.

51 See Goldziher, *op. cit.* p. 88 and especially *Iḥyā*, vol. II, p. 124; cf. also *K. al-iqtiṣād*, p. 96. L. Binder, *op. cit.* n. 18, states that if a qualified Quraishite is the actual holder of power he can appoint himself as *imām* according to Al-Ghazālī. As far as I know Al-Ghazālī nowhere says so explicitly. But Ibn Jamā'a admits as lawful forceful seizure by usurpation. See below, p. 44.

52 Iḥyā, vol. II, p. 124. Cf. also H. A. R. Gibb, "Some Considerations on the Sunni Theory of the Caliphate" in *Archives d'histoire du Droit Oriental*, vol. III (1948), pp. 401–10; A. H. Siddiqi, *Caliphate and Kingship in Medieval Persia* (Lahore, 1942), pp. 126 ff.; and L. Binder, *op. cit.* pp. 232 and 240. The last-named author speaks of a multilateral conception of the caliphate and of multilateral rather than unitary government. But although in practice the functions of governmental authority are carried out by caliph, sultan and *'ulamā*,

the application of the term "multilateral" to the government does not seem justified. Binder's further statement that each of the three "represents a major element of political power in the *Sunnī* Community" is likely to be misunderstood unless the term "political" is used in its Islamic sense of including religion, and not in our modern meaning. The caliphate is a unity and a unitary institution. Pre-Islamic tribal organization in Arabia influenced its constitution as much as Byzantine and Sassanian ideas of absolute monarchy did. In theory, therefore, its authority is ultimately vested only in the *imām*, even with Al-Ghazālī. We must beware of applying modern constitutional terms (and their meaning) to Islamic institutions, especially to the idea of the caliphate itself. The part played by the *'ulamā* in the government (both as advisers, owing to their expert knowledge of the *Sharī'a* and its correct interpretation, and as *qāḍīs*, applying the law) may well be a little overrated. No doubt they would have liked to play such a prominent part. But the repeated admonition addressed to the caliph to seek, listen to and act upon their advice—so freely offered by all the later jurists and the authors of "Mirrors"—is perhaps born of self-interest and desire rather than the result of actual influence in the day-to-day administration of the Muslim state.

53 He was a noted jurist, theologian and teacher and held the office of *qāḍī* in Jerusalem 1288–91, then that of Grand Qāḍī of Cairo and (1294) of Damascus. Later he was Professor of *Fiqh* in Cairo. His treatise under discussion deserves notice as a compendium of political statutes, like Al-Māwardī's *Al-Aḥkām al-sulṭānīya*.

54 *Taḥrīr al-aḥkām fī tadbīr ahl al-Islām*, edited and translated under the title "Handbuch des Islamischen Staats- und Verwaltungsrechtes von Badr- Ad-Dīn Ibn Ǧamā'ah" by Hans Kofler in *Islamica*, vol. VI, pp. 349–414 and vol. VII, pp. 1–64, continued in the "Schlussheft" (1938), pp. 18–129. Both Kofler and Binder emphasize the purely theoretical character of Al-Māwardī's treatise and do not see that he tried as hard in his day to save the Abbasid caliphate and the unity of Islam as Al-Ghazālī and Ibn Jamā'a did in theirs. Political conditions had radically changed in the meantime and the power and authority of the caliph had greatly deteriorated. Compromise in practice was no longer sufficient but had to be carried right into the theory of the *khilāfa*. See also pp. 27f., above.

55 See Kofler, *op. cit.* vol. VII, p. 36, n. 1, for the designations used by Ibn Jamā'a for the sovereign, namely, *imām*, *sulṭān* and *khalīfa*. That he is never called *amīr al-mu'minīn* is not correct, however, since he is so designated in ch. 4, p. 367. *Malik* is also used a few times, though not intended as a title. What is so striking is that Ibn Jamā'a often uses two terms together, joined either by *wa* or *aw*, especially in the first three chapters, e.g. *imām wa-sulṭān* (p. 356 and *passim*); *khalīfa.wa-sulṭān* (p. 358); *sulṭān wa-khalīfa* (p. 359). In the detailed discussion of military and financial matters (*jihād*, *kharāj*, *fay'*, *dhimma*, etc.) only one term is used, chiefly *sulṭān*, and this mostly, but not exclusively, where rights and duties are concerned which belong to the ruler and which we would term "political" rather than "religious". *Imām* sometimes occurs alone, especially where purely religious duties are concerned, such as measures against heretics and rebels (vol. VII, ch. 16, pp. 24ff.). These belong to the religious leader and "Defender of the Faith". The combination *mulūk wa-salāṭīn* naturally refers to the wielders of effective power, as is clear from the qualification *ka-'urf...fī zamāninā* (e.g. vol. VI, p. 359). I venture to suggest that the combination of *imām wa-sulṭān* and *khalīfa wa-sulṭān* in the first chapters dealing with the theory of the *khilāfa* or *imāma* is intentional and should be regarded as an attempt to uphold the supreme authority of the sovereign as the unitary head of the religious-social-political one *ummat-al-Islām* of the *Sharī'a*, irrespective of the man who holds the actual power in the state.

56 This is reminiscent of Al-Ghazālī, see above, p. 39.

57 Nīẓām al-Mulk says in his *Siyāsat nāma* (discussed in the next chapter) that a just king disappears as soon as his subjects no longer obey the ordinances of the *Sharī'a*. He seems, thus, to make a good ruler dependent on law-abiding subjects.

58 See above, p. 42. Cf. *Taḥrīr, op. cit.* vol. VI, p. 355. Ibn Taymīya, *Siyāsa shar'īya* (Cairo, 1951), p. 173, quotes very much the same view with a slightly different wording as a Hadith: Sixty years of an unjust *imām* are better than one night without a *sulṭān*.

59 *Taḥrīr*, p. 356. Kofler asserts (n. 3) that *bay'a is* the conclusion of the contract. But this can hardly be the case since *bay'a* is not synonymous with *'ahd* or *'aqd*. What Ibn Jamā'a means—like his contemporary Ibn Taymīya, and Al-Juwaynī before him—is that only private *bay'a* is necessary, and he thus dispenses with the second, public, *bay'a*.

60 *Taḥrīr*, p. 357.

61 Sir Hamilton Gibb, *op. cit.*, asserts that Ibn Jamā'a "gave the final consecration to secular absolutism" (p. 403) and that "the Ash'arite theory ends up by divorcing the Imamate from the *Sharī'a* and the complete negation of the rule of Law" (p. 404). The first statement seems to call for some qualification, since the term "secular" is hardly applicable to Islam and certainly not in the case of Ibn Jamā'a. As for the second assertion, it may be readily conceded that this was so if we consider the political reality of the Abbasid caliphate from the eleventh, and especially from the thirteenth century onwards. But it was not so in the theory of the *khilāfa*, which at no time abandoned the claim of the *Sharī'a* to supremacy and final authority, no matter how far it dared to compromise with political realities. Even if we were to insist that this theory was but a fiction, we must admit that this particular fiction possessed more reality and staying power than the Abbasid state which it fitted so badly. By legalizing usurpation, it tried to keep the *imāma* within and under the *Sharī'a* and thus to secure the rule of law.

62 *Taḥrīr*, pp. 358f. See also pp. 47f. with notes, below. It is to be noted that by devoting a special chapter to *tafwīḍ*, delegation (of authority), Ibn Jamā'a departs from Al-Māwardī, most likely because the latter was faced with the Buwaihid emirs only. Hence we find Al-Māwardī dealing with the same problem under the heading "Emirate" as a subdivision of the "General Emirate" which he defines in these terms: "the emirate of (forceful) seizure is that which is concluded under duress (lit. from necessity, constraint, *'an iḍṭirārin*), that is, when the emir takes possession of a country by force, the caliph invests him with the emirate over it and delegates to him (or entrusts him with, *yufawwiḍu ilayhi*) the administration and government of it" (*Aḥkām*, p. 54). Ibn Jamā'a, on the other hand, tries to legalize usurpation of independent power by men who are no longer satisfied with calling themselves emirs, but "kings or sultans". The use of the term "*ka-'urf*" points in the same direction: to confer legality on an act of aggression.

63 *Taḥrīr*, p. 359.

64 *Ibid.* p. 365. This is his own reason for the institution and is not found in Al-Māwardī. *Naẓar* here and throughout this chapter stands for overall responsibility within the confines of the caliph's empire. It is not only a general supervision, but includes also the nomination of *qāḍīs*, *muftis* and the chief of police with his officials, as well as the appointment of subordinate officials who execute the vizier's orders and are in charge of departments under his authority. In case of dismissal of the vizier, only those officials immediately under his direct authority are, as a rule, replaced by order of the caliph. A comparison with Al-Māwardī's *Aḥkām* shows here, as almost everywhere, a close resemblance, if not complete identity, in treatment. Ibn Jamā'a naturally uses the same technical terms with the same meaning. As here, he sometimes provides a reason or finds a justification where Al-Māwardī only states the legal position about qualifications, rights and duties. Cf. *Aḥkām*, pp. 33ff.

65 Ibn Jamā'a, *op. cit.* p. 366, reproduces Al-Māwardī's definition and exposition in a more concise form. Kofler, *op. cit.* vol. VII, p. 56, translates the passage I quoted in the text, wrongly as: "...und das, was jener [he means the Vizier] billigt, zu bestätigen und das, was jener abschlägig bescheidet, zurückzuziehen." This is not only grammatically but also logically impossible, since there would be no point in the *imām*—who is the subject, not the vizier—using his *ra'y* and *ijtihād* when in fact, according to Kofler's translation, he uses only a rubber stamp. A comparison between the *Taḥrīr* and the *Aḥkām* establishes complete identity in meaning, as is clear from Al-Māwardī (*Aḥkām*, pp. 38ff.): "...in order to confirm thereof what accords with what is right and proper (*ṣawāb*) and to revoke what runs counter to it, for the government of the *umma* is entrusted to him and is a charge on his (personal) application (*ijtihād*)." We see that Ibn Jamā'a upholds the theory: the caliph is, as sovereign, ultimately responsible.

66 *Taḥrīr*, pp. 366f. Only strong caliphs in effective control of the government would employ this type of vizier.

67 This is not found in Al-Māwardī. As stated in n. 62 Al-Māwardī subdivided the "General Emirate", and we have seen that his "Emirate by Conquest" exactly corresponds to what Ibn Jamā'a called "delegation (of authority)" conferred upon self-appointed "kings and sultans" who have conquered a territory by force of arms. This is not to be confused with the self-appointed *imām* (see p. 45, above). The only difference is that Al-Māwardī thinks of one country or territory, whereas Ibn Jamā'a speaks of *every* country. It is possible that for this reason he called the holder of power *malik* as the *khalīfa* of the *imām*, thus taking account of the change and transformation of power that had occurred since the time of Al-Māwardī. However, the matter is very complicated, for Al-Māwardī explicitly states that the "General Emir" must fulfil the same conditions as the "vizier-in-charge" (lit. "vizier by delegation"), namely, those of the caliph, apart from descent from the Quraish (*Aḥkām*, p. 48). Normally, the vizier is the prime minister, whereas the man on whom the "General Emirate" is conferred—whether by choice or free will (*ikhtiyār*), or under duress—is a ruler, a prince. The conclusion forces itself on the reader of these treatises that although in law a distinction is maintained between vizier and emir, in practice they may be identical, or at least interchangeable.

68 This corresponds to Al-Māwardī's second kind of "General Emirate". Ibn Jamā'a may have classed it "particular" because he had to distinguish it from what he called "General Emirate" and from his legalized *malik*.

69 See *Taḥrīr*, pp. 358f. and pp. 46f., above. *'Urf* or *'āda* is custom, recognized as law, but inferior to the *Sharī'a*, by which it should be replaced (see *EI*, *s.v.*).

70 *Ibid.* pp. 367f. Cf. also Al-Māwardī, *Aḥkām*, pp. 57ff.

71 *Ibid.* p. 369.

72 "*Imāms*" here refers to outstanding or great jurists, such as the founders of the four orthodox rites, and Al-Ghazālī, Al-Juwaynī and others.

73 *Shi'arāhā*. Perhaps we should read *sharā'i'ahā*, "its laws".

74 *Taḥrīr*, pp. 370ff.

75 *Ibid.* p. 360. Here is an echo of Al-Ghazālī's statement in the *K. al-iqtiṣād*, quoted above, p. 39.

76 *Ibid.* pp. 360f.

77 *Ibid.* p. 362.

78 *Ibid.*

79 *Ibid.* p. 363.

80 *Ibid.* pp. 363f. He brings an interesting definition of "sultan" which is presumably his own, unlike that of "vizier" which he reproduces word for word from Al-Māwardī's *Aḥkām*. He says "the term (*sulṭān*) is employed for royalty or kingship and power (*malaka wa-*

qudra), or in the meaning of 'proof'. The sultan is called *sulṭān* because of his kingship and power, or because he is a proof for the existence of God and his unity. The world cannot endure in good order (*ḥukm*) without a wise governor (*mudabbir*). Another explanation is that it [*sulṭān*] comes from the word *salīṭ*, because the sultan shines in his justice and in his government over his subjects like the oil that shines with its light over the people" (pp. 364f.).

81 See pp. 47ff. above, with notes. The classical theory of the *khilāfa* and far-reaching concessions to political realities often stand side by side, only to be reconciled by resorting to expediency. This is already discernible in Al-Māwardī, but is much more glaring in Ibn Jamā'a. There is no real integration, because it is impossible to reconcile the two.

82 See above, pp. 48f.

83 See n. 80 above.

84 Taqī al-Dīn Ibn Taymīya, who was born in 1263, died in prison in 1328. Though poles apart from Al-Ghazālī, he is nevertheless to some extent under his influence, but more under that of Ibn Ḥazm and his *Ẓāhirism* (as I. Goldziher showed in his *Die Ẓâhiriten* (Leipzig, 1884). In direct opposition to Al-Ghazālī, who tried to accommodate all movements and tendencies in contemporary Islam, such as mysticism, rationalism, dogmatism, etc., as legitimate branches of one tree, Ibn Taymīya sought to cleanse Islam from everything which was, to his mind, incompatible with the Sunna and the simple purity of early Islam (see I. Goldziher, *Vorlesungen über den Islam*[2] (1925), pp. 265ff.). His reforming zeal extended also to the day-to-day administration of the Muslim state, which he tried to bring into line with the ideal demands of the *Sharī'a*. He was acutely aware of the defects of contemporary political, social and religious life (see Henri Laoust, *Doctrines Sociales et Politiques d'Ibn Taimīya* (Cairo, 1939)). He was opposed to philosophy, although he betrays some knowledge of Greek political thought and may even have been influenced by it. His views found little favour in his own day but unexpectedly bore fruit more than four centuries after his death in the reformist theology of Muḥammad b. 'Abd al-Wahhāb (d. 1787), whose ideas were put into practice by his son-in-law, the emir Muḥammad Ibn Sa'ūd, who fought with the sword for the restoration of the Sunna and founded a dynasty and a state, Sa'ūdī Arabia. Preceded by Goldziher, M. Laoust, *op. cit.*, deals fully with Ibn Taymīya's influence on Wahhābī doctrine.

According to H. Laoust's informative introduction to his important and valuable study of the author's social and political teaching, Ibn Taymīya stems from a distinguished Ḥanbalī family and continued its tradition in Damascus, where he was born and died, and in Cairo. He served the first Mamluk sultans, notably Muḥammad ibn Qalāwūn. His treatise is meant for this ruler and for the emirs and *'ulamā*. It sets out the doctrine of right government according to the *Sharī'a*, and also aims at large-scale administrative reforms. Some of them, though less radically, were instituted by Muḥammad ibn Qalāwūn. Basing himself on the *K. Bidāya wa-l-nihāya* of the Shāfi'ī Ibn Kathīr, an admirer of our author, Laoust computes the date of our treatise as between 709 and 712 (or 714) A.H. (1309–12).

It was in 1294 that Ibn Taymīya intervened for the first time in politics. He unsuccessfully petitioned the authorities to carry out the prescribed punishment on a Christian accused of insulting the Prophet. They imprisoned Ibn Taymīya. But in 1297 he was to accompany an expedition which sultan Lājūn sent against Armenia, as legal expert and propagandist. Two years later he proved a great resistance leader against the Mongol invaders for several years. But although Muḥammad ibn Qalāwūn was favourably disposed towards him and partially implemented reforms advocated by him, he was essentially guided by self-interest and expediency and did not hesitate to employ in his service Ibn Taymīya's old enemy, Badr al-Dīn Ibn Jamā'a. This, together with Ibn Taymīya's fearless attacks on such contemporary evils as the cult of saints, was responsible for his temporary disgrace and imprisonment. He actually died in prison in his native Damascus after more than two years' incarceration. His influence as a professor of Ḥanbalī law—in which office he succeeded his father—was considerable, and so was his popularity among the masses.

M. Laoust furnishes considerable biographical detail in the Introduction to his French translation of the *Siyāsa shar'īya*, and also in his major work devoted to Ibn Taymīya's doctrines, especially the first book entitled *La formation des Doctrines*. I should like to direct the reader to M. Laoust's well-documented and broadly conceived analysis. He thinks that Ibn Taymīya's doctrine is opposed to the Mamluk state as it developed in his day. But he seems to have accepted its structure, since the emirs and the *'ulamā* were the two most important groups which supported the military dictatorship on which the state was erected. The position which Ibn Taymīya would like to secure for the *'ulamā* will occupy us presently.

My own exposition of Ibn Taymīya's political thought is based on the *Siyāsa shar'īya* only, and no account is taken in this introductory outline of his other political-religious treatise, the *Minhāj al-sunna*. Generally speaking, I would agree with Goldziher's characterization of Ibn Taymīya as not belonging to a definite school of thought but being, so to say, a "Muslim on his own" ("Muhammedaner auf eigene Faust"). See Goldziher, *Die Ẓâhiriten*, pp. 188ff., with quotations from Ibn Baṭṭūṭa, e.g. on Ibn Taymīya, and illustrations of his advocacy of *tajsīm*.

85 Al-Ghazālī also speaks of *ahl al-sunna*. See p. 41 above.

86 This important *Shī'ī* philosopher and theologian (1201–74) was a brilliant exponent of the *Shī'ī* doctrine of the *imāma* and an able commentator and critic of Ibn Sīnā, apart from being a noted mathematician and astronomer. He also wrote expertly on ethics, his *Akhlāq-i Nāṣiri* being extensively used by Jalāl al-Dīn al-Dawwānī in his *Akhlāq-i Jalāli*, which will engage our attention in ch. x. Ṭūsī was vizier under Hūlāgū whom he had accompanied on his successful expedition against Baghdad, as his trusted adviser. Here he set up an observatory, by order of his Mongol master.

87 See *Siyāsa shar'īya* (Cairo, 1951), p. 2 (Laoust, *Le traité de droit public d'Ibn Taimīya* (Beyrouth, 1948), p. 2). The full title is: *K. al-siyāsa al-shar'īya fī iṣlāḥ al-rā'ī wa-l-rā'īya.*

88 *Ibid.* pp. 10f./9f.

89 *Ibid.* pp. 167/165.

90 *Ibid.* pp. 24/22.

91 *Ibid.* pp. 3/2.

92 *Ibid.* pp. 172f./172. This is reminiscent of Ibn Jamā'a, see above, p. 49.

93 *Siyāsa*, pp. 22/20. "Pastor" is a favourite term for the ruler (and flock for his subjects). Abū Yūsuf addresses Hārūn al-Rashīd thus in his *K. al-kharāj*, and the term is met with in many "Mirrors" as well. It goes back ultimately to the Old Testament.

94 *Siyāsa*, pp. 174/174. Cp. also Al-Ghazālī, above, p. 41.

95 *Ibid.* pp. 81/73. "The substance of religion is prayer (*ṣalāt*) and holy war (*jihād*)" (*ibid.* pp. 20/18).

96 *Ibid.* pp. 78f./70ff. "To command the good" extends to the prescribed prayers, almsgiving, fast, pilgrimage, sincerity, honouring father and mother, and good-neighbourly behaviour. "Forbidding the evil" is defined (*ibid.* pp. 172f./172) and includes inflicting the legal penalties (*iqāmat al-ḥudūd*) without fear or favour.

97 *Ibid.* pp. 177/177. "Hierarchy" is a translation of *ba'ḍuhum fawqa ba'ḍin.* Ibn Taymīya goes on "just as the body is not in good order without the head". The appeal to reason is due to Greek political thought.

98 In his *Madīna fāḍila* and especially in his *Fuṣūl al-madanī*. This will be discussed fully in ch. vi.

99 See also above, p. 44, with n. 58 (Ibn Jamā'a).

100 See *Siyāsa*, pp. 140f./136f.

101 See *ibid.* pp. 74/67.

102 See below, ch. vi.

103 See *Siyāsa*, pp. 78/70.

104 From the *Ṣaḥīḥ* of Al-Bukhārī.

105 See *Siyāsa*, pp. 170f./170.

106 *Ibid.*

107 See p. 40, above, with n. 47.

108 See *Siyāsa*, pp. 170/169.

109 See H. Laoust, *Doctrines*, p. 201. It is difficult to understand M. Laoust's qualification that the '*ulamā* have become the heirs of the Prophet as individuals, not as a class (that is, not as the *ahl al-ḥall wa-l-'aqd*), in view of his claim (*ibid.* p. 202) that: "La souveraineté,

dans la doctrine d'Ibn Taimīya, est une souveraineté diffuse. Il en résulte que les '*ulamā*' constituent, en droit, la première classe dirigeante de la communauté et de l'État, avant même celle des émirs." Moreover, it should be clear that "en droit" really means "in law, according to the theory of Ibn Taymīya", not in actual *Fiqh*.

110 M. Laoust may be right when he describes Ibn Taymīya's political philosophy as a policy of the "juste milieu" between the two extremes of the Kharijites and a particular branch of the Shī'ites. Ibn Taymīya contrasts the Prophet as *imām muṭlaq* (imam in the absolute, ideally perfect sense), with the imam—especially as understood by the Shī'a—as *imām muqayyad* (imam in a restricted, relative sense). In other words, Muḥammad was the divinely ordained, ideal ruler of the ideal *umma*, whereas his successors, the first *khulafā rāshidūn*, were of human, that is, of relative, perfection only (see M. Laoust, *Doctrines*, p. 182).

111 See *Siyāsa*, pp. 63/56. M. Laoust translates *umma wasaṭ* by "la nation du juste milieu". It may be asked whether this meaning was actually in Ibn Taymīya's mind. In view of his rigid Ḥanbalism I am rather inclined to give preference to my second translation, "the just, equitable nation", and to take *wasaṭ* in the sense of Aristotle's *mesotes*. The term occurs in the Qur'ān (II, 137) in this sense.

112 At any rate the two classes fulfil the same functions in the theories of the respective states. M. Laoust (*Doctrines*, p. 182) compares the Prophet as the just ruler of "the ideal state which the original community represented" with the "gouverneur philosophe" of Al-Fārābī in these words: "Un législateur souverainement sage doit imposer à tous la discipline d'une loi juste universellement respectée. Le prophète est le législateur idéal dont la fonction est de maintenir l'unité et la paix dans la communauté en s'inspirant directement des ordres de Dieu. Il possède donc un pouvoir autonome de législation: sa fonction rappelle celle qu'al-Fārābī attribuait au sage, gouverneur de la cité, qui, en communication constante avec Dieu et en s'inspirant continuellement de ses ordres, avait pour mission d'édicter les lois (*waḍ' al-nawāmīs*) de la communauté idéale." While in general agreement with this statement I would offer two critical observations. In the first place, the Prophet-lawgiver of Islam promulgates a law which does actually guarantee the unity and peace of the community, but goes far beyond this purpose (which is common to all laws in all states): he legislates for the hereafter on the basis of the transitory, preparatory character of this life. His law embraces *dīn wa-dunya* with the latter clearly subordinate and preparatory to the former. In the second place, Al-Fārābī's philosopher-king is deliberately identified with the prophet, and in his prophetic capacity he acts as lawgiver. But his prophetic quality is the result of his natural perfection, which enables him to receive an emanation of the Active Intellect, in form of a revelation. The Prophet of Ibn Taymīya is the Prophet of the Qur'ān to whom Gabriel mediated by means of *tanzīl* the *Kitāb al-*

'azīz, the "Precious Book". As stated a little earlier, the Qur'ānic concept can only be harmonized with the philosophical concept by allegorical interpretation. This Ibn Taymīya would never concede, since his literalism is of the very essence of his theology and also of the politics he based on it. God sent down the Book, just so; there can be no question of any interpretation other than the literal acceptance of this statement. (See Goldziher, *Vorlesungen*, p. 103 for telling examples from Ibn Taymīya and his disciples, as from Ḥanbalīs generally). M. Laoust states, in fact, that Ibn Taymīya attacks Al-Fārābī for reducing prophecy to a "politique juste".

113 See the later chapters under the general heading of "The Platonic Legacy". Naṣīr al-Dīn Ṭūsī and Jalāl al-Dīn al-Dawwānī occupy a middle position which still awaits a detailed investigation. I shall deal with some relevant points in the chapter devoted to Al-Dawwānī, below.

114 See *Muqaddima*, ed. Quatremère, vol. 1, pp. 342ff.; ed. Beyrouth (1900), pp. 191ff.

115 See E. Tyan, *op. cit.* pp. 234 where the date of the sultanate as effective power is given as approximately 330 A.H./941 C.E.; see also pp. 380ff. for an important discussion of the problem of "Sovereignty" in Islam with definition of *mulk*, *malik*, *sulṭān* in the Qur'ān and under the Umayyads and Abbasids; and pp. 513ff. for a discussion of the relative positions of caliph and sultan from the middle of the tenth (fourth A.H.) century onwards.

CHAPTER III

1 Ṣafī al-Dīn Muḥammad b. 'Alī b. Ṭabāṭabā, known as Ibn al-Ṭiqṭaqa, was born in 1262, of noble lineage. According to Derenbourg (see next note) our author was eighteen generations removed from 'Alī, the son-in-law of the Prophet. His father, Tāj al-Dīn 'Alī b. Muḥammad b. Ramaḍān al-Ṭiqṭaqa, was the 'Alid representative at al-Ḥilla, where he was assassinated in 1281. The son succeeded him in the task of looking after the interests of the 'Alids. In 1298 we find him at Baghdad, in relations with the effective ruler, the Mongol sultan Ghāzān. Making a journey to Tabrīz he was forced by the weather to stop at Mosul at the end of 1301, and was royally received and befriended by its governor, "*malik*" Fakhr al-Dīn 'Īsā b. Ibrāhīm. H. Derenbourg gives a full biographical sketch in the introduction to his edition of the Arabic text. Ibn al-Ṭiqṭaqa is placed at the head of this chapter and not at its end where chronologically he would belong, because the *Al-Fakhrī* is more than a "Mirror for Princes" of the kind described in the second part of this chapter. Though the *adab*-element predominates, the treatise is a work of history and not simply one of a large number of moralizing and entertaining examples of a literary genre. Its main theme is political and its stress is on government based on morals and power.

2 See *Al-Fakhrī*, ed. H. Derenbourg (Paris, 1895), pp. 15 ff. There is a good, recent complete English translation by G. E. J. Whitting (London, 1947).

3 *Ibid.* p. 20.

4 *Ibid.* p. 55.

5 *Ibid.* pp. 23 f.

6 *Ibid.* p. 30.

7 *Ibid.*

8 *Ibid.* p. 31. This advice to the "religious" leaders sounds like implied criticism of their theoretical stand upon the *Sharī'a.* It does not contradict his statement that "The state is guarded by the sword and administered by the pen" (*ibid.* p. 70), which accords well with Ibn Taymīya's claim that the emirs and the '*ulamā* are the two classes in authority (see p. 58, above), a dictum subscribed to by all jurists. "Theologians and jurists" is a translation of *aṣḥābu-l-ra'y wa-l-madhāhib.*

9 *Ibid.* pp. 20 ff. It is noteworthy that '*aql* ranks first as the fundamental qualification preceding '*adl.* He quotes the Persian Buzurjmihr as saying that a ruler should not act independently on his own opinion (*ra'y*), but on good advice. Actually *ra'y* and *shūrā* (or *mashwara*) are not mutually exclusive, as we know from the jurists (who are in favour of *ra'y*) and from the "Mirrors".

10 *Ibid.* p. 80.

11 See *ibid.* pp. 35 ff., 44 ff., 48.

12 See *ibid.* p. 55.

13 See *ibid.* p. 102, for the first four caliphs and pp. 187 f. for the Umayyad dynasty. Like Ibn Khaldūn later, Ibn al-Ṭiqṭaqa characterizes the rule of the Umayyads as a combination of *dīn* with *mulk*, which is equally true of the Abbasids. But he seems to have felt more respect for the Umayyads as rulers and men of affairs (they were Muslims after all), than for the Abbasids whose piety he cannot have taken seriously. He charges them with "deception, ruse and perfidy", no doubt in the first place on account of their treatment of his own 'Alid kinsmen. See also next note.

14 *Ibid.* pp. 201 ff. This passage is characteristic of our author, who distributes light and shade fairly in his verdict on the Abbasids. He appears to have resented their weakness even more than their dishonourable practices, for he stresses the state of dissolution and decay towards the end of the Abbasid caliphate at Baghdad and its loss of control and transfer of authority, in both of which, as tokens of strong government, he was particularly interested.

This is also clear from another passage (p. 42): "Every year, the kings of Syria and Egypt and the master of Mosul are bringing presents to the caliph and request to be invested with the government of their countries in order to exercise authority over their subjects and to demand their obedience. The caliphs gave them corresponding or even more valuable presents in exchange, and all this ⟨merely⟩ to keep up appearances and to ⟨retain the privileges of⟩ *sikka* and *khuṭba* in ⟨those⟩ countries and border-regions, until it became proverbial to say of somebody, who had of a matter ⟨only⟩ the appearance (*ẓāhir*) but nothing of the substance (*bāṭin*), that he was satisfied with the *sikka* and *khuṭba* of a thing. This means that he was satisfied with a name without the reality. And this is the sum total of the affairs of the Abbasid dynasty." On *sikka* (the minting of coins in the name of the reigning caliph) and *khuṭba* (mentioning the caliph first in the public address during Friday prayers) see also Al-Ghazālī, above, p. 43. In contrast to the jurists Ibn al-Ṭiqṭaqa calls this formality simply a pretence; he is not concerned with upholding the fiction of the supreme authority of the *Sharī'a*.

15 Abū Muḥammad Ibn al-Muqaffa', a Persian convert to Islam, was in the service of Umayyad governors and generals and later of the 'Alid uncles of the first two Abbasid caliphs. According to Al-Jahshiyārī, he successfully delayed the change-over when his master Al-Masīḥ al-Ḥawārī was to be replaced as governor of the Kirmān by Sufyān b. Um'āwiya. For this action the latter bore him a grudge which eventually led to his murder in revolting circumstances. See the valuable study by M. Dominique Sourdel in *Arabica*, vol. I (1954), pp. 307–23, entitled "La biographie d'Ibn al-Muqaffa' d'après les sources anciennes", which shows convincingly that Sufyān "removed" our author at the orders of the caliph Al-Manṣūr. Ibn al-Muqaffa' was at that time secretary to the 'Alid 'Īsā b. 'Alī in Basra, in which capacity he drafted an *amān* (safe conduct) for 'Abd Allah b. 'Alī. He included a passage which displeased the caliph, who then made use of his personal enemy, at that time governor of Basra, to rid himself of Ibn al-Muqaffa'; Sufyān avidly seized this opportunity. See also n. 43, below.

G. Richter's literary-critical study of the "Mirrors" gives a good survey of their literary affiliations. See *Studien zur Geschichte der Älteren Arabischen Fürstenspiegel* (Leipzig, 1932). His claim of Greek Hellenistic influences needs further investigation. Moreover, Al-Fārābī's *Madīna fāḍila* certainly cannot be included among "Mirrors", as Richter suggests (p. 107).

16 See *K. adab al-ṣaghīr*, ed. Aḥmad Zakī Pasha (Alexandria, 1911), pp. 5ff. and O. Rescher's translation *Das Kleine Adab-Buch des Ibn el-Moqaffa'* (Stuttgart, 1915), pp. 1ff. G. Richter, "Ueber das kleine Adabbuch des Ibn al-Muqaffa'" in *Der Islam*, vol. XIX (1931), pp. 278–81, denies Ibn al-Muqaffa''s authorship, in which view he is followed by F. Gabrieli in his important survey "L'opere di Ibn al-Muqaffa'" in *RSO*, vol. XI (1931–2), pp. 197–247. Linguistically akin to the *K. adab al-kabīr*, the treatise is said to be far removed from it spiritually. But, to my mind, its religious tone and its stress on *'aql* and *'āqil*, go very well together with the *R. fī-l-ṣaḥāba*, the genuineness of which no scholar has so far challenged. To judge by his writings Ibn al-Muqaffa''s orthodoxy cannot be questioned. He

seems to have left his *zandaqa* behind when he became Abū Muḥammad in place of Abū 'Amr, nor has his Manicheanism anything to do with his death (see previous note). That Ibn Qutaiba speaks in his *Uyūn al-akhbār* of *ādāb ibn al-muqaffa'*, by which he means, according to Richter (*loc. cit.* pp. 280f.) the *K. adab al-kabīr*, is no definite proof that in his day the *K. adab al-saghīr* was not extant. It is not mentioned in Al-Qiftī (ed. Lippert, p. 200) but in the *Fihrist*, p. 118. If any inconsistencies between various writings of Ibn al-Muqaffa' exist they should be attributed to a universal human failing and to different purposes at different times, but should not be interpreted as due to different authorship.

The phrase *salāḥ...ma'ād* is a good "orthodox" definition, common to jurists, (political) philosophers and authors of "Mirrors".

17 See *K. adab al-ṣaghīr*, pp. 21/10. The same idea is expressed in the *R. fī-l-ṣaḥāba*, ed. Muḥammad Kurd 'Alī in *Rasā'il al-bulaghā*[3] (Cairo, 1946), p. 122 (see pp. 72f., below).

18 See *K. adab al-saghīr*, pp. 23/11.

19 *Ibid.*

20 *Ibid.* pp. 23ff./11f. This is an ever-recurring theme in all "Mirrors". Other examples will be found on pp. 76f. and 82, below.

21 *Ibid.* pp. 35f./18. See also *K. adab al-kabīr*, ed. Aḥmad Zakī Pasha (Alexandria, 1912), pp. 8ff.; O. Rescher, "Das Kitâb 'el-adab el-kebîr' des Ibn el-Moqaffa'" in *MSOS*, vol. xx (1917), p. 39.

22 See *ibid.* pp. 37f./19. He shows himself a good Muslim by his distinction between the sources of religion and reason not only, but principally by his making law an integral part of religion.

23 See *ibid.* pp. 41/21.

24 See *K. adab al-kabīr*, pp. 12/41.

25 See *ibid.* pp. 15/42; and also *R. Fī-l-ṣaḥāba*, pp. 129–31.

26 See *K. adab al-kabīr*, pp. 18/43.

27 See *ibid.* p. 19. *Ḥazm* is translated by "will to power": literally, "firmness, determination".

28 See *ibid.* *Ṭa'an wa-tasakhkhaṭ* is translated by "opposition"; literally, "attack and anger".

29 See *ibid.* *Hawan* is translated by "arbitrary rule"; literally, "desire, love, passion, fancy".

30 See *ibid.* pp. 18ff./44f. for the whole passage.

31 See *ibid.* pp. 29/47.

32 This treatise is discussed by S. D. Goitein in his article in *Islamic Culture*, vol. XXIII (1949), entitled "A Turning Point in the History of the Muslim State (apropos of Ibn al-Muqaffa''s Kitāb aṣ-Ṣaḥāba)".

33 The translation "charter" for *amān* (Prof. Goitein translates "catechism") is based on the usual meaning of *amana*, "trust", and points to the relationship between the caliph and his army as one of mutual trust. It is to be understood, in conjunction with the expression "within proper bounds" (*qāṣiran 'an al-ghuluwwi*), and the usual meaning of "safe-conduct", as directives issued by the caliph to his

army to keep them within the religious law of Islam and prevent them from committing excesses, as is clear from the context (*R. fī-l-ṣaḥāba*, pp. 119f.). To connect this *amān* with the *amān* which Ibn al-Muqaffaʿ drafted incurring the caliph's displeasure (see n. 15, above) is perhaps too speculative. In any case, the terminology of Ibn al-Muqaffaʿ presents some difficulty, since he must have been influenced by his native Persian. Apart from this, some of the terms he uses may not then have assumed the legal connotation of later times. As for *ra'y*, in many instances it seems to be equivalent with *ʿaql*, in the sense in which the latter is used in the *K. adab al-ṣaghīr*, that is, in its Qur'ānic connotation and not as the independent, sovereign reason that subjects *dīn* to rational proof.

34 See *R. fī-l-ṣaḥāba*, pp. 123f. All the "Mirrors" stress the necessity of regular pay as a prerequisite of loyal and efficient service.

35 See *ibid.* pp. 121/122. "The good order of this life and of the hereafter" translates *ṣalāḥ al-maʿāsh wa-l-maʿād*, taking *maʿāsh* not in its usual meaning of "livelihood", but rather as identical with *dunya*. *Dīn* comes from God through *tanzīl* mediated to his *rasūl*. See also n. 16 above, on the agreement between this treatise and the first part of the *K. adab al-ṣaghīr*.

36 See *R. fī-l-ṣaḥāba*, p. 127.

37 See *ibid.* p. 121. Prof. J. Schacht deals in *The Origins of Muhammadan Jurisprudence* (Oxford, 1953) with the legal aspects of the *R. fī-l-ṣaḥāba* (see pp. 58f., 95 and 102) and defines *athar* as "authoritative precedent", practically as a synonym of *sunna* or "living tradition".

38 See *ibid.* p. 127. Prof. Schacht (*loc. cit.* p. 95) states that this code ought to be revised by successive caliphs. Prof. Goitein (*loc. cit.* p. 128) is of the same opinion. But to my mind the text on which both scholars base their interpretation is corrupt as we have it on p. 127, line 5, of the *R. fī-l-ṣaḥāba*: *thumma yakūnu dhālika min imāmin ākhara ākhira-l-dahri 'in shā'a-Llāh*. The last five words can only mean "at the end of time if Allah wills" and thus point to the time of the *Mahdī*. This suggests the permanence of the caliph's legislative measures, which are necessitated by the existing divergencies and confusion. *Min imāmin ākhara* seems to be corrupt, but even if the original had words to that effect (the syntax of which I do not understand) they could hardly imply revision by successive caliphs, in view of the end of the sentence. See also next note.

39 This is Prof. Schacht's view, *loc. cit.* p. 95. He understands by "*shay' ma'thūr ʿan al-salaf*" local precedents.

40 See *R. fī-l-ṣaḥāba*, p. 120f.

41 *maʿrūf mustaḥsan*, if it is here used in its legal connotation.

42 See *ibid.* p. 126. Ibn al-Muqaffaʿ uses the term "*a'imma huddā*", not yet the later "*khulafā rāshidūn*".

43 See M. Sourdel (*Arabica*, I (1954), pp. 307–23) and n. 15 above. The great importance of *aṣḥāb* is stressed in the *R. fī-l-ṣaḥāba* on pp. 129ff. They are the aids (*aʿwān*) to his *ra'y* (p. 129). He recommends relatives (*aqrab*) for the offices of viziers, governors and preachers (p. 125), warns against giving secretaries and chamberlains a free hand (p. 130) and commends to the caliph the cause of his own family, of his father's house, of the Banū 'Alī and the Banū 'Abbas in that order (p. 131). He pleads for a careful, well-planned education, the lack of which he thinks responsible for the absence of nobility and judgement. Noble lineage is essential in the companions of the caliph. With courage and temperance, noble birth qualifies an officer to be raised to the ranks of the sovereign's companions. The religious knowledge of the *fuqahā* makes them eligible, together with members of the Arab nobility. Among the latter, Ibn al-Muqaffa' thought in the first place of his masters, the 'Alid uncles of the caliph. Among those specially picked (*khawāṣṣ*) as the caliph's companions and advisers are the *ahl al-dīn wa-l-'uqūl*, that is, the *fuqahā*, whose cause only prospers with the help of the *imām* (p. 134). Yet, apart from his near counsellors and companions, the caliph needs a broadly based support among his subjects. First of all, he must have a reliable army in the Khurasanians; next come the two great cities of Basra and Kufa (where he should mix the Arabs and Persians together); then Iraq, Syria, Hijāz, etc. It is perhaps more than coincidence that Al-Manṣūr should recommend the same groups (relations, Khurasanians) to his son in his testament (*waṣīya*), modelled upon those of 'Omar and Mu'āwiya (see Albert Dietrich, "Das politische Testament des zweiten 'Abbasidenkalifen al-Manṣūr" in *Der Islam*, vol. xxx (1952), pp. 133–65), where the different recensions found in Ṭabarī, III, 443, are quoted and discussed. For these specific recommendations reflect the conditions of his own time, whereas advice to pay the troops regularly, to be a good Muslim by imposing the legal penalties, to defend the faith against heretics, etc., may well go back to the earlier testaments.

The parallels between Ibn al-Muqaffa''s advice to Al-Manṣūr and the latter's to his son are certainly striking, the more so since Ṭabarī's third version goes back to that of Isḥāq b. 'Īsā b. 'Alī in the name of his father, who was Ibn al-Muqaffa''s master. If Al-Manṣūr actually took Ibn al-Muqaffa''s advice seriously an element of irony enters into the latter's tragic end.

Prof. Goitein (*loc. cit.* p. 128) expresses the view that Ibn al-Muqaffa' tried to establish state control over religion and law, but that orthodoxy prevailed, with the result that religious law remained largely theoretical while the state developed a secular jurisdiction of its own. While not disputing the correctness of this view in the realm of practical politics I question the advisability of separating the religious from the secular and would stress again the intrinsic unity of all spheres of life within the Muslim state under the caliph (at any rate in theory). As stated earlier in this book, the theory was real and valid, not only in the writings of the jurists, but also in the formal pronouncements of caliphs, emirs and sultans.

44 See *K. al-kharāj*, pp. 2ff. There is a French translation by E. Fagnan under the title *Le Livre d'Impôt Foncier* (Algiers, 1915). Abū Yūsuf Ya'qūb b. Ibrahīm was born in 113 A.H./731 C.E. and died in 182 A.H./798 C.E. Goldziher, *Muhammedanische Studien*, vol. II, p. 67, calls the introduction to his *K. al-kharāj* a kind of *waṣīya*. Prof. J. Schacht states in *EI*, new edition, vol. I, p. 3, that Harūn al-Rashīd conferred upon Abū Yūsuf the title of Grand Qāḍī for the first time in Islam.

45 Edited and translated by H. Keller (Leipzig, 1908). See also G. Richter, *loc. cit.* pp. 80ff.

46 See *K. Baghdād*, pp. 38f./18. Richter, *loc. cit.* p. 94, thinks that *iqtiṣād* represents Aristotle's *mesotes*.

47 See *ibid.* pp. 39/18 and pp. 41/19.

48 *Ibid.* pp. 44/21 and again pp. 52/24. *Wa-kthar mushāwarata-l-fuqahā'i.*

49 *Ibid.* pp. 46f./22. We are reminded of Abū Yūsuf's *K. al-kharāj*.

50 *Ibid.* pp. 52f./24.

51 Edited by Aḥmad Zakī Pasha (Cairo, 1914); French translation, with introduction and notes by Ch. Pellat, *Le livre de la couronne* (Paris, 1954). Jāḥiẓ was born at Basra in the year 160 A.H./776–8 C.E. and died there in 255 A.H./868–9 C.E. He was perhaps the most distinguished of many distinguished Basran men of letters. Highly cultured and urbane, he was one of the principal Basran representatives of the Mu'tazila and at the court of the caliph Al-Ma'mūn. See Pellat, introduction, pp. 12ff., and his excellent monograph (a model of its kind) *Le Milieu Basrien et la Formation de Ğāhiẓ* (Paris, 1953). For his humanism see *ibid.* pp. ixf. and 63ff. (Until we have such critical assessments of the life and works of the principal Muslim authors, not to mention critical editions of their writings and of their background, surveys like the present must remain mainly descriptive.) Pellat, with Rescher, decides against Jāḥiẓ's authorship, in opposition to Gabrieli and Christensen. The work is dedicated to the Emir Al-Fath b. Khagān, the secretary of the caliph Al-Mutawakkil. Both died in 861, therefore Pellat thinks the date is between 847 and 861. The real author might be Muḥammad b. al-Ḥārith, a Persian who wrote poor Arabic.

52 See F. Gabrieli, "Etichetta di Corte e Costumi Sasanidi nel kitâb Aḫlāq al-Mulūk di Al-Ğāhiẓ" in *RSO*, vol. XI (1926–8), pp. 292–305. Pellat holds that the author considered borrowings from Hellenism safer than from Iranian culture. Gabrieli disagrees, and Jāḥiẓ himself says (*K. al-tāj*, p. 23) that he began with the Persian kings (*mulūk al-'ajam*) because they had introduced such etiquette and because the Muslims had taken over the canons of government from them.

53 See *K. al-tāj*, p. 27. An alternative translation would be: "while... them with indispensable authority" (*amr*). Pellat renders "en employant les moyens convenables".

54 See *ibid.* p. 70. "Foundations" translates *arkān*, pillars.

55 See *ibid.* pp. 127f. Pellat translates *mamlaka* by "pouvoir royal".

56 *Ibid.* This may be an instance of Persian influence in view of the absolute power of the ruler, despite the hereditary dynastic principle. On the other hand, it may simply reflect Abbasid (and earlier Umayyad) practice. The phrase *walī 'ahdi-l-mulk* occurs later in the Sunnī jurists' treatises on constitutional law as a legal technical term.

57 *Ibid.* pp. 139f. Cf. p. 77 below on three kinds of *imām*.

58 See *ibid.* pp. 160ff. Cf. also Niẓām al-Mulk's *Siyāsat-nāma*, ed. Ch. Schefer, e.g. pp. 38ff., 55ff.

59 See *ibid.* pp. 167f., 172. This point is stressed in all "Mirrors", e.g. in the *Qābūs-nāma* and the *Siyāsat-nāma* (see later pp. 79f. and 82, and in Ibn al-Muqaffa''s *R. fī-l-ṣaḥāba* (see p. 71 above).

60 See n. 52 above.

61 See *K. al-tāj*, pp. 173f. For him, the Abbasids are the successors of the Sassanian kings, with the Umayyads, to whom he is fair, in between.

62 See *ibid.* p. 177.

63 This treatise is printed in the *Rasā'il al-Jāḥiẓ* (Cairo, 1933), pp. 241–59.

64 *Ibid.* pp. 247f.

65 *Ibid.* p. 249.

66 *Ibid.* pp. 251f.

67 *Ibid.* p. 257.

68 *Ibid.* pp. 258f. His detailed argument no doubt reflects the current debate on this question.

69 See the discussion in Al-Māwardī and Ibn Khaldūn on the one hand and among the *Falāsifa* on the other.

70 The following summary is based on Prof. R. Levy's English translation, entitled *Kai Kā'ūs, A Mirror for Princes* (London, 1951), of the Persian text, edited by him in 1951 in the E. J. W. Gibb Memorial Series (N.S. vol. XVIII) as *The Naṣīḥat-nāma known as Qābūs-nāma of Kai Kā'ūs*.

71 *A Mirror for Princes*, p. 222.

72 *Ibid.* pp. 228f. This advice is no doubt based on experience; it is important because the Seljuq sultans came to power by force of arms and would naturally look to their army for governors and administrators. They might also be inclined to levy high taxes on the civilian population in order to reward the soldiers who brought them to, and must keep them in, power.

73 *Ibid.* p. 230.

74 *Ibid.* p. 231. This means that "kingship" is absolute rule, which turns into tyranny if the power upon which it is based goes to the ruler's head and becomes an end in itself. We note in the six qualities the balance between religious and moral virtues.

75 *Ibid.* p. 235.

76 *Ibid.* p. 213.

77 *Muqaddima*, ed. Q(uatremère), vol. II, p. 108.

78 Edited by Ch. Schefer under the title *Siasset Námeh, Traité de gouvernement* (Paris, 1891). French translation by the same scholar

1893. Niẓām al-Mulk founded several important seats of learning, mainly for the teaching of the theology of Al-Ash'arī and of *Fiqh*, thus contributing to the official recognition and extension of Ash'arism. Al-Ghazālī exerted great influence at the Niẓāmiya in Baghdad (see the previous chapter, n. 34). See now the new critical edition by H. Darke (*Niẓām al-Mulk's Siyasetname*, Tehran, 1340 [1962]).

79 The author's master Malik Shah is credited with all these qualities to perfection. See *Siyāsat-nāma*, pp. 6f./7f. Hence the prosperous and happy state of his realm, the like of which Islam has never known; revolt and rebellion reared their head in every previous reign. At Malik Shah's orders Niẓām sets out the duties of the ruler. It is significant that the author does not mention the caliph at all, but looks upon the sultan as the Muslim sovereign whose appearance at this juncture he attributes to divine providence.

80 See *Siyāsat-nāma*, pp. 5f./5f.

81 See *ibid.* pp. 9/11.

82 See *ibid.* pp. 38ff./55ff. After describing how Persian kings dispensed justice at their court, he deals with judges, preachers, chiefs of police, etc., who must preserve justice, public morale, equity in the market-place and fair dealing in trade and commerce generally.

83 See *ibid.* pp. 10/12.

84 See *ibid.* pp. 54f./82f.

85 See *ibid.* pp. 18ff. 27ff.; also pp. 57ff. 87ff., with an account of the functions of postmasters and postal services. Cf. also pp. 68ff. 103ff. See also p. 70 (Ibn al-Muqaffa') and pp. 76f. (Jāḥiẓ) above.

Espionage and intelligence are frequently mentioned in the *Shāhnāma*, particularly in the reign of Ardashīr I, cf., for example, p. 1404 (ed. Turner-Macan). Further, Rashīd ad-Dīn's *History of Ghāzān Khān* (E. J. W. Gibb Memorial Series, N.S., vol. XIV) repeatedly deals with intelligence: of foreign countries through ambassadors (p. 171); commercial relations and breaking of foreign monopolies (p. 173); and close examination and supervision of foreign merchants (p. 206). I am indebted to Mr G. M. Wickens for this information.

86 See *ibid.* pp. 72ff./121ff.

87 See *ibid.* pp. 85f./126f. and pp. 91ff./134ff.

88 See *ibid.* pp. 94f./138f.

89 See *ibid.* pp. 110/162f.

90 See *ibid.* pp. 115/169f. This ensures the stability of government and maintains the dynasty in power.

91 See *ibid.* pp. 110/163. According to *ibid.* pp. 151/223 the vizier must be an orthodox Muslim, a Ḥanafī or Shāfi'ī.

92 See *ibid.* pp. 138f./204ff.

93 See *ibid.* pp. 183ff./276ff. It is interesting to note that Al-Ghazālī wrote a treatise against the *Bāṭinīya* while he was teaching at the Niẓāmiya (see ch. II above, p. 39).

94 See *ibid.* pp. 44/68. I am indebted to Mr G. M. Wickens for his help with the Persian text. He also drew my attention to the Persian poets.

Although they did not write "Mirrors" and had no direct interest in politics and certainly not in political theory, men like Firdausī and Sa'dī, sensitive to the disturbing events of their times, could not but write of kings, their fate and duties. A few illustrations may, therefore, be given from Sa'dī's *Gulistan*, taken from Prof. A. J. Arberry's English translation of the first two chapters under the title *Kings and Beggars* (London, 1945). The *Gulistan* was composed in 1258, the very year of Hūlagū Khān's sack of Baghdad and the killing of the last of the Abbasid caliphs.

Of the lust for power Sa'dī has this to say:

"For though ten dervishes upon one blanket can lie down
Within one clime two kings can never wear in peace the crown.
The man of God, when he a loaf receives,
Eats half, the other to the poor he gives;
A king that holds a clime entire in fee
Yet yearns o'er other climes supreme to be." (Arberry, p. 33.)

He describes the evil consequences of a tyrannous king's greed very much as Kai Kā'ūs had done: "The population (through flight abroad) thus declining, the revenue of the province suffered a diminution, the treasury remained empty, and the enemies pressed hard." He counsels generosity and kindness:

"If thou wouldst find a friend indeed
Upon thy day of utmost need,
When fortune smiles upon thee, then
Be generous to other men.

The servant faithful to obey,
Neglected, soon will run away:
If thou a stranger wouldst impel
To be thy servant, treat him well."

When the minister argued with the king, quoting the example of Feridun, who had attained power with the help of the people though he "had neither treasure nor kingdom nor followers", in the hope of persuading him to relax his grip upon the people, he advised him:

"Cherish thine army with a loving hand,
For on his army rests the king's command."

"The king said, 'What causes soldiery and people to rally round their king?' The minister said, 'The king must be generous, so that they will rally about him, and merciful, so that they will sit secure in the shelter of his power; and you have neither of these things.

No monarch makes a trade of tyranny—
The wolf no shepherd of the flock can be.
The king who on oppression founds his sway
With his own hand destroys his empire's stay.'

The king, incensed with this advice, imprisoned his minister. Soon afterwards the king's cousins rose in rebellion and were joined by all those who had suffered from his grasping tyranny. He lost his throne.

'The king who thinks it meet and wise
O'er subject folk to tyrannize,
His friend upon the day of woe
Will prove his formidable foe.

Conciliate thy subjects, then,
And live secure from hostile men:
Such emperors as upright be
Their subjects are their soldiery.' "

(*Ibid.* pp. 38f.)

Sa'dī dwells on this theme of tyranny in several other tales as well, e.g. tales 11 and 12 (*ibid.* pp. 42f.) or tale 20 where the tyrant is the minister who is punished by the just king, with this moral:

"Wouldst thou the sultan's pleasure win?
Then with his subjects' love begin.
Or dost thou seek divine compassion?
Then treat mankind in kindly fashion."

(*Ibid.* p. 55).

Needless to say, many of the tales and stories told with such literary skill belong to the store from which the authors of the "Mirrors" have taken their illustrations. Sa'dī did not intend to give advice, but to entertain and to point a moral from his experience of the transitoriness of life, be it the king's or the dervish's. But he stresses the king's responsibility and duty to his subjects in these words:

"The monarch is the guardian of the poor,
Although his pomp of empire is secure:
Sheep were not made, the shepherd for to keep,
It is the shepherd lives to serve the sheep.

One man is well to-day and thriving,
Another sick at heart for striving:
Wait shortly, till the earth shall eat
The brain puffed up with vain conceit!

King, slave—the mark is lost to view
When fate's decree at last comes true;
Go, disinter the crumbling dead—
Is rich from poor distinguishèd?" (*Ibid.* pp. 63f.)

CHAPTER IV

1 For a fuller account the reader is referred to my monograph *Ibn Khaldûns Gedanken über den Staat* (*KGS*), published in 1932 (R. Oldenbourg, München/Berlin) as Beiheft XXV of the *Historische Zeitschrift*. The political ideas of Ibn Khaldūn are systematically described in his own words, translated from the *Muqaddima* (ed. Beyrouth), corrected with better variants from the Cairo edition and Quatremère's text, and supplied with a running commentary. Passages incorporated in this chapter were translated afresh, based on my earlier study and in the light of criticism and suggestions of learned reviewers. Unfortunately, no critical text based on MSS. described by M. Plessner (*Islamica*, vol. IV (1931), p. 5) is yet available, though Fr. Rosenthal's excellent translation has now appeared. Nor do we have any studies investigating his Islamic or especially his Greek-Hellenistic sources—without which a final assessment of his achievement is impossible. That he was acquainted with the natural sciences and the natural philosophy of the Greeks is obvious, yet his indebtedness to both has not yet been shown in detail although his materialism and empiricism obviously owe much to them. Nor has any explanation been given of the extraordinary gap separating the principles of historical research enunciated in the *Muqaddima* from the exposition in his History (*K. al-'ibar*), which, though an invaluable source for the history of the Maghreb, hardly surpasses earlier Muslim historical writings (see my *KGS*, Vorwort).

A few biographical details from his *Autobiography* may not be without interest in the context of his political ideas:

Born on 27 May 1332 in Tunis into an old Arab family of the Hadramaut which had emigrated first to Spain, then to Morocco and finally settled in Tunisia, Ibn Khaldūn received a thorough education in the theological and philosophical disciplines taught at the University (*madrasa*) of Tunis by outstanding scholars. At the age of twenty he entered upon a long and chequered public career, beginning as secretary to the Hafside sultan of Tunis, and soon changing over to his Merinide rival. He stayed for ten years with the Merinides, often negotiating with the Beduin tribes in the *Ifriqīya* (North Africa) on their behalf. He delighted in intrigues between members of the Merinide dynasty competing for power, and spent two years in prison for conspiring with a Hafside prince who tried to regain power. Released, he tried his fortune in Spain, gaining the confidence of the sultan of Granada who sent him on a diplomatic mission to the court of Peter the Cruel of Seville. This Christian prince recognized Ibn Khaldūn's diplomatic talents and offered to restore to him valuable property belonging to his family if he would enter his service. But Ibn Khaldūn refused and remained in Muslim service until he returned to Bougie to become First Minister to the Hafside prince on whose behalf he had earlier spent two years in prison. He soon lost this office when his master was murdered, and he settled in Biskra where he recruited Berbers for the various dynasties.

Much of his penetrating analysis of Arab and especially Berber character rests on his own experience as servant of princes and negotiator with the Berbers. It was here that he recognized the fundamental difference between nomadic and settled life, between country and cities. He observed and rationalized the driving forces of political power, rooted in psychological factors. From time to time he actually led Berber contingents as their general, hence his appraisal of military tactics and army finance. All his life he was torn between a career as a statesman and soldier and as a scholar working in the quiet atmosphere of the study. For four years he lived in the solitude of a Berber castle, where he wrote his *Muqaddima* and part or the whole of his *Universal History*.

Always longing for a chance to contribute to his "new science of history", he was too restless and perhaps too ambitious and vain to resist for any length of time taking a hand in the game of politics which he had set out to describe. Thus, when in 1383 he left Tunis for Egypt and settled in Cairo, greatly attracted by the splendour of this great city and the court of sultan Barqūq, his hope was a life of teaching and writing. But a year later we find him as Grand Qāḍī of the Mālikī rite, in which office he aroused enmity and such powerful opposition to his determined measures to abolish corruption and bribery that he was dismissed after less than twelve months. He occupied this high office at intervals another five times, appointment and dismissal being closely linked to the political fortunes of his masters no less than to his integrity. In 1387 he made the pilgrimage to Mecca, incumbent on every Muslim.

Perhaps the most dramatic interlude in his troubled life is the historic meeting with the Mongol conqueror Timur (Tamerlane) in 1401. This encounter is the subject of a monograph by Walter J. Fischel (*Ibn Khaldūn and Tamerlane*, Berkeley, 1952), who gives a full translation of the relevant part of the *Autobiography*, based on a critical text, with a detailed and informative commentary. We owe to the same scholar an interesting monograph on "Ibn Khaldūn's Activities in Mamluk Egypt (1382–1406)" in *Semitic and Oriental Studies Presented to William Popper* (Berkeley, 1951), pp. 103–23, which is also based on a MS. of the *Autobiography*. Cf. also Franz Rosenthal, "Die Arabische Autobiographie" in *Studia Arabica*, vol. I. Refusing to enter Tamerlane's service, he returned from captured Damascus to Cairo, where he died in 1406. In view of the continuous alternation between favour and disgrace most students of Ibn Khaldūn are inclined to rate his character rather low, while extolling his intellectual achievement. While it is not our task to sit in judgement over Ibn Khaldūn, it is only fair to remember that if he must be judged then it should be against the background and by the standards of his own times and surroundings. Moreover, effortless and free from moral scruples as his changing of political masters appears, his dismissals from the Grand Qāḍī-ship seem to be attributable rather to his virtues than to his faults. We also know that he was a loyal friend to Ibn al-Khatīb, the vizier of the sultan of Granada and a noted historian and poet (cf. Kamil Ayad, *Die Geschichts- und Gesellschaftslehre Ibn Ḫaldūns* (Stuttgart und Berlin, 1930), p. 11), especially at the time of Ibn al-Khatīb's discomfiture. Ibn Khaldūn, at no small risk, tried his best to save his friend's life, unfortunately without success. To Ibn al-Khatīb we owe a list of Ibn Khaldūn's works, including a treatise on logic and a summary of the works of Ibn Rushd which are presumably lost. His gratitude to his teachers, especially to "the authority on metaphysics, Muḥammad ibn Ibrāhīm al-Ābilī" (cf. Fischel, *op. cit.* n. 88), and his high regard for Al-Mas'ūdī and Al-Ṭurṭūshī (despite frequent criticism of their views), should also be taken into account. Nor can we ignore the importance for the shaping of his views and for evaluation of historical data furnished by his predecessors of his own observation of, and participation in the political life of his time. The reader may be referred to Kamil Ayad's work for a brief sketch of the intellectual background of Ibn Khaldūn. His puzzling personality, torn between ambition and devotion to research in the midst of political confusion and moral and intellectual decline, makes his achievement as a political scientist the more surprising. We are only concerned with this one aspect of his *Summa* of civilization; but his thought cannot be understood except in the context of his active life.

2 This term is the *nisba* of *madīna*, "city, city-state, state", and usually means "political" or "civic" as an adjective, derived from a literal meaning "belonging to the *madīna*". In the context (Q(uatremère) vol. I, pp. 68f./B(eyrouth), p. 41) it is equivalent to "*civilitas*, civilization".

3 See my "Ibn Khaldūn: A North African Muslim Thinker of the Fourteenth Century" in *Bulletin of the John Rylands Library*, vol. XXIV, 2 (1940), pp. 311ff., and Hellmut Ritter, "Irrational Solidarity Groups. A Socio-Psychological Study in connection with Ibn Khaldûn" in *Oriens*, vol. I (1948), pp. 1–44, esp. pp. 3, 19ff., 26ff., 35ff.

4 See ch. I, pp. 14f. above. Cf. *Muqaddima*, Q. vol. II, p. 261/B. p. 374. Here *insānīya* is used in the sense of *civilitas*, identical with *madanīya* and *'umrān*.

5 Cf. Q. vol. II, pp. 126ff./B. pp. 302ff. *Siyāsa dīnīya* or *s. shar'īya* is identified with the traditional *khilāfa* or *imāma*; the second is the power-state which Ibn Khaldūn describes (*s. 'aqlīya*), and the third (*s. madanīya*) is, in his view, a hypothetical and theoretical exercise of the philosophers (*Falāsifa*). See the subsequent treatment, pp. 93ff. and 100ff. Gaston Bouthoul is wrong when he maintains in his stimulating study *Ibn- Khaldoun, Sa Philosophie Sociale* (Paris, 1930) that the Middle Ages (Christian as well as Muslim) had no constitutional theory (*ibid.* pp. 64ff.). Constitutional law in Islam is based

on the theory of the *khilāfa* (considered in ch. II above). If he says (p. 65) that "la théorie du Kalifat a toujours été très controversée", he leaves out of consideration that there was fundamental agreement among Muslim jurists about the origin, significance and scope of the caliphate as the one legally valid constitution of the community of the faithful. Nor is it right to charge this theory with being fatalist and pessimistic; it is other-worldly, and though the jurists increasingly took refuge in expediency and bowed to political reality, they yet upheld the ideal as realized in the original caliphate (see ch. II above). Sovereignty is clearly defined in law, contrary to Bouthoul; nor is he justified in claiming that Muslim ethics are fatalistic, and due to material conditions. This is too sweeping a generalization. Bouthoul is no doubt right when he contrasts Ibn Khaldūn with the Greek thinkers who asked what was the best form of government. But it is clear that Ibn Khaldūn had no need to ask this question; for him as a Muslim the caliphate which he described in terms borrowed from Al-Māwardī *was* the best form of government. His interest and his inquiry were directed to the *mulk*, the power-state.

6 See Q. vol. I, p. 69/B. pp. 41 f. and my "Ibn Jaldūn's Attitude to the Falāsifa" (KAF) in *Al-Andalus*, vol. XX, I (1955), p. 81, n. 4, with reference to Al-Fārābī's *ma'mūra* which is derived from the same root *'mr* as *'umrān*. The Greek equivalent is *oikoumene*.

7 See Q. vol. II, p. 371. This passage is missing in B.

8 See Q. vol. I, p. 71/B. p. 43.

9 See my *KGS*, pp. 1 ff. ("Die 'Aṣabijja als motorische Kraft im staatlichen Geschehen") and *ibid.* pp. 10, 23, 25, 39f., 52, 54, etc. Cf. also the detailed discussion in Fr. Gabrieli, "Il concetto della 'aṣabiyyah nel pensiero storico di Ibn Khaldûn" in *Atti della Reale Academia delle Scienze di Torino*, vol. LXV (1930), pp. 473–512.

10 See Q. vol. I, p. 72/B. p. 43 and esp. pp. 377 ff./B. pp. 187f. and my *KGS*, pp. 39f., for a definition of *mulk* as government based on authority by power. Since it is natural to man, he does not need the prophet and his law, as the *Falāsifa* tried to prove. In fact, the majority of mankind has no revelation. See my article in *Al-Andalus*, *loc. cit.* pp. 82f., with special reference to Ibn Khaldūn's rejection of the psychological and "political" interpretation of prophecy as advanced by Al-Fārābī and Ibn Sīnā. This point is fully dealt with in the following chapters devoted to the *Falāsifa*. Ibn Khaldūn's attitude to prophecy is largely traditional; while he is convinced of the superiority of the state built on the prophetically revealed law, his interest is centred upon the state built on power. His contention, contrary to the views of the *Falāsifa*, is that prophecy is neither natural nor necessary for the origin, development and maintenance of the state. The power-state is the usual form of political organization necessitated by man's natural needs as a gregarious, rational being. See also p. 94 below.

11 See Q. vol. I, pp. 300f./B. pp. 66f.

12 See Q. vol. I, pp. 306ff./B. pp. 170f. and my *KGS*, pp. 15ff., for full references.

13 See Q. vol. I, pp. 314f./B. pp. 175f. It is characteristic of Ibn Khaldūn that he systematizes and reduces everything to a causal nexus. We saw earlier on in Ibn al-Ṭiqṭaqa and the authors of "Mirrors for Princes" (especially Ibn al-Muqaffa') how they had stressed the necessity of the right kind of companions for the sovereign, of regular pay for the army, and how they warned against the sovereign's participation in trade and commerce. But it was left to Ibn Khaldūn to discover the close connection between dynasty, army and finance and to recognize their interrelationship as one of cause and effect. See also my *KGS*, pp. 17ff.

14 For the development of the family as symptomatic for the state see Q. vol. I, pp. 247ff./B. pp. 136f. and my *KGS*, pp. 13ff.

15 See Q. vol. I, pp. 309ff./B. pp. 172ff. Ibn Khaldūn stresses the inevitable transition from *badāwa* to *ḥaḍāra* with the consequent deterioration of manly qualities and extension of luxury and ease. The transformation of human habits goes hand in hand with the transition from rural to urban life and adversely affects political power and authority. The decisive stage is reached when a frugal mode of living gives way to a luxurious life of leisure and a marked decline in morals (see Q. vol. I, pp. 251ff., 301, 309ff.; B. pp. 138ff., 167, 172ff.). Cf. also my *KGS*, pp. 20–45.

16 We must beware of seeing in Ibn Khaldūn a forerunner of Marxism. I refer the reader to my *KGS*, p. 72, n. 1. Although a sound economy is indispensable, it is only one of the foundations of the state. Religious ideas, political ambition and cultural pursuits combine with material prosperity in the development and stability of the state, be it built on the *Sharī'a* of Islam or on political power and authority.

17 See Q. vol. II, pp. 92f./B. p. 286.

18 See Q. vol. II, p. 79 (with a different chapter heading)/B. p. 279. Here the great influence of a religious administration for the good of the state is clearly expressed.

19 See Q. vol. II, pp. 87ff./B. pp. 283ff. The state is here the power-state.

20 See *ibid.* We note that Ibn Khaldūn accepts private property as a matter of course and is against "state-capitalism" (see also n. 16 above). His overriding interest is the good order and welfare of the state and its population in the interests of the state.

21 In addition to the passages quoted and referred to in the previous three notes, see also Q. vol. II, pp. 82f./B. pp. 280ff. For the whole question of the relation of politics to economics, cf. the chapter "Staat und Wirtschaft" in my *KGS*, pp. 71–92, where illustrations from Arab geographers are given.

22 See Q. vol. I, pp. 339ff./B. pp. 188f.

23 See Q. vol. II, pp. 126ff./B. pp. 302ff. Cf. my article quoted in nn. 6 and 10 above.

24 See Q. vol. I, p. 72/B. pp. 43f. He undoubtedly has Ibn Sīnā's

K. al-najāt in mind, and in particular the chapter "Fī ithbāt al-nubuwwa".

25 See Q. vol. I, p. 232/B. pp. 126f. and my KAF, p. 82. Ibn Khaldūn observed the deterioration of the spontaneous faith which dictates the believer's actions, and the gulf that separates the masses from the learned guardians, teachers and interpreters of the religious law which had to be mastered by prolonged, intensive study. Islam, like Judaism, rejects a division into clergy and laity. But it was unavoidable that the ever-increasing differentiation and complexity of life in the ethnically, socially and culturally heterogeneous Islamic empire should call for special skills. Hence a class of scholars grew up who were trained in the science of the all-embracing *Shar'* and all its intricacies and subtle interpretations according to the four recognized schools. This religious law became more and more complex, and its hold over the Muslims more and more precarious, as political considerations increasingly encroached upon Muslim life as represented in the original *khilāfa*.

26 See Q. vol. II, pp. 126f./B. p. 303.

27 Ibn Rushd makes the same distinction. Cf. my "The Place of Politics in the Philosophy of Ibn Rushd" (*PIR*) in *BSOAS*, vol. XV, 2 (1953), pp. 273ff., and also the chapter devoted to his political philosophy. Among Jewish thinkers, Maimonides adopts the same attitude. But whereas he and Ibn Rushd contrast the law of revelation (*Torah* in the case of the Jew, *Sharī'a* in that of the Muslim) with the *Nomos* of Plato, Ibn Khaldūn thinks of political reason, the reason of the autocratic ruler, since for him the philosopher's reason is applied to the state in a purely theoretical and hypothetical fashion. Perhaps one could describe this contrast in terms of the pure reason of the metaphysician versus the practical reason of the political thinker.

28 See Q. vol. I, p. 284/B. p. 157. This is Ibn Khaldūn's interpretation of *Sūra* VIII, 64. But he is realist enough to see the negative side of religion as well; he stresses no less forcefully the adverse effect of religion on the manly virtues which are needed for an active political life, once spontaneous faith has given way to guided obedience and meek submission.

29 See Q. vol. I, pp. 284ff./B. p. 158. Cf. also my *KGS*, ch. "Staat und Religion", pp. 50ff.

30 See Q. vol. I, pp. 286f./B. p. 159. Cf. also my *KGS*, pp. 53f. It is clear from this passage that the dividing line between realism and expediency is very thin.

31 See Q. vol. I, pp. 373f./B. pp. 207f.

32 *Ibid.* Here Ibn Khaldūn's explanation of the transition from *khilāfa* to *mulk* is based on political considerations alone. This is clear from his stress on the '*Aṣabīya*, although it cannot be overlooked that the '*Aṣabīya* itself is permeated with faith and religious conviction. Yet it is the '*Aṣabīya* and not the reality of the *Sharī'a* which preserved the *khilāfa*, even though it was only a shadow of its former self.

Ibn Khaldūn's utterances must be understood and evaluated in their context, and in relation to the particular point he wants to emphasize. In another context they may be openly contradicted, thus giving a strong impression of equivocation and inconsistency. This is the case with the positive and at the same time negative influence of religion on political structure and stability. But apart from the ideal *Sharī'a*-state of the original *khilāfa*, Ibn Khaldūn is not out to pass judgement and to insist for the *mulk* on absolute values such as govern the *Sharī'a*-state. His remarks are always relative and occasioned by a certain situation at a certain stage of a natural political development into which he inquires as a detached observer (cf. also notes 25 and 28).

33 Literally, "a riding animal".

34 See Q. vol. I, pp. 364f./B. p. 202. Here the Muslim speaks and apparently takes sides by stressing the superiority of the divinely revealed law as a guide to individual salvation through a life of justice and righteousness, assuring the believer of the hereafter. Cf. notes 25, 28 and 32 above.

35 See Q. vol. I, p. 366/B. p. 203. Cf. ch. II for Al-Māwardī, Ibn Jamā'a and Ibn Taymīya. Ibn Taymīya, in particular, aimed at a reform of political and social life in accordance with the principles of the *Sharī'a* and its proper application. Ibn Khaldūn was satisfied with observation and diagnosis, although as a Muslim he deplored injustice and tyrannous rule just as much. See also H. A. R. Gibb, "The Islamic Background of Ibn Khaldūn's Political Theory" in *BSOAS* (1933), pp. 31–9, for a discussion of K. Ayad's book and my *KGS*.

36 See Q. vol. I, p. 342/B. p. 190. We note that Al-Fārābī and, following him, Ibn Bājja and Ibn Rushd credit the ancient Persians with an autocratic priestly rule.

37 *Ibid.*

38 *Ibid.* This agrees with an earlier quotation, cf. n. 34 above.

39 See Q. vol. I, p. 354/B. p. 196. *Qudra* here means natural ability as well as the necessary means to enforce his will and authority. This is borne out by the example of the Quraish. It was precisely the weakening of the caliphal power and central authority which confronted the jurists with the grave problem of maintaining the authority of the *Sharī'a*, and the caliph's prerogative and authority based upon it, against the emirs and (later) the sultans who usurped actual authority and power by force of arms.

40 See Q. vol. I, pp. 230ff./B. pp. 126f. Cf. also notes 25, 28, 32, 34 and 35. Prof. Gibb, *op. cit.* pp. 36ff., criticizes my exposition of Ibn Khaldūn's attitude to religion (especially my *KGS*, pp. 59f.) as leaving "an unresolved contradiction" which he resolves by assuming two different senses of the term "religion" in Ibn Khaldūn: religion "in the true and absolute sense..." and "acquired religion", the latter based on the above-quoted passage (in full in my *KGS* on pp. 68f.). I am inclined to interpret Ibn Khaldūn as I have done in the foregoing pages and the relevant notes, and to speak of a trans-

formation of "religion in the true and absolute sense" as the result of the transition from *badāwa* to *ḥaḍāra*. From a spontaneous driving force among the early followers of Muḥammad, religion had become institutionalized; from a living and inspiring example it had become a subject of tuition by experts, in short a science, as Ibn Khaldūn himself says; not forgetting the impetus which '*Aṣabīya* gave to religion, being itself transformed in the process.

41 Naturally, he is dependent for much of the material of early Islamic history down to his own time on the Muslim historians of Umayyad and Abbasid times. But at least in some respects he transcends their interpretation with the help of the principles and concepts which he himself evolved. This is not the place to attempt an assessment of Ibn Khaldūn as an historian of Islam; but such a study is long overdue.

42 See Q. vol. II, p. 251/B. p. 369.

43 *Ibid.* He illustrates his point with many examples taken from the history of the Jews, Greeks and Romans—as it was known to him through Muslim historians—and finally of Islam in East and West.

44 See Q. vol. II, pp. 254f./B. p. 371. Here his interest is predominantly political.

45 See Q. vol. II, pp. 261–5/B. pp. 374–6 and my *KGS*, pp. 101ff.

46 See Q. vol. II, pp. 255–61/B. pp. 371–4 and my *KGS*, pp. 96–101. He stresses the growth, development and decline of culture and civilization within a definite span of time like that of human life, in which growth of every kind comes to a stop at the age of 40; after a standstill of several years decline sets in.

47 See Q. vol. III, pp. 87ff./B. p. 478; Q. vol. II, pp. 364ff., *passim*/B. pp. 429f. (Q. contains the Introductions mentioned in the title of this chapter, which are missing in B: from 376 onwards the text again agrees with B. pp. 430ff.); and my KAF, pp. 76f.

48 See Q. vol. II, pp. 307f./B. pp. 400f.; and for a fuller account my *KGS*, pp. 103f. He compares the highly developed civilization of Cairo with the simpler civilization of the Maghreb, and makes some notable observations on the force of habit and tradition, how they change, and how they account for much of civilization. Cf. also n. 15 above and the passages quoted there.

49 See Q. vol. II, pp. 383f./B. pp. 434f. and my *KGS*, pp. 106f.

50 See pp. 88f. above, with n. 13.

51 It is fully discussed in my KAF, pp. 78ff.

52 See Q. vol. III, p. 210/B. p. 514.

53 See later in the chapter devoted to Ibn Rushd, pp. 178f.; 183ff.; 204.

54 See KAF, pp. 81ff., especially p. 84. Ibn Khaldūn was too censorious and condescending, as will be clear from the discussion of Ibn Rushd's political thought (pp. 189–96 below). Ibn Khaldūn shows no trace of any knowledge of Ibn Rushd's commentary on Plato's *Republic*.

55 See Friedrich Meinecke, *Niccolò Machiavelli. Der Fürst und kleinere Schriften* (Klassiker der Politik, Achter Band, Berlin, 1923), p. 22.

See also *ibid.* p. 21 for an important definition of *virtù*. For a penetrating analysis of Machiavelli's personality and doctrine see H. Butterfield, *The Statecraft of Machiavelli* (London, 1955).

56 See Q. vol. I, pp. 252ff./B. pp. 139f.

57 See my *KGS*, pp. 111ff. A detailed discussion of similarities and contrasts between the two thinkers will be found *ibid.* pp. 43, 53, 55 and 70.

58 See Book I, ch. 11. Cf. also ch. 12 on religion as a positive force for political stability.

59 See *Il Principe*, ch. 3, and my *KGS*, pp. 110f., n. 1. A parallel statement from the *Muqaddima* was quoted above, p. 101.

60 See p. 97, with n. 30 above.

61 See p. 101 above and nn. 25, 28, 32 and, especially, n. 40.

62 See pp. 94f. above.

CHAPTER V

1 See above, *Introduction*, pp. 3–7; pp. 8f. and ch. I. Cf. also on the question of Platonism in Islam: S. Pines, "Some Problems of Islamic Philosophy" in *Islamic Culture*, vol. XI (1937); and Franz Rosenthal, "On the Knowledge of Plato's Philosophy in the Islamic World", *ibid.* vol. XV (1941).

2 See R. Walzer, "Islamic Philosophy" in *The History of Philosophy, Eastern and Western* (London, 1953), pp. 127–48, "Arabic Transmission Of Greek Thought To Mediaeval Europe" in *Bulletin of the John Rylands Library*, vol. XXIX, 1 (1945), and *Greek into Arabic*, Oxford, 1962; and my PIB, pp. 189 f., with notes.

3 Cf. M. Steinschneider, "Die arabischen Uebersetzungen aus dem Griechischen" in *Centralblatt für Bibliothekswesen* (Leipzig, 1893), pp. 75ff. Al-Kindī is credited with a revision of the *Theology* in Porphyry's recension, translated into Arabic by 'Abd al-Masīḥ b. Nā'ima. Baumstark showed that the attribution to Aristotle goes back to a Syriac source, not to Al-Kindī. See P. Kraus, "Plotin chez les Arabes" in *Bulletin de l'Institut de l'Egypte*, vol. 23 (1941), p. 267. G. Graf, *Geschichte der Christlichen Arabischen Literatur*, vol. II (*Studi E Testi*, 133, Vatican City, 1947), pp. 228ff., still maintains that Al-Kindī is responsible not only for a revision of the Arabic translation by the Syrian Christian but also for far-reaching alterations and for the attribution to Aristotle. P. Kraus, *op. cit.*, renders the best and most reliable account of the transmission of Plotinus's *Enneads* IV–VI as the *Theology of Aristotle* in Arabic and Latin and stresses its importance for Islamic philosophy. He expresses serious doubts that Al-Fārābī accepted the attribution as genuine and is of the opinion that the treatise was of little consequence for Al-Fārābī's thought (p. 270). Although Ibn Sīnā mentions that Aristotle may not be its author he wrote extensive notes on passages of the *Theology* (pp. 272ff.). Cf. also G. Vajda, "Les Notes d'Avicenne sur la Théologie d'Aristote" in *Revue Thomiste*, 1951, no. 2. This work is

a translation of the Arabic text edited by A. Badawi. It is preceded by the relevant passages of the *Theology* and accompanied by important notes. Kraus published in his study fragments of the *Theology*, wrongly attributed to Al-Fārābī as *Risāla fī-l-'ilm al-illāhī*, which differ from the text of Dieterici (*Die sogenannte Theologie des Aristoteles*, Leipzig, 1882). For the *Liber de Causis* see O. Bardenhewer, *Die pseudoaristotelische Schrift über das reine Gute, bekannt unter dem Namen "Liber de Causis"* (Freiburg, 1882).

4 See above, ch. I, pp. 15ff.

5 The theory of *the double truth* is wrongly attributed to Ibn Rushd, whose philosophy must be clearly distinguished from the later Averroists who held such a view. Unfortunately, historians of medieval philosophy do not as a rule make this necessary distinction.

6 E.g. what Maimonides calls the Ceremonial Laws.

7 A detailed analysis must be reserved for the chapter dealing with the political philosophy of Ibn Rushd.

8 See my M, pp. 192f.; SAIPT, pp. 9 ff.; AIJT, pp. 67ff., 77ff.; PIR, pp. 259ff., 269f., 273ff.

9 See *Politikos*, 259B. Cf. also E. Barker, *op. cit.* p. 273.

10 Al-Fārābī (*K. al-siyāsā al-madanīya*, p. 39) treats the household (as the smallest unit of association) as a part of a street. Likewise Ibn Bājja (*K. tadbīr al-mutawaḥḥid*, 6, 2ff.) sees in the household, as well as in economics, something which exists for the sake of the state, not an independent science. Economics is part of man's government of himself or part of politics (*ibid.* p. 7). See also my PIB, p. 13, with notes 44–8. Ibn Sīnā and Al-Ghazālī adhere to Aristotle's threefold division of the practical sciences into politics, economics and ethics (Al-Ghazālī), respectively: ethics—taught by Aristotle in his *Nicomachia*, economics—taught in *Bryson*, and politics—taught as far as kingship is concerned in Plato's *Republic* and in Aristotle's *Politica*, and, as far as prophetic revealed law is concerned, in Plato's *Laws*. (Ibn Sīnā, *Aqsām al-'ulūm* in *Tis' rasā'il*, p. 73). Cf. also above ch. II, n. 38.

11 Cf. Averroes' commentary on Plato's *Republic* in my edition (Cambridge University Press, corrected reprint, 1966), p. 22 (Hebrew text)/p. 112 (English translation), §§ 7 and 8.

12 Averroes says: "For the very same reason this art ⟨of politics⟩ is divided into two parts: in the first part acquired habits, volitional actions and behaviour in general are mentioned in a comprehensive exposition. Their mutual relationship is also explained, and which of these habits are due to which others. In the second will be explained how these habits become entrenched in the soul, and which of them are co-ordinated so that the action resulting from the intended habit should be perfect to the highest degree; and which habits hinder one another. Generally, in this part are placed things which are capable of realization, if they are conditioned by general principles" (*ibid.* pp. 21f./112, § 6). Averroes closely follows Al-Fārābī's exposition. Cf.

A. Gonzalez Palencia, *Al-Farabi Catálogo de las Ciencias* (Madrid, 1953), p. 91.

13 Maimonides in his *Guide*, ed. Munk, vol. II, ch. 40, p. 86b, makes the same distinction with regard to divine and human law, and uses the same term *maẓnūna*, "assumed, alleged".

14 Or "rule, dominion". Cf. Palencia, *loc. cit.* p. 92.

15 *Ibid.* p. 93. The Arabic terms are *riyāsa fāḍila*, corresponding to Plato's *Republic* or ideal state, and *riyāsa jāhilīya*, corresponding to Plato's imperfect states.

16 *Ibid.* p. 94. *Khissa* may also be translated by "avaricious" and denotes plutocracy. On this state as well as on *karāma* (timocracy) see the chapters devoted to Al-Fārābī and Ibn Rushd below. Cf. also my PIB, p. 15, n. 51; PF, pp. 168f. with the relevant notes; and *ACR*, pp. 207ff. and 283ff.

17 *Falsafat Aflāṭūn*, edited as *Alfarabius De Platonis Philosophia* by Fr. Rosenthal and R. Walzer (*Plato Arabus*, vol. II, London, 1943). The treatise and its possible Greek source are fully discussed in the "Praefatio". English translation by M. Mahadi, *Alfarabi's philosophy of Plato and Aristotle*, New York, 1962.

18 Op. cit. p. 13 (Arabic text)/pp. 9f. (Latin translation).

19 Cf. *Iḥṣā*, p. 94. "Practical wisdom" translates *hunka*, "prudence". See Ibn Rushd, pp. 118f. above.

20 *Falsafa madanīya*, *op. cit.* p. 95. Al-Fārābī usually employs the term *'ilm* here and in the *K. taḥṣīl al-sa'āda*, or *ṣinā'a* in the *Falsafat Aflāṭūn*.

21 *Ibid.* p. 97. Cf. Ibn Rushd, p. 118 above, taken from ACR, pp. 22/112. There is so far no evidence that any of the *Falāsifa* actually used Aristotle's *Politica*. *Siyāsa* stands for *politike* and *politeia*. For Plato's other political treatises see *Falsafat Aflāṭūn*, §§ 18, 23–5, 27 with the editors' *Notae*.

22 *Riyāsāt fāḍila* and *siyar*, *malakāt jāhilīya*. *Riyāsa*, "authority, rule", may here mean "constitution".

23 *Ibid.* p. 98. Cf. also *Falsafat Aflāṭūn*, p. 13, § 18.

24 *Ibid.* p. 99. The Arabic terms used are *quwwa tajarrubīya*, "experimental faculty", "empiricism as knowledge gained by experience", and *quwwa qarīḥa jaballīya*, "natural talent". I follow the variant reading of the Cairo MS. against the text *quwwa qarīḥīya ḥissīya*.

25 This most mature of Al-Fārābī's political treatises is discussed in the next chapter. It represents his most weighty contribution to the first, theoretical part of political philosophy.

26 "Physical science" includes Aristotle's *De Anima* and psychology in general. See also my *ACR*, p. 255, where I refer to *Iḥṣā* and say: "As far as we know, Alfārābī is the first Muslim thinker to include *De Anima* among the eight Aristotelian treatises making up 'physical science', analogous to the eight parts of the *Organon*."

27 Cf. *K. taḥṣīl*, p. 13.

28 *Ibid.* pp. 14ff.

29 Cf. *ibid.* p. 14 for highest perfection (*kamāl aqṣā*) and p. 16 for final, utmost happiness (*saʿāda quṣwā*). Since Al-Fārābī speaks at the beginning of this treatise of "worldly happiness in the first life and final happiness in the other life" (p. 2), the question may legitimately be asked whether he meant by "the other life" the future life of the Muslim or the life of speculation and contemplation of the philosopher in the ideal state.

CHAPTER VI

1 Abu Naṣr Al-Fārābī was born of Turkish parents in Transoxiana in the district of Fārāb in the last third of the ninth century. He spent a large part of his long life at the court of the Hamdanid ruler Saif al-Dawla at Aleppo and died in Cairo in 339 A.H./950 C.E. His comprehensive knowledge of Aristotle, upon many of whose works he commented, earned him the title of "the second teacher", and he established a reputation as a logician respected by *the* commentator of Aristotle, Ibn Rushd. He also commented on the *Nicomachean Ethics*, as we know from Ibn Rushd. This commentary must be presumed lost; it would be interesting to compare it with Ibn Rushd's commentary.

In our context, his contributions to psychology, science and music—he was a noted composer and performer—are of less interest than his political writings. These are commentaries, paraphrases and free, or more independent adaptations of Plato's political writings, chief among them the *Republic* and the *Laws*. M. Steinschneider's extensive monograph, *Al-Farabi Des Arabischen Philosophen Leben und Schriften* (S. Pétersbourg 1869), is still invaluable. Some writings were wrongly attributed to him, as, for example, the *R. fuṣūṣ al-ḥikam* which S. Pines showed to be by Ibn Sīnā (see *Revue des Études Islamiques*, 1951), and S. M. Stern, in his review of *Plato Arabus*, vol. III, throws doubt on Al-Fārābī's authorship of the *Compendium Legum Platonis* (see *BSOAS*, vol. XVII (1955), p. 2). His mystical tendency is relevant to our problem; he is said to have lived the life of a Sufi, and traces of Sufism are undoubtedly to be found in his *Siyāsa madanīya* (see p. 138 below).

Of the many studies in recent years, showing a heightened interest in his writings, which are by no means easy to understand and to interpret, those by L. Strauss must be singled out for their stress on Al-Fārābī's outstanding importance, especially "Maimunis Lehre von der Prophetie und ihre Quellen" (*Le Monde Oriental*, vol. XXVIII, 1934). I stated Al-Fārābī's influence on Maimonides' political ideas independently in my "Maimonides' Conception of State and Society" in *Moses Maimonides* (ed. I. Epstein, London, 1935). In a famous letter addressed to his Hebrew translator Maimonides explicitly recommends the study of Al-Fārābī. Hebrew translations of Al-Fārābī's works enjoyed wide currency in the Middle Ages (see M. Steinschneider, *Die Hebräischen Uebersetzungen des Mittelalters und die Juden als Dolmetscher*, Berlin, 1893) and did much to spread his influence and to stimulate philosophical study. Cf. also L. Strauss, "Eine vermisste Schrift Farâbîs" (*MGWJ*, 1936). As far as we know, Al-Fārābī led a sheltered life of study, contemplation and philosophical discussion at the court of his patron, apart from making music which greatly moved and delighted his audience. His interest in politics, with the possible exception of his *Al-fuṣūl al-madanīya*, was theoretical, and an attempt is made in this chapter to describe his political ideas and to place them in the context of Platonism and Islam, on the lines of my article "The Place of Politics in the Philosophy of Al-Fārābī (PF)", published in *Islamic Culture*, vol. XXIX, no. 3 (Hyderabad, 1955).

2 For a fuller treatment see my PF, pp. 157ff., with notes and the explanatory notes in my *ACR*, pp. 255ff., also my M, PG, SAIPT, PIB, PIR and AIJT, *passim*.

3 Published in *Alfarabi's Philosophische Abhandlungen* (*Abhdln.*) by Fr. Dieterici (Arabic text, Leiden, 1890; German translation, 1892).

4 See previous chapter, pp. 119f. and notes 17, 18 and 21.

5 *Op. cit.* p. 53, §§ 4, 5. See also p.118 of the previous chapter, and note 10. Al-Fārābī significantly stresses action (moral behaviour) based on knowledge. By this he means scientific knowledge acquired by the study of physics (?) and mathematics (?) in that order, since nature is easier for us to understand (*ibid.*). Maimonides holds the same view about *Imitatio Dei*. The translation "physics" requires reading *ṭabī'iyāt* for *ṭabāi'*; "mathematics" is literally "geometry" (*handasa*).

6 176 *B*.

7 *Enneads*, I, ii.

8 Cf. *Abhdln.* p. 25.

9 See my M, pp. 197ff.; SAIPT, pp. 6ff.; PIB, pp. 193f.; AIJT, pp. 67ff.; PF, p. 165; and especially PIR, pp. 261f., 273ff. Cf. also above, ch. V, pp. 115ff.

10 Cf. *Abhdln.* pp. 25ff.

11 It helped the emergence of a theosophy of the type represented by Al-Suhrawardī (see H. Corbin, *as-Suhrawardi's Opera Metaphysica et Mystica*, vol. II, Teheran, 1952). It is particularly evident among *Falāsifa* with a mystical bent, beginning with Al-Fārābī and becoming stronger with Ibn Sīnā, Ibn Bājja and Ibn Ṭufail.

12 *Alfarabis's Abhandlung Der Musterstaat* (Leiden, 1895).

13 I, ii, 1094b. This passage has already been cited in chs. I and V.

14 In his *Faṣl al-maqāl*, pp. 7ff., and *Tahāfut al-tahāfut*, ed. M. Bouyges, pp. 219ff. See my PIR, pp. 256ff. Cf. also *ACR*, pp. 185ff., 272, 274. English translation by S. Van den Bergh, London, 1954.

15 The medieval Jewish thinkers share this intellectualism, which should not be confused with rationalism. Cf. my AIJT, pp. 67ff.

16 When this book was first printed only D. M. Dunlop's English translation of a Bodleian fragment of this treatise was available. (*Iraq*, vol. XIV part 2, 1952.) I have now used his edition of the complete text with translation and notes, *Fusul al-madani*, Cambridge, 1961.

17 See *Mad. fāḍ.* p. 53, ll. 7ff.; *Siyāsa*, p. 39, ll. 10ff. Al-Fārābī adds in the *Mad. fāḍ.* (pp. 1ff.) that the first association in which the highest good and the utmost perfection are attainable is the (city)-state, not a smaller political unit. Since man is guided by free will and choice, happiness is attainable only in the ideal state (*al-madīna al-fāḍila*). For only in it do men help each other in promoting good rather than evil.

18 *Taḥṣīl*, p. 14, ll. 5ff.

19 *Ibid.* p. 14, ll. 9ff. Cf. also previous chapter, p. 121.

20 See my PF, p. 161 with note 1, and PIR, p. 265.

21 See *Mad. fāḍ.* p. 54, ll. 5ff. in continuation of the passage quoted in note 17 above. Al-Fārābī compares the states (city, nation, cultivated world) to the body and its members. Just as these co-operate to achieve and preserve perfect health, so the parts of a city, the city-states of a nation, and the nations of an empire (equivalent to the whole inhabited Earth, *ma'mūra*) co-operate to guarantee and maintain happiness through virtues and good deeds. *Ma'mūra* probably translates *oikoumene*, as *umma* does *demos*, and *madīna* stands for *polis*.

22 See *ibid.* p. 46, ll. 7ff. Happiness can be attained only by volitional actions and habits, that is, by those which are conducive to it and not those which are a hindrance. Al-Fārābī says much the same thing here as in the *Iḥṣā*, quoted in the preceding chapter, p. 119, when defining political science.

23 See *Taḥṣīl*, pp. 13ff., as quoted in the preceding chapter, p. 121, and, with regard to the ruler of the ideal state, *Mad. fāḍ.*, p. 57, l. 18 to p. 58, l. 4.

24 See *Taḥṣīl*, p. 2 and note 29 of the preceding chapter. An alternative interpretation would be to look upon speculative perfection, reached in this world by the metaphysician, as the highest stage attainable by mortal man immediately preceding the ultimate happiness of the world to come (?).

25 Cf. *Republic*, Book IV, especially 427C–434D and 441C–445B.

26 Literally "deeds". Cf. *Taḥṣīl*, pp. 32f. and 40ff. and *ACR*, pp. 117ff. and 257f.

27 Cf. *Taḥṣīl*, p. 29. Al-Fārābī devotes pp. 22–9 to a detailed description of the fourfold perfection in ethical, intellectual and speculative virtues, and practical arts, the possession of which makes up ultimate happiness. The description is based on Aristotle's *Nicomachean Ethics* seen in the light of Plato's views on education of philosophers and guardians.

28 See my *ACR*, p. 119 and pp. 257f. Al-Fārābī's distinction between principal and subordinate arts, repeated by Ibn Rushd, goes back to *NE*, I, I, 1094a; cf. also Plato, *Politikos*, 304. The same applies to his distinction between *mulūk* (rulers, masters) by will-power and nature, and *Khadam* (ruled, servants) by nature and free will.

29 See *Mad. fāḍ.* pp. 54–7 for a detailed analogy of the ruler of the body and its serving parts, and the ruler of the state and the hierarchy of his servants down to those who serve but are not served (*ibid.* p. 55, l. 3). The excellence of the ruler—both in the human body and in the state—cannot be matched even by those nearest him (p. 55, ll. 13ff.), and the excellent habits of his subjects are due to his example; towards him and his aim all actions in the ideal (excellent) state are directed, "he becomes *intellect* and *intellectum* in actuality" (*ibid.* p. 57, l. 18: *'aql wa-ma'qūl bi-l-fi'l*). He is nearest to the Active Intellect, being midway between it and the Passive Intellect without intermediary (p. 58, l. 4).

30 See *Mad. fāḍ.* p. 57, l. 18 to p. 59, l. 8 and *Siyāsa*, p. 3, l. 19 and p. 49, l. 11 to p. 50, l. 5. In the latter passage the three intellects (Active, Passive and Acquired) are related to the *K. al-nafs*, that is, *De Anima*, probably in the form of Alexander of Aphrodisias' commentary. Cf. also my PF, p. 162 with note 2. "His imaginative faculty is by nature disposed to receive, be it in a state of waking or of sleep, from the Active Intellect the particulars...and then the *Intelligibles*.... When man has perfected his passive intellect with all the *Intelligibles* he becomes *intellectus* and *intellectum in actu*...his stage is above the passive intellect most completely removed from matter and near to the active intellect, and he is then called acquired intellect, midway between the active and passive intellects. There is nothing else [that is, no barrier any longer] between him and the active intellect." Then the revelation is mediated to him, as summarized above. It is noteworthy that "*Allah tabāraka wa-ta'āla*" of the *Mad. fāḍ.* (p. 58, l. 21) is in the *Siyāsa* (p. 50, l. 3) "the first cause". This implies an identification of the God of Islam with the god of Aristotle; Al-Fārābī here goes further than Ibn Sīnā and Ibn Rushd, to my mind.

31 See *Mad. fāḍ.* p. 59, ll. 11ff. For this whole section cf. *ibid.* p. 57, l. 17 to p. 59, l. 13; particularly p. 58, l. 14 to p. 59, l. 9 for inspiration and highest perfection.

32 See *Siyāsa*, p. 50, ll. 7f.: *al-nāsu-l-fāḍilūn wa-l-akhyār wa-l-su'adā.*

33 See for a fuller account my PF, pp. 164f. with notes 1–5, p. 165. The most important qualification of the ideal ruler of the ideal state is the possession of speculative virtue as the essence of philosophy (*Taḥṣīl*, p. 42, ll. 12ff.). He acquires these virtues by the assiduous study of the speculative as well as of the practical sciences for which he is predisposed by his nature. What this entails cannot be summarized here in every detail; Al-Fārābī discusses the perception of the *Intelligibles* by means of certain proof at great length (*ibid.* p. 38, ll. 7ff.), significantly in connection with the indispensable philosophical qualification of the first ruler. As for the lawgiver, his qualifications are described *ibid.* p. 41, l. 17 to p. 42, l. 18. Since the king must have perfect capacity for a comprehensive knowledge and perception of the theoretical and practical sciences and arts, as well as for the virtues leading to good deeds, he is identical with the philosopher

and lawgiver (*ibid.* p. 43, ll. 1–8). "As for the meaning of *imām* in the Arabic tongue it points to one whom one follows..." (p. 43, l. 9). Hence it is imperative that his qualifications should be as comprehensive as those of the philosopher, so that his actions serve as a real example which will lead to happiness (*ibid.* p. 43, ll. 10–17). Ibn Rushd adopted Al-Fārābī's definitions and equations, cf. *ACR*, p. 177.

34 Cf. *Taḥṣīl*, p. 29, l. 11 to p. 38, l. 9, for education in the state, in particular p. 29, ll. 18ff. for the speculative sciences which the *imāms* and kings must study in order to fit themselves by stages for the exercise of their functions. On the king as the teacher, educator and instructor of his people, see p. 31, ll. 16ff. to p. 32, l. 9; for a summing up of the results of education and instruction as the responsibility of the first ruler, who alone can bring utmost happiness to nations and city-states, see p. 36, l. 8 to p. 38, l. 9. Such happiness consists in man's possession to perfection of "the four human things" (ethical, intellectual and speculative virtues and practical arts) in proportion to man's inborn capacity for them. The two classes of citizens, the elect few and the masses, are taught by the two methods of demonstration and persuasion (cf. p. 36, ll. 14–17), and in detail p. 36, l. 18 to p. 37, l. 15, the first two lines being given over to the masses and everything else to the elect, who exercise political leadership under the first ruler by applying themselves to a civic art for which they are individually suited. "The most elect of the elect is necessarily the first ruler" (p. 37, l. 16). The aim of all the other elect who enjoy political authority is to achieve completely the end of the first ruler by serving him (p. 37, l. 19 to p. 38, l. 1). His alone is the first rule since he does not serve anybody; but theirs is the second or third rule in proportion to their degree of knowledge: certain knowledge by means of demonstrative proof, or knowledge by means of persuasion (rhetoric) and imagination. Cf. also below, Ibn Rushd, pp. 179ff., 207, for the same distinction and division, and also *ACR*, pp. 117ff. and 257f.

35 Cf. *Republic* 376E–412B for the education of the guardians in general and of those selected to be rulers 521C–541B, and also for the philosophers in particular 471C–480; 484A–487A.

36 See *op. cit.* p. 4 and cf. also my PF, p. 163 with note 2, and PIR, p. 273.

37 See below, ch. IX, p. 180.

38 See *Taḥṣīl*, p. 37, l. 16 to p. 38, l. 13 and note 34 above.

39 *Ibid.* p. 38, l. 14 to p. 39, l. 18. Ibn Rushd (*ACR*, p. 120) similarly points out that philosophy as a natural aptitude is not confined to the Greeks, but individuals predisposed for speculative perfection are also to be found in Spain, Syria, Iraq and Egypt.

40 See *Taḥṣīl*, p. 42, ll. 3ff. and note 33 above.

41 *Ibid.* p. 43, l. 18.

42 See *Taḥṣīl*, p. 41, ll. 17f.

43 *Ibid.* p. 42, ll. 3–11.
44 *Ibid.* p. 44, ll. 7ff.
45 *Ibid.* p. 42, l. 11.
46 *Ibid.* p. 42, l. 19; p. 43, l. 8.
47 *Ibid.* p. 43, ll. 18f.
48 See my M, pp. 197ff.; SAIPT, pp. 6ff.; PIB, pp. 193f.; PIR, pp. 261f. and 273ff. on this important point. Cf. also above, ch. v, p. 117.
49 Cf. *Taḥṣīl*, p. 44, ll. 16f. *Siyāsa* is the Arabic term for Plato's *Republic*. We know from the *Iḥṣā*, p. 97 (quoted in the previous chapter, p. 120), that Aristotle's *Politica* was also called *K. siyāsa*.
50 See *Mad. fāḍ.* p. 59, l. 14 to p. 60, l. 11 for twelve (actually thirteen) qualifications.
51 *Ibid.* p. 57, l. 17 to p. 59, l. 13. Cf. also note 30, above.
52 See *Taḥṣīl*, p. 45, ll. 6f.
53 See *Republic*, 474B–480.
54 See *Ta'rīkh al-ḥukamā*, ed. Lippert, p. 116.
55 See note 50. Ibn Rushd lists the same conditions except for the physical qualifications which are identical with those demanded of the guardians; hence he counts only ten (*ACR*, pp. 178f. with notes). They are deprived from Plato's *Republic*, 485–487A, with the addition of the orator's gift, and not discussed in the *Siyāsa madanīya*.
56 This means that, like the caliph, he must be a *mujtahid*, that is, capable of independent decision (in contrast to the *muqallid* who entirely relies on earlier authorities). It is interesting to note that Al-Fārābī introduces a new political consideration: the best interests of the state, like the jurists we have considered, since their stress on *ṣalāḥ ma'āsh wa-ma'ād* means the same as his *ṣalāḥ ḥāli-l-madīna*, only that he explicitly mentions the state, to which Al-Māwardī's *maṣāliḥ 'āmma* offers the nearest parallel.
56a See now *Fuṣūl*, ed. Dunlop, pp. 15ff.
57 See *Mad. fāḍ.* p. 61, ll. 9–11; *Fuṣūl*, p. 137, § 54B. In the latter the group of *aristoi* seems to consist of four men who possess between them the six qualifications of the *Mad. fāḍ.* and of the "first chief" of § 54A. But "wisdom" in A becomes "provides the end" in B; "perfect intelligence" in A becomes "provides what leads to the end" in B; "excellence in persuasion" and "excellence of imagination" in A become "a third possesses excellence of persuasion and excellence of imagination" in B; and lastly "power to fight the holy war in person" and "that there should be nothing in his person to prevent him attending to matters which belong to the holy war" in A become simply a shortened "another possesses the power to fight the holy war" in B. Ibn Rushd reproduces five by keeping the third and fourth separate and by being more explicit in the first and second by adding "through his wisdom" and "through his intelligence" respectively (*ACR*, p. 208).
58 See *Mad. fāḍ.* p. 61, ll. 11–15. This is reminiscent of the *Politikos*, e.g. 259. But we cannot be sure that Galen's summary of the *Politikos*

was known to the *Falāsifa*. There the "statesman" is either the ruler or his effective adviser.

59 Cf. above, note 57, and my PF, pp. 167 and 174–7.

60 Cf. *Republic*, 445 D, E and 544 C.

61 See *Mad. fāḍ.* p. 61, l. 17, *madīna jāhilīya*; *Siyāsa*, p. 58, ll. 7 ff., *madīna jāhila*.

62 See *Republic* 444 B. Cf. also *ACR*, p. 163, n. 3.

63 See *Mad. fāḍ.* p. 62, ll. 4 ff.; *Siyāsa*, p. 58, l. 11 to p. 59, l. 2, where he mentions agriculture, hunting, pasturage and brigandage as the means of providing for the necessities of life, such as housing, clothing, food and drink. All the terms for the imperfect states are dealt with in my PIB and in the notes in *ACR*. Cf. *ACR*, pp. 217 f. and 289, based on Al-Fārābī, and *Republic* 369 C, D for "necessity".

64 See *Siyāsa*, p. 59, ll. 3–12. See also my PF, p. 168, n. 5. *Baddala* of *Mad. fāḍ.* p. 62, l. 6 must be changed to *nadhāla*. Cf. also my PIB, p. 201 with note 51. Ibn Rushd briefly touches upon this state in *ACR*, pp. 211 f. and 285 ff. Plato discusses oligarchy 550 C–555 B.

65 See *Mad. fāḍ.* p. 62, ll. 8 ff., where Al-Fārābī employs the terms *khissa* and *shaqwa*; *Siyāsa*, p. 59, ll. 12–19, where we find *khasīsa* in place of the two terms of the *Mad. fāḍ.* This state is the one "in which men help each other to enjoy sensual pleasure such as games, jokes and pleasantries...and this is the enjoyment of the pleasures of food, drink and carnal gratification". They are not sought in order to preserve and benefit the body but only for the sake of the pleasure one derives from them. "This state is the happy and fortunate state with the people of ignorance (*al-ahl al-jāhilīya*), for this state only aims at attaining pleasure after obtaining ⟨first⟩ the necessities ⟨of life⟩ and ⟨then⟩ wealth and abundant money to spend" (*Siyāsa*). See also p. 279, n. 71.

66 See for a full description *Siyāsa*, p. 60, l. 16 to p. 64, l. 2, whereas the *Mad. fāḍ.* has a much shorter account, p. 62, ll. 10–14, which is slightly enlarged as far as *madīna karāma* is concerned in the *Siyāsa*, p. 59, l. 20 to p. 60, l. 15, immediately preceding the details about the various kinds of honour. Cf. also Ibn Rushd's more concise and far more discerning treatment, though it is undoubtedly based on Al-Fārābī's diffuse exposition, in *ACR*, pp. 209 ff. and 220 ff. with pp. 284 f. and 290 f. The source for both Muslim writers is *Republic* 548, 549. Ibn Rushd treats of timocracy and oligarchy in Plato's order, first in a summary fashion and later in detailed comment on Plato. In the former treatment he is much more dependent on Al-Fārābī than in the latter. For example, *Siyāsa*, p. 60, l. 16 to p. 61, l. 3, speaks of *victory* as one of the things most desired and deserving of honour. This is taken over by Ibn Rushd in a much more concise statement (*ACR*, p. 210, with note 2 and p. 284, the note on this passage). For honour due to noble descent or wealth see *Siyāsa*, p. 61, l. 18 to p. 62, l. 3, which is paralleled in *ACR*, p. 210. Such honour entitles its holder to be in authority as king.

Al-Fārābī stresses (e.g. p. 62, ll. 9–14) that he is considered the best ruler who promotes the aim of the ruled, such as wealth and pleasures, but wants nothing but honour for himself. In order to achieve this, he must possess greater wealth than anybody else, either through taxes or foreign conquests. If such a ruler is concerned about the advantage and welfare of the citizens in matters of honour through wealth, etc., such a state resembles the ideal state because its citizens are graded in rank on account of the honour accorded them. Ibn Rushd expresses the same idea in *ACR*, p. 209, yet he insists on the basic distinction between the two states when he says (*ibid.* p. 210): "...the difference between them is that in the ideal state honours follow virtues and worthy things that are in truth worthy things; honour is not aimed at for itself, but is rather a shadow linked with virtue." Al-Fārābī ends his account of timocracy with the extraordinary claim that if the love of honour becomes excessive in it, it is transformed into tyranny. This tallies neither with Plato's nor with Aristotle's order of transformation. Ibn Rushd does not accept this view (p. 64, ll. 1 f.).

67 Cf. *NE*, VIII, 10, 1160b.

68 See *Mad. fāḍ.* p. 62, ll. 14ff.; *Siyāsa*, p. 64, l. 3 to p. 69, l. 3. Al-Fārābī first describes the desire for victory and brute force, and how the strongest with a gift for authority gains the ascendancy and becomes the master and king. Often he finds like-minded helpers. Al-Fārābī then sets out to distinguish between despotic states, and defines tyranny or despotism according to the aim: mastery, over others or over their possessions for power's sake, within or externally, by force and conquest or by persuasion and achieving enslavement. He does not, however, sufficiently distinguish between the impulse to gain victory, mastery and absolute power for their own sake, that is, tyranny in the strict sense, and for other ends, particularly to gain honour or wealth or pleasure. Hence his despotic rule is a mixed one and thus often resembles timocracy or plutocracy. Ibn Rushd avoids this by following Plato's description of tyranny and the tyrannical man, and the transition from democracy to tyranny and of the democratic to the tyrannical man (562A–580C). But due to their common source both Al-Fārābī and Ibn Rushd similarly define tyranny as absolute power. Ibn Rushd in his systematic way distinguishes clearly between timocracy, plutocracy, a hedonistic state, and tyranny in the strict sense of the term. Cf. *ACR*, pp. 232–45 and the notes on this section, pp. 294–7. He is also more exact in his definition of liberty, as can be seen from the order in his commentary, which follows the *Republic*, compared with Al-Fārābī who treats of democracy after tyranny.

69 See *Mad. fāḍ.* p. 62, ll. 16ff.; *Siyāsa*, p. 69, l. 4 to p. 71, l. 5. Again the source is Plato for Al-Fārābī and Ibn Rushd, *Republic* 555B–562A. But whereas Ibn Rushd follows Plato more closely (although he values certain features of democracy higher than his master, probably because of his Muslim milieu), Al-Fārābī lacks precision, as in the case of timocracy and tyranny. See *ACR*, pp. 212f. and 287, 227–31 and 293f. Since democracy is "a free-for-all", Ibn Rushd paraphrases *Republic* 557C–E thus: "So there will come into being in this state all the things which are separate in those ⟨other⟩ states. There will be among them men who love honour, men who love the possession of property, and men who love tyranny. But it is not impossible that there will be among them those who possess virtues and are moved by them" (*ibid.* p. 213). But naturally the state is still a democracy, and not a timocracy, plutocracy or tyranny. This point is not clear from Al-Fārābī's description. Ibn Rushd continues, reminiscent of Al-Fārābī's view (*Siyāsa*, p. 70, l. 20 to p. 71. l. 5): "Therefore, all arts and dispositions will come into being in this state; it will be destined that out of it the ideal state and each of the other states may come into being." Since Aristotle holds that democracy is "the least bad of the deviations" (*NE*, VIII, 10, 1160b) both Al-Fārābī and Ibn Rushd possibly follow him rather than Plato, whom Ibn Rushd criticizes in his commentary on the *NE*, though he does not challenge his opinion on the transformation of states one into another in his commentary on the *Republic* (cf. *ACR*, p. 294, where Ibn Rushd's comment on *NE* 1160b is cited). The sequel in Plato is: monarchy-timocracy-oligarchy (plutocracy)-democracy-tyranny; in Aristotle: monarchy-tyranny; aristocracy-oligarchy; timocracy-democracy.

70 Timocracy, 543A–550C; oligarchy, 550C–555B, called by Ibn Rushd also plutocracy; democracy, 555B–562A; tyranny, 562A–576B.

71 See *ACR*, p. 209, for "the government of the pleasure-seeker"; "the association based on money...this rule is known as the rule of the few" (p. 212); "the plutocratic and the hedonistic state belong to the same category" (p. 227); "the leadership of the few and this is rule based on money, also known as the leadership of vice" (p. 207); "the constitution of the vicious" (p. 211); "this rule is a vile, despicable and base rule" (p. 224).

Shahwa is an emendation. The text of the *Mad. fāḍ.* (ed. Dieterici, p. 62, l. 8) reads *shaqwa* which is no satisfactory complement to *khissa*. I thought first to read *shawqa* since a term expressing "desire, appetite, lust" is required in the context and in view of Ibn Rushd's term used for the hedonistic state in his commentary on Plato's *Republic*. But no feminine noun is known to exist of *shāqa*. Mr G. M. Wickens with whom I discussed this passage and the possibilities of *shāqa* and *shaqā* suggested reading *shahwa* which yields the required meaning.

72 They occur in the following order in the *Mad. fāḍ.*: *mad. fāsiqa*, *mutabaddala* (variant *mubaddala*), *ḍālla*, p. 61, ll. 7f.; *mad. mubaddala*, p. 63, l. 1 and p. 80, l. 5; *sāqiṭa*, p. 80, l. 5; and in the *Siyāsa*: *mad. fāsiqa*, p. 57, l. 11; and *mad. ḍālla*, p. 57, l. 12; for *mubaddala* (*mutabaddala*) of the *Mad. fāḍ.* where it makes good sense, we find in the *Siyāsa* the term confirmed by Ibn Rushd: *nadhāla* (p. 59, l. 3).

73 See *Siyāsa*, p. 73, l. 16 to p. 74, l. 3 (*mad. fāsiqa*); *Mad. fāḍ.* p. 62, ll. 21 ff.

74 See *Mad. fāḍ.* p. 63, ll. 1 ff.

75 See *Mad. fāḍ.* p. 63, ll. 3–16; *Siyāsa*, p. 74, ll. 4–7, much abbreviated.

76 Cf. *ACR*, pp. 296f., where I discuss in detail this absence in Ibn Rushd and give as a possible reason that as commentator on Plato he concentrated on Plato's constitutions and was concerned only with those states and their corresponding individuals. Moreover, Ibn Rushd's equivalent to *ḍālla* seems to denote error in the sense Plato has in mind when he speaks of the deviation of the imperfect states from the ideal republic. For Al-Fārābī *ḍālla* means "holding erroneous beliefs and convictions", whereas *fāsiqa* denotes "right beliefs and convictions", yet the actions and morals of the citizens of this state are those of the *jāhilīya*. On the other hand, *nadhāla* recurs in Ibn Rushd; it is not to be found in the Qur'ān and clearly represents Plato's oligarchy or plutocracy. A further point must be made: as we have so far not discovered Ḥunain b. Isḥāq's Arabic version of the *Republic* (presumably a translation of Galen's *Summary*) it is impossible to decide the exact degree of dependence of Ibn Rushd on Al-Fārābī. A good many correspondences may go back to their common source.

77 Cf. *Republic* 428, 514–541B. See also pp. 124f., 127f., 129f. above and *ACR*, pp. 187ff., especially pp. 193–7, 199–203. The principal discussion in Al-Fārābī is in *Taḥṣīl*, pp. 22–9.

78 *Republic* 514–516C. Cf. also *ACR*, pp. 197f.

79 Cf. *Mad. fāḍ.* p. 69, l. 6 to p. 73, l. 16; *Siyāsa*, p. 71, l. 6 to p. 73, l. 15.

80 See *Mad. fāḍ.* p. 61, l. 18; *Siyāsa*, p. 57, ll. 11 ff.

81 *Siyāsa*, p. 74, ll. 20 ff. The whole discussion from p. 74, l. 8 to the end of the treatise is relevant.

82 See my PIB, pp. 203 ff. with notes 55–59 for a fuller treatment of the *nawābit*.

83 See *Siyāsa*, p. 50, ll. 7–12.

84 See L. Massignon, *La Passion d'Al Hallaj* (Paris, 1914–21), pp. 740 and 751 on *ghurabā*, and also H. Corbin, *as-Suhrawardi's Opera Metaphysica et Mystica*, vol. II (Teheran, 1952), pp. 86 and 97f. (*Qissat al-Ghurbat al-Gharbiya*).

85 See *Tadbīr al-mutawaḥḥid*, ed. Asín Palacios (Madrid-Granada, 1946), p. 11. Ibn Bājja held, contrary to Al-Fārābī before and Ibn Rushd after him, that the *ghārib* = *nābit* could reach happiness in isolation even in imperfect states. Cf. my PIB, p. 205 with note 63. He equates the "stranger" with his *mutawaḥḥid* and thinks that such persons can help in bringing about the ideal out of the imperfect states. We are reminded of Al-Fārābī's (and Ibn Rushd's) view that democracy can thus promote the ideal state (cf. note 69 above).

86 See my PF, pp. 176ff., for a detailed treatment of the qualifications of the rulers as demanded in the *Fuṣūl*, preceded by a discussion of

Ibn Rushd's indebtedness to Al-Fārābī, with special reference to the *Fuṣūl* (pp. 174ff.). Cf. also note 57 above.

87 See pp. 133f., 202f. above and cf. also *ACR*, pp. 207ff. and 283.

88 So on the basis of *ACR*, p. 208; Dunlop translates "king according to the law" *op. cit.* p. 51; it is legal qualification as a *mujtahid* which determines the type of ruler and of the state which he rules. On Plato's *Politikos*, see *ibid.* pp. 17 f.

89 Cf. Al-Fārābi's *Compendium Legum Platonis*, ed. F. Gabrieli, p. 22, especially line 19 (divine laws), a summary of *Laws* 709c–711b.

90 See also pp. 131f. above, with note 48 to which the following references may be added: M, pp. 192ff., 204ff.; PIR, pp. 255, 259ff.

91 Cf. *Gorgias*, 466c, 520B. Cf. Al-Fārābī's summary of the *Gorgias* in his *Falsafat Aflaṭūn.* Ibn Bājja accorded to rhetoric only secondary importance, as an auxiliary art to philosophy, as the art of persuasion (*iqnā*', cf. also *Iḥṣā*, p. 25).

92 Some aspects of Al-Fārābī's political thought will be considered again when we compare Ibn Rushd's treatment of the Platonic ideal and imperfect states with Al-Fārābī's (in the chapter devoted to the political philosophy of Ibn Rushd). Similarity and contrast emerge from the previous notes, though they stressed the dependence of the later upon the first "political" philosopher in Islam. Although it is much more than literary dependence it was not strong enough, as we shall see, to tie Ibn Rushd to the metaphysician's detached attitude which we encounter in Al-Fārābī. This will become clear when we have occasion to stress the political realism and criticism of contemporary Islam to be found in Ibn Rushd's *Commentary on Plato's "Republic"*.

93 See p. 131 above.

94 Cf. *Taḥṣīl*, p. 43, ll. 9ff. and note 33 above. "Accomplishments" translates *ṣinā'at*.

95 Cf. *Siyāsa*, p. 50, l. 3 and see pp. 128f. above, with the end of note 30.

96 See my PF, pp. 164f.

97 See once more ch. v above, pp. 115ff.

CHAPTER VII

1 Avicenna (Abū 'Alī al-Ḥusain b. 'Abd Allah Ibn Sīnā) was born in the province of Bukhara in 980 and died in Isfahan in 1037. We know from his autobiography that although the political turmoil of Persia in his lifetime seriously affected his personal fortunes, he managed to make himself master in medicine, jurisprudence and philosophy. Possessed of a rare intellect and fired by a consuming zeal for knowledge he aspired to and achieved in the most original form that synthesis between the divine law and human reason after which all the *Falāsifa* from Al-Kindī to Ibn Rushd had striven. Indebted to Al-Fārābī who, as he himself tells us, helped him to understand Aristotle's *Metaphysics*, he soon left his teacher far behind in an

original blending of Greek-Hellenistic philosophy, Muslim theology and mysticism and achieved a philosophical monotheism such as no other Muslim thinker could boast. Ibn Rushd's own synthesis may be logically more satisfying, but it is not his equal in depth of religious feeling. His medical encyclopaedia, the *Qānūn*, remained the text-book for centuries in Europe, partly through Hebrew translations. Similarly, his philosophical *Summa*, the *Shifā'*, exerted a lasting influence on Jews and Christians alike. His style is sparkling as the wine which he enjoyed, and matches the profundity of his religious insight and philosophical understanding.

The millenary of his birth has reawakened modern interest in his many-sided achievements and produced a spate of books, monographs and articles. Some aspects of his thought are touched upon in a Cambridge symposium, edited by G. M. Wickens under the title *Avicenna: Scientist & Philosopher* (London, 1952), and the reader will find an excellent selection, in a fine English translation, from his ideas about himself, God and man as a religious being in A. J. Arberry's *Avicenna on Theology* (London, 1951). Mlle A.-M. Goichon deals with his principal ideas and his influence on medieval Europe in her *La Philosophie d'Avicenne et son influence en Europe médiévale* (Paris, 1951) and L. Gardet has placed all students of Islamic and general philosophy and religion under a special debt with his profound study on *La Pensée Religieuse d'Avicenne* (Paris, 1951); see especially chs. IV and V ("Le prophétisme et les vérités religieuses" and "La mystique avicennienne et ses fondements philosophiques").

We are concerned with his political ideas as they are embedded in his philosophical and theological writings; they are very briefly set out in this short chapter.

2 See above, ch. VI, pp. 130f., and cf. Al-Ghazālī, *Tahāfut al-falāsifa* (ed. M. Bouyges, 1927), pp. 27ff.

3 See *Rasā'il Ikhwān al-ṣafā'* (ed. Cairo, 1927), Book IV, ch. 6, on law and lawgiver.

4 A considerable literature has grown round this term, e.g. C. A. Nallino, "Filosofia 'orientale' od 'illuminativa'" in *RSO*, 1923–5, and recently S. Pines published an important study (in *Archives d'histoire doctrinale et littéraire du Moyen Age*, 1953) entitled "La 'Philosophie orientale' d'Avicenne et sa polémique contre les Bagdadiens", especially pp. 23–34 (of offprint). This writer is of the opinion that Ibn Sīnā professed his own views, as distinct from peripateticism, under the guise of an "oriental" school, ancient but not Greek. P. Kraus, in "Plotin chez les Arabes" (see ch. V, n. 3), anticipated Pines in this view. According to Pines Ibn Sīnā's "Oriental philosophy" is not Zoroastrian, nor does it belong to a school flourishing at Sassanian Gondeshapur, but is his own invention in his polemics against the "Western" Muslim philosophers of Baghdad. In fact, Al-Suhrawardī, the foremost exponent of *ishrāq* (illumination), reproaches Ibn Sīnā for not paying heed to this ancient wisdom (*ibid.* p. 33). Cf. also Mlle

Goichon's Introduction to her translation of Ibn Sīnā's *K. al-ishārāt wa-l-tanbīhāt* (*Livre des Directives et Remarques*, Paris, 1951).

5 See above, ch. v, n. 10.

6 See *K. al-najāt* (i.e. the abbreviated *Shifā'*), 1331 A.H., pp. 498ff. Here Ibn Sīnā confines himself to a general exposition of political organization under a prophetic lawgiver which agrees with the second and third chapters of the tenth section of the *Shifā'*; the latter, however, then continues with a brief discussion of economics and politics proper. These two chapters, which form the conclusion of Ibn Sīnā's *Metaphysics* in the *Shifā'*, are summarized at the end of the present chapter.

7 See *Tis' rasā'il* (Constantinople), pp. 85f.; *K. al-ishārāt*, ed. J. Forget, p. 200; and *K. al-najāt*, p. 406, where we read of the prophet "this man is rich⟨ly endowed⟩ to administer (*tadbīr*) the affairs of men in such a way that their livelihood is provided and their future life well ordered". This formulation is in accord with the accepted definition of the purpose of the *Sharī'a*: to secure the believer's well-being in this life and his "salvation" in the next.

It is noteworthy that, similar to the *Shifā'*, this statement occurs in a treatise devoted to an exposition of the contents and scope of metaphysics.

8 Cf. S. Landauer, "Die Psychologie des Ibn Sina" in *ZDMG*, vol. XXIX (1875), pp. 410ff.; and now the English translation of the sixth chapter of the *K. al-najāt* under the title *Avicenna's Psychology* by F. Rahman (Oxford, 1952). Ibn Sīnā, speaking of immediate intuitive perception, says of the prophetic nature: "Thus there might be a man whose soul has such an intense purity and is so firmly linked to the rational principles that he blazes with intuition, i.e. with the receptivity of inspiration coming from the active intelligence [that is, the Active Intellect] concerning everything. So the forms of all things contained in the active intelligence are imprinted on his soul either all at once or nearly so, not that he accepts them merely on authority but on account of their logical order which encompasses all the middle terms. For beliefs accepted on authority concerning those things which are known only through their causes possess no rational certainty. This is a kind of prophetic inspiration, indeed its highest form and the one most fitted to be called divine power; and it is the highest human faculty" (Rahman, pp. 36f.). In the passage quoted from the chapter on prophecy Ibn Sīnā ends with these words: "he is a man distinguished from all other men by his divine nature." Rahman, *op. cit.* pp. 93ff., comments on Ibn Sīnā's theory of prophecy and thinks that while its main element is Aristotle's *anchinoia*, "quick-wittedness", i.e. "intuition", its elaboration is probably Avicennian.

9 Ed. J. Forget (Leiden, 1892); Fr. trans. Mlle Goichon under the title *Livre des Directives et Remarques* (Paris, 1951).

10 See *K. al-najāt*, pp. 499f. The whole chapter is translated in *Avicenna* *on Theology* on pp. 42–9. In view of the distinction between the few elect and the masses, stressed in ch. VI above, p. 129, it may be of interest to quote or paraphrase at greater length from Ibn Sīnā: "He need not impart to them anything of the knowledge of God beyond ⟨the fact⟩ that He is One, the Truth and without like." It is not for him to define God's existence as unverifiable in space and in or out of the world because the majority of the people cannot fathom this without taking great pains. "For only few men are able to perceive the true significance of this unity (*tawḥīd*) and remoteness" (*tanzīh*), i.e. God is exempt from all these notions of time, space, likeness, etc. Otherwise, error sets in and people hold "opinions at variance with the weal of the state" (*ṣalāḥ al-madīnati*). Metaphysics is beyond the ken of most people, and it is, therefore, sufficient to teach the masses, by hints and parables, of the majesty and grandeur of God. These hints are understood by the masses in their simplicity, but there may be employed hints and allusions which will enable those capable of philosophical speculation to inquire into the deeper meaning of observances and their advantage in this life and the next. But the prophet must not give the impression that he possesses a (philosophical) knowledge of truth which he withholds from the masses. Next, he discusses the usefulness of prayer, fasting, holy war and pilgrimage, not only for the sake of true worship and right belief, but also—and this is important in our context—for the spirituality of man as such and for his future life. Needless to say, the acquiring of virtues will be beneficial for life in society. Man realizes, through the divine origin of the prophet's law, that God commands him to obey this law to ensure his life in this world and his survival in the world to come. At the same time, only the law commanded by God through his messenger-prophet can guarantee the survival of mankind (*ibid.* pp. 500ff.).

11 Cf. *Tis' rasā'il*, pp. 73ff. (chapter "On the divisions of practical philosophy"). He stresses, as at the beginning of the chapter on prophecy in the *K. al-najāt*, man's need of association with others to obtain the necessities of life, first in the household and then in "political association" in the state. See also above, ch. V, n. 10, and for Ibn Khaldūn my KAF, pp. 81ff.

12 See *K. al-ishārāt*, and my KAF, pp. 79f.

13 Cf. *Tis' rasā'il*, p. 85.

14 See *Siyāsa*, p. 50, ll. 7–12 and above ch. VI, pp. 138f. *Qissat al-ghurbat al-gharbīya*, pp. 97f. In view of Pines's contention (see n. 4 above) that Ibn Sīnā's *Oriental Philosophy* has no connection with those ideas of "oriental" provenance which Al-Suhrawardī blended with Islamic notions, it is an open question, without a detailed examination of the relevant Avicennian texts, whether Ibn Sīnā's remark about the Greek "prophets" will really help to settle the point.

15 See A. E. Taylor, *The Laws of Plato* (London, 1934), p. li.

16 See *ibid.* p. 296 (*Laws*, 902 end, 903).

17 See "Avicenna: His Life and Times" by A. J. Arberry in *Avicenna: Scientist & Philosopher*, ed. G. M. Wickens (London, 1952), p. 13.

18 *Laws*, 715 end, 716 (Taylor, *op. cit.* p. 100).

19 See *K. al-ishārāt*, p. 200 and also *K. al-najāt*, pp. 498f.; Arberry, *op. cit.* pp. 42ff., 46ff.

20 Cf. above ch. VI, pp. 140f. where the same question was asked with regard to Al-Fārābī. The later pages of the *R. fī ithbāt al nubuwwa*, giving a metaphysical interpretation of the prophecy of Muḥammad, present the same difficulty; cf. also above, ch. V, n. 29.

21 See, for example, AIJT, p. 68, and PIR, pp. 254ff.

22 Cf. MS. Or. 1245 of the Cambridge University Library, fols. 163a–167a, of which this part is a summary. Cf. also M. Horten, *Die Metaphysik Avicennas* (Halle and New York, 1907), a German translation of the sections dealing with metaphysics, theology, cosmology and ethics contained in the *Shifā'*, accompanied by notes. The relevant chapters corresponding to the Arabic text are found on pp. 671–85. Since the *K. al-najāt* contains only the more general statements from the *Shifā'*, the two chapters here extracted are only extant in the *Shifā'*. They are headed: "The formation (*'aqd*) of city-states and of the household, namely ⟨the conclusion⟩ of marriage, and the general laws concerning this", and "The caliph and *imām* and the duty to obey both; indication to politics, ethics and social relations". These chapters are important for Ibn Sīnā's political thought since they offer an interesting blend of Islamic and Platonic concepts.

23 Cf. *Republic*, 407–10. These passages are commented upon by Ibn Rushd, who seems to refer to Ibn Sīnā, though not by name, in his statement: "As for those with defects who are able to live without being cured, but unable to contribute anything to the maintenance of the State, some are of the opinion that they should be put to death, while others think that they should survive" (*ACR*, p. 139). Ibn Sīnā seems to be included among "others".

24 As far as idleness, the playing of games of chance, and such crimes as theft and robbery are concerned, the agreement with Plato need not be taken as showing the influence of the *Republic* on Ibn Sīnā, since these precautions to protect society from undesirable elements and against loss of property are natural and necessary in any society. But as far as idleness and games are concerned, and especially the care of the incurably sick and infirm, such influence, either positive or negative, cannot be excluded.

25 See M. Plessner, *Der Oikonomikos des Neupythagoreers 'Bryson' und sein Einfluss auf die islamische Wissenschaft* (Heidelberg, 1928). Ibn Sīnā's *K. al-siyāsa* was published by Cheikho in *Al-Mashriq* (1906). In his *Aqsām al-'ulūm* he distinguishes three practical sciences, as quoted above in ch. V, n. 10, and says of economics that it is set out in *Bryson* which deals with the regimen of the household which man shares with his wife, children and servants (see my PIB, p. 200, n. 48).

26 *Ḥusn tadbīr* means literally "goodness of rule of self and others".

27 This view seems to spring from the Muslim claim to bring the whole inhabited earth to the worship of Allah in Islam, based on the distinction between the *dār al-islām* and the *dār al-ḥarb*. The latter has to be conquered: therefore *jihād*, holy war, is one of the cardinal duties of every Muslim. It is the God-ordained means by which to reduce and finally eliminate the *dār al-ḥarb* and to turn it into the *dār al-islām*.

28 "The mean" is Aristotelian; cf. also Ibn Taymīya on *umma wasaṭ*, ch. II, p. 56 above.

29 Ibn Sīnā is, to my knowledge, the first among the *Falāsifa* to make this distinction between practical and theoretical wisdom (as distinct from that between practical and theoretical reason, common to all *Falāsifa*) under the aspect of politics. Unless Ibn Rushd's "knowledge" (*ACR*, p. 116) means "practical wisdom", Ibn Sīnā may actually be the only one. "Practical wisdom" is defined in *NE*, VII, x, 1152a (cf. *ACR*, p. 257). Intellectual perfection finds its highest expression in the knowledge of God, reserved to the metaphysician. It seems that Ibn Sīnā's *'ārif* is above the *failasūf*, thanks to his mystical quality which enables him to attain intuitive perception in a flash.

CHAPTER VIII

1 Born in Saragossa towards the end of the eleventh century, Ibn Bājja is said to have died of poison at the hands of his personal enemies in 1138. He was for many years vizier of a brother-in-law of the Almoravid ruler of Muslim Spain.

We owe the first comprehensive account of his philosophy to S. Munk, based chiefly on Hebrew translations of the *Tadbīr al-mutawaḥḥid* and of the *Risālat al-wadā'* (in his classic *Mélanges de philosophie juive et arabe*, Paris, 1859). For my PG I had only these two treatises at my disposal, the former in a Bodleian MS. under the title *Hanhaghath hammithbōdhēdh* (Or. 116), edited by D. Herzog (Berlin, 1895), the latter in a Paris MS. (Hébreu 959) under the title *Iggereth happeṭīrah*. The Hebrew version of the *Tadbīr* is only a summary, by Moses Narbōnī, contained in his commentary on Ibn Ṭufail's *Ḥay b. Yaqẓān*. The two treatises and a third, *K. ittiṣāl al-'aql bi-l-insān* were edited in the Arabic original by Asín Palacios several years after my PG and used by me in a more detailed but still preliminary study in my PIB. The reader is referred to this article for a fuller treatment than is here possible. There and in PG attention is drawn to Ibn Bājja's Greek sources (Plato, Aristotle, Alexander of Aphrodisias and Galen, cf. PG, n. 11 and PIB, n. 13). A comprehensive treatment of this many-sided Muslim philosopher of the West is badly needed.

In addition to his own writings there are frequent references to them in Ibn Rushd's commentaries on Aristotle (*De Anima*, in particular) and in Narbōnī's commentary on Ibn Ṭufail, as well as in

Maimonides' *Dalālat al-ḥā'irīn* (*Guide of the Perplexed*). Ibn Bājja is a thinker in his own right in addition to being an important influence on Ibn Ṭufail and a link between Al-Fārābī and Ibn Rushd, who valued his treatise on the union of the human with the Active Intellect so highly that he wrote a commentary on it. Maimonides recommended Ibn Bājja to his translator Ibn Tibbōn. Unfortunately, the Berlin MS. of Ibn Bājja's writings which contains his commentary on *De Anima* must now be considered lost. The late Asín Palacios did most to make the work of Ibn Bājja known by his editions with introductions and summaries of their contents. The three treatises mentioned above form the basis for the present chapter. Asín published "El filosofo zaragozano Avempace" in *Revista de Aragon* (1901), which I was unable to consult.

2 To this theme he devoted his *K. ittiṣāl al-'aql bi-l-insān*, ed. Asín Palacios in *Al Andalus*, vol. VII (1942), pp. 1–47. See also preceding note and my PG, p. 160, with note 21 and PIB, pp. 192f.

3 PG, PIB and also briefly SAIPT. The difficulty of isolating Ibn Bājja's political ideas was stressed in PIB.

4 The *Risālat al-wadā'* is edited by Asín Palacios in *Al Andalus*, vol. VIII (1943) as "La 'Carta de Adios' de Avempace", pp. 1–87, with translation and notes; the *Tadbīr* under the title "El Régimen del Solitario por Avempace" (Madrid-Granada, 1946); and the *K. ittiṣāl* as "Tratado de Avempace sobre la union del intelecto con el hombre" (see n. 2 above). The title of this treatise means literally "Contact of Reason [that is, of the Active Intellect] with man [that is, with the human intellect]". See also PIB, p. 187, n. 3.

5 See n. 1 above. Narbōnī adds to his qualification of the *mutawaḥḥid*: "whether he be isolated or a citizen, whether his state be 'ideal' or non-excellent (imperfect), for they are in a majority." Al-Fārābī uses *mutawaḥḥid* in his *Mad. fāḍ.* p. 73, l. 17, of a person completely isolated, without any help. The term goes back to *NE*, I, vii, 1097b and IX, ix, 1170a (*monotes*).

6 See PIB, pp. 192f. for a tentative assessment of the possible development of Ibn Bājja's thought and a chronological attribution of the three treatises.

7 Cf. *Risālat al-wadā'*, p. 30, ll. 19–27.

8 Cf. *Siyāsa*, p. 48; p. 69, ll. 14ff.; on "heads" of other states p. 59, ll. 9ff.; p. 61, ll. 13ff.; p. 65, ll. 4ff.

9 Cf. *Risālat al-wadā'*, p. 34, ll. 19–26. "Guardians" translates *'urafā'*, which is rendered in the Hebrew version by *shōṭᵉrīm*. In fact, Plato's Guardians, who have to be philosophers, are meant, hence *'urafā* in Ibn Bājja. Asín translates by "inspectores", which misses the link with the *Republic*. This is certainly intended by Ibn Bājja. "Ethical virtues" translates *faḍā'il shaklīya* (in Hebrew, *ma'alōth middōthiyōth*; Asín, "virtudes morales"); and "social relations" renders *mu'āshara* (in Hebrew, *massā u-mattān*, i.e. commerce; Asín, "la buena convivencia social", which is perhaps a little too free).

10 Cf. *Taḥṣīl*, p. 28, ll. 6ff.
11 Cf. *Risālat al-wadā'*, p. 35, ll. 3–6; and above, ch. VI, p. 140 with note 91.
12 Cf. *Risālat al-wadā'*, p. 37, ll. 7–16.
13 *Ibid.* p. 38, l. 24 to p. 39, l. 14. This is not inconsistent with his neglect of the *Sharī'a* as the constitution of the ideal state; he never speaks of a lawgiver in connection with it, since he is only interested in the philosopher. For him the messenger (*rasūl*) does not primarily promulgate God's law as the norm by which man must live, but mediates true knowledge. On the other hand, he speaks of the *imām*-state in the *Tadbīr* which, though not the ideal state of the philosopher, is probably equivalent to Plato's aristocracy or rather timocracy, at any rate on a higher level than the other imperfect states, as we shall see later in this chapter.
14 See *Faṣl*, ed. Mueller, p. 5. Ibn Rushd says it is foolish if man is prevented from study as a means to the knowledge of God; such action leads to an estrangement from God.
15 Cf. *Risālat al-wadā'*, p. 39, ll. 24ff. We note that mutual help and co-operation are stipulated for intellectual and spiritual ends, not for the satisfaction of the needs of physical life.
16 See n. 6 above.
17 Cf. *K. ittiṣāl*, p. 17, ll. 25ff. Cf. also Al-Fārābī, *Taḥṣīl*, p. 15, ll. 14ff.
18 Cf. *K. ittiṣāl*, p. 18, ll. 12ff. See also p. 161 above and Al-Fārābī on the *su'adā* in his *Siyāsa*, p. 50, ll. 7f. and later in this chapter, pp. 166f.
19 Cf. *Tadbīr*, p. 29, ll. 10f.
20 Cf. *ibid.* p. 4, ll. 13ff. and Al-Fārābī, *Abhdln.* p. 25.
21 Cf. *Tadbīr*, p. 5, ll. 3ff. and above, ch. VI, p. 129 with note 34.
22 Cf. *Tadbīr*, p. 5, l. 18 to p. 6, l. 2.
23 Cf. *Abhdln.* p. 5.
24 Cf. *Tadbīr*, p. 6, ll. 2ff.; p. 7, ll. 8f., and Al-Fārābī, *Siyāsa*, p. 39. See also above, ch. V, p. 118 with note 10; and PIB, p. 199 with notes.
25 Cf. *Tadbīr*, p. 57, ll. 1f.
26 *Ibid.* p. 8, l. 6 to p. 9, l. 2.
27 *Ibid.* p. 9, ll. 2–5.
28 Cf. *ACR*, pp. 137ff. and 262.
29 See PIB, pp. 200f. with notes.
30 Cf. *Tadbīr*, p. 54, ll. 6f.
31 Cf. *ACR*, pp. 205 and 281, and also PIB, p. 208, n. 72.
32 In Messer Leon's *Rhetoric* (in Hebrew, *nōfeth ṣōphīm*) "priestly" is identified with 'the rule of the best", that is, aristocracy. Cf. also *ACR*, pp. 205, 215f., 281, 288.
33 Cf. *Tadbīr*, p. 54, ll. 3–7.
34 Cf. *Risālat al-wadā'*, p. 37, ll. 7–16; p. 38, ll. 24 to p. 39, l. 14, quoted on pp. 161f. above.
35 Cf. *Republic*, 487B–497A, especially 489 and 491 A.B. By contrast, Al-Fārābī and Ibn Rushd are in full agreement with Plato, who holds that the philosophers may only retire to the "Islands of the Blest"

after they have fulfilled their civic duties, namely, "ruling for the public good" (*Republic*, 519 and 540).

36 Cf. *Tadbīr*, p. 9, ll. 6ff. Both enable every citizen to attain "the best which his natural disposition warrants". Ibn Bājja refers to *NE*.

37 Cf. *ibid.* p. 10, l. 3.

38 Cf. *ibid.* p. 10, l. 7 to p. 11, l. 2. Ibn Bājja uses the term *kāmila* (perfect) for the more common and usual *fāḍila* of Al-Fārābī, Ibn Sīnā and Ibn Rushd. By contrast, in Al-Fārābī's *Siyāsa*, the *nawābit* arise in the *madīna fāḍila* as a menace, as we saw in ch. VI above.

39 Cf. *ibid.* p. 11, ll. 3–14. Ibn Bājja continues: "The Sufis allude to them by their term *ghurabā* (the strangers). For although they live in their own countries and among their friends and neighbours, they are strangers in their opinions; they travel in their thoughts to other planes which are for them like homelands."

40 Although Ibn Ṭufail's philosophical novel, as his *Ḥay ibn Yaqẓān* has been styled, represents an important contribution to the problem of faith and reason, or rather of revelation and reason, it falls outside our purview. Its central figures stand for unquestioning obedience to the revealed law in all its aspects on the one hand, and for independent philosophical speculation leading to the mystical union with God on the other.

41 However, see ch. VI above, p. 136 with note 69. Both Al-Fārābī and Ibn Rushd think it possible that the ideal state may emerge from democracy which, like a many-coloured coat, can harbour a sufficient number of "philosophers" capable of starting an ideal state. Al-Fārābī does not speak of *nawābit*, but of "most excellent" persons (*afāḍil*), and explicitly denies happiness (*sa'āda*) to those among them living scattered over many places. Happiness is only attainable in a closely knit state ruled over by a philosopher/king/lawgiver/*imām* (*Siyāsa*, p. 50, ll. 7ff.). It is Ibn Bājja who identifies such strangers with the *nawābit*.

42 Cf. *Tadbīr*, p. 12, ll. 2–9.

43 Cf. *Siyāsa*, p. 57, l. 11. Here he speaks of *madīna jāhila*, *madīna fāsiqa* and *m. ḍālla* in opposition to the *m. fāḍila*.

44 Cf. *Tadbīr*, p. 15, l. 15 to p. 16, l. 2; p. 16, ll. 6–13. The four "ways of life" are those opposed to the ideal state in Al-Fārābi's *Ṣiyāsa*, pp. 58–71. Cf. also PIB, p. 206 with notes.

45 Cf. *Tadbīr*, p. 19. The universal intelligibles are the active and the acquired intellects.

46 Cf. *ibid.* p. 29, ll. 6–15. Ibn Bājja summarily points out that this subject is treated in "political science", that is, in the books of Plato and Aristotle devoted to it. He may have in mind particularly *Republic*, 381 to end of Book II and Book III. Obviously, education did not concern him, except of the philosopher in isolation. Cf. also *NE*, VI, v; viii; xii.

47 Cf. *Tadbīr*, p. 37, ll. 9–15.

48 Cf. *ibid.* p. 54, l. 11 to p. 55, l. 1. See p. 166, above, on the *imām*-state.

Whether this state corresponds to Plato's aristocracy or timocracy, it is the second best after the ideal state and (for Ibn Bājja no less than for Ibn Rushd) the Muslim state. Cf. *ACR*, pp. 209ff., especially p. 211: "...this kind of constitution is often found among us"; on p. 223 Ibn Rushd, after Plato, says: "You may understand what Plato states concerning the transformation of the ideal constitution into the timocratic constitution... from the case of the government of the Arabs in the earliest period. For they used to imitate the ideal constitution, and then were transformed in the days of Mu'āwiya into timocratic men. It seems to be the case with the constitution that exists now in these islands" ⟨Spain⟩. He has in mind the Almoravids (p. 227): "at first they imitated the constitution based on the law (*Sharī'a*) —this under the first of them—then they changed ⟨it⟩ under his son into the timocratic ⟨constitution⟩...." These passages would suggest that the *imām*-state of Islam corresponds to Plato's timocracy. However, the possibility cannot be entirely ruled out that here and in the passage quoted on p. 166, above, in the eyes of Ibn Bājja the *imām*-state is actually the Muslim ideal state, the *khilāfa* or *imāma*.

49 Cf. *Tadbīr*, p. 55, ll. 2–9.

50 Cf. *Siyāsa*, p. 57, ll. 16ff.

51 Cf. *Tadbīr*, p. 61, ll. 9–17.

52 Cf. *ibid.* p. 78, ll. 6–16. "In principle" translates *bi-l-dhāti*, literally "in essence"; "in certain circumstances" translates *bi-l-'arḍi*, literally "by accident". For political science (*'ilm madanī*) see n. 46 above. To the books mentioned there add Plato's *Laws* and perhaps *Politikos*, and Al-Fārābī's political writings, especially the *Taḥṣīl*, where political science is defined, as quoted in ch. v, above, pp. 118ff. with notes.

53 Cf. *K. al-ishārāt wa-l-tanbīhāt*, pp. 199 ff. Ibn Sīnā here discusses the stages of intellectual endeavour and perfection of the *zāhid*, the ascetic, that is, the ordinary Sufi; the *'ābid* who practises Islam by fulfilling the *'ibādāt*, the religious duties, with sincere piety and devotion; and finally the *'ārif*, the speculative mystic. To the best of my knowledge, Ibn Bājja does not quote Ibn Sīnā and was not familiar with his writings, though his views may have come to him through Al-Ghazālī, whom he attacks several times.

54 Cf. *K. ittiṣāl*, p. 20, ll. 3f.

55 540A–C. This and the following passages are quoted from the translation of the *Republic* by F. M. Cornford (*The Republic of Plato*, Oxford, 1941).

56 *Ibid.* 519D–520A.

57 *Ibid.* 520B.

58 *Ibid.* 520B–D.

CHAPTER IX

1 Abū-l-Walīd Ibn Rushd was born at Cordoba in 520 A.H./1126 C.E. Both his father and his grandfather of the same name (Abū-l-Walīd) were jurists and held office as *qāḍī* (judge). Ibn Rushd, like his grandfather, was Grand Qāḍī of Cordoba, but the elder Ibn Rushd served the Almoravids while the grandson was in the service of their successors, the Almohads. Trained in *Fiqh* and representing the school of Mālik, Ibn Rushd was equally well versed in theology, philosophy and medicine. He succeeded Ibn Ṭufail as body-physician to the Almohad Caliph Abū Ya'qūb Yūsuf, an office he retained under the caliph's son and successor, Abū Yūsuf Ya'qūb al-Manṣūr. He owed this position to his medical skill, but not less to his philosophical attainment; for we have it on his own authority from the historian Al-Marrākushī that Ibn Ṭufail introduced Ibn Rushd to Abū Ya'qūb Yūsuf, who engaged him in a long philosophical discussion. He was then charged to write commentaries on Aristotle's principal works. This encounter took place, according to L. Gauthier, in 1169 and was followed by Ibn Rushd's appointment to Seville as *qāḍī*. In 1171, he was appointed to the same office at Cordoba and in 1182 he became body-physician to the caliph at Marrakesh and subsequently Grand Qāḍī at Cordoba.

The atmosphere in Muslim Spain was anything but favourable to the pursuit of philosophy, in spite of the great interest the Almohad rulers took in it. The jurists and especially the theologians (*mutakallimūn*) frowned upon philosophical speculation. Ibn Rushd joined battle with them all his life, and his polemical as well as his philosophical treatises bear witness to this struggle. To it we owe Ibn Rushd's most important treatise, the *Faṣl al-maqāl*, in which the Muslim philosopher attempts to reconcile revelation and philosophy. He vindicates philosophy as the only legitimate discipline which leads to a true understanding of the inner meaning of the *Shar'* or revealed law. He denies both jurists and theologians, who are restricted to the use of dialectical and rhetorical arguments, the right or the ability to rise to demonstrative proof of the truth of revelation. Only the metaphysician is capable of this certainty, within limits, as will be apparent from this chapter. L. Gauthier gave us a penetrating analysis of the *Faṣl*; I dealt with his conclusions in my PIR (pp. 253ff.).

But while Ibn Rushd may have defeated his opponents by his pen, they had their practical revenge in his temporary banishment to Lucena, on the eve of his master's and patron's departure for the holy war against the Christians. L. Gauthier is, to my mind, right in attributing Ibn Rushd's exile to the caliph's attempt to soothe the jurists and theologians as well as the populace at large by dissociating himself from the *Falāsifa* who stood in such bad odour. Ibn Rushd was soon restored to favour, though, and died in 1198 at the court at Marrakesh. With his passing, philosophy in Muslim Spain declined;

but his influence was considerable and lasting, as every page of the Schoolmen shows. Although his contemporary Maimonides shows some affinity in important aspects of religious philosophy, there is no truth in the frequent claim that he was Ibn Rushd's disciple. In fact, Maimonides states in the letter in which he recommends to his pupil and Hebrew translator the study of Al-Fārābī, Ibn Sīnā and Ibn Bājja, that he had not yet had time to study the works of Ibn Rushd.

I must repeat that Averroes should not be confused with the Averroists and that for him there was only one Truth, the truth of revelation at one with the truth of reason. But if there are things that reason cannot explain, yet they are nevertheless true since they come from God through His Prophet. This is not the place to deal even in a summary fashion with Ibn Rushd, the Muslim philosopher and theologian, and *the* commentator of Aristotle, the more so since important legal and theological writings of his are not at present available (assuming that they are still undiscovered in North African libraries and await discovery and scholarly edition and interpretation). What is relevant for Ibn Rushd's political philosophy is set out in this chapter. The reader is also referred to my PIR and *ACR*. E. Renan's *Averroès et l'Averroïsme* (Paris, 1861) is still of great value and interest, and L. Gauthier's study of the *Faṣl*, *La théorie d'Ibn Rochd sur les rapports de la religion et de la philosophie* (Paris, 1909) as well as his biography *Ibn Rochd* (*Averroès*) (Paris, 1948) are indispensable, even if one cannot agree with his rationalistic interpretation.

2 First made known by S. Munk in his *Mélanges*, p. 388. Cf. my PG, p. 154.

3 Cf. Camb. MS. Add. 496, f. 156b.

4 *Ibid.* f. 9b. Similarly f. 135a on *NE*, IX, ix, 1170a.

5 See R. Dozy after al-Warrān, Appendice xxv, pp. lxxiii f. of his *Recherches sur l'histoire et littérature de l'Espagne pendant le Moyen Age*[2] (Leiden, 1860); E. Renan, *op. cit.* pp. 12f. and my PIR, p. 248.

6 *Averroes' Commentary on Plato's "Republic"*, University of Cambridge Oriental Publications, No. 1, corrected reprint (Cambridge, 1966). Hebrew text, English translation, introduction, notes and glossaries.

7 Cf. PIR, pp. 253–64, 273ff.

8 Cf. *Tahāfut al-tahāfut*, ed. M. Bouyges, Beyrouth, 1930; S. van den Bergh, *Averroes' Tahāfut al-tahāfut*, translation with introduction and notes, 2 vols. (London, 1954); *Faṣl a-maqāl*, ed. L. Gauthier (Alger, 1948); *K. kashf 'an manāhij al-adilla fī 'aqā'id al-milla*, ed. M. J. Mueller (München, 1859); *ACR*, *passim*; now also G. F. Hourani, K. Fasl al-Makal (Leiden, 1959), translated as *Averroes on the Harmony of Religion and Philosophy* (London, 1961).

9 See *ACR*, p. 185 and PIR, p. 252.

10 See *Faṣl*, p. 9, ll. 3–7 and also p. 3, ll. 3–8 on *qiyās fiqhī* and *q. 'aqlī*; cf. also PIR, pp. 257f.: "Averroes also adopted Ibn Ḥazm's stand on the interpretation of words in legal texts in accordance with their grammatical meaning (cf. *Faṣl*, p. 9)...." He draws this conclusion

from the *'arabīya*: "if this is the practice of the *faqīh* how much more is the *failasūf*, who possesses knowledge by proof, entitled to interpret in conformity with Arabic usage. For the *faqīh* works only with *qiyās ẓannī*, whereas the *'ārif* works with *q. yaqīnī*. ... This juxtaposition of syllogism based on (subjective) opinion, and syllogism of certainty, i.e. demonstrative proof, sums up tersely the difference between the *failasūf*, who as *'ārif* has certain knowledge, and the *mutakallim*, who lacks certainty." It is obvious that Ibn Rushd's *'ārif* is not on a level with Ibn Sīnā's *'ārif* of the *K. al-ishārāt*; the mystical element is entirely lacking in Ibn Rushd's *failasūf*.

11 See *Faṣl*, p. 32.

12 Cf. *ACR*, p. 185 and PIR, p. 253. For prophecy see PIR, pp. 258–64.

13 Cf. *Faṣl*, pp. 22f. Ibn Rushd continues: "The knowledge of these actions is called practical science; they are divided into two, external, physical action, and the science concerning them is called *Fiqh* (jurisprudence); and the actions of the soul, like gratitude, patience and other virtues which the *Sharī'a* recommends or prohibits, and the science concerning them is called *Zuhd* (asceticism) and the sciences of the hereafter."

14 Cf. *Faṣl*, p. 11. Ibn Rushd defends Al-Fārābī and Ibn Sīnā against al-Ghazālī's accusation of unbelief.

15 Cf. *Faṣl*, pp. 17ff.

16 Cf. *ibid.* pp. 21f., 33.

17 Cf. *ibid.* pp. 7f.

18 See 'Abd al-Wāḥid al-Marrākushī, *History of the Almohads*, ed. R. Dozy (Leiden, 1847), p. 134; (French translation by E. Fagnan, *Histoire des Almohades*, Alger, 1903), p. 134.

19 Cf. *Faṣl*, p. 33. See also I. Goldziher, *Mohammad Ibn Toumert et la Théologie de l'Islam dans le Nord de l'Afrique au xie· Siècle* (Alger, 1903). This is the introduction to Luciani's edition of *K. muḥammad b. tūmart mahdī al-muwaḥḥidīn*.

20 Cf. I. Goldziher, *Die Ẓâhiriten* (Leipzig, 1884); and "Materialien zur Kenntnis der Almohadenbewegung" in *ZDMG*, XLI (1887) on which my brief remarks are based. Cf. also PIR, pp. 256ff.

21 See n. 10 above.

22 Cf. *Manāhij*, p. 98.

23 Cf. *Tahāfut al-tahāfut*, p. 516.

24 Cf. *Manāhij*, p. 101.

25 Cf. *Tahāfut*, p. 582. Religion is not a substitute for philosophy, nor can the philosopher who happens to be an adherent of a revealed religion dispense with the religious law, its teachings and commands. This statement must not be taken in isolation; on the contrary, we must take account of its context, the book as a whole; this aims at defending *falsafa* and the *Falāsifa* against Al-Ghazālī's charge of irreligion, of being a menace and in opposition to the *Sharī'a*.

26 Cf. *ACR*, p. 204. We are reminded of Ibn Sīnā's statement about a state apart from the ideal state, which after a long time achieved a good constitution (see above, ch. VII, p. 155).

27 Cf. Camb. MS. Add. 496, f. 17b corresponding to *NE*, I, xiii, 1102a. *Mudabbir* is the Arabic equivalent of the Hebrew *manhīg* of Samuel b. Yehūdā's translation. Aristotle uses the term *politikos*, that is, statesman.

28 Cf. *ibid.* ff. 70b, 71a which corresponds to *NE*, V, vi, vii, 1134b. But where Ibn Rushd speaks of "men who are either rulers or ruled" Aristotle says "who share equally (*isotes*) in ruling and being ruled".

29 Cf. *ACR*, pp. 154 and 265.

30 Cf. Camb. MS. Add. 496, f. 71a. Ibn Rushd's comment on *NE*, V, vii, 1135a adds prayers, sacrifices, etc., thus clearly adapting Aristotle to Islamic conditions. See also *ACR*, p. 155 with characteristic modification of Plato's religious terms and their replacement by Islamic ones.

31 Cf. *Tahāfut al-tahāfut*, p. 581.

32 Cf. *ACR*, p. 112.

33 Cf. Camb. MS. Add. 496, f. 156b. Cf. above, p. 175.

34 Cf. *ACR*, pp. 154f. and *NE*, V, x, 1137b concerning a general law and a special ordinance. See also p. 196, below.

35 Cf. *ACR*, pp. 156 and 265f., concerning *Republic*, 428.

36 See *NE*, VI, xiii, 1144b–1145a.

37 Cf. *Siyāsa*, p. 4, l. 8; p. 43, ll. 10ff. *Taḥṣīl*, p. 32, ll. 19ff. and other passages in both treatises as well as in the *Madīna fāḍila*.

38 Cf. *ACR*, pp. 159ff. and 266.

39 See p. 186, above.

40 With one notable exception, his reference to Muslim war in his comment on *NE*, V, x, 1137b, which is discussed on p. 196 below.

41 He concludes his Commentary on *De Partibus Animalium* (ed. Venice, 1550, f. 103b) on this personal note: "Nobis tamen non est concessa huiusmodi facultas hac nostra tempestate, neque in hac provincia nostra, immo si aliquid incidentur scivimus de his rebus, est quid minimum. Cuius rei veritatem cognoscet qui nostram hanc tempestatem viderit, vel hanc provinciam nostram, scil. Andalugiae: et quot damna passi sumus nos, et alij homines sunt passi multos labores ad necessarias res adipiscendas, quibus conservatur sanitas corporea...." It is the more surprising that he found time to write so many commentaries on Aristotle's numerous treatises, apart from his own independent works, being so preoccupied with earning his living and preserving his health.

We may compare this statement with his tribute to his patron, at the end of his commentary on the *Republic*: "This then—may God make your honour endure and prolong your life—is the sum of the theoretical statements necessary for this part of the science ⟨of Politics⟩, which those treatises ascribed to Plato comprise. We have explained them in the briefest possible manner as time was pressing. [Or: "because of the troubled times", which is perhaps better and more likely.] In this we succeeded only because you have helped us to understand them, and because of the boon of your sharing in all we have longed for of these sciences. Your help in ⟨mastering⟩ them was to us the most perfect kind of help in every respect. You are the cause not of our achieving and possessing this good alone, but also of all the human good things we have acquired, and which God Almighty has bestowed upon us for your sake. May God make your honour endure!" (*ACR*, p. 250).

42 See ch. VI above, pp. 135–138 with notes 62–64, 66–71, 76–78 and pp. 138f. with notes 86–88; cf. also pp. 198–203 of this chapter.

43 See ch. VIII above, pp. 165f.

44 Cf. *ACR*, pp. 133 and 260f. where reference is made to Miskawaih, who in his *K. tahdhīb al-akhlāq* severely censures Imrū-l-qais and al-Nābigha, and to al-Ṭūsī's *Akhlāq-i-Nāṣirī* (see M. Plessner's *Bryson*, p. 79) condemning Imrū-l-quais and Abū Nuwās. Plessner stresses Ṭūsī's dependence on Miskawaih, and *Bryson* as the source for both.

45 Cf. *ACR*, pp. 133ff. and 261f.

46 Cf. *ibid.* pp. 152f.

47 Cf. *ibid.* p. 166. We note Ibn Rushd's utilitarian attitude. See also *PIR*, pp. 251f.

48 Cf. *ACR*, pp. 182f. and 272f.

49 Cf. *ibid.* pp. 180 and 272. For the philosopher/lawgiver/*imām* see Al-Fārābī (*Taḥṣīl*, p. 43, ll. 18ff.) and for the true philosopher *ibid.* p. 45, ll. 5ff. Ibn Rushd is more positive than Al-Fārābī, since he insists that the ideal state is a practical proposition.

50 A similar view of Ibn Sīnā was referred to in n. 26 above.

51 Cf. *ACR*, pp. 205 and 281.

52 *Ibid.* Ibn Rushd omits the characteristic of "excellent convictions" upon which Messer Leon insists, for whom aristocracy is the Greek equivalent. But Ibn Rushd simply follows Al-Fārābī's definition of *imām* here; this leads him to distinguish from this *imām*-state another one, probably a modification of the first, which, in view of the quotation on p. 194, below, seems to correspond to timocracy. But even if we are justified in speaking of two such states—it would perhaps be more correct to speak of one and its debased offshoot—they have one important element in common, namely, their designation as *imām*-states.

53 Cf. *ACR*, pp. 215f. Ibn Rushd has in mind the state of the Almoravids and especially of the Almohads whom Leo Africanus called *pontifices*.

54 Cf. *ibid.* p. 216, and also Ibn Bājja, *Tadbīr*, p. 54; PIB, nn. 72 and 74, and above, ch. VIII, p. 166.

55 Cf. *ACR*, p. 177. The source is Al-Fārābī, *Taḥṣīl*, p. 43, l. 9, where we also find the equation between philosopher, lawgiver and king (p. 43, ll. 7f.).

56 Cf. *ACR*, pp. 223 and 291.

57 Cf. *ibid.* pp. 227 and 292.

58 *Ibid.*

59 Cf. *ibid.* pp. 235 and 295. He specifically mentions his native Cordoba and a member of the Banū Ghāniya who formed the rallying centre of opposition to the Almohads, remaining loyal to their former masters, the Almoravids, under whose rule they had occupied important positions in army and administration. See A. Bel, *Les Benou Ghânya* (Paris, 1903). Cf. also PIR, p. 248.

60 Cf. *ibid.* p. 237.

61 Cf. *ibid.* pp. 247 and 298f., and also once more pp. 223 (ix, 13–end) and 227 (xi, 5).

62 Cf. Camb. MS. Add. 496, f. 123a, where Ibn Rushd, commenting on *NE*, VIII, x, xi, 1160b, 1161a, replaces Zeus by "king" and Agamemnon by "rulers", only leaving Homer as calling Zeus (king) "father" and Agamemnon (rulers) "shepherd".

63 Cf. Camb. MS. Add. 496, f. 76a on *NE*, V, x, 1137b (Latin, f. 39b). The Hebrew text is obscure and probably corrupt, the Latin translation different; hence I offer only a paraphrase and hope that I have brought out the meaning correctly.

64 Cf., for example, *ACR*, pp. 213 (*Laws*, 697); 215 (*Laws*, 903*c*, 961*e*, 962*a*). Other examples are listed in my Introduction (*ibid.* p. 18). Whether Ibn Rushd drew on Al-Fārābī's *Compendium on the Laws* is difficult to decide, the more so since he must have used passages which are not to be found in Al-Fārābī. I may be permitted to quote from p. 18 of *ACR*: "No doubt both Al-Fārābī and Averroes used the same extensive *Summary*, and any agreement between them may well be due to their common source. Averroes' approach...was quite different from that of his predecessor...his purpose was not only to describe, but also to interpret Plato with a fuller and keener insight into politics...."

65 Cf. *ACR*, p. 153. See also next note and p. 187, above for similar adverse criticism.

66 Cf. Camb. MS. Add. 496, f. 116a on *NE*, VIII, x, 1160b. See also *ACR*, p. 294 where the Latin translation of the commentary is quoted (ed. Venice, 1550, f. 59b r.). Ibn Rushd's criticism ends with the words "ut dixit Arist. non ut dicit Plato".

67 Cf. my "Notes on some Arabic Manuscripts in the John Rylands Library. 1. Averroes' Middle Commentary on Aristotle's 'Analytica Priora et Posteriora'" in *Bulletin of the John Rylands Library*, vol. XXI, no. 2, October 1937, pp. 482f.

68 Cf. *ACR*, pp. 111f. "The first and second parts of this science ⟨of Politics⟩ stand in the same relationship to each other as do the books of *Health and Illness* and the *Preservation of Health and Removal of Illness* in Medicine." See also the continuation of this passage which is quoted above on p. 187.

69 See ch. VI above, pp. 125 with note 16; 133f. with notes 57–59; 139f. with notes 86–89.

70 Cf. Al-Fārābī, *Taḥṣīl*, p. 2, which is compounded of *NE*, I, vii, 1098a; I, xiii, 1103a; and X, vii, 1177b. See also *ACR*, pp. 112f. and 256.

71 Cf. *ACR*, p. 119.

72 Cf. *ibid.* p. 125.

73 *Ibid. passim*; and PF, pp. 171–8; cf. also M, SAIPT, PIB and PIR, *passim.*

74 *Mad. fāḍ.* p. 54.

75 *Taḥṣīl*, p. 26, l. 11 to p. 27, end.

76 In *ACR*, many examples are given in the notes, pp. 283–98, particularly pp. 286, 292 ff., 296 f.

77 In his *Republic*, 369C, D, Plato speaks of the state which owes its existence to our daily needs. Therefore it is a necessity. But while man needs the help and co-operation of others to obtain the means of his physical life and survival, and must form political associations to that end, such a combination of men is only the *basis* for a state as understood by Plato. Necessity does not provide a constitution, nor is it sufficient to assure man's end, happiness.

78 Cf. for Al-Fārābī his *Madīna fāḍila* and *Siyāsa*, *passim*, especially *Siyāsa*, pp. 58–74; for Ibn Rushd *ACR*, pp. 163 f. with 266 f. ("ignorant states"); and pp. 205 f. with 282 ("states in error"). For Ibn Rushd the terms "ignorant" and "in error" are synonymous. As with "necessity" so it is here also with "ignorance"; the term is used by Plato to characterize the four non-perfect states, but not as a constitutional term. It simply means "deviation, error, mistake" in relation to the ideal state, which is excellent in convictions and actions alike. Ibn Rushd, though accepting the term from Al-Fārābī, uses it in the Platonic sense. Al-Fārābī seems to understand *jāhilīya* in both senses, as Plato's *amartia* and in the meaning it has in Islam, namely to denote the "ignorance" of the Arabs before Muḥammad brought them belief in one God and his "precious book".

79 Cf. *ACR*, pp. 205 f. and 282. Ibn Bājja uses the term "four simple states" in his *Tadbīr*, p. 9, l. 3 and *passim*. See also PIB, p. 201. Ibn Rushd speaks of "the four or five simple states" in the epilogue to his commentary on the *NE* (Camb. MS. Add. 496, f. 156a). Plato distinguishes between "simple" and "composite" states in his *Politikos* (292B, 300B, 301B) and in his *Laws* (693*b*, *d*) he counsels against "over-powerful or *unmixed* sovereignties". He speaks of the "two matrices of constitutions: monarchy and democracy...the strands...of which all other constitutions...are woven".

80 Cf. *NE*, VIII, x, 1160b; and n. 52, above.

81 Cf. *ACR*, pp. 292 and 294.

82 See, for example, his treatment of *Republic* 554B–555A (*ACR*, pp. 226 f.) where he divides Plato's plutocratic man into plutocratic and hedonistic, as soon as wealth or any other desire becomes the goal. Plato counsels keeping these "base desires" at bay. Al-Fārābī's confused and imprecise description (*Siyāsa*, pp. 62 and 69) is possibly responsible for Ibn Rushd's inconsistency. Further, Ibn Rushd, following Al-Fārābī, takes Plato's ironical praise of democracy seriously in *ACR*, p. 230 (xiii, 3–4), but then repeats Plato's

disapproval in the following two paragraphs (5–6). On the other hand, there is Plato's own designation of democracy as one of the two "matrices" for the other constitutions in his *Laws* (693*d*; see n. 80) and Aristotle's reference to it as "the least bad of the deviations" (*NE*, VIII, x, 1160b).

It is, perhaps, not so surprising that Ibn Rushd did not succeed in reconciling Plato with Aristotle and both with the ideal *Sharī'a*-state of Islam. It is also possible that he simply followed Al-Fārābī (*Siyāsa*, p. 70, l. 20 to p. 71, l. 5) in the first passage and then commented literally in the following one; or he deliberately allowed for different views and possibilities of the emergence of the perfect and imperfect states. A similar inconsistency seems to prevail in the matter of the *imām*-("priestly") state or a part of it, discussed earlier.

83 Cf. *ACR*, p. 177.

84 Cf. *ibid.* p. 208.

85 See for this treatise ch. VI, n. 16, especially pp. 133f. with note 57, where reference is made to *ACR*, p. 208; also pp. 139f. with notes 87–9.

86 A detailed comparison would fall outside the scope of this chapter. I have made it in my PF, pp. 174–8 and also, in a more restricted form, in ch. VI above, n. 57.

87 The words in italics represent what I assume to be the Arabic original of obscure Hebrew words in Ibn Rushd; I have arrived at them by comparison with the *Fuṣūl*. The Hebrew translator did not understand their legal or technical meaning, but simply reproduced the basic meaning of the Arabic root by a corresponding Hebrew word.

88 Cf. *ACR*, pp. 207f. and 283. Ibn Rushd has *ACR*, p. 81, 1–5 *melekh ha-huqqīm* = *malik al-sunan* for Dunlop's *malik al-sunna* (*op. cit.*, p. 138, 1–9).

89 *Ibid.* pp. 208f. Al-Fārābī's joint rule of the *Mad. fāḍ.* is reminiscent of the *Politikos*: the philosopher advises the "tyrant".

90 See ch. III above.

91 Cf. *ACR*, pp. 250f.

92 S. Van den Bergh, *op. cit.* vol. II, p. 98 traces the three classes to Aristotle's *Metaphysics* A, 3.995*a*, *b*: "those who accept only mathematical proof, those who accept proof by example, and those who accept proof by poetical quotation", but thinks that Averroes' concept of "religion as threefold, the religion of the masses, of the lawyers and of the philosophers" is dependent on the Stoic theory. He quotes among others Plutarch who distinguishes "poets, lawgivers and philosophers". We know from Ibn Rushd that the three classes of arguments (poetical or rhetorical, dialectical and demonstrative) belong to the masses, jurists and theologians, and metaphysicians respectively, but all three share in one and the same religion.

93 Cf. *ACR*, p. 250 and see also p. 300.

94 See also my PIR, pp. 246–53 for a discussion of the practical aspect of his political thought.

95 Cf. Camb. MS. Add. 496, f. 90a on *NE*, VI, xiii end, 1145a (Latin, f. 46a), echoing *NE*, I, i, 1094b.

96 Cf. *ibid.* f. 115a on *NE*, VIII, ix, 1160a (Latin, f. 59b) on associations as a part of the association of the state. Ibn Rushd uses the term "partnership", according to the Hebrew version, for Aristotle's *koinonia*. See also n. 4 above, and *ACR*, pp. 214 and 287f.

97 Cf. *ibid.* Ibn Rushd explains "sacrifices" as "festivals of pilgrimage". I assume that the Hebrew *ḥaggīm* is simply a transliteration for Arabic *ḥajj*. The Latin translates *Pascha*.

CHAPTER X

1 I am greatly indebted to my colleague G. M. Wickens for his ready help with the Persian texts of the *Akhlāq-i Jalālī* and *Akhlāq-i Nāsirī*. See now his translation of *Ṭūsī, The Nasirean Ethics* (London, 1964), introduction and notes, especially those on my Chapter X.

Muḥammad b. As'ad Jalāl al-Dīn Al-Dawwānī was born at Dawwān, where his father was *qāḍī*, in 1427 C.E. and died in 1501 C.E. (907 or 908 A.H.). He became *qāḍī* of Fars and taught at the Madrasa al-Aitām in Shīrāz. He wrote philosophical commentaries and treatises, one of which—the subject of this chapter—is an adaptation of Ṭūsī's treatise on practical philosophy. In addition he wrote theological works, among them a commentary on the creed of al-Ījī, and left a number of mystical writings. Although Ṭūsī would have deserved consideration in his own right in this survey of political thought in Islam his contribution is approached through his epitomizer and popularizer, Al-Dawwani. For while Ṭūsī wrote when Islamic philosophy was already in decline after the death of Ibn Rushd, he still writes as a philosopher and in the manner of the *Falāsifa*. Al-Dawwānī, separated from Ṭūsī by two centuries and great changes in the political and spiritual climate of the Muslim world, writes as an eclectic harmonizer in a fluent, easy style and succeeds in making philosophy respectable and presentable as part of a pleasant, interesting mixture of traditional beliefs and convictions, with appropriate quotations from Qur'ān and Hadith and suitable sayings from Plato and Aristotle.

2 See ch. II above, pp. 48f., 51f. with note 84; 54 with note 97; and 58 with notes 110 and 111.

3 It was published in London in 1839. A new translation with references to Ṭūsī's original and locations of quotations is desirable. Thompson often paraphrases and leaves out long passages. His notes are interesting, especially his references to Cicero, since Stoic influence on Islamic philosophy is strong and since the Stoics are often nearer to the *Falāsifa* than Plato's and Aristotle's texts. His references to Aristotle's *Politica* are misleading since, as far as we know at present, this work was not known to the *Falāsifa*. But as parallels they are instructive. The same applies to Cicero, who was certainly not known to the *Falāsifa*. Unfortunately the Greek sources common to Stoics and *Falāsifa* are no longer extant.

4 So C. Brockelmann in *EI*, *s.v.* al-Dawwānī. Cf. also *GAL*, vol. II,

p. 217. See for Ṭūsī also ch. II, above, nn. 86 and 113. I have used the Lahore edition of the *Akhlāq-i-Nāṣirī*, published in 1952 (quoted as Ṭ henceforth) and M. K. Shirazi's edition of the *Akhlāq-i Jalālī* (Calcutta, 1911) (quoted as D henceforth).

5 See M. Plessner, *Der Oikonomikos des Neupythagoreers 'Bryson' und sein Einfluss auf die islamische Wissenschaft* (Heidelberg, 1928) pp. 104ff. who says of his version, based on Ṭūsī: "popularisiert und trägt den Stoff pädagogischer vor...er lässt den Leser seine Lehren sich mühelos und unter ästhetischem Genuss aneignen." Ṭūsī adopts Ibn Sīnā's division of practical philosophy into ethics, economics and politics, cf. ch. v above, n. 10.

6 Cf. D, p. 52/Ṭ, p. 117, based on *NE*, v, v, 1133a.

7 D, p. 53/Ṭ, p. 117. For the saying "Religion and temporal power are twins" see also above, ch. II, p. 39 and n. 43 (Al-Ghazālī); and ch. III, n. 11 (Ibn al-Ṭiqṭaqa), as well as Introduction, p. 8.

8 *Ibid.* Thompson incorrectly translates the two terms by "discipline and correction". Throughout he renders *Sharī'a* by "the Institute".

9 *Ibid.* The quotation comes from *Sūra* lvii, 25. Ṭūsī only quotes the verse while Al-Dawwānī explains it.

10 Cf. *ibid.* D, p. 53/Ṭ, p. 118.

11 Cf. D, pp. 54ff. This is not in Ṭ. "Temporal" refers to matters of government and administration in accordance with the requirements of the time.

12 See *NE*, v, vi, vii.

13 Cf. D, p. 57/Ṭ, p. 118.

14 Cf. D, p. 58. This interesting passage does not occur in Ṭūsī, at any rate not in this context. It can only be understood as a "vote of confidence" in the *Falāsifa*, a move to take them back into the fold after they had been treated with suspicion and open hostility in previous centuries. In my opinion it is appropriate to Ibn Rushd and perhaps Ibn Sīnā, but less to Al-Fārābī, although it can hardly be said, as Al-Dawwānī does, that they withdrew from the Greek and Hellenistic philosophers. There would have been no point in claiming "agreement" between *falsafa* and *Sharī'a*, nor in Al-Dawwānī's quoting Plato and Aristotle and their views. Thompson's note 46 on p. 139 of his translation attributes the change to Al-Ghazālī: "The twelfth century seems to have been the aera of this reaction. Ghazaly, we know, after the sciences had been perfected by the aid of Greek translations, reflected on his predecessors for adopting them." [!]

15 Cf. D, p. 59.

16 Cf. H. A. R. Gibb, "Some Considerations on the Sunnī Theory of the Caliphate" in *Archives d'Histoire du Droit Oriental*, vol. III (1948), pp. 401–10; and also H. A. R. Gibb and Harold Bowen, *Islamic Society and the West*, vol. I, pt. I (Oxford, 1950), p. 32. See also the end of this chapter, p. 222f., below.

17 Cf. D, p. 116/Ṭ, p. 243. Ṭūsī uses the terms *ijtimā'* and *tamaddun* synonymously.

18 Thompson translates it here by "restraining influence" [!].

19 Cf. D, p. 117/Ṭ, p. 243. Al-Dawwānī says that this was explained in the section on justice. There it was stated that justice depended on these three kinds of *nāmūs*. That he uses identical terms here shows the close connection between politics and law. *Dīnār*, money, here means economy based on money, as the means of exchange.

20 It is very likely that Ṭūsī bases his exposition on the *NE* itself or perhaps on Al-Fārābī's or Ibn Rushd's commentary on it. The constitutions are not discussed in this order in Al-Fārābī's *Madīna fāḍila* or *Siyāsa*.

21 D, p. 117/Ṭ, pp. 244f. They quote Plato as saying that "they are possessed of important and superior [supranatural] powers" which Al-Dawwānī explains as possessing theoretical and practical knowledge and, thanks to divine inspiration, ability to examine the hidden things and to perceive the world of generation and corruption. Aristotle said of them that they are most favoured by divine Providence.

22 Thompson translates: "the absolute sovereign and his directions the sovereign function", p. 324.

23 Cf. D, p. 117/Ṭ, p. 245. This is of course in the tradition of Al-Fārābī and Ibn Rushd.

24 Cf. D, p. 117. This is not in Ṭūsī, who also leaves out "in harmony... *Sharī'a*". See also note 50 in ch. II above, for the use of this title by Al-Ghazālī. "Shadow of God" and "*Khalīfa* of God" are in general use by poets and authors of "Mirrors" especially during the decline of the Abbasid caliphate; the more shadowy the power of the caliph, the more exalted became his titles. Cf. also above, ch. II, nn. 19, 33, 55 and 80.

25 I am unable to locate this expression in Plato. It is indeed baffling since it is otherwise applied to God the creator, as quoted in ch. VIII, p. 165 from Al-Fārābī (*mudabbir jamī'i-l-'ālam*). Ibn Jamā'a, on the other hand, gives as one of the definitions of the term "*sulṭān*" that from "kingship and power" (see n. 80 of ch. II) and gives as his reason that the world (*'ālam*) cannot endure without a wise governor (*mudabbir ḥakīm*). Ibn Jamā'a may have been acquainted with the term used by Al-Dawwānī and his source Ṭūsī, but if so then hardly from his own reading of Plato. His knowledge of philosophy came to him more probably from his rival Al-Ghazālī. From the context it is clear that *mudabbir 'ālam* corresponds to *insān madanī* which Al-Dawwānī explains as "the man who watches over the affairs of the *madīna*", that is, the statesman. It would therefore seem plausible to look for the possible source in Plato's *Politikos*. This treatise, as mentioned above, in n. 58 of ch. VI, may or may not have been known to the *Falāsifa*, and "the world" may represent a Hellenistic interpretation of Plato's revised definition—to use J. B. Skemp's subheading in his translation, *Plato's Statesman* (London, 1952), preceded by an excellent Introduction—276 b–e. Plato does not use the term *oikoumene*, but only talks there of "all men", which could not be

rendered by "'*ālam*". The usual rendering of *oikoumene* into Arabic is *ma'mūra*, as we find it in Al-Fārābī (see above, ch. VI, p. 126). Galen's summary of the *Politikos* is lost, but it is possible that Proclus' commentary on the *Republic* in which reference is made to the *Politikos* (cf. *De Platonis Philosophia*, notes to § 18), can help us. Al-Dawwānī likens the ruler to the physician: the ruler of the world is at the same time "the physician of the world" (*ibid.* p. 118). Taking the passage as a whole we remember that Ibn Rushd, while accepting Al-Fārābī's equation between philosopher-king, lawgiver and *imām*, left the question open whether he ought to be a prophet as well.

26 Cf. D, p. 118. "This science" is Politics. Ṭ has a long section on *ḥikma madanīya*, entirely on the lines of Al-Fārābī and Ibn Sīnā, in strictly philosophical terminology.

27 *Ibid.* Al-Dawwānī continues: "this science is a term for the principles to which the general welfare of mankind is attached. Without co-operation there is no true perfection."

28 Ibn Jamā'a already uses the three terms synonymously, cf. above, ch. II, n. 55.

29 Cf. D, p. 130/Ṭ, p. 275.

30 Cf. D, p. 131/Ṭ, p. 278.

31 Cf. D, p. 132/Ṭ, p. 279, in general, but not literal agreement. This is also the attitude of Ibn Rushd.

32 Cf. D, p. 133/Ṭ, p. 281. The classes enumerated may perhaps represent a mixture of those who serve the statesman in the *Politikos* (287*c*–290*e*) and the three classes of the *Republic*, adapted to Islam. The first class are clearly Plato's philosopher-kings; the second seem to be borrowed from Ibn Rushd as far as *'ulamā* and *fuqahā* are concerned, from the Muslim administration and the jurists who, as we know, stress the importance of associating the *'ulamā* with the government, and from Plato (*Politikos*, 290*b*) [?]. The inclusion of orators and poets is strange in view of Plato's strictures—repeated, as far as poets are concerned, by Bryson, Miskawaih and Ibn Rushd, yet their role as educators of the masses is significant, bearing in mind Plato on the one hand and Ibn Rushd on the other, at least as far as their use of arguments is concerned.

33 Cf. *Siyāsa*, pp. 74ff. Ṭūsī and Al-Dawwānī are more concise than their source.

34 Cf. D, p. 130/Ṭ, p. 296. Al-Dawwānī incorporates only Ṭūsī's summary in his own version, prior to his treatment of the ideal state. See also above, ch. VI, pp. 134ff. and *ACR*, pp. 289f. and 296f.

35 Cf. D, p. 134/Ṭ, p. 282 (without the titles, however).

36 Cf. Ṭ, pp. 282f.

37 Cf. D, p. 135.

38 Cf. D, pp. 138ff./Ṭ, p. 304. Ṭūsī is less explicit and less "Islamic". The five "pillars" are here reduced to four political "elements"; the philosophical qualification has disappeared, unless, as stated in the text, the *'urafā al-ḥaqīqa*, *awliyā* and *philosophers* are only different groups of men possessing a true knowledge of reality and from there proceeding to knowledge of God. As far as the four groups are concerned, they resemble the "servants" of the *Politikos*, adapted to Islam.

39 Cf. D, p. 144. As stated earlier the possibility cannot be ruled out that sometimes "*ḥukamā*" may simply denote "the wise" in general, so perhaps here.

40 Cf. D, pp. 144f./Ṭ, p. 308 in general, but not in literal agreement.

41 Cf. D, p. 145.

42 Cf. D, pp. 146f./Ṭ, pp. 309f.

43 Cf. D, p. 149/Ṭ, p. 314.

44 *Op. cit.* p. 405, n. 16. Sir Hamilton refers to the '*Aqīda* of Al-Nasafī who lets the *khilāfa* come to an end after 30 years when it is followed by the *imāma*. Al-Taftazānī's comment on this passage is relevant to my point: "And were it admitted that the period of the Khalifate was for 30 years only, then perhaps after it the era of the Khalifate ends without the era of the Imamate ending, on the basis that 'Imam' is a more general term than 'khalīfa'....But after the Abbasid Khalīfas the matter of the Khalifate is a dubious affair (*mushkil*)" (quoted from *A Commentary on the Creed of Islam. Al-Taftazānī on the Creed of Najm al-Dīn al-Nasafī*, by E. E. Elder, N.Y., 1950, p. 146).

45 I was unable to locate this saying attributed to Plato, in his *Laws*, but *Laws* 715 *c*, *d* come very near to it, whether condensed from Plato's own words or from a Hellenistic summary or apocryphal. The passage follows that adduced two pages before, D 145.

This quotation, together with those on pp. 215, 217 and in nn. 21 and 25 above, as well as references to "the philosophers" in general pose the problem of the reception of Platonic ideas and formulations in Islam in its acutest form. It must, however, be remembered that Al-Dawwānī's knowledge of Greek and Hellenistic philosophy was second-hand; it came from Al-Ghazālī and Ṭūsī. Where he simply copies Ṭūsī or acclimatizes his formulations to traditional Muslim concepts, the problem is simply removed one stage and complicated, since Ṭūsī's philosophical attainment is considerable and due to first-hand study, at least in part, as far as I can judge. A detailed study of Ṭūsī is necessary, not least in the context of the Platonic legacy. While the difficulties are serious and numerous—the absence of Hellenistic sources in their original Greek and in Arabic translations is only the first and most important of them—only the close co-operation between specialists in Greek and Hellenistic philosophy and Arabists and experts in Islamic philosophy will substantially advance their solution. The principal obstacle is the terminology of the *Falāsifa* and their popularizers like Al-Dawwānī, and, after its establishment, consistency in its use. Apart from the *Falāsifa* themselves quotations contained in the works of historians like Al-Bīrūnī and Abū-l-Fidā must be collected and examined systematically. Modern critical editions, such as those of Averroes by M. Bouyges and by the contributors to the *Corpus Averrois* of the Medieval Academy of America and to the *Plato Arabus* of the *Corpus Platonicum Medii Aevi* of the Warburg Institute, offer much material and help. Terminology and philosophical argument will enable us to separate Platonic from later Hellenistic material to an as yet uncertain extent, and to determine more accurately and completely the Platonic legacy. Within the narrower confines of political thought the authors studied in this outline supply us with a reliable guide to the *Republic* and the *Laws*. But it is still an open question what is pure Plato and what Neoplatonic revision; in the direct quotations this can be ascertained more easily than in paraphrases and sayings attributed to Plato. Al-Dawwānī offers examples of the latter group.

How far the *Politikos* comes into the legacy is difficult to say, and it cannot at present be decided whether this important political treatise was known *in extenso* (in Galen's summary) or only through quotations of greater or lesser precision and of Platonic or later origin and colouring (see also nn. 32 and 38, above, on this point).

APPENDIX

1 Some examples of seventeenth-century Sunnī political thought are offered in the form of an *Appendix*. The three treatises under discussion, accessible to me in translation only, have in common that they owe their existence to an acute crisis of the Ottoman state and have therefore a predominantly practical purpose. In this they differ from the authors and writings which form the subject of this book. They are neither concerned with the theory of government in the strict sense of Part I, nor do they fall within the category of the Platonic legacy of Part II. But the advice which they offer to the sultan is based on a definite concept of a Muslim state which is founded upon and centred in Muslim law. The practical remedies suggested are closely related to the spirit and also largely to the letter of this law. The authors of the memoranda as well as Ḥājjī Khalīfa, who couched his advice in the form of a theoretical treatise, have a clear idea of what the government of a Muslim state ought to be. The two memoranda stress the importance of a return to the administration of the early Ottomans, which implies a recognition of the dual nature of Ottoman law, namely the *Sharī'a* and the *Qānūn* of the reigning monarch.

Ḥājjī Khalīfa is in a category of his own, although the same crisis produced his treatise and although he tenders practically the same advice in order to resolve the crisis and restore the power and stability of the Ottoman empire. This distinction is due to the theoretical superstructure, frame and form in which he presents his views. This character of his *Dustūr al-'amal* establishes a definite link with authors and works of both parts of the book. He follows an intellectual and literary tradition which justifies his inclusion in our survey.

2 The description which follows is based on the German translations made by W. F. A. Behrnauer between 1857 and 1864 and published in the *ZDMG* in this order: (1) "Hâǵî Chalfa's Dustûru' l- 'amal. Ein Beitrag zur osmanischen Finanzgeschichte", XI (1857), pp. 111–32, 330. (2) "Koǧabeg's Abhandlung über den Verfall des osmanischen Staatsgebäudes seit Sultan Suleiman dem Grossen", XV (1861), pp. 272–332. (3) "Das Naṣîḥatnâme. Dritter Beitrag zur osmanischen Finanzgeschichte", XVIII (1864), pp. 699–740. F. Babinger calls Kōja Beg "the historian of the decline of the Ottoman empire" in his article in *EI* and also "the Montesquieu of the Ottomans". Kōja Beg, who had served successive sultans from Aḥmad I to Murād IV, died during the reign of Meḥmed IV. His fearless analysis of the reasons for the decline of Ottoman power and the suggestions contained in the treatise under discussion were presented to Murād IV, whose complete confidence he enjoyed and whom he loyally advised.

For Ḥājji Khalīfa see J. H. Mordtmann's article in *EI*. Muṣṭafā b. 'Abdu-llah Ḥājji Khalīfa was born in 1608, the son of a soldier and himself a soldier for the best part of his short life which ended in 1657. At the same time he occupied a minor post as clerk in the administration of the army, resigned because he was not promoted, but rejoined in a somewhat higher category, whereupon he called himself Ḥājji *Khalīfa*. He retired from the Office of Control in 1645 so that he could devote all his time to literary studies and writing. He left a considerable number of historical studies and is best known for his encyclopaedic biographical and bibliographical work *Kashf al-ẓunūn* on which he is said to have worked for twenty years. He was a scholar of no mean attainment, of extensive knowledge based on a deep and wide education. He mentions Al-Dawwānī, to whom I think he is indebted, with appreciation and high respect.

3 Behrnauer's translation is based on MSS. in the libraries of Vienna and Leningrad and is accompanied by notes and explanations. There are modern editions available. I have here given only the barest outline and concentrated on the general content and on what is relevant for the problem under discussion. The reader will find much valuable information on the Ottoman army and finance, with figures for the size of the army and for the pay of the officials.

4 The reader is referred to the whole treatise, which contains an interesting account of the financial and legal administration of the Turkish state.

5 Cf. *Dustūr*, *loc. cit.* p. 116.

6 Cf. *ibid.* p. 118. See above, ch. IV, pp. 87ff.

7 Cf. *ibid.* p. 119. See above, ch. X, p. 217.

8 Behrnauer explains *rijāl* as combining the meaning "statesmen" with that of "soldiers" (*ibid.* p. 119, n. 3).

9 Literally "money".

10 See above, ch. X, pp. 220f.

11 Cf. *Dustūr*, *loc. cit.* p. 120.
12 Literally "law of reason".
13 Cf. *Dustūr*, *loc. cit.* pp. 121 ff.
14 Cf. *ibid.* p. 124.
15 Cf. *ibid.* pp. 124 ff. with detailed figures about the strength of the army and its pay.
16 Cf. *ibid.* pp. 126 ff. with figures for expenditure.
17 Cf. *ibid.* p. 129. He repeats earlier suggestions and admonitions.
18 Cf. *ibid.* p. 132.
19 Cf. *ibid.* p. 115.
20 In their assessment of the situation and in their suggestions of practical measures to stop the decline by energetic reforms the three authors show remarkable similarity. The special character of his own work, showing the double legacy, is described on pp. 227 f., above.

GLOSSARY

A

ʿābid, pious, worshipper, servant (of God)
ʿabīd (*ʿabd*), slaves
adab, good manners, *mores*, etiquette, belles-lettres
ʿadāla, *ʿadl*, justice, equity
ʿādāt (*ʿāda*), habits
ʿādila, *madīna ʿādila*, just state. *ʿādila* is used synonymously with *fāḍila* and *ḥasana* (see *s. vv.*), meaning "ideal state"
afāḍil (*afḍalu*), most excellent, virtuous men
afḍal, preferable
ʿahd, contract, treaty, pact between caliph and community
aḥkām, statutes, ordinances, laws (see *s. v. ḥukm*)
  aḥkām wāziʿa, restraining statutes
ahl, men, people, possessors of
  ahl al-ḥall wa-l-ʿaqd, men with power to bind and to loosen, i.e. spiritual leaders representing the Muslim community
  ahl al-dīn, men of religion, god-fearing men
  ahl al-kitāb, people, possessors of a book (of revelation), adherents of Judaism, Christianity and Zoroastrianism who enjoy privileged status under Islam
  ahl al-mashwara, counsellors
  ahl al-shūrā, counsellors; applies to the six companions of Omar who formed a council of electors to elect one among themselves caliph. *shūrā* means consultation and is a duty imposed on the caliph and persons in authority
  ahl al-sunna, adherents of Sunnī Islam, orthodox Muslims
  ahl al-sunna wa-l-jamāʿa, members of the (orthodox) Muslim community
ākhira, al-, world to come, the hereafter
akhlāq (*khulq*), morals, ethics
ʿālam, world
  ʿālam arḍī, terrestrial world
amān, safe conduct, charter
amīr al-muʾminīn, Commander of the Faithful, title of caliph or *imām* referring to his military duties
amr, command, authority, power
anbiyā (*nabī*), prophets
anṣār, companions of Muḥammad in Medina
ʿaqd, contract, pact
ʿaqīda, faith, article of faith, dogma, religious conviction
ʿaql, reason, intellect, intelligence
ʿaql faʿʿāl, active intellect

aqwāl (*qawl*), words, utterances, statements
arbāb (*rabb*) *amwāl*, owners of wealth, the rich
'ārif, man of knowledge, discernment, (speculative) mystic
arkān (*rukn*), pillars
'aṣabīya, collective driving force giving staying and striking power to a group animated by loyalty, a common outlook, or ideal, based initially on physical kinship, becoming spiritual
'askar, army
athar, trace, tradition
āthār, traditions, examples, monuments
awliyā (*walī*), saints
awqāf (*waqf*), pious bequests

B

ba'da-l-ṭabī'īyāt, "beyond the natural things", metaphysical
badāwa, rural life, activity, character; in contrast to *ḥaḍāra* (see *s.v.*)
badw, desert; territory used for rural activities like agriculture, cattle breeding
basīṭ(*a*), simple
bāṭin, inner, hidden (meaning)
bay'a, investiture, installation through oath of loyalty, of allegiance
bid'a, innovation (tantamount to heresy)
burhān, proof, argument, demonstration

D

ḍālla, erring, in error; applied to an imperfect state
dār, dwelling, house, realm
dār al-ḥarb, the realm of war, i.e. lands which are as yet outside Islam and must be conquered and incorporated in the Islamic empire
dār al-islām, the realm of Islam, in contrast to *dār al-ḥarb*
ḍarūrīya, necessity; applied to a state which provides and guarantees the necessities of life to its citizens
da'wa, call, appeal
dawla, dynasty, state, power
dhimma, protection extended to "possessors of a book" (*ahl al-kitāb*) living under Muslim rule
dhimmī, protected, enjoying *dhimma*; second-class citizen of Muslim state
dīn, religion
dīnār, gold coin (*denarius*), money
dunya, world, this life (on earth)

F

fāḍila, excellent, virtuous, ideal; of city-state, corresponding to Plato's ideal state of his *Republic*
falāsifa (*failasūf*), Muslim philosophers, disciples of Plato and Aristotle
falsafa, philosophy dependent on Greek-Hellenistic philosophy

faqīh, *fuqahā*, Muslim jurists, expert in law (*fiqh*)
fāsiqa, vicious, wicked (of state, *madīna*)
fay', legal booty (of Muslims engaged in *jihād*, holy war)
Fiqh, jurisprudence, science of Muslim law
furū' (*far'*), branches, derivations, consequences of *uṣūl* (principles of jurisprudence)

G

ghaḍab, anger, applied to the irascible part of the soul
ghurabā (*gharīb*), strangers

H

ḥaḍāra, urban life, civilization; used synonymously with *madanīya* and *tamaddun* (see *s.vv.*)
ḥadīth, tradition, body of authentic traditions going back to Muḥammad
ḥākim, governor, ruler
ḥanafī, teacher, adherent of orthodox law school of Abū Ḥanīfa
ḥanbalī, teacher, adherent of orthodox law school of Ibn Ḥanbal
ḥaqīqa, truth, reality
ḥaqq, truth, right, certain thing
  ḥaqq yaqīnī, certain knowledge, certain truth
ḥarb, war
ḥasana, beautiful; of state, used synonymously with *'ādila* and *fāḍila* (see *s.vv.*)
ḥayā', modesty
ḥayāt, life
  al-ḥayāt al-ākhira, *al-ukhrā*, the after-life, future life
ḥayawān, living thing (animal, man)
  ḥayawān insī, human being; *insī* is used synonymously with *madanī*, political
  ḥayawān madanī, political being, citizen
ḥayawānīya, animal nature, applied to the concupiscent part of the soul
ḥikma, wisdom, philosophy
  ḥikma 'amalīya, practical wisdom, philosophy; prudence
  ḥikma madanīya, politics, political philosophy
  ḥikma naẓarīya, theoretical wisdom, philosophy
ḥisba, supervision of markets and morals, police (see *s.v. wilāya*)
ḥiyal (*ḥīla*), devices, legal fictions
ḥujja, argument, documentary proof
ḥukamā (*ḥakīm*), sages, philosophers
ḥukm, statute, ordinance, legal rule, regulation, authority, government
  ḥukm wāzi', restraining authority
ḥusn, beauty, good quality
  ḥusn tadbīr, "goodness of rule", "right conduct" (in Ibn Sīnā used for "justice"; in Al-Fārābī meaning "thrift")

I

'ibād (*'abd*), servants (of God)
'ibāda, service, cult, piety
'ibādāt, duties to God, religious duties
ijmā', consensus; ideally of the *umma* (or *jamā'a*); in practice of the leading *'ulamā* of a generation, the *ahl al-ḥall wa-l-'aqd* (see *s.vv.*)
ijtihād, independent legal decision, judgement arrived at by knowledge and reasoning
ikhtiyār, choice, freedom of choice, free will
ilāhīyāt, divine things; metaphysics
'ilm, knowledge (of tradition), science, wisdom
'ilm ṭabī'ī, natural science, physics
imām, chief, leader in prayer; synonym of *khalīfa*
imāma, imamate; synonym of *khilāfa* (caliphate). Muslim state ruled by the *Sharī'a*, the ideal state of Islam
imāmīya, belonging to *imām*, "priestly"; term applied to state
infirād, isolation, without rival (in authority, power); see also *s.v. majd*
insān madanī, statesman
insānīya, humanity (*humanitas*)
iqnā', persuasion
iqtiṣād, moderation
ishrāq, illumination
ishrāqī(yūn), adept in illumination, theosophist (?)
istibdād, independence, independent rule, sovereign power, absolute monarchy
i'tiqād, *i'tiqādāt*, (religious) convictions

J

jadal, dialectic, dialectical argument
jāhil(a), ignorant, applied to imperfect state
jāhilīya, state of ignorance, pagan idolatry prior to Islam
jamā'a, Muslim community
jamā'īya, belonging to the people, community
madīna jamā'īya, democracy
jamīl(a), good, beautiful
jihād, holy war, one of the cardinal duties of a Muslim
jizya, poll-tax, levied on *dhimmīs* (see *s.v.*)
jumhūr, *al-*, the people, *vulgus*, the masses

K

kalām, dialectic, anti-philosophical theology (word, *logos*)
kamāl, perfection
karāma, respect, honour
madīna karāma, timocracy

khalīfa, caliph, vicegerent of Prophet Muḥammad
  khalīfat-allah, vicegerent of God; title given to later caliphs
kharāj, land-tax
khārijī, secessionist, rebel
khasīsa, greedy, vile, debased
  madīna khasīsa, plutocracy
khilāfa, caliphate; equivalent of *imāma*
khissa, equivalent of *khasīsa*
khulafā rāshidūn, term applied to the first four caliphs as the ideal rulers who guide the Muslim community on the right path (to Allah)
khuṣūma, debate, dispute
khuṭba, sermon, address in Friday public prayer
kifāya, sufficiency, satisfying material conditions of caliphal office
kitāb, al-, book, revealed book
  al-kitāb al-ʿazīz, the precious book, i.e. the Qur'ān

M

maʿād, return, future life
maʿāsh, livelihood, this life
  maʿāsh wa-maʿād, this world and the next; in conjunction with *ṣalāḥ* (*iṣlāḥ*), welfare in...
mabda', principle
  mabda' awwal, first principle
madanīya, belonging to the city-state, political, civic, civilization; synonym of *ʿumrān* and *ḥaḍāra* (see *s.vv.*)
madīna, city, state
  madīna fāḍila, see *s.v. fāḍila*
mahna malakīya, royal office
majd, glory, nobility, rank, authority
  infirād bi-l-majd, being alone, unrivalled in authority, exercising sovereign power
māl, wealth, finance (see also *s.v. arbāb*)
malak, angel
malik, king, "temporal" ruler
mālikī, teacher, adherent of orthodox law school of Mālik b. Anas
mamlaka, kingdom, realm
maʿmūra, cultivated, inhabited part of the earth; the inhabited world
maʿqūlāt, metaphysics
maʿrifa, knowledge
maṣāliḥ (*maṣlaḥa*), *maṣāliḥ ʿāmma*, *maṣāliḥ mushtaraka*, } public interest, common weal, welfare
mashwara, counsel
mawālī (*mawla*), clients, freedmen, companions, friends
mawjūdāt, al-, existing things, reality
maẓnūna, assumed, alleged

milla, religion, religious community
mu'ākhāt, brotherhoods, inaugurated by Muḥammad in Medina
mu'āmalāt, commercial transactions, social relations, duties of man to man
mubaddala, *mutabaddala*, transformed, changed, applied to an imperfect state
mudabbir, administrator, governor, leader, ruler
  mudabbir fāḍil, ideal ruler
muhimmāt, practical affairs
mufti, he who gives legal decisions (*fatwā*), judge
mujtahid, capable of exercising *ijtihād* (see *s.v.*), independent decisor
mulk, royal dignity, kingship, rule, government, "temporal" authority, state
mu'min(*ūn*), believer(s), Muslims
munākaḥāt, married life, family life
muqallid, practising *taqlīd* (see *s.v.*), dependent on previous decisors
murshid, spiritual guide
mushārakāt, general affairs, what men have in common
mustabidd, exercising independent authority, absolute monarch (see *s.v. istibdād*)
mutaghallib, exercising tyranny, tyrant
mutakallim(*ūn*), adherent of *kalām*, dialectic theologian
mutawaḥḥid, isolated (philosopher), solitary, abandoning society, neglecting civic duties
mu'tazila, philosophical, anti-Aristotelian sect

N

nabī, prophet
nābit mufarrad, isolated *nābit*
nadhāla, base, vile, contemptible
  madīna nadhāla, oligarchy
najda, prowess
nāmūs (*nawāmīs*), law(s)
  nāmūs ilāhī, divine law
nawābit (*nābit*), plants, weeds, self-grown in alien soil (term applied by Al-Fārābī and Ibn Bājja to certain individuals or groups)
naẓar, supervision, attention, speculation
  naẓarīy, theoretical, speculative
niẓām, custom, rule, order, harmony
  niẓām al-dīn, good order of religion

Q

qabīḥ, ugly, detestable, ignominious
qāḍī, judge
qahr, force, violence, victory
qawānīn (*qānūn*) *siyāsīya*, political laws, ordinances
qisṭ, justice

qiyās, analogy, principle of exegesis
qiyās 'aqlī, logical deduction by analogy
qiyās shar'ī, legal deduction by analogy
qiyās yaqīnī, syllogism of certainty
qiyās ẓannī, syllogism of conjecture
qudra, power
quwwa, power, faculty
quwwa tajarrūbīya, experimental faculty

R

ra 'āyā, subjects
rabb, master, lord (see also *s.v. arbāb*)
raḥma, compassion
ra'īs, chief, ruler, master
ra's, ruler
rasūl (*rusul*), (prophetic) messenger, apostle
ra'y, opinion, judgement based on one's own opinion
ri'āsa, rule, dominion, principate
riyāl, army
riyāsa, authority, rule, dominion
riyāsa fāḍila, excellent authority, ideal rule, state
riyāsa jāhilīya, ignorant authority, imperfect rule, state
rūḥ, spirit
rūḥ ḥayawānī, spirit of life

S

sa'āda, happiness, blessedness
sa'āda ākhira, ultimate happiness
sa'āda quṣwa, utmost happiness
ṣadaqāt, alms, charity prescribed by law
ṣaḥāba, friends (of the Prophet), companions
ṣāḥib al-shar', lawgiver
sā'is, governor, administrator
salaf (*salaf al-umma*), first generation of Muslims
ṣalāḥ, good order, good working, welfare
salāma, physical fitness (demanded of caliph), soundness
ṣāliḥ, sound, good, decent
sānin, lawgiver (see *s.v. sunna*)
sāqiṭa, vile, debased (applied to state)
shāfi'ī, teacher, adherent of orthodox law school of Al-Shāfi'ī
shahwa, desire, passion for pleasures
shajā'a, courage
shar', divine, divinely revealed law
shāri', lawgiver (prophetic)
sharī'a, divinely revealed, prophetic law of Islam
shawka, force, power

shaykh (*sheikh*), chief, elder
shī'a, heterodox Islam, followers of 'Alī and his descendants as rightful caliphs
shī'ī, doctrine, follower of *Shī'a*
sikka, coin minted in name of caliph
siyar (*sīra*), ways of life
siyāsa, government, administration, politics
  siyāsa 'ādila, just (ideal) government
  siyāsa 'aqlīya, government based on reason and rational human laws
  siyāsa dīnīya / *siyāsa shar'īya*, religious government based on the *Sharī'a*
  siyāsa madanīya, politics, political government, government of the city-state, of the *madīna fāḍila*
su'adā (*sa'īd*), the happy, blessed
sulṭān, secular power, ruler
sunan, laws
  sunan hādiya, right-guiding laws
sunna, custom, law, exemplary life of the Prophet Muḥammad
sunnī, follower of *sunna*, orthodox Muslim

T

tadbīr, regime, government, rule, administration
tafwīḍ, delegation, vizierate of
taghallub, subjugation, tyranny (imperfect state)
tajjār, traders, merchants
tamaddun, to live, associate in cities, civilization
tanfīdh, execution; vizierate of execution of caliph's orders, in contrast to *tafwīḍ* when the caliph delegates his powers to vizier
tanzīl, sending down; divine communication of Qur'ān to Prophet Muḥammad through the angel Gabriel
taqlīd, legal decision based on authority of predecessors capable of *ijtihād* (see *s.v.*)
tawḥīd, (absolute) unity of God
ta'wīl, (allegorical) interpretation

U

ukhrā, see *s.v. ḥayāt*
'ulamā, scholars, learned, masters of traditional Muslim sciences, spiritual leaders of Muslim community
'ulūm shar'īya, sciences based on and dealing with the *Sharī'a*, traditional sciences
'ulūm siyāsīya, political sciences
umma, *ummat al-islām*, nation, Muslim nation, community of Muslims, founded by Muḥammad
  umma wasaṭ, nation of the middle road or just, equitable nation

'umrān, human culture, comprising material civilization and spiritual culture, population
'urafā ('arīf) al-ḥaqīqa, those who possess true knowledge, speculative mystics
'urf, custom, contemporary practice, law founded on custom
uṣūl (-al-fiqh), the principles (of jurisprudence)

W

wāḍi'u-l-nawāmīs, lawgiver (usually of rational laws)
-l-sharā'i', lawgiver of revealed laws
waḥy, revelation
walī-l-'ahd, *walī 'ahdi-l-mulk*, heir presumptive
wara', fear (of God)
wasaṭ, mean, middle, just, equitable
wasāṭa, mean, (golden) mean
waṣīya, testament
wāzi', restraining authority, ruler with power to restrain men from harming one another
wilāya, prefecture, authority
wilāyatu-l-ḥisba, police of markets and morals

Z

zāhid, ascetic
ẓāhir, external, plain, clear (meaning)
zakāt, poor-tax, obligatory alms
zandaqa, Manicheanism, dualism, atheism
ẓann, opinion, conjecture
ẓannī, based on opinion, conjecture (see *s.v. qiyās*)
zuhd, asceticism

INDEX

Bold figures indicate a main entry